The Glannon Guide to Professional Responsibility

Published by Wolters Kluwer in New York.

Wolters Kluwer serves customers worldwide with CCH, Aspen Publishers, and Kluwer Law International products. (www.wolterskluwerlb.com)

To contact Customer Service, e-mail customer.service@wolterskluwer.com,
call 1-800-234-1660, fax 1-800-901-9075, or mail correspondence to:

Wolters Kluwer
Attn: Order Department
PO Box 990
Frederick, MD 21705

Printed in the United States of America.

1 2 3 4 5 6 7 8 9 0

ISBN 978-1-4548-6215-4

Library of Congress Cataloging-in-Publication Data

Stevenson, Dru, author.
The Glannon guide to professional responsibility : learning professional responsibility through multiple-choice questions and analysis / Dru Stevenson, Professor of Law, Harry and Helen Hutchens Research Professor and Baker Institute Scholar at the Rice University James A. Beard III, Institute for Public Policy, South Texas College of Law.
pages cm
Includes index.
ISBN 978-1-4548-6215-4
1. Legal ethics—United States—Problems, exercises, etc. 2. Attorney and client—United States—Problems, exercises, etc. 3. Confidential communications—Lawyers—Problems, exercises, etc. I. Title.
KF306.S79 2015
174'.3076—dc23

2015018886

The Glannon Gui
to Professional Responsibility

Learning Professional Responsibility Through Multiple-Choice Questions and Analysis

Dru Stevenson
Professor of Law
South Texas College of Law

About Wolters Kluwer Law & Business

Wolters Kluwer Law & Business is a leading global provider of intelligent information and digital solutions for legal and business professionals in key specialty areas, and respected educational resources for professors and law students. Wolters Kluwer Law & Business connects legal and business professionals as well as those in the education market with timely, specialized authoritative content and information-enabled solutions to support success through productivity, accuracy and mobility.

Serving customers worldwide, Wolters Kluwer Law & Business products include those under the Aspen Publishers, CCH, Kluwer Law International, Loislaw, ftwilliam.com and MediRegs family of products.

CCH products have been a trusted resource since 1913, and are highly regarded resources for legal, securities, antitrust and trade regulation, government contracting, banking, pension, payroll, employment and labor, and healthcare reimbursement and compliance professionals.

Aspen Publishers products provide essential information to attorneys, business professionals and law students. Written by preeminent authorities, the product line offers analytical and practical information in a range of specialty practice areas from securities law and intellectual property to mergers and acquisitions and pension/benefits. Aspen's trusted legal education resources provide professors and students with high-quality, up-to-date and effective resources for successful instruction and study in all areas of the law.

Kluwer Law International products provide the global business community with reliable international legal information in English. Legal practitioners, corporate counsel and business executives around the world rely on Kluwer Law journals, looseleafs, books, and electronic products for comprehensive information in many areas of international legal practice.

Loislaw is a comprehensive online legal research product providing legal content to law firm practitioners of various specializations. Loislaw provides attorneys with the ability to quickly and efficiently find the necessary legal information they need, when and where they need it, by facilitating access to primary law as well as state-specific law, records, forms and treatises.

ftwilliam.com offers employee benefits professionals the highest quality plan documents (retirement, welfare and non-qualified) and government forms (5500/PBGC, 1099 and IRS) software at highly competitive prices.

MediRegs products provide integrated health care compliance content and software solutions for professionals in healthcare, higher education and life sciences, including professionals in accounting, law and consulting.

Wolters Kluwer Law & Business, a division of Wolters Kluwer, is headquartered in New York. Wolters Kluwer is a market-leading global information services company focused on professionals.

Contents

Introduction: Preparing for the MPRE

All but three U.S. jurisdictions (Maryland, Wisconsin, and Puerto Rico) require a passing score on the Multistate Professional Responsibility Exam (MPRE) for admission to the bar. This means that nearly every law student in the country needs to pass the MPRE—even law graduates in Maryland and Wisconsin usually seek admission to the bar of a neighboring state with a large metropolitan area (Virginia or Illinois, respectively) in order to be more marketable.

The MPRE contains 60 multiple-choice questions (a, b, c, or d)—no essays or short answers. The multiple-choice questions have a hypothetical situation, one to three paragraphs in length. They usually have two affirmative answers with different rationales ("Yes, because . . .") and two negative answers, also having distinct rationales ("No, because . . ."). Like the Multistate Bar Exam, there are *never* any answer choices such as "all of the above," "none of the above," or "a & b above, but not c." The questions do not give the characters names, but instead refer to "the attorney" and "the client."

The National Conference of Bar Examiners (NCBE) publishes the topics tested on the MPRE, as well as the proportions. These are as follows: conflicts of interest (12–18%); litigation and other forms of advocacy (10–16%); the client-lawyer relationship, including formation, scope, and fees (10–16%); client confidentiality (6–12%); regulation of the legal profession (6–12%); competence, legal malpractice, and other civil liability (6–12%); communications about legal services (advertising and solicitation) (4–10%); different roles of the lawyer (4–10%); safekeeping funds and other property (2–8%); transactions and communications with persons other than clients (2–8%); lawyers' duties to the public and the legal system (2–4%); and judicial conduct (2–8%). For example, there are always exactly 2 questions out of 60 pertaining to judicial conduct, but around 10 or 12 questions out of 60 on conflicts of interest. Many of the MPRE questions use the same hypothetical problems discussed in the official comments to the Model Rules, so the comments are very important.

This book arranges topics around the MPRE coverage ratios, covering the most heavily tested subjects first, and in the greatest depth. The least important subjects are covered toward the end of the book (and there are no questions on the Code of Judicial Ethics, which appears in only one to three questions on the MPRE). These are the same subjects covered by every professional responsibility or legal ethics casebook, though casebooks tend to arrange the chapters (and allocate coverage) differently. This book is useful for preparing for both the MPRE and a law school final exam in professional responsibility.

The Glannon Guide to Professional Responsibility

PART I

Heavily Tested Topics

1

Conflicts of Interest: Introduction

CHAPTER OVERVIEW

A. Conflicts Between Current Clients — Adverse Parties
B. Conflicts Between Current Clients — Joint Representation
C. Conflicts Between Current Clients — Representing Corporations and Their Employees
D. Former Clients and New Clients
E. Former Clients and New Clients — Unrelated Matters
F. Third-Party Compensation and Influence — Relatives
G. Consent to Third-Party Compensation and Influence
H. Conflicts Between Lawyer and Client — Sex with a Client
I. Rule 1.9 — Duties to Former Clients
J. Rule 1.10 — Imputation of Conflict of Interest
K. Rule 1.11 — Special Conflicts of Interest for Former and Current Government Officers and Employees
L. Rule 1.12 — Former Judge, Arbitrator, Mediator
M. The Closer
Stevenson's Picks

Lawyers act as agents of their clients, so there will inevitably be some overlap between the lawyer's own self-interest and the goals of the client, as well as points where their respective interests or goals diverge. At the same time, lawyers are part of a professional association — the bar — and have certain duties to the profession that sometimes require sacrifice or putting the greater good ahead of their own wants or needs.

In learning the rules that govern conflicts of interest, it is helpful to categorize potential scenarios (or exam hypotheticals) along the lines of the relationship affected. Conflicts of interest arise hierarchically, between a lawyer and an individual client (the lawyer's personal interests and those of the client), as well as laterally, between different clients (one client's interests in tension with another client's interests). These lateral conflicts can arise between current clients, between a former client and a current client, and between prospective clients and current (or future) clients. Third parties can also have conflicts with current clients, as when family members of the client pay the lawyer's fees for representation, or when an insurance company pays a lawyer to represent an insured. Of course, judges can have conflicts of interest, between the judge and parties in a case, or between the judge and lawyers representing parties in that court. The rules are easier to remember when sorted along the lines of client-lawyer, client-client, client-third party, and so on. An additional category of problems in this area is that we "impute" a conflict of interest to the lawyer's co-workers, especially the other lawyers at that firm or agency. Thus, the issue of "imputed conflicts" arises when lawyers work together—one lawyer's conflict could disqualify all the other lawyers employed there. Some imputed conflicts, however, are easy to eliminate, as we will see in the discussion about those particular rules.

Thinking about the policy concerns behind the rules can help make the rules seem more intuitive. Of all the rules of professional conduct, those pertaining to conflicts of interest have the most connection to traditional morality and ethics. From a subjective moral standpoint, conflicts of interest seem inherently unfair, introducing bias into the administration of justice. Proceeding with representation when a conflict is present also shows a lack of loyalty where loyalty is due—in other words, a conflict of interest is a nascent breach of one's duty to another. Even from a purely utilitarian perspective, conflicts essentially facilitate exploitation—they hurt one party in order to benefit the other. Lawyers should be professionals, not merely practitioners, and a conflict of interest will cloud the lawyer's judgment, so it becomes harder to be objective, realistic, or competent. Conflicts taint the lawyer's professional reputation and, by association, the reputation of the profession overall. Finally, remember that conflicts overlap with concerns about confidentiality, as will be seen with the rules for eliminating imputed conflicts.

What do the rules require lawyers to do when facing potential conflicts of interest? The default rule is that the lawyer must refuse to take the case, if the conflict is apparent at the outset, and must withdraw from the representation if a conflict of interest emerges later (either because the parties' situations change, or new information brings to light an existing conflict that was previously unknown). The rules also provide exceptions, the most important of which is waiver or consent. Many conflicts (but not all) are curable if the clients give informed consent, in writing, with the opportunity for outside legal counsel about the risks involved. Of course, such informed consent applies only where the lawyer reasonably believes that unbiased, competent representation is indeed possible. The rules' other important exception applies to imputed conflicts, and this generally involves "screening" the lawyers from one another when it comes to communication about the representation. These rules and exceptions—as well as some other more specific exceptions—will each feature in the subsections that follow.

The consequences for violating the conflicts rules are far broader than they are for violations of most of the other rules. While most of the rules carry the threat of disciplinary action by the bar (the conflicts rules included), a lawyer who proceeds despite a conflict may find herself "disqualified" from that particular case. The opposing party may file a motion to disqualify the lawyer based on the conflict. In other words, a court may order a lawyer to withdraw, upon threat of dismissing the client's case, due to the lawyer's conflict of interest. Obviously, having to find a new lawyer on the eve of trial is incredibly inconvenient for the client, and potentially prejudicial. Disqualification is a sanction unique to the conflicts rules. In addition, conflicts of interest are a rapidly growing area of legal malpractice claims; in fact, many of the largest malpractice cases in recent years have resulted from the lawyer's conflicts of interest rather than incompetence or negligence in representation. Thus, from the standpoint of one's legal career, conflicts are particularly important to understand, as they pose perils and risks for attorneys beyond the usual punishments for violations of the rules.

The Multistate Professional Responsibility Examination (MPRE) tests conflicts of interest more heavily than it tests any other subject—it currently constitutes 14 percent of the test. Students preparing for the MPRE should therefore devote special attention to this topic. Professional Responsibility casebooks also tend to devote one or more lengthy chapters to this subject, and it is a favorite topic for course final exams. The MPRE examiners suggest that test-takers should expect questions on the following types of conflicts:

Current client conflicts—multiple clients and joint representation
Current client conflicts—lawyer's personal interest or duties
Former client conflicts
Prospective client conflicts
Imputed conflicts
Acquiring an interest in litigation
Business transactions with clients
Third-party compensation and influence
Lawyers currently or formerly in government service
Former judge, arbitrator, and so forth

This list provides students with a useful checklist when studying for the exam—as you read down the list, ask yourself if you can articulate the rules for each type of conflict, and if you can anticipate some of the facts that are likely to appear in hypotheticals that test the rules for each.

Note that the rule—absolutely prohibiting representation of directly adverse parties, regardless of client consent—applies to transactional work as well as litigation. The comments in Section 7 observe:

> Directly adverse conflicts can also arise in transactional matters. For example, if a lawyer is asked to represent the seller of a business in negotiations with a buyer represented by the lawyer, not in the same transaction but in

another, unrelated matter, the lawyer could not undertake the representation without the informed consent of each client.

The most obvious form of conflicts is between two current clients who are adverse parties in the same matter. The rules are very clear on this point, and in real life, lawyers usually avoid such scenarios, but it is a helpful starting place for students to learn the rules about conflicts of interest. We will turn to that situation first, and then work through the more nuanced problems that arise.

A. Conflicts Between Current Clients—Adverse Parties

It should be intuitively obvious that a lawyer cannot represent the plaintiff and the defendant in the same litigation. Not only would this present logistical problems (one imagines a television sitcom in which the lawyer switches back and forth between the defense table to the plaintiff's table throughout the trial and objects to his own remarks and questions), but the Model Rules absolutely forbid it.

Rule 1.7(a)(1) forbids representation of a client if "the representation of one client will be directly adverse to another client." Most conflict-of-interest scenarios permit clients to consent to representation despite the conflict (in which case the lawyer may proceed with representation). In contrast, directly adverse clients *may not consent* to joint representation. In other words, this type of conflict is "nonconsentable," in the jargon of the ABA Comments, and as set forth in Rule 1.7(b)(3): "[Consent is permissible if] the representation does not involve the assertion of a claim by one client against another client represented by the lawyer in the same litigation or other proceeding before a tribunal." Even if the clients both consent, a lawyer cannot represent the defendant and plaintiff in the same matter. The comments (Section 6) explain:

> Loyalty to a current client prohibits undertaking representation directly adverse to that client without that client's informed consent . . . The client as to whom the representation is directly adverse is likely to feel betrayed, and the resulting damage to the client-lawyer relationship is likely to impair the lawyer's ability to represent the client effectively. In addition, the client on whose behalf the adverse representation is undertaken reasonably may fear that the lawyer will pursue that client's case less effectively out of deference to the other client, i.e., that the representation may be materially limited by the lawyer's interest in retaining the current client. Similarly, a directly adverse conflict may arise when a lawyer is required to cross-examine a client who appears as a witness in a lawsuit involving another client, as when the testimony will be damaging to the client who is represented in the lawsuit.

Consider the following problem as an illustration of these rules.

QUESTION 1. **Directly adverse parties.** Mrs. Kramer met with a lawyer to discuss a physical assault by her estranged husband, who had broken into the house of Mrs. Kramer's, friend, where Mrs. Kramer was now living to avoid contact with her husband, and had assaulted her, leaving minor injuries and damaging some of her personal property. The lawyer agreed to represent her in seeking a restraining order against her estranged husband. The next day, upon hearing about this meeting, the estranged husband appeared in the lawyer's office, also seeking representation in the same matter. Mr. Kramer expressed his desire for reconciliation and asked the lawyer to represent him in mediation with his estranged wife, and to defend him at the restraining order hearing. The lawyer accepted a retainer fee from Mr. Kramer and agreed to represent him, just as he had done with Mrs. Kramer. Both the husband and wife were aware that the same lawyer represented them and proceeded with scheduling a hearing and mediation meetings, but neither signed paperwork actually consenting to the joint representation. Mrs. Kramer is unhappy that the husband hired her lawyer, but she feels she cannot do anything about it. What sanction could the lawyer face because of this dual representation?

A. The lawyer is not subject to any sanction because both parties verbally consented to the representation.
B. The lawyer is subject to disqualification by the court from representing one or the other client, but can then proceed with representing the other, whichever one the court allows.
C. The lawyer is subject to discipline, but only because he did not obtain written consent from both parties to the dual representation.
D. The lawyer is subject both to discipline and to disqualification for violating the Model Rules, as the parties are directly adverse in the same proceeding.

ANALYSIS. This story presents the classic scenario of a lawyer trying to represent two adverse parties in the same matter, one of the clearest conflicts of interest imaginable— and these are the facts of an actual case! Where parties are directly adverse in the same matter (whether a transaction or litigation), the Model Rules do not even permit the parties to consent to the arrangement. There is an absolute prohibition against representing opposing parties in the same litigation matter, regardless of what the parties want. In this type of situation, the lawyer is subject both to disqualification and to discipline. If one party decides at the beginning of trial to have the lawyer disqualified, a court will certainly agree in this type of case, and will probably disqualify the lawyer from representing *either* party, given that he probably has enough confidential information from each side to be prejudicial to the other. Moreover, the lawyer is clearly subject to disciplinary action (the lawyer in the case above received a public reprimand), as this is a blatant violation of the Model Rules.

A is wrong because consent is irrelevant in cases where the parties are directly adverse in the same matter. The comments to Rule 1.7 describe this situation as "nonconsentable." Other less egregious conflict scenarios allow for the parties to consent to the representation—and in those cases, the consent must be in writing, so A would be wrong even if this were a "consentable" conflict.

B is wrong because the lawyer is not merely subject to disqualification in this case, but is also subject to disciplinary action for a clear violation of the rules. In addition, the disqualification would probably apply to *both* parties, because by working on the case for each side, the lawyer has presumably received confidential information from each that would be prejudicial to the other.

C is wrong because the problem is not the lack of written consent—this type of conflict is "nonconsentable," so it would not have solved the problem even if the lawyer had obtained written consent in this case. With other types of conflicts that do not involve opposing parties in the same matter, parties can usually consent in writing to the conflict.

D is correct because the lawyer in this case is subject both to discipline and to disqualification. Similar consequences apply when lawyers try to represent both the debtor and creditor in bankruptcy, the plaintiff and defendant in tort, or even adverse parties engaged in some transaction, such as resolving a dispute over the ownership of property.

B. Conflicts Between Current Clients—Joint Representation

Conflicts also arise between current clients even when they are not opposing parties in a matter. Co-defendants or co-plaintiffs can have different interests at stake, or different goals in a case, which would lead them to respond differently to a settlement offer or plea bargain. Rule 1.7(b) permits a lawyer to provide joint representation as long as certain factors are present: informed, written consent by all parties, and the lawyer having a reasonable belief that she can provide competent and diligent representation to each of the co-clients (and where there is no other statute prohibiting joint representation in that specific type of case).

Watch for problems in which the parties agreed only verbally to the joint representation instead of providing written, informed consent, or where one party visits the lawyer alone and hires her to represent a group of friends or relatives—several co-defendants or co-plaintiffs. In addition, watch for the conflicts that arise as a matter of fact, rather than as a matter of principle, even after the parties have all consented to the joint representation. Often parties have different responses to offers to settle a case or enter a plea bargain, and such deals can benefit some of the jointly represented parties more than others—or can be more detrimental to some parties than to others. Rule 1.7(g) provides:

> A lawyer who represents two or more clients shall not participate in making an aggregate settlement of the claims of or against the clients, or in a criminal case an aggregated agreement as to guilty or nolo contendere pleas, unless each client gives informed consent, in a writing signed by the client. The lawyer's disclosure shall include the existence and nature of all the claims or pleas involved and of the participation of each person in the settlement.

In other words, not only must each of the clients consent in writing to joint representation at the outset, they will each have to consent in writing to any agreement that resolves the matter. The following problem illustrates this issue.

QUESTION 2. **One for all and all for one.** Miranda and her two sisters, Lisa and Nancy, all received injuries in a car accident last year. Because they did not have enough money to get separate attorneys, they decided to consent to using the same lawyer, Joseph. After months of trial preparation, the defense counsel approached Joseph with a settlement offer. Miranda sustained severe injuries, but fortunately Lisa and Nancy only received a few bumps and bruises. Joseph believed that the settlement offer was a reasonable offer and that it would be in the clients' best interest to accept it because of how all-consuming and costly trial can be. Even so, Joseph also knew that Miranda would be a hard sell on accepting a settlement offer because she believed she could get a larger judgment if she presented her case in front of a jury. If Joseph obtains consent from both Nancy and Lisa to accept the defendant's settlement offer, will he be subject to discipline for accepting the offer without first discussing it with Miranda?

A. No, because when a client retains a lawyer, they authorize the lawyer to accept or reject settlement offers on their behalf.
B. Yes, because an attorney must inform each client about all the material terms of the settlement before accepting any settlement offer on behalf of multiple clients.
C. Yes, because an attorney must inform and obtain written consent from each client about all the material terms of the settlement before accepting any settlement offer on behalf of multiple clients.
D. No, because the three sisters consented to being represented by the attorney and he believed it was in their best interest as a whole.

ANALYSIS. This scenario depicts the dangers of accepting multiple clients in the same case despite having their written informed consent. Although the rules permit the attorney to accept settlement offers for multiple clients, he or she must have informed each client that he or she represents before doing so. Comment 15 to Rule 1.8 states that before accepting any settlement offer or plea bargain on behalf of multiple clients, the lawyer must inform each client about all the material terms of the settlement, including what the other clients will receive or pay if the settlement or plea offer is accepted.

A is incorrect because every settlement offer must be disclosed to the client, unless the client expressly waives this requirement. Furthermore, in multiple client settings, the lawyer must disclose the offer to each client individually to ensure compliance with the rules.

B is incorrect because it is not enough merely to inform each client of a settlement offer before the lawyer accepts it. The lawyer must obtain each client's written informed consent in addition to disclosing all material elements of an offer.

C is correct because it states the applicable rule, Rule 1.8(g), that "a lawyer who represents two or more clients shall not participate in making an aggregate settlement of the claims of or against the clients . . . unless each client gives informed consent, in a writing signed by the client. The lawyer's disclosure shall include the existence and nature of all the claims or pleas involved and of the participation of each person in the settlement."

D is incorrect because although Joseph may reasonably believe that this settlement offer is in the best interest for all three of the sisters, he may not selectively disclose some information to some sisters and not the rest of them for fear of foregoing a settlement offer.

C. Conflicts Between Current Clients—Representing Corporations and Their Employees

A special type of current-client conflict arises when lawyers represent a company as corporate counsel, usually as in-house (though not necessarily—some corporations outsource their entire legal department to a nearby firm). On a day-to-day basis, as employees, corporate counsel generally follows the orders of the corporate managers, whoever is above the attorney in the corporate organizational chart. Managers make decisions for the corporation about product lines, outsourcing, marketing, investments, hiring and firing, purchases, and mergers, and assign the legal department to draft the pertinent documents, research the legal ramifications of various proposals, and handle liability issues that arise.

Almost inevitably, some managers start thinking that the corporate counsel represents *them*—that is, the managers themselves—partly because of the

daily experience of having the lawyers follow their orders and handle matters they assign. Moreover, the managers may have hiring and firing authority over the lawyer. The lawyer, however, represents the corporation, not individual managers (see Rule 1.13). Corporate counsel, therefore, often face a type of conflict unique to their situation—the person who hires them, could fire them, and gives them regular work assignments at the corporation (their "boss," for practical purposes) may have goals and objectives that differ from the goals and objectives of the corporation itself. When such conflicts arise, the lawyer's duty is to the corporation. The rules encourage lawyers to go up the chain of command when a conflict emerges, in an attempt to do what is best for the corporation. Remember that accommodating the wishes of a wayward manager—even the boss—could end up subjecting the corporation to enormous regulatory fines or liability to third parties, which the lawyer has a duty to avoid. Consider the following problem.

QUESTION 3. **Going up the chain of command.** Attorney Adams is in-house counsel for a large international corporation and has daily contact with higher-level executives and managers. One day, a senior executive mentions casually to Attorney Adams that he has offered lucrative stock options, worth millions of dollars, to a foreign government official who has agreed to give the firm an exclusive contract to provide certain goods and services to the foreign state. The executive seems to think this is normal and good for the company, but Adams believes it constitutes bribery of foreign officials, which would violate the Foreign Corrupt Practices Act, and could subject the company to enormous fines and penalties. Attorney Adams explains her concerns to the executive, including her concern that he could face personal criminal charges in addition to bringing liability on the corporation, and she reminds him that she represents the corporation, not him personally. The executive is dismissive of her concerns, even though she approaches him several times about the matter. How must Attorney Adams proceed?

A. She should report the matter immediately, in writing, to the Department of Justice, and tell no one in the company that she has done so.

B. She should keep her conversations with the executive confidential but try to document everything that she knows about the situation in case the Department of Justice brings an enforcement action.

C. She should approach the executive's immediate corporate superior, advising those next up the chain of authority to stop the transaction and take appropriate actions against the executive involved.

D. She should immediately notify the company's Board of Directors, advising them about the potential liability and threatening to report the activities to the Department of Justice if they take no action.

ANALYSIS. In-house lawyers represent the firm itself and have a duty of loyalty to the company overall, rather than to individuals within the company, according to Rule 1.13. In cases where one manager or executive is jeopardizing the company's future by committing federal crimes (like bribery of government officials), an attorney should try to correct the problem, and should start working up the chain of command if the individuals in charge are uncooperative.

A is incorrect because the rules do not encourage lawyers to report misconduct to the enforcement agencies immediately, but rather to try to resolve the matter internally first. Essentially, this is an attempt to balance the lawyer's duties of confidentiality and loyalty to clients with the lawyer's duty to uphold the law and maintain the integrity of the profession. Note that Rule 1.13(c) permits lawyers to disclose such information (that is, break their confidences) if they have exhausted all avenues for remedial action within the organization and the conduct would result in serious harm to the company, such as facing millions of dollars in fines.

B is incorrect because the lawyer's duty is to the corporation, not to the individual, so there is no reason to keep a conversation confidential that pertains to behavior that would expose the company to criminal prosecution and hefty fines or penalties.

C is correct. Rule 1.13 directs the lawyer to report the matter to the next level of authority above the manager who is being problematic, and to keep working up the chain of command to try to find someone who will address the situation.

D is incorrect because even though the lawyer may have to notify the Board of Directors eventually, this is a last resort, after trying to work with the executives and managers first. A lawyer may need to resign or threaten to resign at some point, but under these facts, doing so would be premature.

D. Former Clients and New Clients

Conflicts arise between new clients and a lawyer's former clients—for example, when a new client wants to sue one of the lawyer's former clients after the representation of the latter has long since ended. Normally, the lawyer can resolve the problem by obtaining written consent from the former client to represent the new client. While some former clients may refuse to allow their previous lawyer to represent their new opponent, other former clients would prefer to have someone they know as opposing counsel instead of a complete stranger.

Conflicts between new and former clients are imputed to all the lawyers in a firm. When a lawyer moves laterally to a new firm, her new employer's lawyers could encounter conflicts with that lawyer's former clients. The Model

Rules allow the new firm to "screen" the lawyer from the cases involving former clients as a way to remedy this problem. Keep in mind that this type of conflict presents special confidentiality issues, and a lawyer confronting this type of conflict could simultaneously violate the rules pertaining to conflicts *and* the rules pertaining to confidentiality. A lawyer must not use previously obtained confidential information to injure a former client, nor disclose the information to other lawyers who are representing the former client's opponents in a matter—the same matter or a new matter.

Generally, a lawyer cannot switch sides in a particular matter—this would presumably be "nonconsentable" under the rules. In other words, if the lawyer worked on a plaintiff's matter at a particular firm, the lawyer cannot work as opposing counsel for the defendant in the same case after switching to a different firm. Similarly, if a lawyer withdraws from representation or the client fires the lawyer, that lawyer cannot go represent the opposing party in the same matter, or even a substantially similar matter. If it is a completely new matter, the lawyer should still obtain his former client's consent in writing. Otherwise, the former client could have a reasonable fear that some of the confidential information the lawyer learned during the previous representation could be at the opponent's disposal in the new matter. Let's try a problem involving the most common type of former-client conflicts.

QUESTION 4. Former clients and new clients. Lawyer Laura worked at the Abel & Bentley firm for five years, and specialized in real estate. During the last three years, Lawyer Laura has worked extensively on Client Cain's properties and disputes that arose related to them. Before leaving the Abel & Bentley firm, Lawyer Laura handled a new real estate deal for Client Cain that facilitated the erection of a new apartment complex. Lawyer Laura now works at the Davis & Eldridge firm. One of her first assignments is a case in which a Client Seth, a new client of the first, is suing Cain over a disputed right of way through the very property that now holds the new apartment complex—Seth and Cain are neighbors. Can Laura represent Client Seth against her former client, Cain?

A. Lawyer Laura may represent Client Seth if Client Cain consents in writing to her doing so.
B. Lawyer Laura may not represent Client Seth in the same or substantially the same matter unless Client Cain consents in writing.
C. Lawyer Laura may not represent Client Seth in the same or substantially the same matter unless Client Seth consents in writing.
D. Lawyer Laura may represent Client Seth because Lawyer Laura left Abe & Bentley and no one in Davis & Eldridge has confidential information about Client Cain.

ANALYSIS. This illustrates conflicts between former clients and present clients, which are especially common when lawyers move laterally between firms. The general rule is that this creates an impermissible conflict of interest for the lawyer, but that the parties themselves can consent to the arrangement if they believe the conflict will not prejudice them in the case.

A is correct because even though the lawyer will now have an adversarial role against her former client, as long as the former client consents in writing (waives the conflict), and Laura reasonably believes she can provide fair representation and will not have to reveal confidential information from her former client, she may proceed with the representation.

B is incorrect because it is too narrow and misstates another rule. The rule for the "same or substantially the same matter" is that lawyers cannot represent an adversarial client—that is, one with a direct conflict to the previous client—regardless of whether the parties consent.

C is wrong for the same reason as B—the prohibition against representing adverse parties in the same or substantially the same matter is so strong that parties cannot waive it merely by consent. In addition, it would not make much sense to allow the new client to waive the previous client's rights when it is the previous client who is most likely to feel prejudiced by the representation of an opponent.

D is wrong because it does not address the need to obtain informed consent from one's former clients. Even though the information issue would be relevant for deciding whether to input Laura's conflict to others in her firm, in the facts here, it is Laura's conflict of interest that is the concern.

E. Former Clients and New Clients—Unrelated Matters

Many types of conflicts are "consentable"—that is, the lawyer can resolve the problem by obtaining written consent from the former client to represent the new client, even in a matter where the former client will be the opposing party. Of course, the former client may be indignant and refuse to allow his former lawyer to represent his new opponent, but such agreements are relatively common. The prior representation may have occurred years in the past, or the client may have been unsatisfied with the lawyer's services and does not mind if an opponent hires him instead, or the client may have a good working relationship with the former lawyer and would prefer to have this lawyer as opposing counsel instead of someone unknown.

A few points are important to remember. First, the consent must be in writing and must be informed. Watch out for exam questions that mention verbal consent, or tacit consent, because anything less than written, informed consent is insufficient.

Second, remember that the lawyer must reasonably believe that the conflict would not interfere with diligent representation of the new client. Watch for problems with facts that are particularly egregious—where no reasonable person could possibly have thought that it would be possible to be objective, diligent, and fair. In most cases, however, the lawyer will claim that it seemed possible to proceed and be adequately loyal to the new client.

Third, remember that confidentiality concerns still apply here—in fact, confidentiality is particularly important in cases with former clients and new clients, because the earlier client could not foresee the lawyer would someday represent an opposing party, and therefore might have been more forthcoming with private information than otherwise would have been the case. Concurrent clients are more likely to be aware of each other and therefore have the opportunity to be more careful about what they disclose. Even if a former client consents to the lawyer's representation of a new adversary, the lawyer still has a duty of confidentiality to the former client. The lawyer cannot disclose confidential information to the new client, or use the information he knows about the previous client to gain some strategic advantage.

Fourth, remember that we *impute* most conflicts of one lawyer to the entire firm where the lawyer works—especially in cases like this, with former clients and new clients. Imputed conflicts are often solvable through "screening" the lawyer with the direct conflict from the matter so that no confidential information will spread to the other lawyers that might injure the former client.

Finally, remember that some situations will involve completely unrelated matters—the lawyer may have handled a simple real estate closing for the first client and now may be handling an unrelated business contract dispute for the new client. Unrelated matters are the easiest to obtain consent and the least likely to pose hazards for the lawyer as she proceeds. Other situations, however, involve substantially related matters, where the lawyer might need to challenge or impeach the very documents that he drafted for the previous client. Let's consider a scenario where the lawyer's representation involved a related matter.

QUESTION 5. The past comes backs to haunt. Attorney Albert worked at Ricks, Sawyer & Thompson for five years and specialized in real estate. During the last three years, Albert has worked intensively on Client Callahan's properties and disputes that arose. Before leaving Ricks, Sawyer & Thompson, Albert handled a new real estate deal for Callahan that resulted in the erection of a new apartment complex. Albert now works at Friedman & Grisley and receives a new case assignment. Albert discovers that the new client, Raymond Bradley, is a small business owner located next to Callahan's apartment complex and is suing Callahan for a disputed right of way.

- **A.** Albert may represent Bradley if Callahan consents in writing to him doing so.
- **B.** Albert may not represent Bradley in the same or substantially the same matter unless Callahan consents in writing.
- **C.** Albert may not represent Bradley in the same or substantially the same matter unless Bradley consents in writing.
- **D.** Albert's firm may represent Bradley because Albert has left Ricks, Sawyer & Thompson and no one in Friedman & Grisley has confidential information about Callahan.

ANALYSIS. After a client-lawyer relationship terminates, a lawyer still has continuing obligations with respect to confidentiality and conflicts of interest. In situations where a lawyer has a new client whose interests are directly adverse to a former client, Rule 1.9 governs the duties that the lawyer has to his former client; Rule 1.9(a) states "A lawyer who has formerly represented a client in a matter shall not thereafter represent another person in the same or a substantially related matter in which that person's interests are materially adverse to the interests of the former client unless the former client gives informed consent, confirmed in writing." Here, the matters are substantially similar, or relate to each other, because they involve the same transaction or legal dispute: the real estate transaction.

A is correct because Albert, who has represented Callahan in the past, is permitted to represent Bradley, even though his interests are materially adverse to Callahan's, if Albert obtains written informed consent from Callahan, his former client.

B is wrong because it states the inverse of the rule. If Callahan, the former client, consents in writing to Albert's representation of the current client, Bradley, then Albert may represent Bradley, even if it is in the same or substantially related matter.

C is incorrect because it calls for the current client to give the informed written consent of Albert's representation. Rule 1.9(a) requires the former client to give the consent, not the current client.

D provides a partly true, but incorrect answer. Although Albert has confidential information about the former client, no one else in his firm has confidential information about Callahan, and thus will not be disqualified. Albert's knowledge of the client will not be imputed to the whole firm because he can be adequately screened. The policy of not imputing Albert's knowledge to his new firm and thus disqualifying the whole firm goes against promoting the movement of lawyers between firms or clients freely changing counsel. However, Albert is still required to obtain Callahan's consent in order to represent his new client, making D incorrect.

F. Third-Party Compensation and Influence—Relatives

Sometimes, lawyers represent a client whose legal fee payments will come from another source—the client's parents, employer, insurer, a friend, or a non-profit entity interested in this case or this client (e.g., the NRA, the ACLU, the Sierra Club, or the Anti-Defamation League). The potential conflict of interest lies in the fact that the client (the person the lawyer is representing) may have goals or interests in the case that differ from the goals of the third party that is paying the lawyer. Sometimes, the party paying the lawyer also hired the lawyer in the first place and sees itself as the lawyer's client, but the client is the person whom the lawyer represents, not the person writing the checks.

The comments to Rules 1.7 and 1.8(f) address this commonplace conflict-of-interest situation. "Lawyers are frequently asked to represent a client under circumstances in which a third person will compensate the lawyer, in whole or in part. The third person might be a relative or friend, an indemnitor (such as a liability insurance company) or a co-client (such as a corporation sued along with one or more of its employees)." (Comment 11, ABA MR 1.8). The comments on Rule 1.7 explicitly endorse such arrangements as long as the client (the person who actually needs representation) consents to the arrangement (as Aaron apparently did in Question 6). The comments on Rule 1.8, however, qualify this by warning, "[L]awyers are prohibited from accepting or continuing such representations unless the lawyer determines that there will be no interference with the lawyer's independent professional judgment and there is informed consent from the client."

Try to solve the following problem involving parents who hire a lawyer to represent their sort-of-adult child.

QUESTION 6. **Parents hiring lawyers for their college kids.** Aaron, a college sophomore, is facing criminal charges related to a drunk driving accident the previous night. To his great relief, Aaron's parents visit the firm of Lawyer Lucas, and retain him as defense counsel for their son, agreeing to cover all fees and expenses. The criminal charges in this case allow for jail time or hefty fines as potential punishments. The prosecution offers a plea bargain—a $2,000 fine, a few hours of community service, and six months' probation, but no jail time. Aaron, the defendant, is thrilled, but his parents insist that Lawyer Lucas decline the plea bargain and go to trial, which Lucas is certain will result in a conviction and a short jail sentence. The parents believe a short jail term will be good for their son and teach him a lesson, and paying the $2,000 fine on top of the lawyer's fees will force them to forego their vacation plans that year. A loud argument ensues in the conference room between the parents and Aaron over the best course of action. How should Lawyer Lucas proceed?

A. The lawyer should represent the wishes of the parents, as they retained him for his services, and they are paying his fees.
B. The lawyer should follow his own judgment about what would be the best result in this case, given that there is a disagreement between the party he represents and the party paying his fees.
C. The lawyer must follow the decision of Aaron, who is his real client, and accept the plea; he should have explained to the parents in advance that they could not control the case even if they paid his fees.
D. The lawyer has a duty to both Aaron and his parents as joint clients, and must wait until they reach an agreement about how to proceed.

ANALYSIS. This problem illustrates the situation in which the parents hire a lawyer to represent their teenaged or twenty-something child. Conflicts are common as the parents may have a different agenda than the child, who is the actual client. This case includes a special wrinkle because it is a criminal matter, involving a plea bargain, and there are more cases about plea bargain scenarios than about many other third-party conflict situations. Let's work through the possible answers in light of the rules.

A is wrong, because Rule 1.7(a) explicitly directs lawyers to follow the client's decisions about such questions, and a line of Supreme Court decisions about plea bargains reinforces this view. In addition, Rule 5.4(c) provides, "A lawyer shall not permit a person who recommends, employs, or pays the lawyer to render legal services for another to direct or regulate the lawyer's professional judgment in rendering such legal services."

B is also wrong, because it contradicts Rule 1.7; moreover, Rule 1.2(a) provides that the client, not the lawyer, must decide whether to accept a plea bargain: "In a criminal case, the lawyer shall abide by the client's decision, after consultation with the lawyer, as to a plea to be entered, whether to waive jury trial and whether the client will testify."

C is the correct answer. Rule 1.2(a) specifically requires lawyers to follow the client's decision about plea bargains in criminal cases, and Rules 1.7(a) and 1.8(f) contemplate the scenario where someone else is paying the lawyer's fee—and still require the lawyer to go with what the client wants, not the party funding the case.

D is incorrect, although it might be prudent for the lawyer in such a case to spend some time trying to resolve the disagreement and remind the parents that his retainer agreement requires him to follow Aaron's choice. The rules mandate that the lawyer follow the wishes of the client, or withdraw from representation where the conflict of interest interferes too much with the lawyer's ability to provide appropriate representation. There is no provision in the rules for a lawyer simply to stall indefinitely and wait for a consensus to emerge among parties with conflicting interests.

G. Consent to Third-Party Compensation and Influence

In situations where one party is paying for a lawyer to represent another (parents-children, employer-employee, insurer-insured) the represented person must consent to the arrangement in writing at the beginning of the representation, according to the comment to Rule 1.8(f). In some situations, as with insurers or parents, clients typically consent readily to the compensation arrangement. Less common is the situation where an anonymous third party offers to pay the lawyer, but it does occur (both in real life and on the MPRE or law school exams).

Anonymous donors, secret admirers, or well-meaning friends and neighbors cannot fund the legal representation unless the client actually gives informed consent, because the client may be aware of strong conflicts of interest that are unknown to the lawyer at the outset. Note that this does not apply to situations where the funding is more remote and not directed at an individual client—for example, a neighborhood legal aid clinic may receive all its funding from two or three wealthy donors, who pay the clinic to represent indigent clients in that area generally.

It is important to recognize the multiple issues created by the third-party conflict situation—not only must the lawyer pursue the goals and wishes of the client (not the third-party payer), but the arrangement must have the client's consent at the outset. In other words, even where the lawyer fully represents the goals and interests of the client exclusively, there may still be a conflict problem (and a rule violation) if the client did not agree to having the third party pay the lawyer's fees. Some clients would decline the lawyer's representation under such circumstances, either because they fear that the third party will exert inappropriate influence over the lawyer (due to their financial control of the case), or because the client does not want to feel indebted to the third party thereafter, for a variety of reasons. On the other hand, remember that merely obtaining the client's consent does not eliminate all the potential issues here regarding conflicts. As the previous problem illustrated, even where a client consents to the arrangement, the lawyer has to be vigilant to honor to goals and interest of the client instead of the goals or desires of the party paying the lawyer. Consider the following scenario as an illustration of consent issues.

QUESTION 7. Secret admirer. Lindsey is a single mother working as a cashier in a liquor store. She is behind on her rent, and her landlord has provided written notice of his intent to evict her from her apartment; a complicating factor in the eviction is that the landlord did not fully honor the terms of the lease regarding conditions in the apartment parking lot. She meets with a lawyer for a free initial consultation, but realizes she cannot possibly afford the lawyer's fees, so she leaves and starts planning to move home with her parents. Lindsey also discusses her problems with one or two of her friendly customers. To her surprise, the lawyer calls her the next day and offers to represent her free of charge, and she returns to the office and signs a retainer to this effect. Unbeknownst to Lindsey, a regular customer at the liquor store, Richard, is infatuated with her, and having learned of her plight, Richard contacted the lawyer and offered to pay all the fees for the lawyer's representation of Lindsey, on the condition that Lindsey never know about it. Richard wants to keep Lindsey in the neighborhood so that he might someday win her affections. Under the Model Rules, how should the lawyer handle this situation?

A. The lawyer can represent Lindsey under this arrangement as long as he explains to Richard that Lindsey will have ultimate control over the case decisions, not Richard.

B. The lawyer absolutely cannot represent Lindsey without obtaining her written consent, even though she would receive free legal help and the lawyer would represent her diligently.

C. The lawyer can represent Lindsey as long as he discloses to her that someone else is paying his fee, but he should keep Richard's identity confidential.

D. The lawyer should decline the representation because Lindsey clearly has no case here, given that she is behind on rent, and the eviction is a legal certainty.

ANALYSIS. This scenario describes an anonymous third party who tries to hire a lawyer to represent a client. The anonymous donor scenario is helpful to illustrate the requirement of client consent, a point that may be less clear when looking at third-party compensation arrangements that the client expected (such as parents) or bargained for ahead of time (insurers, employers). As mentioned above, in situations where one party is paying for a lawyer to represent another (parents-children, employer-employee, insurer-insured), the represented person must consent to the arrangement in writing at the beginning of the representation, according to the official comment to Rule 1.8(f).

A is wrong because the arrangement of a secret funding source is not permissible under the Model Rules. The tricky part about this answer is that in other situations, where the client consents to having another person pay the legal fees, the lawyer indeed has a duty to explain to the funder that the client (the person the lawyer represents) has control over the decisions in the representation, not the funding source.

B is correct. Even though it seems like there would be a social benefit in helping the poor receive legal representation, and despite a lawyer's intentions to provide adequate, conscientious representation, the Model Rules forbid this scenario because of the conflicts of interest that are likely to arise. For example, in this case it might be better for Lindsey in the long run to relocate, and if she knew Richard's intentions, she might be uncomfortable with the situation. This includes the likelihood that Richard will later feel that Lindsey owes him a debt of gratitude, or that Richard will try to control the course of the eviction proceedings to keep Lindsey in his neighborhood. As a general rule of thumb, lawyers will need to obtain written consent from clients whenever there is a potential conflict of interest—between two clients, between the lawyer and the client, or between the client and a third party, as in this hypothetical.

C is incorrect because Comment 12 on Rule 1.8 says that lawyers must obtain "informed consent," that is, the client must know about "the identity of the third-party payer." It is not enough to tell a client that she has a secret admirer or that an anonymous donor is graciously covering her legal fees. Clients have a right to know *who* is paying the lawyer. This makes sense from a policy standpoint, because clients are usually aware of the nuance of their relationship with the third-party payer, especially when it is a friend or relative, and will often have a better sense than the lawyer has about whether the other party will try to push an agenda and control the course of the representation. The lawyer could face discipline, or malpractice liability, for failure to disclose the identity of the payer as part of obtaining the client's written consent.

D provides an incorrect reason for declining the case, even though the lawyer should decline representation for other reasons—the secret third-party payer. Rule 1.8 and the accompanying comments preclude the lawyer from taking the case under these circumstances, regardless of the merits of the case. In addition, D is incorrect because the facts state that the eviction case is complicated—both parties are in partial breach of the lease, and depending on the seriousness of the landlord's breach, a court might waive or reduce the amount of back rent due. The real problem here is the lawyer hiding from his client that a third party is paying him to represent her.

H. Conflicts Between Lawyer and Client—Sex with a Client

Rule 1.8(j) plainly prohibits sexual relationships between lawyers and their clients unless the relationship already existed when the representation commenced. Comments 17–19 on Rule 1.8 provide policy rationales for the rule—the inherent imbalance of power in the lawyer-client relationship means sexual contact is likely to be exploitative, and even where it is not, the intimate relationship will probably cloud the lawyer's judgment in the case and prevent objectivity in the representation.

When approaching exam problems, watch for two exceptions. First, the prohibition applies only to sexual relationships that start after representation has begun. If a lawyer chooses to represent someone who is already his sexual partner, we handle the situation as if the lawyer were representing a close friend or family member. Lawyers should be careful about their objectivity in such cases, but they do not have to cease their relationship with the person in order to provide representation.

Second, this is one type of conflict that is *not imputed* to the other lawyers in a firm, and this is an exception frequently tested on the MPRE. Consider the following problem.

QUESTION 8. "I have needs." Lucille Bluth hires attorney Wayne Jarvis to represent her and her family in a complex federal case involving the family business and charges of securities fraud and racketeering. Early in the representation, Lucille and the lawyer, Wayne, start dating and become sexually involved, to the consternation of the rest of the family. Lucille and Wayne rationalize the relationship by saying that they each have "needs" that their new romantic partner meets, and they have even discussed marriage as an eventuality. Is the lawyer subject to discipline for this relationship?

A. No, the Constitution does not allow a state bar or the judiciary to interfere in private matters such as a lawyer's consensual sexual relationships.

B. Yes, the lawyer is representing the other family members as well, and they disapprove of the relationship at this time; if they approved of the relationship, it would be fine.

C. No, because it appears this will be a long-term or permanent relationship, perhaps leading to marriage, so there is very little risk of the lawyer exploiting his client or the lawyer having clouded judgment.

D. Yes, unless the sexual relationship predates the beginning of legal representation, the lawyer absolutely cannot represent a client with whom he has such a relationship.

ANALYSIS. This problem presents the scenario in which a lawyer has commenced a sexual relationship with one of his clients. This violates a clear rule, and the lawyer could face disciplinary action. Also, keep in mind that such relationships often end in a malpractice action against the lawyer by the client-sexual partner.

A is wrong, because at least up to the time of this writing, the Supreme Court has never held that prohibiting sexual relationships in certain settings (employment relationships, military, professor-student, or lawyer-client) would violate the Constitution, and such prohibitions are fairly common. The courts have upheld numerous rules that pertain to the integrity of the legal profession and avoiding conflicts of interest.

B is also incorrect, although it makes a good point that there is a potential conflict of interest here between the members of the family as co-clients and co-defendants in the federal enforcement proceedings. Even if the relationship between Lucille and Wayne were permissible, it would create questions of loyalty between Wayne and the other family members that he represents. Nevertheless, Wayne would be subject to discipline even if the rest of the family (and all his clients) approved of the relationship, because Rule 1.8(j) provides no consideration for acceptance by the others involved.

C is wrong because it does not matter if the relationship promises to become permanent or lead to marriage—in fact, based on the policy concerns about the lawyer's objectivity and the potential for exploiting clients, a permanent relationship would raise the stakes for both individuals, making the lawyer even less objective and the client even more vulnerable.

D is correct, because according to Rule 1.8(j), the lawyer, Wayne Jarvis, could be subject to discipline for starting a sexual relationship with a client, and it would undermine his defense if other family members sued him for malpractice later on. Note that the rules contain a single exception—sexual relationships that start before the representation begins.

I. Rule 1.9—Duties to Former Clients

Even though a lawyer no longer represents a former client, a lawyer still owes certain duties to the former client. This duty may interfere with a lawyer's representation to a prospective client. In this chapter, you will learn about the duties that lawyers owe to former clients and how those duties may affect the relationship between lawyers and their prospective clients.

According to the Model Rule of Professional Conduct, Section 1.9, a lawyer may not represent a prospective client in a matter that is "the same or substantially related matter" in which the prospective client's interest is materially adverse to the interest of the former client, *unless* the former client gives informed written consent.

A lawyer is not prohibited from representing a prospective client in a matter that is factually distinct from the former client's representation. However, the lawyer is prohibited from representing the prospective client if it involve the same transaction, legal dispute, or if a substantial risk that the confidential information obtained in the prior presentation would help the prospective client's case in a subsequent matter. The passage of time may render some confidential information obsolete.

A lawyer may represent a prospective client, regardless the general rule, as long as the former client gives informed written consent. Informed written consent requires that the former client know of the consequences of giving the lawyer consent to representing the prospective client.

QUESTION 9. **Former prosecutor.** Attorney began her career as a prosecutor at the District Attorney's Office. During her tenure as a prosecutor, she brought charges against an individual suspected of sending ricin, a deadly toxin, in an envelope to a prominent politician, apparently in an unsuccessful attempt to assassinate the public official. The jury found the evidence too attenuated, and acquitted the defendant. Shortly thereafter, another person, who was a member of a terrorist organization, confessed to sending the ricin and provided extensive evidence of his plot to kill the politician to make a political statement. Attorney resigned from the District Attorney's Office, partly out of humiliation over this case, and went into private practice. Eighteen months later, the accused individual decides to sue the government over wrongful arrest, slander, libel, and wrongful prosecution over the case in which he obtained an acquittal. Attorney feels that her superiors at the D.A.'s Office had pressured her to press charges in order to satisfy the public uproar over the ricin letters, despite having scanty evidence that the accused individual was actually guilty. Attorney offers to represent the accused individual in his lawsuit against the government, partly to make amends or atone for her role in what she now views as an abuse of government power and a great injustice. Would it be proper for Attorney to handle this case, given her good intentions?

A. Yes, because the test for determining if an improper conflict of interest exists between former clients and a new client is the lawyer's subjective motivations in undertaking the new representation, and in this instance, Attorney is merely trying to make amends for her past mistakes.

B. Yes, because Attorney has a duty to repudiate her previous wrongful actions, and her representation of the individual will send a strong message to other prosecutors, which in turn serves the public interest.

C. No, a lawyer who has prosecuted an accused person could not properly represent the accused in a subsequent civil action against the government concerning the same transaction.

D. No, because a prosecutor cannot ethically "switch sides" and start representing criminal defendants in public practice, regardless of whether the same individuals are involved as clients.

ANALYSIS. The issue in this case is whether Attorney can represent the accused individual against her former client, the state.

A is incorrect in this situation because Attorney is planning on being adverse with the state and suing the state based on the same case that she tried. Furthermore, the answer misstates the law; nowhere in the rules does it state that the test for determining improper conflict does not involve a lawyer's subjective motivation.

B is also incorrect because it gives weight to Attorney's subjective motivation. It does not matter what Attorney felt. This rule was created to preserve a former client's confidential information, not give weight to attorney sympathy.

C is the correct answer because it recognizes the conflict of interest. Attorney cannot represent the accused individual because the accused individual wants to sue the state for the same case that the Attorney trialed.

D is incorrect because it gives weight to Attorney's subjective ability to competently represent the accused individual. The general rule does not impose a presumption that a prosecutor can't switch sides. As you will see later on, Attorney could have represented the accused individual if Attorney had written informed consent from the state to represent the accused individual.

QUESTION 10. **The defendant.** Client consults with Attorney regarding a criminal case in which Client is the defendant. Attorney previously represented Client's friend, who is a co-defendant in the current case, in another matter. Attorney does not believe that the previous representation of Client's friend will disable him from providing competent and diligent services to Client, and the parties are not making any claims against each other. May Attorney represent Client in this case?

A. Yes, attorneys may represent conflicting parties as long as both clients give informed consent and have had the opportunity to consult with independent counsel regarding the matter.
B. Yes, attorneys may represent conflicting parties as long as both clients give informed consent and both parties confirm their consent in writing.
C. No, attorneys shall not ever represent conflicting parties, as it is impossible for attorneys to provide competent and diligent services when representing conflicting parties.
D. No, attorneys cannot represent conflicting parties when the parties are co-defendants in criminal matters.

ANALYSIS. The issue in this case is whether Client's interest is materially adverse to the Client's friend interest. Does Client and Client's friend interest differ in a criminal suit? Can Attorney's representation of Client in this criminal matter adversely affect Client's friend? If Client and Client's friend's interest are materially adverse, then Attorney cannot represent Client, unless the exception applies. Is there consent? What type of consent is effective?

A appears to be correct because it recognizes that Client and Client's friend are adverse. As co-defendant for the same crime, they can blame each other for the alleged conduct or even make a plea deal to testify against one another. Because they are adverse, Attorney can only represent Client if Attorney gets the parties' consent. Even so, Client's friend (Attorney's former client) must give informed *written* consent. The answer insinuates that any consent, whether oral or written, is sufficient. But oral consent is not effective for the purpose of this rule. It is also not necessary for Client and Client's friend to consult with independent counsel. Thus A is incorrect.

In this situation, **B** is the correct answer because it also recognizes that the parties are adverse and that Attorney can only represent both parties if the parties give written informed consent.

C is incorrect because Attorney is allowed to represent Client, if Attorney obtains Client's written informed consent. This answer ignores the exception, therefore it is incorrect.

Lastly, **D** is another version of **C** as it ignores the written informed consent exception. The rules do not make any exception between civil and criminal cases.

Firm Imputation

A lawyer cannot knowingly represent a prospective client in a matter that is the "same or substantially similar" related matter, where the prospective client's interest is materially adverse to a client of the lawyer's former law firm. Furthermore, a lawyer is prohibited from representation only if they have actual knowledge of the information protected in Sections 1.6 and 1.9(c).

Like the general rule, a lawyer may represent the prospective client, regardless of the former firm imputation, if the former client gives informed written consent.

QUESTION 11. **The patent lawyer.** Attorney worked for Big Firm in their intellectual property department, specializing in patent applications and patent enforcement, as well as some trademark disputes for clients. Unbeknownst to Attorney, the regular litigation department at Big Firm undertook representation of a Trucking company in defending against a personal injury lawsuit over a roadway accident involving one of the trucks. Attorney worked in the Washington, D.C. office of Big Firm, near the United States Patent and Trademark Office, and the litigators handling the truck accident are in the firm's Dallas office. Each office of Big Firm has its own local computer network for sharing documents and files between lawyers there. It is possible for lawyers at Big Firm to access the networks of other satellite offices, however, with a special login that most lawyers never use. Attorney has never accessed the files of the Dallas office except for one trademark case four years ago. Attorney did not make partner at Big Firm, so he left and went to work for a small plaintiff's firm in Kansas. One of Attorney's first case assignments was the same truck accident case in which Big Firm was defending Trucking Company; Attorney's new firm represents Plaintiff in the case. Attorney was not aware of the case or that Big Firm represented Trucking Company until the new firm assigned him to the case as second chair on the litigation. Is Attorney subject to disqualification in this matter?

A. Yes, because even though Attorney did not have actual knowledge of confidential information about the trucking company, he had the ability to access the files if he had used a special login while he was at Big Firm, and this creates the appearance of impropriety.

B. Yes, because Attorney's work in the patent enforcement division of Big Firm gave him some exposure to Big Firm's behind-the-scenes approach to litigation generally, as well as familiarity with Big Firm's litigators, thus providing Attorney with an unfair advantage, therefore both Attorney and the other lawyers in the new firm would be subject to disqualification.

C. No, because Attorney now works for a firm in Kansas, and both offices of Big Firm mentioned were in other states, where many of the lawyers would not have licenses to practice law in Kansas, so Attorney would be subject to disqualification, but not the other lawyers in the new firm.

D. No, if a lawyer while with one firm acquired no knowledge or information relating to a particular client of the firm, and that lawyer later joined another firm, neither the lawyer individually nor the second firm are disqualified from representing another client in the same or a related matter even though the interests of the two clients conflict.

ANALYSIS. Like all the previous questions in this chapter, the issue is whether Attorney may represent a client, Plaintiff. May Attorney still represent Plaintiff despite the fact that the two matters are adverse? What does Attorney know about Trucking Company? Does access count as knowledge?

A is the wrong answer because it doesn't matter that the Attorney had access to Trucking Company's files. The rule is that Attorney is prohibited from representing Plaintiff if Attorney has actual knowledge of any information gained during his employment at Attorney's former firm. Since Attorney worked in the intellectual patent department and not the litigation department, Attorney did not have access to Trucking Company's file.

B is similar to **A** in that it ignores whether Attorney has actual knowledge of Trucking Co. It does not matter that Attorney had exposure to the litigation department or that familiarity with the previous law firm would give Attorney unfair advantage. There is no fact that indicates that Attorney has actual knowledge of Trucking Company's confidential information.

C is also incorrect, because the location of the firms is irrelevant. The location of the firm in no way indicates whether Attorney has knowledge of Trucking Company's confidential information.

D is the correct answer because it correctly restates the law and correctly applies the facts to the law. Attorney may still represent Plaintiff, even though Plaintiff's interest is directly adverse to Trucking Company, because the facts do not indicate that Attorney has actual knowledge of Trucking Company's confidential information.

Former Client's Confidential Information

Even if a lawyer has permission to represent a prospective client, he may be limited in using and revealing the former client's confidential information. A lawyer is prohibited from using information gained in relation to the representation of the former client to her disadvantage. The information protected by this rule is any confidential information gained during representation of the former client. In addition, a lawyer may use the information if the rules allow it or when the information has become general knowledge. There are many situations where the Model Rules of Professional Conduct allow lawyers to use former clients' confidential information. For example, the attorney may disclose a former client's confidential information when there is a dispute between the former client and the attorney, where a judge orders disclosure, and in order to protect others from imminent death or serious bodily injury.

A lawyer may not reveal information relating to the representation of the former client. This prohibition deals with revealing the former client's information, regardless of whether or not it is to the disadvantage of the former client. Similarly a lawyer may disclose the client's information if the rules allow disclosure.

QUESTION 12. **The third wife.** Attorney represented Husband twenty years ago in a divorce with Husband's first wife. Husband is a well-known local celebrity, a retired professional athlete who became a semi-successful actor and an outspoken advocate of a radical political cause. Recently, Husband's third wife approached Attorney asking him to represent her in obtaining a divorce from Husband. There are no children from the marriage—their children from previous marriages are now adults—and the distribution of assets will follow the terms of a carefully drafted prenuptial agreement between Husband and his third wife, which Husband's new lawyer drafted for them. Husband long ago provided written informed consent for future conflicts of interest if Attorney represented another party with adverse interests to Husband. Attorney does not believe that any confidential information learned from representing Husband twenty years ago in his first divorce will be relevant to the pending third divorce. On the other hand, there is regular media coverage of Husband's trysts and on-and-off sexual relationships with various actresses and female socialites in the area, and marital infidelity could trigger certain exception clauses in the prenuptial agreement. Can Attorney use the information about Husband's recent indiscretions in representing the third wife?

A. Yes, as long as the Husband's new lawyer provides written informed consent to the use of the information in the divorce proceeding.
B. Yes, the fact that a lawyer has once served a client does not preclude the lawyer from using generally known information about that client when later representing another client.
C. No, not if Attorney learned confidential information about Husband having a pattern of marital infidelity during his prior representation of Husband.
D. No, the fact that there is a prenuptial agreement with exceptions triggered by marital infidelity should preclude Attorney from using such information.

ANALYSIS. This question involves the use of Husband's recent indiscretion against him. Remember, the rule states that a lawyer may not use an ex-client's confidential information against the client. So the issue is whether the Husband's recent indiscretion is considered confidential.

A is incorrect because the answer assumes that Husband's recent indiscretion is confidential. Remember the confidential information must be obtained during representation. Husband's recent indiscretion was obtained after the representation of Husband was over. Therefore, the information is not protected under this rule and written informed consent is not necessary.

B is the correct answer because it recognizes that Husband's recent indiscretion is not confidential. The information is public information that is regularly disseminated in the media. Since it is public, Attorney does not need Husband's written informed consent to use Husband's recent indiscretion against him.

C is wrong because it assumes that Attorney learned about Husband's indiscretion during Husband's representation. The term "recently" indicates that Attorney found out about Husband's indiscretion after Husband's representation ended. Answer **D** is wrong because the facts do not mention anything about prenuptial agreement being triggered by a marital infidelity.

D is wrong because it focuses merely on the consequences of the potential disclosure, overlooking the nature of the original communication. If the information is not confidential in the first place, the mere fact that its disclosure might have legal consequences (such as triggering a clause in the prenuptial agreement) does not prevent the lawyer from making the disclosure.

J. Rule 1.10—Imputation of Conflict of Interest

A lawyer shall not represent a client with whom they have conflict of interest with under Model Rules 1.7 and 1.9. In addition to those rules, a disqualified lawyer's conflict of interest may be imputed to the other lawyers in the firm and those lawyers will also be disqualified from representing a client. Model Rule 1.10 governs such imputation: from lawyer to lawyer, and from lawyer to firm.

Lawyer-to-lawyer imputation occurs when two or more lawyers work in a firm and all the lawyers are disqualified from representing a potential client because one lawyer in the firm has a conflict of interest with the potential client. The general rule for lawyer-to-lawyer imputation is that a lawyer is prohibited from representing a client, where a fellow lawyer from the same firm is disqualified from representing that client due to a conflict of interest. Yet there are two instances in which the conflict of interest is not imputed: (1) a disqualified lawyer's conflict of interest is based on personal interest of the disqualified lawyer, or (2) a disqualified lawyer's conflict of interest is due to the disqualified lawyer's association with his or her prior firm.

The personal interest exception generally arises in cases where a lawyer has strong political or religious belief that may impair the lawyer from effectively representing a client. The Model Rules suggest that other lawyers in the firm should not be prohibited from representing a client where question of loyalty to a client and protection of confidential information is not a problem. Therefore, if a disqualified lawyer's conflict of interest is due to (1) personal interest of the disqualified lawyer, and (2) there is not a significant risk of materially limiting the client's representation, the remaining lawyers in the firm may represent the prospective client.

QUESTION 13. **The abortion clinic.** Attorney works for a firm. She also describes herself as an outspoken advocate for the rights of unborn children, that is, she passionately favors legal restrictions on abortion. A local abortion clinic asks the firm to represent it in litigation over recent zoning measures that would significantly limit its hours of operation and therefore the number of clients the clinic could accept. The firm agrees to the representation. Attorney firmly refuses to have any part in the representation, and though no formal screening measures are in place, everyone else in the firm avoids discussing the case with her or around her because they are afraid of receiving another lecture about the wrongfulness of abortion. Early in the litigation, the judge considers disqualifying the firm because it employs Attorney, who has a reputation in the community for her advocacy against legalized abortion. Neither the clinic nor the opposing party (the municipal zoning authority) provided written consent to a conflict of interest. Should the firm be subject to disqualification in this case?

A. Yes, because the firm did not implement formal screening measures to ensure that Attorney receives no confidential information about the case and cannot influence the other lawyers working on the case.
B. Yes, because the firm did not obtain informed written consent from both parties to the potential conflict of interest.
C. No, the firm should not be disqualified where one lawyer in a firm could not effectively represent a given client because of strong political beliefs, but that lawyer will do no work on the case and the personal beliefs of the lawyer will not materially limit the representation by others in the firm.
D. No, because preserving women's access to legalized abortion is such an important fundamental right that it would be improper to limit the abortion clinic's options for representation in the matter, and other firms may also have conflicts of interest that would preclude representation.

ANALYSIS. This case is clearly about the personal interest of a lawyer being imputed onto another lawyer in the same firm. Model Rule 1.10 Comment 3 states that where a lawyer cannot effectively represent a client because of his beliefs, other lawyers in the firm may represent the potential client as long as the belief of the disqualified lawyer does not materially limit the representation by other lawyers in the firm, and that the disqualified lawyer will do no work on that client's case.

A sounds correct because it recognizes that there is a conflict of interest between the Abortion Clinic and the Attorney, but it is wrong because Attorney is not working on the case and she is not limiting the firm's ability to represent Abortion Clinic. Furthermore, **A** incorrectly talks about implementing formal screening measures and confidential information. Model Rule 1.10(a) states nothing about the need to implement formal screening measures and receiving confidential information in such circumstances.

For the same reasons as stated in **A**, **B** is also incorrect. **B** would be correct if Attorney did materially limit the firm's representation of Abortion Clinic or if Attorney did work on Abortion Clinic's case. One of the ways that Attorney could have materially limited the firm's representation is if Attorney was a partner of the firm because then the loyalty of the other lawyers is torn between the Client and the Attorney.

C is correct. The other lawyers in the firm may represent Abortion Clinic because Attorney refuses to work on the case and Attorney's personal belief on abortion is not limiting the other lawyers' ability to effectively represent Abortion Clinic.

D is incorrect because it states policy reasons as a justification for not disqualifying the other lawyers in the firm. Remember, Model Rule 1.10 is used to protect the relationship between a lawyer and client and protect the client's confidential information. It is not created to further women's access to abortion or other political or religious beliefs. Furthermore, it does not apply the rule to the fact of the problem.

Lawyer's Prior Firm Exception

This exception allows a law firm to represent a client, regardless of what a disqualified attorney did in the prior representation, under certain circumstances. Model Rule 1.9 states that a lawyer is generally prohibited from representing a prospective client, whose interest is adverse to a former client or a client of a former firm that the lawyer was associated with. Model Rule 1.10 states that where a lawyer in a firm is disqualified from representing a client, all other lawyers in the firm are also disqualified. Even so, according to the lawyer's prior firm exception, a disqualified lawyer's conflict of interest is not imputed onto another lawyer in the firm as long as:

1. The conflict of interest is based on the disqualified lawyer's association with a prior firm;
2. The disqualified lawyer is timely screened from representation;
3. The disqualified lawyer may not receive direct compensation from the fee; A lawyer may receive a fee or salary according to an agreement established prior to the representation.
4. Written notice is promptly given to the former client which shall include:
   a. Description of the screening procedure
   b. Statement of the firm about compliance with Model Rule 1.10
5. Certification of compliance with Model Rule 1.10 and screening procedure at reasonable intervals upon the request of the former client.

There are a few minor details to remember along with two exceptions. First, the personal interest exception applies only to current lawyers in a firm. Second, the lawyer's prior firm exception only applies to a lawyer moving from one firm to another. Third, this rule does not affect non-lawyers, such as law clerks or secretaries. A lawyer is not prohibited from representation due to events before the lawyer became a lawyer, for example, when a lawyer is doing work as a law student. Fourth, even if neither of the two exceptions applies, a lawyer may still represent a potential client, regardless of Model Rule 1.10, if the affected or former client gives informed consent, confirmed in writing.

QUESTION 14. Married to the lawyer. A legal secretary in a law firm is married to the owner of an independent retail-clothing store. The firm undertakes representation of a clothing wholesaler, who is suing the same independent clothing store over nonpayment for shipments of merchandise. The legal secretary's husband hires another firm to represent his store in the lawsuit, and his lawyer asks the court to disqualify the legal secretary's firm because of her position there. Should the firm be subject to disqualification?

A. Yes, because the conflict of interest is too great where the defendant's spouse works for the opposing counsel's firm.
B. Yes, because the lawsuit involves nonpayment for a shipment of merchandise, and the legal secretary indirectly benefited from her husband keeping these unpaid funds.
C. No, as long as the firm screens the legal secretary from any involvement in the case or from access to any confidential information about the case.
D. No, because the legal secretary is not a lawyer, so the Rules of Professional Conduct do not apply to her personal conflicts of interest.

ANALYSIS. Model Rule 1.10 states that a lawyer may be prevented from representing a client because of a disqualified attorney's conflict of interest. While analyzing this problem, think about: Who has the conflict of interest? Who does this rule apply to? Is loyalty to a client or disclosure of confidential information a problem? If there is a conflict of interest, does the exception apply?

A is wrong because there is no conflict of interest. The secretary has no loyalty to the client. Furthermore, although she works in the firm it does create a presumption that she has access or knows of any confidential information. The major reason why **A** is incorrect is because the Model Rule 1.10 Comment 4 specifically states that the rule does not apply to non-lawyers.

B is also wrong for the same reason as **A**. It does not matter that the secretary received an indirect benefit from being married to her husband.

C is tricky. Answer **C** assumes that there is a conflict of interest. Is there a conflict of interest? If so, what is it? **C** is wrong because there is no conflict of interest. Furthermore, it does not matter that the secretary has a conflict with the clothing wholesaler, because the imputation rule does not apply to non-lawyers.

D is the correct answer, because it correctly states the model rule and recognizes that Model Rule 1.10 does not apply to the secretary. Remember, Model Rule 1.10 seeks to protect the relationship between a lawyer and a client. Nonlawyers have no relationships with clients, and the Model Rules seek to govern the conduct of lawyers; therefore, the rule does not apply to non-lawyers.

Lawyer-to-Firm Imputation

Lawyer-to-firm imputation occurs when a lawyer leaves a firm and the firm is prohibited from representing a prospective client because the former employee has a conflict of interest with the prospective client and the conflict of interest is imputed onto the firm. Model Rule 1.10(b) states that a firm is not restricted from representing a potential client when the former employee-lawyer had a conflict of interest unless (1) "the matter is same or substantially related" to the former employee-lawyer's representation, and (2) any lawyer in the firm has protected information under Model Rules 1.6 and 1.9(c). Similar to the lawyer-to-lawyer imputation, a former or affected client may consent to the conflict of interest if they give informed written consent. The Model Rules allow firms to present potential clients whose interests are directly adverse to a former employee-lawyer of the firm.

QUESTION 15. **The lateral move.** Lawyer worked for Law Firm and represented Client. Sometime after the conclusion of the case, Lawyer left Law Firm. Potential Client consults with Firm after Lawyer left and discusses a potential case with Attorney, another attorney at the firm. Potential Client's interests would be materially adverse to those of Client. Attorney accepts Potential Client's case. Is Attorney subject to discipline?

A. Yes, attorneys are imputed with knowledge of current or previous members of the firm, and attorneys with imputed knowledge shall not accept cases of potential clients whose interests would be materially adverse to those of a prior client of the firm.
B. Yes, an attorney shall obtain the informed consent, confirmed in writing, of a client of a prior attorney's clients if the attorney is going to represent a different client with materially adverse interests.
C. No, when an attorney leaves a law firm, the rules regarding conflicts of interest and imputation do not apply.
D. No, prior attorneys' knowledge is not imputed unless the matter is the same or substantially related and another lawyer in the firm has information that is material to the matter.

ANALYSIS. The issue here is whether a firm is prohibited from representing a potential client because the firm's former employee represented Client in a former case and Potential Client's case is materially adverse to Client. Model Rule 1.10(b) states that a disqualified lawyer's conflict of interest is not imputed onto his former firm, unless (1) the matter is "substantially or materially" related to the disqualified lawyer's representation, and (2) any lawyer remaining at the firm has any protected confidential information.

A is wrong because there are not enough facts to establish that any lawyer remaining at the firm has actual knowledge of Client's confidential information. **A** also incorrectly states the rule. Under Model Rule 1.10, only actual knowledge of protected communication is protected. The rule does not protect imputed knowledge.

B is incorrect because it assumes that the matter is substantially related and that there is a lawyer at the firm with knowledge of Client's protected information. As stated in **A**, there are not enough facts in the problem to establish that any lawyer remaining at the firm has any of Client's confidential information. Therefore, the second prong fails, and **B** is incorrect.

C is wrong because it completely ignores Model Rule 1.10.

D is correct because it correctly states the rule and accurately presents Model Rule 1.10(b).

Imputation of Conflicts of Interest in General

Rule 1.10 sets forth provisions for the imputation of one lawyer's conflict of interest to all the other lawyers in that firm. The main focus is on lawyers who have moved laterally between firms—the primary remedy for conflicts in these situations is "screening" the individual lawyer from any involvement in the matter and informing the affected client from the former firm. There are numerous exceptions, as one might expect, and students should study Rule 1.11 (and its associated comment) before the MPRE.

QUESTION 16. The victim. An attorney works for a firm where another lawyer is representing the defendant in a personal injury lawsuit. The other lawyer has represented the defendant for a long time on unrelated, non-litigation matters, but the personal injury lawsuit is a new case. The victim, the plaintiff in the same personal injury lawsuit, was a college classmate of the attorney and he asks the attorney to represent him in the litigation. The attorney has not learned any confidential information yet about the defendant from his fellow associate at the firm, nor has the attorney learned any confidential information from the victim during their preliminary consultation. The firm decides to undertake the representation of the victim as well. The firm will carefully screen the attorney and lawyer from one another, forbidding them to discuss the case with each other or anyone else in the office, and ensuring that they do not have access to each other's files for the case. In addition, neither lawyer will receive a bonus from the fees received for this litigation. Under the Rules of Professional Conduct, is it proper for the attorney to represent the victim, given these circumstances?

A. Yes, as long as the firm provides notice to the defendant and the victim about the specific screening procedures it has in place, and gives periodic certifications of compliance with the screening procedures.

B. Yes, as long as both the clients provide written informed consent to the conflict of interest, after receiving a detailed explanation of the problems with common representation, and neither party has its fees paid by a third party.

C. No, because the Rules of Professional Conduct impute the conflict of the other lawyer to the attorney, and screening procedures do not apply to conflicts between current clients.

D. No, unless the attorney has already represented the victim in previous unrelated matters while working at another law firm, and joined the new law firm only recently.

ANALYSIS. Comment 2 for Rule 1.10 suggests that imputation of conflicts of interest should be considered as though a single lawyer in the firm owes a duty of loyalty to her client that vicariously binds the other lawyers in the firm. One lawyer who worked at the firm represented the defendant. Any other lawyers within the firm, including the attorney, would be subject to the duty of loyalty to the defendant.

A is incorrect because the victim was never the attorney or the firm's client so the rules requiring notice to the affected former clients is not applicable.

B is incorrect because conflicts of interest between directly adverse clients are considered so strong that they are not waivable. Third-party payment of fees is irrelevant.

C is correct because the defendant is a current client of the firm with a directly adverse interest to the victim. The representation of the victim in this situation would violate the duty of loyalty owed to the defendant.

D is incorrect because it incorrectly applies the "substantially unrelated" test, as the victim is not a former client of the attorney.

QUESTION 17. The shareholder. An attorney is a partner in a law firm, and owns $100,000 worth of stock in Conglomerate Corporation, the named defendant in a new antitrust suit. The attorney's total compensation from the firm is around $15 million per year, including bonuses, and his net worth is around $500 million. His home is worth about $7 million and the attorney inherited it, so the property is unencumbered by any mortgage or liens. The attorney works in a specialized area of law at the firm and does not have much interaction with the other lawyers, except at parties and occasional partners' meetings. Another lawyer in the firm seeks to represent the plaintiffs in the antitrust action against Conglomerate Corporation, which is not a client of the firm. Would it be proper for the firm to represent the plaintiffs in litigation against Conglomerate Corporation?

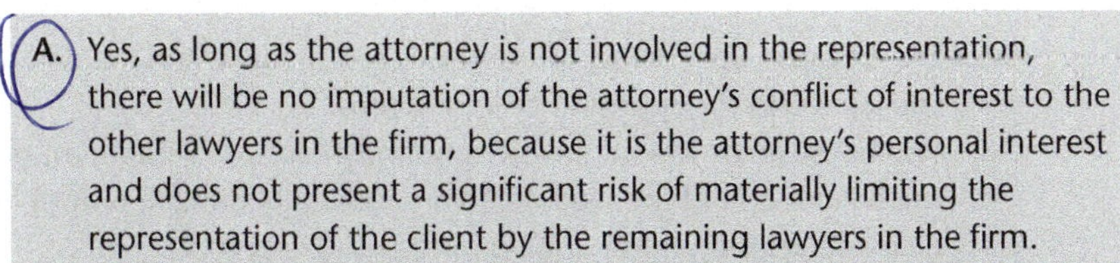

A. Yes, as long as the attorney is not involved in the representation, there will be no imputation of the attorney's conflict of interest to the other lawyers in the firm, because it is the attorney's personal interest and does not present a significant risk of materially limiting the representation of the client by the remaining lawyers in the firm.

B. Yes, as long as the plaintiffs provide written informed consent to the potential conflict of interest, and the firm carefully screens the other lawyer representing them from the rest of the firm.

C. No, because the personal interest of the firm's managing partner in Conglomerate is so great, relative to his earnings and assets, that there is a significant risk of materially limiting the representation of the plaintiffs in their cause of action against Conglomerate.

D. No, because it is a non-consentable conflict of interest for the firm to represent both adverse parties in litigation.

ANALYSIS. When determining whether a conflict of interest would prohibit representation, consider whether the client loyalty or protection of confidential information is at stake. Here, Conglomerate Corporation is not a client of the attorney or his law firm so no duty of loyalty is owed to Conglomerate. Furthermore, if the attorney does not participate in the representation of the plaintiffs any confidential information received by the firm would be protected.

A is correct because the attorney's interest is personal and he will not be involved in the representation of the plaintiffs, therefore no conflict is imputed to the firm or other lawyers in the firm.

B is incorrect because there is no significant risk that the representation of the plaintiffs will be materially limited, therefore the need for written informed consent will not be triggered.

C is incorrect because the attorney's interests are not imputed to the firm and therefore do not limit the remaining lawyers' ability to represent the plaintiffs.

D is incorrect because the firm is not representing Conglomerate and therefore not attempting to represent adverse parties.

QUESTION 18. The secretary's husband. A legal secretary in a law firm is married to the owner of an independent retail-clothing store. The firm undertakes representation of a clothing wholesaler, who is suing the same independent clothing store over nonpayment for shipments of merchandise. The legal secretary's husband hires another firm to represent his store in the lawsuit, and his lawyer asks the court to disqualify the legal secretary's firm because of her position there. Should the firm be subject to disqualification?

A. Yes, because the conflict of interest is too great where the defendant's spouse works for opposing counsel's firm.
B. Yes, because the lawsuit involves nonpayment for a shipment of merchandise, and the legal secretary indirectly benefited from her husband keeping these unpaid funds.
C. No, as long as the firm screens the legal secretary from any involvement in the case or from access to any confidential information about the case.
D. No, because the legal secretary is not a lawyer, so the Rules of Professional Conduct do not apply to her personal conflicts of interest.

ANALYSIS. Conflicts of interest arising from a non-lawyer in the firm do not prohibit the firm from representation so long as the non-lawyer is screened from any personal participation and confidential information is protected. Here, though the legal secretary is married to the adverse party, the firm may represent the clothing wholesaler if it screens the legal secretary from personal participation and confidential information regarding the case.

A is incorrect because the degree of the legal secretary's conflict of interest is not relevant to whether her firm will be disqualified. Because she is a non-lawyer, the firm may represent the clothing wholesaler so long as the legal secretary is screened from any personal participation in the representation.

B is incorrect. Although her indirect benefit creates a conflict of interest, the legal secretary is a non-lawyer and that conflict does not disqualify the firm from representing the clothing wholesaler so long as the legal secretary is screened from any personal involvement and confidential information.

C is correct because it correctly states that a non-lawyer's conflict of interest does not prohibit representation.

D is incorrect because the Rules of Professional Conduct nonetheless apply to the firm that is required to prevent any communication of confidential information. The firm may undertake the representation so long as it screens the legal secretary from personal participation and confidential information.

QUESTION 19. **Client of the lawyer who left.** An attorney represented Small Business Associates while working at Big Firm, her first law firm after law school. When the attorney did not make partner at the firm, she ended her employment there and started her own new firm. The attorney took some of her clients with her, including Small Business Associates, whom she continues to represent. Big Firm no longer has Small Business Associates as a client. Big Firm then agrees to represent Conglomerate Corporation in a trademark infringement case against Small Business Associates, the first such case that the latter has ever faced. Can Big Firm represent Conglomerate in a case against its former client, Small Business Associates?

A. Yes, as long as the matter is not the same or substantially related to that in which the attorney formerly represented the client; and no lawyer remaining in the firm has confidential information about Small Business Associates from when the attorney represented them at that firm.

B. Yes, because otherwise the disqualification of the firm would constitute an agreement not to provide representation to particular clients in the future, which would violate the Rules of Professional Conduct.

C. No, unless the attorney's new firm screens her from the litigation according to the procedures set forth in the Rules of Professional Conduct.

D. No, unless Conglomerate provides written informed consent to the potential conflict of interest.

ANALYSIS. A law firm may represent a party with interests directly adverse to those of a former client so long as the current matter is not the same or substantially related to the prior matter and any lawyers remaining in the firm do not have confidential information that is material to the current matter. Big Firm may represent Conglomerate Corporation in a trademark infringement case against Small Business Associates because the matter is not the same or substantially related to any work the attorney performed for Small Business Associates while she worked for Big Firm.

A is correct because the trademark infringement claim is unrelated to any of Big Firm's prior work performed for Small Business Associates and none of Small Business Associates' confidential information remains at Big Firm.

B is incorrect because Big Firm would not be disqualified under these circumstances.

C is incorrect because the attorney is not the entity with a conflict of interest and would not need to be screened.

D is incorrect because written informed consent is not required here as the matter is not the same or substantially related to that in which the attorney formerly represented the Small Business Associates and no lawyer remaining in the firm has confidential information about Small Business Associates from when the firm represented it.

QUESTION 20. **The law student intern.** Years ago, as a law student, the attorney worked on a case for the client during a law firm internship. Now, the attorney's firm is representing a defendant in a lawsuit in which the client is the plaintiff. The client's new lawyer moves to disqualify the attorney's firm from the representation when it learns that the attorney worked for another firm on behalf of the client when the attorney was still a law student. Is the attorney's firm subject to disqualification in this case?

A. Yes, because when lawyers are associated in a firm, none of them shall knowingly represent a client when any one of them practicing alone would be prohibited from doing so.
B. Yes, unless both parties provided written informed consent and waived the conflict of interest at the beginning of representation.
C. No, as long as the firm screens the attorney from any personal participation in the matter to avoid communication to others in the firm of confidential information that both the non-lawyers and the firm have a legal duty to protect.
D. No, because the attorney was not yet a lawyer during the law student internship, and therefore did not actually provide legal representation for the client in the previous matter.

ANALYSIS. When a law student performs work for a firm, he is a non-lawyer for purposes of the Model Rules. A firm may represent a client when a conflict of interest arises with a non-lawyer so long as the firm screens the non-lawyer from personal participation and confidential information. Though the attorney is now a lawyer, any conflict of interest that may arise from events that occurred while he was a law student will be treated as though he is a non-lawyer.

A is incorrect. Comment 4 to Rule 1.10 clarifies that a conflict of interest with a non-lawyer will not prohibit representation by others in the firm so long as the non-lawyer is screened from any personal participation in the matter.

B is incorrect because as long as the attorney is screened, there is no significant risk that representation of the defendant will be materially limited. The need for written informed consent will not be triggered.

C is correct because the events that give rise to the conflict of interest occurred while the attorney was a non-lawyer. So long as the firm screens him from personal participation and confidential information, the firm will not be subject to disqualification.

D is incorrect because it does not state the screening requirement necessary in a conflict of interest arising from a non-lawyer in the firm.

K. Rule 1.11—Special Conflicts of Interest for Former and Current Government Officers and Employees

Rule 1.11 is similar to Rule 1.10 in that it sets forth screening procedures for lawyers who make lateral moves during their careers—but in this case, specifically a lateral move between the private and public sectors. The intent of the current version of Rule 1.11 is to facilitate such moves, so that it will not be too difficult to attract lawyers to positions in government. The following series of questions are very similar in order to emphasize the importance of noticing a small detail in the facts that changes the outcome under the conflicts rules, especially under Rule 1.11.

QUESTION 21. **Former agency lawyer.** Attorney worked for several years for a federal government agency in regulatory enforcement. Big Firm then hired the attorney for a substantially higher salary, and the attorney accepted the position and left her government position. One of the attorney's first assigned cases at Big Firm was a new action by the client against the same government agency for which the attorney had previously worked, challenging the constitutionality of a new regulation that the agency had recently promulgated. While at the agency, the attorney had not been involved with the review and promulgation of any new regulations, including the one at issue in the client's challenge, but instead worked exclusively on enforcement litigation matters. Is the attorney subject to disqualification in the client's matter against the attorney's former employer?

A. Yes, because Big Firm gave the attorney an unreasonably large salary increase for leaving her public service position and joining Big Firm in the private sector, which creates a conflict of interest.
B. Yes, unless the federal government agency is willing to provide written informed consent to the attorney's representation in the case.
C. No, because the attorney did not participate personally and substantially in the matter as a public officer or employee.
D. No, because the case involves a constitutional challenge to the validity of a regulation, not the financial interests of the client or government as would be recognized if the case involved fines, fees, or penalties.

ANALYSIS. A lawyer will not be allowed to represent a future client in any matter the lawyer personally and substantially participated in during her former employment as a public officer or employee of the government. The attorney is asked to represent the client on a constitutionality claim against a federal government agency while she works for Big Firm. Though the claim is against the same government agency that previously employed the attorney, the attorney worked exclusively on matters not related to the claim the client now brings, therefore the attorney may represent the client in this new matter.

A is incorrect because when the attorney worked for the government agency, she worked exclusively on enforcement litigation matters and therefore was not personally and substantially involved in the matter brought by the client to Big Firm.

B is incorrect because written informed consent from the government agency is not required here because while the attorney was employed at the government agency she was not personally and substantially involved with the matter the client is now bringing to Big Firm.

C is correct because it properly states that if the attorney was not personally and substantially involved with the current matter during her previous employment at the government agency she may represent the client.

D is incorrect because it is not the type of claim which triggers the conflict of interest, but whether or not the lawyer participated personally and substantially while in her previous employment at the government agency.

QUESTION 22. **Challenging the constitutionality of the statute.** An attorney worked for several years for a federal government agency in regulatory enforcement. Big Firm then hired the attorney for a substantially higher salary, and the attorney accepted the position and left her government position. One of the attorney's first assigned cases at Big Firm was a new action by the client against the same government agency for which the attorney had previously worked, defending against an enforcement action that the attorney had initiated while at the agency. The defense will involve challenging the constitutionality of a new regulation that the agency had recently promulgated. While at the agency, the attorney had not been involved with the review and promulgation of any new regulations, including the one at issue in the client's challenge, but instead worked exclusively on enforcement litigation matters. The government agency gives informed consent, confirmed in writing, to the representation. Is the attorney nevertheless subject to disqualification in the client's matter against the attorney's former employer?

A. Yes, because allowing Big Firm to give government lawyers an unreasonably large salary increase for leaving her public service position and joining Big Firm in the private sector creates a conflict of interest for all lawyers in government service.

B. Yes, because the attorney participated personally and substantially in the matter as a public officer or employee.

C. No, because the case involves a constitutional challenge to the validity of a regulation, and the attorney was not personally and substantially involved in the drafting or promulgation of the regulation.

D. No, because the appropriate government agency gave its informed consent, confirmed in writing, to the representation.

ANALYSIS. Rule 1.11(a)(2) provides the answer to this question. Generally, a former public officer or employee of the government will not be able to represent future clients in matters in which the lawyer personally and substantially participated. Even so, there is an exception if the appropriate government agency gives written informed consent to the representation. Here, the attorney was able to obtain written informed consent from the government agency, and therefore will not be disqualified from the representation of the client.

A is incorrect because it is the attorney's personal and substantial participation, initiating the enforcement action, which triggers the conflict of interest. The attorney may undertake the representation because she obtained written informed consent from the appropriate government agency.

B is incorrect because it does not consider the exception for allowing representation by obtaining the written informed consent from the appropriate government agency.

C is incorrect. The attorney was in fact personally and substantially involved because she initiated the enforcement action that she is now being asked to defend.

D is correct because once the attorney obtained written informed consent from the government agency, she will fall under the exception to the rule that will allow her to represent the client despite the conflict of interest.

QUESTION 23. **Refusing to consent.** An attorney worked for several years for a federal government agency in regulatory enforcement. Big Firm then hired the attorney for a substantially higher salary, and the attorney accepted the position and left his government position. One of the attorney's first assigned cases at Big Firm was a new action by the client against the same government agency for which the attorney had previously worked, defending against an enforcement action that the attorney had initiated while at the agency. The defense will involve challenging the constitutionality of a new regulation that the agency had recently promulgated. While at the agency, the attorney had not been involved with the review and promulgation of any new regulations, including the one at issue in the client's challenge, but instead worked exclusively on enforcement litigation matters. The government agency refuses to consent to the attorney representing the client, who is the adverse party to the agency, in this matter, and seeks to disqualify Big Firm from representing the client. Is Big Firm subject to disqualification in the client's matter against the attorney's former employer?

A. Yes, because allowing Big Firm to give government lawyers an unreasonably large salary increase for leaving his public service position and joining Big Firm in the private sector creates a conflict of interest for all lawyers in government service.

B. Yes, because the attorney participated personally and substantially in the matter as a public officer or employee, and cannot recuse himself from representing the client, and the appropriate government agency gives its informed consent, confirmed in writing, to the representation.

C. No, as long as Big Firm has policies and procedures in effect to supervise the attorney's work closely enough to ensure compliance with the Rules of Professional Conduct.

D. No, as long as Big Firm screens the attorney in time from any participation in the matter and provides the agency with prompt written notice about the screening measures in effect.

ANALYSIS. Rule 1.11(b) is helpful here. In this scenario, the government agency does not give written informed consent for the attorney to represent the client. Big Firm may be able to represent the client even without the written informed consent if Big Firm timely screens the attorney and provides prompt written notice of the screening measures taken to the government agency.

A is incorrect because the conflict is not created by the attorney's increased salary but by the attorney's personal and substantial involvement with the claim while he worked at the government agency.

B is incorrect because the attorney may in effect recuse himself by being screened from the matter while at Big Firm. If he is screened and Big Firm gives notice to the government agency of the screening measures taken, Big Firm will not be disqualified from representing the client.

C is incorrect because it is not enough to merely supervise the attorney's work. Big Firm will have to screen the attorney from working on the matter completely.

D is correct because Big Firm will not be disqualified from representing the client as long as the lawyer who would be disqualified is screened from participation in the matter and notice of those screening measures are provided to the government agency.

QUESTION 24. **Having confidential information.** An attorney worked for several years for a federal government agency in regulatory enforcement. Big Firm then hired the attorney for a substantially higher salary, and the attorney accepted the position and left her government position. One of the attorney's first assigned cases at Big Firm was a new action by the client against Conglomerate Corporation. The attorney had worked on an enforcement against Conglomerate Corporation and learned confidential government information about the entity during the litigation. The government agency gives its informed consent, confirmed in writing, to the representation. Is the attorney nevertheless subject to disqualification in the client's matter against the attorney's former employer?

A. Yes, the attorney has confidential government information about a person acquired while working for the government agency, and therefore may not represent a private client whose interests are adverse to that person in a matter in which the information could be used to the material disadvantage of that person.

B. No, because the attorney did not previously represent the client or Conglomerate Corporation, so there is no attorney-client privilege or conflict of loyalties here between two clients that the attorney is representing or has represented.

C. No, because the appropriate government agency gave its informed consent, confirmed in writing, to the representation.

D. No, as long as Big Firm has policies and procedures in effect to supervise the attorney's work closely enough to ensure compliance with the Rules of Professional Conduct, including training sessions about the conflict-of-interest rules.

ANALYSIS. Rule 1.11(c) is the operative provision for this question. When an attorney works for a government agency and learns confidential information regarding an entity, she cannot later represent an adverse party when the confidential information could be used to materially disadvantage the entity. The attorney has learned Conglomerate's confidential information while she was working for the government and is now trying to represent the client, an adverse party. The attorney will not be able to obtain a waiver to represent the client in this matter in order to protect Conglomerate's confidential information.

In order to prevent the attorney from using the confidential information to disadvantage Conglomerate in a material way, the attorney will not be able to obtain a waiver to represent the client in this matter.

A is correct because the client's interest is adverse to Conglomerate's. The attorney has learned Conglomerate's confidential information, and there is no waiver or exception to this kind of disqualification.

B is incorrect because while there is no conflict of loyalties, the attorney has learned Conglomerate's confidential information. In order to protect Conglomerate's confidential information the attorney will be disqualified from representing any future adverse clients of Conglomerate in matters where the confidential information might be used to materially disadvantage Conglomerate.

C is incorrect because this conflict of interest cannot be waived.

D is incorrect because it is not enough to supervise the attorney. The attorney is disqualified from participating in the client's representation completely.

QUESTION 25. It is all out in the open now. An attorney worked for several years for a federal government agency in regulatory enforcement. Big Firm then hired the attorney for a substantially higher salary, and the attorney accepted the position and left her government position. One of the attorney's first assigned cases at Big Firm was a new action by the client against Conglomerate Corporation. The attorney had worked on an enforcement against Conglomerate Corporation and learned confidential government information about the entity during the litigation, but the attorney does not know, and has no reason to know, that the information is confidential government information. The attorney is under the reasonable impression that all the information she learned about Conglomerate Corporation is now public information. The government agency gave its informed consent, confirmed in writing, to the representation. Is the attorney nevertheless subject to disqualification in the client's matter against the attorney's former employer?

A. Yes, the attorney has confidential government information about a person acquired while working for the government agency, and therefore may not represent a private client whose interests are adverse to that person in a matter in which the information could be used to the material disadvantage of that person.
B. No, because the appropriate government agency gave its informed consent, confirmed in writing, to the representation.
C. No, because the attorney does not have confidential government information about Conglomerate that she knows is confidential government information.
D. Yes, because the attorney did not previously represent the client or Conglomerate Corporation, so there is no attorney-client privilege or conflict of loyalties here between two clients that the attorney is representing or has represented.

ANALYSIS. Rule 1.11(c) applies here as well. A lawyer must know that the information she learned about a future adverse party is confidential in order for the lawyer to be disqualified from representing the current client. The attorney reasonably believes the information she learned about Conglomerate is public information, therefore it is not true that the attorney has information that she knows is confidential and may represent the client.

A is incorrect because it leaves out the requirement that the attorney must know the information is confidential before she can be disqualified from representing the client.

B is incorrect because the attorney was not personally or substantially involved in a related matter while she was working for the government agency, which would otherwise require written informed consent. Furthermore, the conflict of interest here stems from Conglomerate's confidential information.

C is correct because the attorney reasonably believes the information she learned about Conglomerate was public information and therefore does not know that it is confidential.

D is incorrect because while there is no conflict of loyalties, the conflict of interest here stems from Conglomerate's confidential information.

QUESTION 26. Job hunting. An attorney worked for several years for a federal government agency in regulatory enforcement. The attorney was involved in several enforcement matters against Conglomerate Corporation. Big Firm has always represented Conglomerate Corporation in all its litigation and regulatory compliance matters. The attorney made a good impression on the Big Firm partners when serving as opposing counsel in the same litigation. At the end of a deposition of Conglomerate Corporation's executives during the discovery phase of an enforcement proceeding, Big Firm partners approached the attorney privately and asked if the attorney would be interested in leaving the agency for a position at Big Firm. The attorney explained that they would have to match his current salary at the government agency in order for him to consider the proposal. Big Firm then scheduled an employment interview with the attorney, at the end of which they offered to double his salary if he left the agency and accepted a position at Big Firm. The attorney decided to postpone making a decision until the pending agency enforcement matters against Big Firm's client were complete, in order to avoid the appearance of a conflict of interest. The matters dragged on for another year, however, and Big Firm eventually withdrew its offer. Is the attorney subject to discipline?

A. No, because the attorney decided to postpone making a decision until the pending agency enforcement matters against Big Firm's client were complete, in order to avoid the appearance of a conflict of interest.

B. No, because Big Firm eventually withdrew its offer and the attorney never actually went to work for Big Firm.

C. Yes, because a lawyer currently serving as a public officer or employee shall not negotiate for private employment with any person who is involved as a party or as lawyer for a party in a matter in which the lawyer is participating personally and substantially.

D. Yes, because Big Firm offered to double the attorney's salary instead of merely matching his current government salary, which creates a substantial conflict of interest for the attorney in any pending or future matters.

ANALYSIS. Rule 1.11(d)(2)(ii) has a specific provision for this (rather commonplace) scenario. The attorney will be subject to discipline if while working as a public officer or government employee he attempts to negotiate for private employment with a party to a matter the attorney is participating in personally and substantially. Here the attorney negotiates with Big Firm for private employment by letting them know he would leave his employment at the government agency under certain circumstances. The attorney will therefore be subject to discipline even though he postponed his decision and eventually lost the offer.

A is incorrect because the attorney negotiated for private employment with a party in which the attorney was participating personally and substantially.

B is incorrect because it is not necessary for the attorney to accept the employment position. Negotiation alone is enough to subject the attorney to discipline.

C is correct because it states all the correct elements that will subject the attorney to discipline for his actions.

D is incorrect because the amount offered in the negotiation is irrelevant. Negotiation alone creates the conflict of interest.

QUESTION 27. **Same claim, different sector.** An attorney spent several years working for the state Office of the Attorney General in its environmental litigation division. While there, the attorney began a case against a scrap metal facility for burying toxic materials on its grounds. The attorney then left government service and went to work for Big Firm. There, the attorney began representing a group of neighboring landowners in a lawsuit against the same scrap metal facility over the same burying of toxic material, as it had polluted the groundwater and had migrated to adjacent properties underground. Is it proper for the attorney to represent these plaintiffs?

A. Yes, as long as the new clients provide written informed consent.
B. Yes, because the new clients' interests match those of the attorney's government employer, and there is no indication of adverse interests being present between them.
C. No, a lawyer who has pursued a claim on behalf of the government may not pursue the same claim on behalf of a later private client after the lawyer has left government service, except when authorized to do so by the government agency.
D. No, because the attorney is using the prestige of having worked in government service to attract new clients, which creates a conflict between the attorney's self-interest and the public interest represented by the government agency.

ANALYSIS. Comment 3 clarifies that Rule 1.11 also exists to prevent a lawyer from exploiting public office for the advantage of another client. Here, because of the attorney's prior work at the State Office of the Attorney General, he may know information regarding the government's claim against the scrap metal facility, which may benefit the suit now brought by neighboring landowners against the scrap metal facility for the same actions. Before being able to represent the neighboring landowners, the attorney would have to obtain written informed consent from the State Office of the Attorney General.

A is incorrect because it is the government agency, not the new client, that would need to provide written informed consent for this representation.

B is incorrect because although there are no adverse interests represented between the new client and the government employer, the attorney participated personally and substantially in a matter connected to the new client's claim. Because the attorney has not obtained written informed consent from the State Office of the Attorney General, he may not represent the new client in this particular claim.

C is correct because it states that generally a lawyer will not be allowed to represent a client under these circumstances whether or not the lawyer obtains written informed consent from the government agency.

D is incorrect because it does not consider the exception for allowing representation when the attorney has received approval by the government agency.

L. Rule 1.12—Former Judge, Arbitrator, Mediator

Rule 1.12 has similar provisions to Rule 1.10, but there are special restrictions in the case of former judges and arbitrators. All parties to a matter, not merely a former client, must consent to the representation.

QUESTION 28. **The former mediator.** An attorney, who often serves as a court-appointed mediator, was appointed to mediate the divorce case between a husband and wife. The case settled in mediation and the divorce was finalized soon after. A year later, the husband sought to retain the attorney to represent him in a modification suit against his wife. The attorney accepted the case and sent a letter to the wife advising her that the attorney had been retained by the former husband to represent him in a modification suit. Are the attorney's actions proper?

A. Yes, the attorney who previously served as a third-party neutral may represent any party in a suit connected to the previous matter if the attorney provides proper notice to the other party in writing.

B. Yes, an attorney who previously served as a third-party neutral may represent any party in a suit connected to the previous matter if the

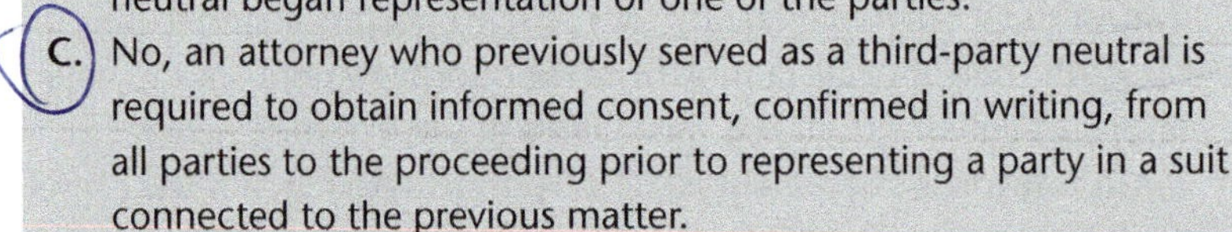

previous case occurred more than one year before the third-party neutral began representation of one of the parties.

C. No, an attorney who previously served as a third-party neutral is required to obtain informed consent, confirmed in writing, from all parties to the proceeding prior to representing a party in a suit connected to the previous matter.

D. No, an attorney who previously served as a third-party neutral shall not represent any party in a suit connected to the previous matter.

ANALYSIS. Comment 2 for Rule 1.12 applies to this situation. A lawyer shall not represent anyone in connection with a matter in which the lawyer participated personally and substantially as a third-party neutral unless all parties to the proceeding give written informed consent. As the court-appointed mediator the attorney participated personally and substantially as a third-party neutral for the matter between husband and wife. The attorney would be required to obtain written informed consent from Wife before representing Husband.

A is incorrect because since the attorney participated personally and substantially as a third-party neutral, written informed consent, and not just notice, will be required in order for the attorney to represent Husband.

B is incorrect because the "one year" fact is irrelevant.

C is correct because it correctly states the rule and what the attorney will be required to do before commencing representation of Husband.

D is incorrect because it does not state the rule completely. An exception is allowed if all parties to the proceeding give written informed consent.

QUESTION 29. **The hearing officer.** An attorney was a state hearing officer for the Workers Compensation Board. The attorney left that position and opened his own law firm, primarily representing parties before the state Workers Compensation Board. One of the cases is the final rehearing of a case in which the attorney had presided as hearing officer at an initial preliminary hearing and ruled on preliminary matters, but the attorney left the Board without issuing any final decision in the case and the Board transferred the matter to another hearing officer. The attorney represents the injured worker, the client, and the employer is Manufacturer. All the parties involved give informed consent, confirmed in writing, for the attorney to represent the client. Is the attorney subject to discipline for representing the client in this matter?

A. Yes, because a lawyer shall not represent anyone in connection with a matter in which the lawyer participated personally and substantially as a judge or other adjudicative officer.

B. Yes, because the type of conflict of interest described here is non-consentable, so it is irrelevant that all the parties provided informed written consent.

C. No, because all the parties involved provided informed written consent to the representation, despite the obvious conflicts of interest at stake.

D. No, the conflict-of-interest rules do not apply to merely administrative hearing officers who are not actual judges, arbitrators, or mediators.

ANALYSIS. Although the attorney did not make a final ruling on the matter he participated personally and substantially, which creates a conflict of interest in his future representation of the client. However, because he was able to obtain written informed consent from all parties involved he will be allowed to continue representation of the client.

A is incorrect because it does not fully state the rule. An exception is allowed if all parties to the proceeding give written informed consent.

B is incorrect because the conflict of interest here is not non-consentable. The rule allows the parties to waive the conflict of interest so long as all parties give written informed consent.

C is correct because it correctly states what the attorney would be required to do in order to continue representation of the client.

D is incorrect because the rule does apply to adjudicative officers.

QUESTION 30. The appellate judge. An attorney spent several years working on the state intermediate appellate court as one of its nine justices in a state in which such judges run for election in the general elections every four years. When the attorney ran for re-election, she lost, and needed to return to private practice. The client wants the attorney to represent her in her appeal of a state trial verdict. The case previously came up on appeal before the state intermediate appellate court, but the attorney was not on the panel that decided the case. The state Supreme Court subsequently reversed the decisions of both the appellate court and the trial court, and remanded the case for a new trial. The new trial resulted in an unfavorable verdict for the client, so she wants to appeal the case again. Would it be proper for the attorney to represent her in this matter?

A. No, because the appeal will come before the very court for which the attorney worked as a judge, and the panel could include some of the attorney's former colleagues.

B. No, because the state Supreme Court already reversed the decision of the state intermediate appellate court, so it is improper for the client to appeal the remanded case back to the same state intermediate appellate court again, as this could thwart the intentions of the Supreme Court.

C. Yes, because it was not the judge's fault that the state Supreme Court reversed the previous appellate decision, making a new trial and subsequent appeals necessary, and that the opposing party has not settled the case in the meantime.

D. Yes, because a judge who was a member of a multimember court, and thereafter left judicial office to practice law, is not prohibited from representing a client in a matter pending in the court, but in which the former judge did not participate.

ANALYSIS. A judge who is part of a multimember court and later leaves to practice law may represent the clients with pending matters in the court so long as the judge did not personally and substantially participate in the matter. Although the client's case was heard before the attorney's court, the attorney was not on the panel that decided the case. Therefore, the attorney did not participate in the client's case personally or substantially and may undertake representation of the client.

A is incorrect because the attorney did not participate personally or substantially in the matter since she was not on the panel that decided the case. The fact that the future panel could include some of the attorney's former colleagues is irrelevant.

B is incorrect because these facts are irrelevant to whether the attorney would be disqualified from representing the client due to her status as a former judge.

C is incorrect because it is irrelevant to whether the attorney would be disqualified from representing the client due to her status as a former judge.

D is correct because the rule requires that the lawyer participated personally in the previous matter in order to be disqualified from representing a client. The attorney was part of the multimember court but was not part of the panel that decided the case.

QUESTION 31. **Court administrator.** An attorney was a judge for several years. Near the end of her tenure as a judge, she functioned in the role of the chief administrative judge in that court, assigning cases to the other judges and supervising their work, and had only a limited docket of her own trials. The attorney then left the bench and opened her own law practice. The attorney agrees to represent the client in a matter in the same courthouse where the attorney formerly served as a judge.

The attorney even remembers the case, but only the names of the parties and the nature of the action, because she assigned it to the trial judge who currently has the case on his docket, but the attorney had no other involvement in the matter. The client's previous lawyer in the matter was subject to disqualification at the motion of the opposing party due to a conflict of interest. Is it proper for the attorney to represent the client in this matter?

A. Yes, the fact that a former judge exercised administrative responsibility in a court does not prevent the former judge from acting as a lawyer in a matter where the judge had previously exercised remote or incidental administrative responsibility that did not affect the merits.
B. Yes, as long as all the parties to the matter provide informed consent, confirmed in writing, to the representation.
C. No, because she previously supervised the trial judge hearing the case, and even assigned the case to that judge.
D. No, because the client's previous lawyer was already subject to disqualification due to a conflict of interest in the matter.

ANALYSIS. Comment 1 to Rule 1.12 explains that a former third-party neutral will not be considered as having personally and substantially participated in a matter if his involvement did not affect the merits of the case. Remote or incidental administrative responsibilities or actions on a matter will not prevent a former judge from representing a client on that matter.

A is correct because the attorney had no personal participation in the case while she was a judge.

B is incorrect because written informed consent will not be required since the judge was not personally participating in the action when she was a judge.

C is incorrect because although she previously supervised the trial judge, she did not personally participate in the case and her responsibility did not affect the merits of the case.

D is incorrect because the facts do not state why the previous lawyer was disqualified. The former judge's potential conflict of interest could be completely unrelated to the previous lawyer's conflict of interest. Additionally, the judge will not be disqualified because she did not personally participate in any actions affecting the merits of the case.

QUESTION 32. **Screening at the firm.** An attorney was a judge but has left that job and joined Big Firm. Another lawyer at Big Firm represents the client in a case on the docket at the same court where the attorney worked as a judge. In fact, as a judge, the attorney ruled on some of the pretrial motions in the case, mostly evidentiary motions. The firm has screening measures in place to screen the attorney from any participation in the matter. The attorney will receive no part of the fee from the matter, and timely notice went to the parties about the screening measures in place. The other parties, however, did not provide informed written consent to Big Firm's representation of the client. Is it proper for the other lawyer at Big Firm to continue representing the client in this matter?

A. No, because a lawyer shall not represent anyone in connection with a matter in which the lawyer participated personally and substantially as a judge, and if a lawyer is disqualified, no lawyer in a firm with which that lawyer is associated may knowingly undertake or continue representation in the matter.
B. No, because a lawyer shall not represent anyone in connection with a matter in which the lawyer participated personally and substantially as a judge, and the other parties did not provide informed consent, confirmed in writing, to the representation.
C. Yes, as long as Big Firm also provides timely notice to the appropriate tribunal as well, so that the tribunal may ascertain compliance with screening measures.
D. Yes, as long as the attorney is not receiving a salary or partnership share established by prior independent agreement.

ANALYSIS. Rule 1.12(c)(2) governs this situation. This scenario illustrates an imputation of conflict to a firm where the attorney is disqualified from representing the client because she is a former judge that participated personally and substantially in the client's matter. Another lawyer in the firm will be allowed to continue the representation under certain circumstances.

A is incorrect because it does not state the exception to the rule which would allow Big Firm to represent the client so long as the attorney is timely screened from any participation, apportioned no part of the fee, and written notice is given to all parties and appropriate tribunals.

B is incorrect because the attorney is the disqualified lawyer. Lawyer will be allowed to continue representation of the client so long as the attorney is timely screened from any participation, apportioned no part of the fee, and written notice is given to all parties and appropriate tribunals.

C is correct because it correctly states the rule and what further steps would be required for Big Firm to continue representation of the client.

D is incorrect because it fails to list the notice requirement.

M. The Closer

QUESTION 33. The former colleague's conflict. An attorney used to work at Big Firm, and three years ago moved laterally to Medium Firm. One of the attorney's former colleagues at Big Firm also left and started a solo practice. While working at Big Firm, the solo received an assignment of literary rights from one of his clients about the client's high-profile case, immediately after the end of the case and the conclusion of the representation. That client also assigned any remaining literary rights to Kingpin Publishers in exchange for a hefty payment. The solo is now suing Kingpin Publishers to establish exclusive literary rights in the story. The first attorney's current firm, Medium Firm, represents Kingpin Publishers, and the solo represents himself. Another publisher is interested in acquiring the solo's book or movie script, and is funding the litigation expenses for the solo, even though it is not a client and does not yet have any ownership rights over the story. The case that gave rise to the literary rights occurred while both the solo and the first attorney were working together at Big Firm. The attorney performed some preliminary work on the case—reviewing and indexing a single deposition transcript before the client's trial—but the lawyer who is now the solo actually represented the client at trial.

A paralegal at Big Firm is currently engaged to an editor at Kingpin Publishers, and the two are already living together. The attorney at Medium Firm, who is representing Kingpin Publishers, is in a sexual relationship with another lawyer at his own firm, and both are working in some capacity on the case. Executives at Kingpin Publishers have informed the first attorney that if his firm wins this case, they will hire Medium Firm for all their future legal work, which could be very lucrative in the long term. The solo has just filed a motion to disqualify the first attorney and the rest of Medium Firm from representing Kingpin Publishers in the case, alleging simply that there is a conflict of interest. Does Medium Firm have a disqualifying conflict of interest in representing Kingpin Publishers in this particular litigation?

A. Yes, because the firm's attorney worked on the case that gave rise to this litigation, and because the solo took literary rights in the client's case.

B. Yes, because the firm's attorney is in a sexual relationship with another lawyer working on the case, and because a third party without a true stake in the case is paying for the solo's legal expenses.

C. No, as long as Medium Firm screens the attorney from the case involving the literary rights and obtains consent from the opposing party.

D. No, because neither the attorney nor Medium Firm have any disqualifying conflict of interest in this case.

ANALYSIS. This question ties together several of the rules about conflicts of interest. It also illustrates that readers must carefully follow the lines of imputed conflicts and decide at each point whether facts that sound like a conflict are indeed a disqualifying event for one of the lawyers.

A is incorrect. It is possible that working on the same matter at a previous firm could create a conflict, but the matter was not the same at all. The current litigation is over which party received legal assignment of the literary rights, and the original matter was over a different issue or dispute, and there is no overlap in the parties. In addition, the solo took literary rights after the conclusion of his representation, which puts the transaction outside the coverage of Rule 1.8's prohibition regarding such rights.

B is also incorrect. First, the Model Rules do not prohibit sexual relationships between lawyers in the same firm, but only between lawyers and their clients and (by implication) between a lawyer and the opposing party or opposing counsel. Second, even if there were a personal conflict of interest for the attorney based on a sexual relationship, such personal conflicts do not impute to the other lawyers in the firm. Third, while it is possible (though very unlikely) that the third-party publisher paying the solo lawyer's legal expenses could create a conflict, the conflict could only apply to the solo lawyer, not to Medium Firm (on the opposite side in the case).

C offers an incorrect condition for Medium Firm to avoid disqualification. Medium Firm does not need to screen the attorney from the case because the attorney has no conflict of interest, and there is no need to seek consent from the opposing party.

D is correct. Despite the many facts here that might sound like a conflict of interest, they either do not apply to the attorney or they fall outside the rules (or within one of the exceptions). Given that there is no conflict of interest that applies to the attorney, there is no conflict imputed to Medium Firm.

Stevenson's Picks

1. Directly adverse parties	**D**
2. One for all and all for one	**C**
3. Going up the chain of command	**C**
4. Former clients and new clients	**A**
5. The past comes back to haunt	**A**
6. Parents hiring lawyers for their college kids	**C**
7. Secret admirer	**B**
8. "I have needs"	**D**
9. Former prosecutor	**C**
10. The defendant	**B**
11. The patent lawyer	**D**
12. The third wife	**B**

13.	The abortion clinic	C
14.	Married to the lawyer	D
15.	The lateral move	D
16.	The victim	C
17.	The shareholder	A
18.	The secretary's husband	C
19.	Client of the lawyer who left	A
20.	The law student intern	C
21.	Former agency lawyer	C
22.	Challenging the constitutionality of the statute	D
23.	Refusing to consent	D
24.	Having confidential information	A
25.	It is all out in the open now	C
26.	Job hunting	C
27.	Same claim, different sector	C
28.	The former mediator	C
29.	The hearing officer	C
30.	The appellate judge	D
31.	Court administrator	A
32.	Screening at the firm	C
33.	The former colleague's conflict	D

2

The Client-Lawyer Relationship

A. Rule 1.2—Scope of Representation and Allocation of Authority Between Client and Lawyer

The Multistate Professional Responsibility Examination (MPRE) lists the second-most heavily tested subject as "the client-lawyer relationship," generally covering Model Rules 1.2 (scope and allocation of authority), 1.4 (communications), 1.5 (fee arrangements), 1.14 (clients with diminished capacity), and 1.16 (termination of representation). These Model Rules furnish the basis for 10 to 16 percent of the MPRE, which translates into somewhere between six and nine questions on each test.

Rule 1.2 pertains to the scope of representation and the allocation of authority between the client and lawyer. "Scope" refers to what the lawyer actually agreed or promised to do for a particular client. For practitioners, this issue is a common source of misunderstandings between clients and their attorneys. Did the lawyer agree to handle a case through the entire course of litigation, from pretrial discovery and settlement negotiations through all posttrial appeals? Alternatively, did the lawyer agree only to do the trial, and refer the client to another firm if the case goes up on appeal? Many lawyers specialize, and even within practice areas like litigation there are some who mostly do pretrial discovery and motion practice, others who prefer courtroom work, and still others who are appellate lawyers. An appellate lawyer, for example, may not want to handle the new jury trial of the matter after an appellate court orders a reversal and remand. Thus, the scope of the representation—the extent of the lawyer's intended work on the client's matter—should be part of the representation agreement (often called the "retainer agreement") from the outset. For purposes of avoiding malpractice suits or grievances from clients, attorneys must ensure that clients understand what the lawyer will do (say, handle a particular case or transaction) and what the lawyer will not do (say, address all other potential legal issues the client may have).

Model Rule 1.2(c) gives lawyers and clients wide latitude in setting the scope of representation: "A lawyer may limit the scope of the representation if the limitation is reasonable under the circumstances and the client gives informed consent." For purposes of testing, watch for questions that describe a significant limitation on the representation (such as a lawyer hired to represent an insured limiting her work to matters covered under the insurance policy), and look for the two critical elements: whether the limitation is reasonable, and whether the client really understood and agreed to the limitation ahead of time. The ABA's official comment for Rule 1.2 provides an example to clarify "reasonable" limitations on the scope—a client who merely has a quick, simple legal question could agree that the "representation" will be a simple phone call, during which the lawyer answers the question and advises the client (see Comment 7 for Rule 1.2). For simple, quick legal questions that the lawyer could easily answer without doing research, most clients would not want the lawyer to engage in extensive research and writing (thus generating higher bills) unnecessarily. At the same time, the telephone conversation must entail reliable advice—it would *not* be reasonable for the lawyer to agree to limit the matter to a simple phone call if the attorney does not really know the answer and must make a guess.

"Allocation of authority" is a more complicated issue—this refers to which decisions the client must make (and to which the lawyer must defer) and which decisions that the lawyer can make, often without asking the client. Overall, the provisions of Model Rule 1.2 have three types of decisions: things the lawyer should decide, things the client must decide (lawyer cannot decide), and things the lawyer must refuse to do (participate in illegal activities, fraud, etc.). The lawyer usually can decide the means for achieving the client's objectives—for example, whether to file a motion for summary judgment or proceed directly to trial. The caveat to this provision is that a client may instruct the lawyer not to use certain means that run up the client's costs, such as hiring an expert witness or a jury consultant. If the lawyer and client strongly disagree about methods or means, and they reach an impasse, the lawyer must withdraw from the representation.

The client *must* decide the overall objectives of the representation—for example, does the client want injunctive relief, or money damages? Is the client more concerned about retaining custody of her children, or obtaining a more favorable distribution of the marriage assets? Clients *must* approve settlement decisions or plea bargains (pre-approving or pre-rejecting certain settlement offers or plea deals can be acceptable). It is *very* common for the MPRE to include a question about a lawyer who fails to ask a client before accepting or rejecting a settlement offer or a plea bargain.

According to Model Rule 1.2(b), representing a client does not necessarily mean that the lawyer endorses the client's political, religious, or moral views. A lawyer may represent a client with unpopular, controversial, or even offensive views and practices, even if the lawyer disagrees with the client strongly about such things.

QUESTION 1. **Waiving the right to a jury trial.** An attorney represents a client who is a defendant in a criminal matter. The defendant faces felony charges. The attorney is very experienced in handling this type of case, and knows from experience that defendants receive acquittals far more often in jury trials than in bench trials, at least with this type of case. The client, however, does not want to incur the legal fees involved in jury selection (voir dire, etc.), and cannot really afford it, so the client tells his attorney that he does not want a jury trial, but rather a bench trial. The attorney is convinced that his client is innocent of the crimes charged, and that a bench trial is likely to result in a wrongful conviction in this particular case, given some of the evidentiary issues. The attorney postpones notifying the court that the defendant will waive his right to a jury trial, in hopes of changing the client's mind. The court schedules jury selection, and the attorney appears and participates in the voir dire without telling his client, because he still hopes and believes that he will change his client's mind about the issue. On the first day of trial, the client arrives in court and is shocked to see a jury seated. The defendant stands and objects loudly to the jury and explains that he wants to waive his right to a jury trial and have a bench trial instead. The judge refuses to dismiss the jury at this point, informing the defendant that his opportunity to request a bench trial has passed. The trial proceeds and the jury acquitted the client of all charges, as the attorney had expected, and to the apparent dismay of the judge, who would have ruled to convict if it were up to him. Is the attorney subject to discipline in this situation?

A. Yes, because the client missed the important opportunity to participate in voir dire and the selection of the jury, and will have to pay legal fees that he did not want to incur.
B. No, because the defendant suffered no harm from the attorney's decision, as the jury gave a complete acquittal and the judge apparently would have given an unfavorable verdict.
C. Yes, because in a criminal case, the lawyer shall abide by the client's decision, after consultation with the lawyer, as to whether to waive the right to a jury trial.
D. No, as long as the attorney does not bill the client for the day spent on jury selection, because clients normally defer to the special knowledge and skill of their lawyer with respect to the means to be used to accomplish their objectives, particularly with respect to technical, legal, and tactical matters.

ANALYSIS. Rule 1.2(a) includes, among other requirements, "In a criminal case, the lawyer shall abide by the client's decision, after consultation with the lawyer, as to a plea to be entered, whether to waive jury trial and whether the client will testify." In civil litigation, lawyers must abide by the client's wishes regarding accepting or rejecting settlement offers (which means lawyers should check with the client whenever the opposing party extends an offer). In the criminal context, there is a heightened concern to let the client control certain major decisions—whether to plead guilty, whether to demand a jury trial, and whether to testify. Even though lawyers will often have strong opinions on these issues, the client has the final say on these matters.

A is incorrect because it gives the wrong reason for the lawyer being subject to discipline. The problem was not that the client missed voir dire—the Model Rules do not require lawyers to include clients in the jury selection process. Nor were the additional legal fees the real issue here, although that may be a secondary problem in this instance. The problem was that the client did not make the decision about whether to have a bench trial or jury trial.

B is incorrect because the Model Rules do not follow this "no-harm-no-foul" approach. A lawyer can be subject to discipline even if the lawyer's conduct protected the client from an adverse outcome or resulted in a significant benefit for the client. Of course, in the real world of legal practice, clients who receive good outcomes are unlikely to complain or file grievances against their lawyers, so disciplinary actions may not occur. Nevertheless, for purposes of the MPRE, rules are rules.

C is the correct answer—it restates the rule from 1.2(a) nearly verbatim. Even where the lawyer is certain that a jury trial would be better (or worse) in a given case, the client must have the final say in this decision. Note that this is true even when the lawyer is correct and the client is wrong (as in this problem). This question also highlights the fact that the lawyer could be subject to discipline even when his unauthorized decisions worked out well for the client—the Model Rules focus on whether the lawyer complied with the Rules, not on the actual consequences of the lawyer's actions.

D is incorrect because, as stated above, the main problem here is not the legal fees, but rather that a jury trial is an important personal right under constitutional law, and a defendant must have the final say on this point. In addition, watch out for answers on the exam that suggest a lawyer may rectify a violation of the Model Rules merely by waiving fees for the client. A lawyer may be subject to discipline for a violation of the rules even if the lawyer did not charge the client for the time spent on the activity that constituted the violation.

QUESTION 2. "Don't even call me." An attorney represented a client in litigation over a breach of contract. After a long period of discovery, as the trial date approaches, the two parties make a new attempt at settlement negotiations, with each party's lawyer acting as representative. The client is the plaintiff in the case, and has told the attorney on several occasions that she will not consider any settlement offer less than $100,000. The client is a sophisticated business owner who has weathered litigation many times in the past, including litigation over a breach of a nearly identical contract term. Based on her experience, the client has made an informed estimate that her chances of winning a $250,000 verdict at trial are almost exactly 50 percent, and that trial expenses are likely to be around $50,000 whether she wins or loses, and from there she derived her reserve amount of $100,000. The attorney met with the client the evening before Attorney would meet with opposing counsel for negotiations, and the client reiterated her reserve amount to the attorney, adding, "Do not even call me if the opposing party offers less than $100,000—I will not accept it, and I want you to simply decline lowball offers." The next day, the client leaves on a business trip, and the attorney heads to the settlement negotiation meeting, where opposing counsel offers $90,000 to settle plus a written apology from the defendant to Client for breaching their contract. May Attorney reject this offer without first consulting with Client?

A. Yes, because Client has a right to dictate the overall objectives of the representation, but the lawyer has a right to decide the means of achieving that objective.

B. No, because a lawyer who receives from opposing counsel an offer of settlement in a civil controversy must promptly inform the client of its substance.

C. Yes, because the client has previously indicated that the proposal will be unacceptable and has authorized the lawyer to reject the offer.

D. No, because Client's method of deriving her $100,000 reserve amount is obviously unreasonable.

ANALYSIS. The MPRE often includes a question about lawyers accepting or rejecting settlement offers without checking first with the client. The general rule is that lawyers must *always* check with the client before accepting or rejecting settlement offers or plea bargains, even if the lawyer personally believes the offer is unfavorable and unreasonable (and the lawyer is free to explain such concerns to the client). Even so, the Model Rules permit pre-authorization by a client to accept or reject certain offers, as in this case.

A is incorrect because a lawyer does not have the right to decide the means of achieving the objective without first discussing it with his client. A lawyer is not required to disclose every detail technique that he would utilize to achieve the objective but in a situation such as this, where the client has given specific instructions, the lawyer is authorized to take those specific actions.

B is not the right answer in this situation because the client has already authorized the lawyer to reject the offer if the offer is less than $100,000.

C is the correct answer. Comment 3 for Rule 1.2 states, "At the outset of a representation, the client may authorize the lawyer to take specific action on the client's behalf without further consultation." Here, the client specifically instructed the lawyer not to call her if the opposing party offers less than $100,000. Therefore, the attorney may reject the offer without first consulting with his client.

D is incorrect because the client's method of deriving the amount is irrelevant. The facts indicate that the client is a sophisticated business owner and has made informed estimates of her chances for winning the case. Rule 1.2 allows clients to authorize their lawyer to reject any offers and the lawyer may rely on such advance authorization.

QUESTION 3. **Insurers and attorneys.** An insurer retained an attorney to represent it in a matter, and requested a retainer agreement that limited the representation to matters related to the insurance coverage. The insurance was a homeowner's policy for damage to the policyholder's residential real estate, and included a rider for premises liability. The incident that triggered the claim, however, involved the brutal murder of a woman and her two young children across the street from the house in a neighbor's driveway. Due to the limited scope of his representation, however, the attorney ignored the horrific deaths and the fact that the known killer had escaped conviction on a technicality. In a cool and calculated matter, the attorney focused his work exclusively on the property damage from the incident and the premises liability, and obtained a favorable outcome for the insurer. Was it proper for the attorney to limit the scope of his representation in this way?

A. Yes, when an insurer retains a lawyer to represent an insured, the representation may be limited to matters related to the insurance coverage; a limited representation may be appropriate because the client has limited objectives for the representation.

B. Yes, because investigating the murders after the suspected killer obtained a conviction would violate the double jeopardy clause of the Constitution.
C. No, because a lawyer may limit the scope of the representation only if the limitation is reasonable under the circumstances and the client gives informed consent, and here the limitation was not reasonable.
D. No, because an attorney has a duty to investigate and discover the truth about what happened, and it would violate public policy to allow lawyers to act in a cool and calculated manner when human lives are at stake.

ANALYSIS. Comment 6 to Rule 1.2 states, "The scope of services to be provided by a lawyer may be limited by an agreement with the client." It is very common for insurers to hire the lawyers representing either plaintiffs or defendants in tort litigation. While the lawyer in such a case does have a duty of loyalty to the individual policyholder represented, the scope of such representation typically confines itself to the coverage of the original insurance policy. The situation differs from one in which a client finds her own lawyer, and would normally want the lawyer to bring other legal considerations to the attention of the client besides the immediate objective of the current representation.

A is the correct answer. In this case, the lawyer has been retained by an insurer—the client to represent the insured (the client). This limited representation is appropriate because the client has limited the objectives for the lawyer, specifically pertaining to the insurance coverage.

B is incorrect because double jeopardy is not the issue here. The issue here is whether it was proper for the attorney to limit his representation specifically only for the insurance claim.

C is incorrect because Comment 6 has given an example of limited representation. That scenario in the example is the same here. The representation is limited to matters related to the insurance coverage, and the scope of services to be provided by a lawyer may be limited by agreement with the client.

D is incorrect because it is not the attorney's duty to investigate and discover the truth. In this case, the lawyer does not have duty to investigate because he is neither the prosecutor nor the client's criminal defense attorney. The lawyer's task is to represent the client in matters related to the client's insurance coverage.

QUESTION 4. **Client Uses Lawyer's Advice to Commit Fraud.** A client met with an attorney to discuss certain financial decisions that the client was considering making in the future. The attorney discussed the pros and cons of making the decisions, but did not give a recommendation to the client. The client went on to make the financial decisions and ultimately came under investigation by the IRS for tax fraud. Is the attorney subject to discipline?

A. No, because an attorney may analyze and give an opinion about the likely consequences of a client's conduct.
B. No, because attorneys are authorized to give opinions and provide any recommendations to their clients, and the attorneys are not held liable for the decisions of their clients, even if made at the recommendation of the attorney.
C. Yes, because the attorney's advice constitutes assisting a client in committing fraud.
D. Yes, because an attorney shall not give advice to clients for actions they anticipate making, especially if those actions might expose the client to criminal or fraudulent liability.

ANALYSIS. This question focuses on your understanding of Rule 1.2(d). Subsection (d) distinguishes the difference between a lawyer discussing with the client legal consequences (whether positive or negative) as opposed to assisting a client to engage in unlawful conduct. Lawyers may not advise clients to do anything fraudulent or criminal, nor may lawyers assist clients in committing fraud or other crimes (destruction of evidence, falsified business records, money laundering, and so on). On the other hand, lawyers may advise clients on whether proposed courses of action violate the law. It is perfectly appropriate, therefore, for lawyers to conduct research in good faith about the validity of existing law, or about whether some "questionable" proposed conduct really falls under the law's verbiage.

A is the best answer because lawyers are allowed to give an honest opinion about the actual consequences that appear likely to result from a client's conduct. The fact that a client uses advice in a course of action that is criminal or fraudulent does not make a lawyer a party to the course of action. There is a critical distinction between presenting an analysis of legal aspects of questionable conduct and recommending the means by which a crime or fraud might be committed with impunity.

B is wrong, as the issue is whether the lawyer knowingly gave advice to assist the client in an unlawful act. The issue is not how the client construed the lawyer's advice. A lawyer must not knowingly counsel or assist a client in committing a crime or fraud. The facts do not indicate that the lawyer knowingly counseled the client to assist the client to commit tax fraud.

C is wrong for reasons the same as B.

Finally, **D** is incorrect because it is too broad. The rule is not that the lawyer may give "any" recommendations to their client. A lawyer shall not counsel a client to engage, or assist a client, in conduct that the lawyer knows is criminal or fraudulent. A lawyer may discuss the legal consequences of any proposed course of conduct with a client and may counsel or assist a client to make a good-faith effort to determine the validity, scope, meaning, or application of the law.

B. Rule 1.4—Communication with the Client; Counsel and Assistance within the Bounds of the Law; and Formation of the Client-Lawyer Relationship

Model Rule 1.4 covers communications with clients, and the MPRE examiners include it in the group of subjects tested second-most heavily on the exam. In terms of real-world impact for practitioners, failure to communicate adequately with a client (along with neglecting client matters) is the most common grounds for attorney reprimand, suspension, and disbarment by state disciplinary authorities. Rule 1.4(a) requires that an attorney "promptly inform the client of any decision or circumstance with respect to which the client's informed consent" is necessary under the Model Rules. In addition, an attorney must "reasonably consult with the client about the means by which the client's objectives are to be accomplished," "keep the client reasonably informed about the status of the matter," "promptly comply with reasonable requests for information," and "consult with the client about any relevant limitation on the lawyer's conduct when the lawyer knows that the client expects assistance not permitted by the Rules of Professional Conduct or other law." Rule 1.4(b) requires attorneys to explain matters to clients in a way that enables the client to make an informed decision.

Note the repeated use of "reasonable/reasonably" in the subsections of the rule—Rule 1.4 does not have bright lines, but instead uses this term to allow disciplinary authorities to take a case-by-case approach. For purposes of testing with multiple-choice questions, as on the MPRE, this means the questions will have to posit facts that are fairly extreme one way or the other, so that examinees can recognize situations that are clearly reasonable or unreasonable. On the other hand, an essay question on an exam in a Professional Responsibility course is likely to present an ambiguous scenario so that students will have to argue why the actions of the attorney, or the demands of the client, were reasonable/unreasonable.

For multiple-choice questions, always remember that a duty to confer with the client (or respond to inquiries promptly) is the default rule, with a number of specific exceptions. As mentioned above, the fact that the Model Rules expresses the basic duty to communicate with repeated qualifications of reasonable and reasonably makes it difficult for examiners to draft multiple-choice questions without using extreme scenarios. The exceptions to the rule, however, are more specific, and as a result, it is easier for examiners to draft multiple-choice questions about the exceptions. When studying for the MPRE, therefore, pay close attention to the specific exceptions mentioned in the rules or in the official comments.

QUESTION 5. **Discussing negotiation strategies with the client.** An attorney is a litigator and represents a client in a civil lawsuit in which the client is the defendant. The attorney explains the general strategy and prospects of success, and consults the client on tactics that are likely to result in significant expense, such as the hiring of experts or jury consultants. At the same time, the attorney believes their best shot at winning the case will be to elicit an admission from the plaintiff during cross-examination when the plaintiff testifies at trial. More specifically, the attorney plans to elicit a mild, relatively innocuous admission during the first round of cross-examination, expecting opposing counsel to rehabilitate the witness on re-direct examination. The attorney then plans a short, direct, re-cross consisting of three yes-or-no questions that should elicit a devastating admission from the plaintiff, which opposing counsel is probably not anticipating. Attorney has not discussed this plan for cross and re-cross with Client. Even if the re-cross does not go as well as the attorney hopes, they might prevail in the case by several other ways. Is it proper for the attorney to leave the client out of the planning for the cross-examination and re-cross of the plaintiff?

A. Yes, because a lawyer ordinarily will not be expected to describe trial or negotiation strategy in detail.
B. Yes, because the client might try to interfere with Attorney's strategies and tactics, which would put the attorney under the control of the client.
C. No, because a lawyer should explain the general strategy and prospects of success and ordinarily should consult the client on tactics that are likely to result in significant expense or to injure or coerce others.
D. No, because lawyers should consult with clients about their plans for direct examination, but not cross-examination, because it is impossible to plan a cross-examination until one first hears the witness's testimony during direct examination.

ANALYSIS. Comment 5 for Rule 1.4 provides an example that served as the basis for this question:

> For example, when there is time to explain a proposal made in a negotiation, the lawyer should review all [the] important provisions with the client before proceeding to an agreement. In litigation, a lawyer should explain the

> general strategy and prospects of success and ordinarily should consult the client on tactics that are likely to result in significant expense or to injure or coerce others. On the other hand, a lawyer ordinarily will not be expected to describe trial or negotiation strategy in detail. The guiding principle is that the lawyer should fulfill reasonable client expectations for information consistent with the duty to act in the client's best interests, and the client's overall requirements as to the character of representation.

In other words, overall objectives and general strategies are items lawyers should discuss with clients, as well as decisions that involve significant additional costs, such as hiring experts or jury consultants. On the other hand, lawyers *do not* have to ask clients about whether to cross-examine a witness, whether to object to questions from the opposing party, or how to present an opening or closing argument.

A is therefore correct because the question asks whether the lawyer can make decisions about cross-examinations without consulting with the client. This is exactly the type of scenario envisioned by the comments to Rule 1.4.

B is incorrect in the reason it gives for permitting the lawyer to exclude the client from such decisions. First, the Model Rules do not express concerns about clients interfering with the lawyer's approach—instead, the reason given in the official comments focuses more on the role of the lawyer in representation and an implicit duty to rely on the lawyer's own training and experience, which the client normally would lack. The phrase "put the lawyer under the control of the client" as a negative should be a giveaway that this is the wrong answer, because throughout the Model Rules there is a pervasive emphasis on the need for clients to have control of the representation.

C is incorrect but tricky—it uses a true statement, borrowed directly from the comments to Rule 1.4, but the statement is inapplicable to this fact pattern. Lawyers indeed have a general duty to consult with clients about decisions that will significantly increase the client's costs, such as hiring experts, or that could injure others. Examples of "injuring others" would be unnecessarily humiliating or disgracing a third party (or even the opposing party) by revealing secret personal failings, such as adultery, previous unwanted pregnancies, past addictions and rehabilitation treatment, and so on. Watch for incorrect answers on the exam that cleverly use verbiage that would be correct for a different question.

D is also incorrect, and this should have been the easiest answer to eliminate. The Model Rules never draw a distinction between direct examination and cross-examination for purposes of ethical or professional behavior. The final clause may sound correct—that it is difficult to plan cross-examination questions without hearing the direct testimony that precedes it—but in reality, litigators often know what to expect from witnesses during direct examination beforehand, because of the prevalence of pretrial depositions and affidavits. Many litigators would actually have their cross-examination questions for each witness in mind before the trial begins.

QUESTION 6. Several ways to structure a large donation.
A client hired an attorney to handle a transactional matter. The client, a billionaire, wants to devote several million dollars to philanthropy. There are several alternative ways to achieve the client's goals—incorporating a 501(c)3 charitable corporation, establishing a private foundation, creating a charitable trust, operating a nonprofit unincorporated association, or simply donating the money to an existing charity of some kind. Each alternative has different pros and cons regarding immediate tax benefits for the donor versus tax deductions for subsequent contributors, permissible activities for the charitable entity, donor control versus independence, eligibility for government grants, and administrative costs related to accounting and recordkeeping. The attorney does not discuss all of these details with the client, though, because the client said at the outset that he trusted his attorney's judgment, and the attorney believed the client would find the details tiresome and confusing. The attorney set up a private foundation for the client because this seemed to provide his client with the greatest immediate tax benefits and the highest degree of control in the long term. The downside was that the private foundation option involved burdensome paperwork and reporting to the IRS every year, imposed annual spend-down requirements, and limited the tax benefits for any other philanthropists who wanted to donate to the foundation later. The attorney believed the pros outweighed the cons in this case, but the client was unhappy because he wanted to start something that would grow and attract other wealthy philanthropists who might get involved, and the administrative costs drained some of the funds that the client had hoped would go directly to charitable causes. Could the attorney be subject to discipline for how he handled the matter?

A. Yes, because the lawyer in this case is merely helping the client avoid his tax obligations on millions of dollars, and a lawyer should not assist a client in shirking his fair share of taxes.

B. Yes, because the Rules of Professional Conduct require a lawyer to consult with the client about the means to be used to accomplish the client's objectives.

C. No, because a lawyer ordinarily will not be expected to describe transactional strategy in detail, according to the Rules of Professional Conduct.

D. No, as long as the attorney was objectively correct that the pros outweighed the cons in this situation, based on his professional judgment and experience.

ANALYSIS. Comments 2 and 3 for Model Rule 1.4 require a lawyer to have a "reasonably" thorough discussion with the client about which means to use in achieving the objectives of the client. Legal transactions and legal disputes normally present several alternative approaches that a lawyer could take. Each approach offers a set of tradeoffs in terms of financial cost, time/delay, risk, and potential payoffs. A lawyer may not need to clear every methodological decision with a client (e.g., which day of the month is best for filing applications with government agencies, or what language to use in a letter to another party). Nevertheless, the choice of which approach to take overall should rest with the client, who must personally shoulder the costs, risks, delays, and so on. This problem illustrates the point with a rather common scenario—a wealthy client who wants to donate a large sum to charity, and who must balance various tax consequences with the desire to control how the money is used, as well as balancing short-term versus long-term impact. A client has a right to make these delicate decisions, with the attorney's advice and counsel.

A is incorrect because it suggests the wrong reason for the lawyer to be subject to discipline in this case. While lawyers cannot knowingly assist clients in committing tax fraud, a lawyer may (and probably should) assist a client in minimizing the tax consequences for a transaction. **A** suggests a political view—that wealthy people should pay higher taxes and have fewer deductions and exemptions available—rather than an ethical or professional approach.

B is correct, and uses the same verbiage found in Comment 3 for Rule 1.4—lawyers must discuss with their clients the means they will use to achieve the goals of the representation. A lawyer could be subject to discipline (reprimand, license suspension, or disbarment) for making such a choice without consulting the client.

C is incorrect given the facts in this problem, though the rationale is true in the abstract. Lawyers indeed are free to proceed with the representation without asking the client about every detail of strategy—the timing of each letter or phone call, the arguments to use in advocating for a position, and so on. The problem is that the question asks about the overall approach to take in this transaction, a decision that involves difficult tradeoffs in terms of costs, risks, client control, and short-term versus long-term impact—this is not just a minor strategic maneuver.

D is incorrect, because the Model Rules do not focus on whether the attorney is ultimately correct in his assessment of a situation, but whether the attorney complied with the rules and allowed the client to make the decisions that the client should make.

QUESTION 7. **What he doesn't know can't hurt him.** An attorney receives a report from a psychologist that provides the psychologist's professional opinion that the client is unstable. The psychologist's report indicates that the client believes himself to be perfectly sane, and that the client has indicated he will cause harm if the psychologist submits a report stating the client is not stable and sane. The attorney chooses not to provide the report to his client when he receives it. Is the attorney subject to discipline?

A. Yes, because the attorney is required to keep the client reasonably informed about his case, especially if a certain event might bear significant weight on the outcome of the case.
B. Yes, because Attorney refused to supply Client with a copy of the report because of his own personal interest.
C. No, because attorneys can withhold or delay information from clients if the information would be harmful to the client or would inconvenience the attorney.
D. No, because immediately providing the report to the client may cause harm to the client.

ANALYSIS. This question addresses a specific exception in the Model Rules to the duty to communicate with clients, and in recent years, the MPRE has tested this specific exception. Comment 7 for Rule 1.4 states, "In some circumstances, a lawyer may be justified in delaying transmission of information when the client would be likely to react imprudently to an immediate communication. Thus, a lawyer might withhold a psychiatric diagnosis of a client when the examining psychiatrist indicates that disclosure would harm the client."

A is incorrect, though the rationale is true in the abstract. Normally, a lawyer indeed has a duty to keep a client reasonably informed, and this report could have significant implications for the case eventually. Nevertheless, there is a specific exception for scenarios like the one described here.

B is also incorrect. There is no indication in the problem that the lawyer was acting in his own interest rather than trying to protect his client.

C is incorrect, but only because of the final phrase in the answer—the "inconvenience of the attorney." In fact, Comment 7 to Rule 1.4, which carves out the narrow exception that is the focus of this problem, specifically says that inconvenience to the lawyer cannot be the basis for withholding the information from a client: "A lawyer may not withhold information to serve the lawyer's own interest or convenience or the interests or convenience of another person."

D is correct. This is exactly the type of situation contemplated in Comment 7 to Rule 1.4—one of the rare scenarios in which a lawyer may withhold information from his own client. The psychologist warned the lawyer that the client might do something dangerous if he were to see the report, and in such a case, it is reasonable for the lawyer to withhold the information, at least for the time being.

QUESTION 8. **Waiting for the second offer.** An attorney represented a client in litigation over a breach of contract. After jury selection but before the opening arguments of trial the following Monday, the opposing party contacted the attorney with a settlement offer. The attorney, an experienced litigator, was familiar with opposing counsel from previous cases, and knew that opposing counsel always follows up an initial settlement offer with a better offer a day or two later. Therefore, the attorney declined the offer immediately, knowing from experience that a better offer was forthcoming. When the attorney met his client at the courthouse the following Monday for the first day of trial, he mentioned that he was encouraged by the opposing party's initial offer the previous week, which he had declined, because it meant that a more generous offer was on the way any time. The client was surprised that his attorney had not consulted with him about the offer, but he accepted the attorney's explanation for declining it and agreed they would wait for the next offer. As both parties and their lawyers took their places in the courtroom, the opposing counsel passed a note to the attorney with a new settlement offer, and just as the attorney expected, it was much more generous. The attorney and his client agreed to settle the case right then, and avoided the inconvenience of going through the whole trial. Is the attorney subject to discipline?

A. Yes, because waiting to settle the case until the last minute before trial meant a lot of inconvenience for the judge, the jury, and other court personnel that could have been avoided if the lawyer had engaged opposing counsel in negotiations at the time of the first offer, the previous week.

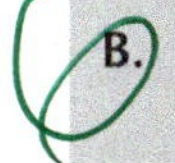

B. Yes, because a lawyer who receives from opposing counsel an offer of settlement in a civil controversy must promptly inform the client of its substance prior to taking any action.

C. No, because Attorney obtained a more favorable outcome for his client by waiting for the follow-up offer on Monday, and the case still ended up settling before trial.

D. No, as long as Client would have agreed anyway to let Attorney decline the initial offer, if Attorney had explained opposing counsel's consistent pattern with offers.

ANALYSIS. This question returns to the basics of Rule 1.4(a) and the important rule that lawyers should always check with clients before accepting or rejecting a settlement offer, regardless of how unreasonable the offer seems, unless the client has explicitly pre-approved or pre-rejected such an offer. Comment 2 to Rule 1.4 offers a similar scenario as an example: "For example, a lawyer who receives from opposing counsel an offer of settlement in a civil controversy or a proffered plea bargain in a criminal case must promptly inform the client of its substance . . . " This rule reflects important policy considerations as well as a bit of realism about legal practice—lawyers often focus on maximizing the payoff in a case, but clients may be trying to balance a number of other considerations as well. An unsophisticated client, unfamiliar with legal disputes and courts, may find litigation extremely stressful and would appreciate any opportunity to end the matter sooner rather than later; the stress level they feel from continuing may outweigh the additional value of waiting for a better settlement offer. On the other hand, even a sophisticated client (i.e., a large corporation that litigates frequently), may feel that the marginal value of a better settlement offer is still less than certain opportunity costs involved with waiting to resolve the case. Suppose the initial settlement offer was $50,000 and the second offer is double—$100,000. Now suppose that the client, a corporation, is simultaneously in merger talks with another company, or on the verge of an initial public stock offering, which might be worth tens of millions—an immediate windfall—to the corporation and its shareholders. If a merger or the stock offering has stalled because of this pending litigation, and the uncertainty about its eventual outcome, the $50,000 in additional money from waiting for a later settlement may be far less than the lost income from delaying a merger or stock offering even a few days or weeks. A corporate buyer or major investor could lose interest and move on in the meantime. A lawyer may indeed be correct that the opposing party will follow up with a much better offer, but the client may have other considerations that offset the value of waiting—and a litigator might not even know about his client being in secret merger talks with another corporation on the side. The client has a right to choose.

A is incorrect because the rule does not take into account the inconvenience for the judge, the jury, and other court personnel. In a client-lawyer relationship, the attorney must consult with the client prior to taking any action unless the client has previously given explicit instructions about accepting or rejecting certain offers.

B is the correct answer. Rule 1.4, Comment 2, states that a lawyer must promptly consult with and secure the client's consent prior to taking action unless prior discussions with the client have resolved what the client wants.

C is also incorrect. The issue is not whether Attorney obtained a more favorable outcome or not, but rather that the attorney did not consult with his client before declining the opposing counsel's offer.

D is similarly incorrect. Even if the client would have agreed anyway with the attorney's decision to decline the initial offer, unless there were prior discussions between the attorney and the client, the attorney must promptly inform the client of any settlement offers from the opposing party.

C. Rule 1.5—Fees

The MPRE covers Model Rule 1.5 under two subheadings: "fees" and "client-lawyer contracts." The ABA titles the rule simply "Fees," though it includes provisions about the contracts (often called "retainers," though that term can mean a variety of things).

Rule 1.5 is lengthy and complicated. For purposes of studying for exams, divide the provisions and subsections into absolute rules versus the ambiguous factors for courts to use in deciding whether fees are "reasonable." The clear, absolute rules (including a few specific exceptions in the comments) are far more likely to appear in multiple-choice questions, such as those on the MPRE. The various factors constituting reasonableness are more likely to be the subject of an essay question on a law school Professional Responsibility exam.

The clear, absolute rules contained in Model Rule 1.5 are as follows:

- Contingent fees are *never* permissible in criminal defense cases.
- Contingent fees are *never* permissible in divorce or child custody cases (but are permissible in subsequent actions to enforce child support or alimony orders after the divorce).
- Agreements to split fees between lawyers at different firms who work on the same case *must always* be in writing.
- Contingent fee agreements *must* be in writing at the outset of representation (other types of fee arrangements do not have to be in writing, though it is preferred).
- Any written agreement about a contingent fee must state the percentage(s) and must state whether court costs and other expenses (copying, hiring experts, etc.) are deducted before or after calculating the contingent fee.
- At the end of the representation, lawyers *must* provide clients with a *written statement* about the outcome of the matter and the fees charged.

Note that fees (whether contingent fees, fees-per-service, or hourly fees) *must* be reasonable, but "reasonable" is an inherently ambiguous term, and Rule 1.5 proceeds to give eight separate factors or considerations for assessing reasonableness—and it is difficult for examiners to write multiple-choice questions about balancing a host of factors.

In legal practice, states vary in the percentages allowed for contingent fees (one-third is common, but some states allow more or less), and in the cases in which contingent fees are permissible. Fee arrangements in practice can become much more complex than many law students realize. For example, litigators may charge different percentages of contingent fees depending on whether the case settles before trial, goes to a trial verdict, or goes through an appeals process. Contingent fees also appear outside the litigation context—some transactional lawyers may receive a contingent fee for helping consummate a major business deal (such as the sale of a small company), and may have a structured agreement that gives the lawyer a higher percentage if he or she negotiates an exceptionally good price for the client. Hourly fees are more common, of course, and are the most common type of arrangement for litigation defense lawyers. Remember, however, that hourly fees are a relatively recent (i.e., twentieth-century) innovation in our legal system, and continue to be controversial because of the way they impact firm practices and the type of perverse incentives they create.

QUESTION 9. Contingent fees in criminal cases. A client retained an attorney to represent him in two cases: a criminal case and a divorce case. The attorney required that the client pay a retainer fee for the family law case, which billed at the attorney's hourly rate. The attorney then arranged for the client to pay him based on a contingency fee for the criminal case. The attorney and the client both signed the combined contract, which detailed each fee arrangement for each case, and the attorney's representation began. Are the attorney's actions proper?

A. No, as attorneys cannot charge a contingent fee for representing a defendant in a criminal case.
B. No, because attorneys must have separate contracts for each separate case the attorney is handling for a client.
C. Yes, because attorneys can charge hourly rates for domestic relations matters and can charge contingency, hourly, or flat fees for criminal cases.
D. Yes, because attorneys are restricted from charging contingency fees only in domestic relations matters when the payment is contingent upon the securing of a divorce or upon the amount of alimony, support, or property settlement.

ANALYSIS. Rule 1.5(d)(2) states that a lawyer may not charge "a contingent fee for representing a defendant in a criminal case." For example, a lawyer cannot offer to charge a fee only if the defendant obtains an acquittal. Representation of criminal defendants must involve either hourly billing or a flat fee for certain types of cases (e.g., charging $100 for challenging traffic tickets, regardless of the time involved). This rule is absolute and applies to the pretrial stage (plea bargain negotiations and discovery), trials, and appeals of criminal convictions. Note that Rule 1.5(d) states that a lawyer cannot even agree to charge a contingent fee in a criminal case, even if the lawyer ends up not charging the contingent fee or decides to waive the fee entirely at some point.

A is the correct answer. Rule 1.5(d)(2) states that Attorney shall not enter into an arrangement for, charge, or collect a contingent fee for representing a defendant in a criminal case.

B is incorrect because even if there are two separate contracts, Attorney still may not enter into a contingent fee arrangement with a defendant in a criminal case. Separating or merging the types of representation cannot cure a violation of the Model Rules.

C is not the correct answer, because even though an attorney may charge hourly rates for domestic relations matters, it is still impermissible to charge contingency fees for criminal cases. It does not matter that there are two different types of cases for Client—one civil and one criminal—Rule 1.5(d)(2) still applies to the criminal case. On the MPRE, watch out for "bundled" rule violations and tricky false answers like this one.

D is the incorrect answer for this question. Even though this answer correctly states the rule about fees in domestic relations cases, this is not the real issue for this question. The issue here is that the lawyer entered into an arrangement with the client charging a contingent fee for the client's criminal case; this is impermissible.

QUESTION 10. **Enforcing child support orders.** A court orders that a particular client should receive child support from her ex-husband. The client's ex-husband stopped making child support payments twelve months ago. The client hires an attorney to handle the enforcement of child support against the client's ex-husband. The attorney agrees to take the case on a contingency basis because the client cannot afford to hire an attorney since she has not been receiving child support from her ex-husband. The client also asks the attorney to pay her court costs, as she cannot afford those either. The attorney prepares a contract that states the attorney will only be paid for his representation if the client prevails on the enforcement motion, but that court costs will be reimbursed by the client within thirty days of the finalization of the case regardless of whether the client prevails. Is the attorney's conduct proper?

A. Yes, because attorneys may represent clients, regardless of the type of case, on a contingency basis, as long as clients are required to reimburse the attorney for the actual expenses paid by the attorney for the client.
B. Yes, because attorneys may accept cases on a contingency basis in domestic relations issues if the case is merely to enforce a prior order, and attorneys may pay for court costs for clients.
C. No, because attorneys cannot advance funds to clients for any expenses, whether or not those expenses are related to the case.
D. No, because contingency fees are specifically prohibited in any case involving domestic relations, including enforcement of prior orders.

ANALYSIS. Rule 1.5(d)(1) prohibits contingent fees in divorce or child custody cases. The policy concern behind this rule is to avoid giving family law attorneys any incentive to make a divorce or child custody proceeding more acrimonious than it already is, or more melodramatic, merely to earn a higher fee. Nevertheless, Comment 6 to Rule 1.5 qualifies this prohibition with a specific exception: "This provision does not preclude a contract for a contingent fee for legal representation in connection with the recovery of post-judgment balances due under support, alimony or other financial orders because such contracts do not implicate the same policy concerns." The MPRE in the recent past has included a question about this specific exception.

A is incorrect, because the Model Rules place clear restrictions on the types of cases in which lawyers may charge contingent fees.

B is correct, as it restates the exception delineated in Comment 6 to Rule 1.5. After a divorce or custody battle is already over, in which the court has ordered child support payments, when the payor becomes delinquent, the receiving party may retain an attorney on a contingent fee basis to seek enforcement of the order. This is more analogous to a contract enforcement action than a dissolution of marriage. Presumably, the amount of the award is already set, so a contingent fee arrangement would give the lawyer no financial incentive to worsen the resentment between the parties.

C is also incorrect, as Model Rule 1.8(e)(1) allows attorneys to advance court costs or fees to clients, with the understanding that the client will reimburse the lawyer for these costs and fees after prevailing in the litigation.

D is incorrect because it contradicts Comment 6 to Rule 1.5, which specifically allows for contingent fees in actions brought solely to enforce existing child support or alimony orders.

QUESTION 11. **After it's over.** An attorney agreed to represent a client as plaintiff in a patent infringement lawsuit. The attorney was part of a partnership that specialized in intellectual property law. The attorney prepared, and the client signed, a written fee agreement that specified the attorney would receive a tiered contingent fee in the case: 25 percent if the case settled before trial, 30 percent if they went to trial and won, and 35 percent if the case went up on appeal and they prevailed in the appellate stage. In addition, the agreement specified that the contingent fee would come from total award before court costs and other expenses, and that the client would be responsible for court costs and expenses out of his own pocket, either along the way as expenses arose during the proceedings, or from the client's share of the award after the attorney received his contingent fee. The attorney never revealed that his partnership agreement required him to share his part of the fees with three other partners in the firm, or that his fees would go toward a general firm operating budget from which the partnership paid the salaries of non-lawyer staff, such as paralegals and secretaries. The attorney obtained a favorable settlement before trial. He telephoned Client with the good news, and explained that he would deduct his 25 percent contingent fee, as they had agreed, and would send Client the remainder of the settlement funds. At that time, there were no outstanding unpaid expenses or court costs. The client was glad to hear the news, and the attorney promptly sent the client a check for 75 percent of the total amount received from the other party. The attorney and the client had no other contact except to exchange holiday greeting cards. Were the attorney's actions improper?

A. Yes, because the attorney failed to obtain written informed consent from the client to share fees with other lawyers in the firm, and because the attorney charged a tiered contingent fee in a patent litigation case.

B. No, because contingent fees in patent litigation are proper as long as there is a written fee agreement at the beginning of the representation.

C. Yes, because the attorney failed to provide the client with a written statement stating the outcome of the matter and showing the remittance to the client and the method of its determination.

D. No, because the attorney properly followed the agreement with the client, and there were no outstanding court costs or unpaid expenses at the time of the settlement.

ANALYSIS. Rule 1.5(c) requires attorneys to provide a written statement at the conclusion of the representation, stating the outcome and delineating any unused retainer funds that the lawyer is returning. This requirement avoids client confusion about the outcome of their case (for example, a client may not understand that a "remand" means they will have to go through another trial), and it avoids misunderstandings about whether the lawyer is continuing to represent the client going forward. The MPRE regularly tests this rule.

A is incorrect—the Model Rules do not require that attorneys explain to clients that they share fees with other lawyers in their own firm, although sharing fees with lawyers from other firms (when firms collaborate on a case) would require written, informed consent from the client. In addition, the Model Rules do not prohibit tiered contingent fees, and these are relatively common in legal practice today.

B is also incorrect, but only because it misses the requirement about a written statement at the end of representation.

C is correct. In this case, the lawyer failed to send a written statement at the conclusion of the matter, so the lawyer's actions were improper.

D is wrong for the same reason as **B**—it overlooks the requirement of a written statement at the conclusion of the representation.

QUESTION 12. It all worked out in the end. An attorney has represented his client in the past on various transactional matters. They have always operated under an oral agreement about the fees, and they have never had a dispute over fees in the past—the attorney would send the client a bill, and the client would pay it. Recently, the client contacted the attorney by phone about representing him as a plaintiff in a personal injury lawsuit. The attorney agreed, and then explained that he would charge a contingent fee in the case, so that the client did not have to worry about how much time his attorney had to put into the case, as the client would still receive the same share of whatever amount they won. Given their long history of working together, the attorney offers to set the contingent fee below the rate charged by other attorneys in the area, and they agree over the phone on a 25 percent contingent fee for the attorney, after costs and expenses. They never formalize this agreement in writing, though at the end of the case, after they prevail and win a large verdict, the attorney sends the client a written statement about keeping 25 percent of the award for his fee. The client is very happy with the outcome of the case and they have no dispute over this fee. Would the attorney be subject to discipline in a situation like this?

A. Yes, because contingent fees must always be formalized in writing at the beginning of representation.
B. Yes, because a lawyer cannot charge a contingent fee in a personal injury case.
C. No, because the lawyer agreed to charge a contingent fee far below the rate that most lawyers receive for this type of case.
D. No, because the lawyer provided an accounting at the end of the case and there was no dispute over the fees.

ANALYSIS. The Model Rules merely express a "preference" for written fee agreements in general, but contingent fee agreements must always be in writing at the outset of the representation. This is a clear-cut rule that lends itself easily to multiple-choice questions. Do not let the extra facts mislead you—an attorney's conduct (such as a failure to put contingent fee arrangements in writing) can constitute a violation of the Model Rules even if the client is pleased with the outcome and there appear to be no adverse consequences. Remember that other lawyers (including those in one's own firm) who learn of rule violations may have a duty to report their colleague to the disciplinary authorities.

A is the correct answer to this question. Rule 1.5(c) states the rule in absolute terms:

> A contingent fee agreement shall be in a writing signed by the client and shall state the method by which the fee is to be determined, including the percentage or percentages that shall accrue to the lawyer in the event of settlement, trial or appeal; litigation and other expenses to be deducted from the recovery; and whether such expenses are to be deducted before or after the contingent fee is calculated. The agreement must clearly notify the client of any expenses for which the client will be liable whether or not the client is the prevailing party.

B is not the correct answer. Attorneys may charge a contingent fee in a personal injury case—this is the current norm for plaintiffs' lawyers, in fact.

C is incorrect, because it misses the point that contingent fees are simply impermissible in criminal cases. This answer may trick some readers because it appears to allude to the "reasonableness" factors in Rule 1.5(a). The "reasonable fee" requirement certainly applies to criminal cases—it would be unreasonable, for example, for defense counsel to charge a defendant fifty times the normal hourly rate in that jurisdiction for a simple misdemeanor charge, under normal circumstances. Here, however, the fee is supposedly too low, which is unlikely to constitute a violation of the rules.

D is also incorrect; even though the lawyer appropriately provided an accounting at the end of the representation, and even though there was no conflict about the contingent fee, the contingent fee itself constitutes a violation of Rule 1.5.

QUESTION 13. **Written agreements not always required.** An attorney has represented a client on various small matters in the past. The client now needs representation for a more substantial matter involving a business transaction. During a phone call, the attorney agrees to represent the client at a slightly higher hourly rate, given the complexity of the matter, and when they meet to discuss the transaction in more detail, the attorney double-checks with the client about the fee arrangement verbally, explaining it carefully and answering any questions the client may have. The attorney and the client never formalize the fee arrangement in writing, but the attorney does send printed bills to the client periodically. Eventually, the client starts to feel that the representation is costing too much, and objects to one of the bills. Was it permissible for the attorney to have an oral agreement over hourly fees, without putting the fee agreement into writing?

A. Yes, because the matter is more complex than the previous work Attorney has done for the client.

B. No, because fee arrangements must be in writing, in order to avoid disputes between lawyers and their clients later on.

C. Yes, because even though it is always preferable to have fee agreements in writing, it is not required in this type of case.

D. No, because the attorney should have reduced his hourly fee, rather than raising it, if the matter is more complex and will generate more hours of work for the lawyer.

ANALYSIS. The purpose of this question is to remind students that the absolute requirement for written fee agreements applies in only two scenarios—contingent fees and fees shared between lawyers from different firms that worked on the case. There is a strong preference for written fee agreements in all other situations (and it is certainly a prudent habit in legal practice), but it is not an absolute requirement.

A is incorrect, because there is no rule that complex cases require a written fee agreement, even if it is probably prudent in practice to use written agreements when cases become more complex.

B is also incorrect, because the Model Rules do not require all fee agreements to be in writing; only contingent fees and shared fees must be in writing, and neither of those elements is present here.

C is correct. This is the type of scenario in which fee agreements do not have to be in writing, even though it is preferable to have them memorialized in text to avoid future misunderstandings.

D is incorrect, because there is no rule requiring attorneys to reduce their fees for more complex legal work—in fact, it is more common for fees to increase for more complex legal matters.

QUESTION 14. **A share of the divorce proceeds.** An attorney agrees to represent a client in a divorce proceeding against her husband. The client is particularly concerned about obtaining her fair share of the marital property or assets—as much as possible, in fact—as well as a suitable level of child support for their children. The client agrees to pay the attorney his usual flat fee for divorce cases, $5,000, but also offers to pay him 10 percent of whatever he wins in terms of payments and distribution of assets, on top of his usual fee. After a protracted, acrimonious divorce proceeding, the attorney obtains a settlement worth approximately $2 million for the client. Is the attorney subject to discipline in this scenario?

A. No, because the client proposed the arrangement and agreed to it beforehand.

B. No, because the contingent fee was much lower than the typical contingent fee in personal injury cases, and the trial was protracted and acrimonious.

C. Yes, because the attorney entered into a mixed flat-fee/contingent-fee arrangement, which is improper under the Rules of Professional Conduct.

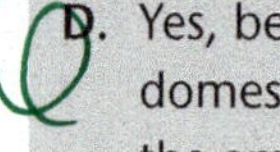

D. Yes, because the attorney entered into an arrangement for a fee in a domestic relations matter, the amount of which was contingent upon the amount of alimony, support, or property settlement.

ANALYSIS. Rule 1.5(d)(1) strictly forbids contingent fees in domestic relations cases. The policy rationale for this prohibition is that contingent fees would give lawyers a perverse incentive to make the divorce more acrimonious or unnecessarily traumatic for the parties in order to obtain a larger share for their client, and therefore, a larger sum for the lawyer. This is a bright-line rule that lends itself easily to multiple-choice questions, so students should prepare to encounter it on the MPRE.

A is incorrect, because Rule 1.5(d) states that a lawyer is not allowed to enter into such an arrangement. When the Model Rules use the word "shall" as opposed to "may" it means that a lawyer is prohibited or limited from doing such act and a client's written agreement to do otherwise does not create an exception.

B is incorrect because the reasoning is irrelevant. Model Rule 1.5(d) states that "a lawyer shall not enter [in]to a contingent fee agreement contingent upon the securing of a divorce or upon the amount of alimony or support, or property settlement in lieu thereof." Whether or not the contingent fee is lower than a typical contingent fee is not an exception to this rule.

C misstates the rule. According to Rule 1.5(d), lawyers may not enter into an arrangement for, charge, or collect any fee in a domestic relations matter, the payment or amount of which is contingent upon the securing of a divorce, or upon the amount of alimony or support, or property settlement.

D correctly paraphrases Rule 1.5(d)(1): "A lawyer shall not enter into an arrangement for, charge, or collect any fee in a domestic relations matter, the payment or amount of which is contingent upon the securing of a divorce or upon the amount of alimony or support, or property settlement in lieu thereof."

D. Rule 1.16—Declining and Terminating Representation

The MPRE examiners include "terminating representation" under the heading of "client-lawyer relationship," which overall is the most-tested subject area after conflicts of interest. Model Rule 1.16 governs both declining representation (refusing to take a case) and terminating representation. The client-lawyer relationship may end when the client "fires" or discharges the lawyer, or when the lawyer concludes a matter or withdraws from representation. The MPRE does not purport to test the provisions about *declining* representation, so those provisions will receive no attention here. A law school course, on the other hand, may give more emphasis to the duty of lawyers to take undesirable or inconvenient cases, especially for indigent clients.

For purposes of answering test questions, keep in mind the most basic (or default) rule: a client can normally discharge a lawyer at any time, for any reason, with one narrow exception (a court forbids it). Lawyers, on the other hand, have more restrictions on their freedom to quit working for a client. If litigation is underway, a lawyer will nearly always have to obtain the court's permission to withdraw from a case; even outside the litigation arena, lawyers may not be able to withdraw if doing so would be excessively prejudicial to the client.

The Model Rules delineate a few situations in which it is presumptively appropriate for lawyers to withdraw (clients refusing to pay their bills, and so on). At the same time, attorneys *must* withdraw when continuing with the representation would violate the Model Rules (as when a lawyer discovers a non-obvious conflict of interest only after taking a case), or when the representation involves perpetrating a fraud or other crimes.

QUESTION 15. **A conflict of interest discovered during representation.** An attorney agreed to represent a plaintiff in a personal injury lawsuit, and the next day agreed to represent a defendant in litigation where the defendant faces vicarious liability. Only after the attorney has conducted some investigation of the case, and has obtained confidential information from each client, does the attorney discover that the plaintiff client is actually suing another of the attorney's clients, under a theory of vicarious liability. The two clients are actually adverse parties in the same litigation. Must the attorney withdraw from representing both clients?

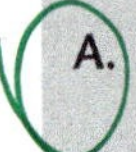

A. Yes, a lawyer shall withdraw from the representation of a client if the representation will result in violation of the rules of professional conduct.

B. Yes, the lawyer must withdraw unless both clients consent to the conflict of interest.

C. No, the lawyer may withdraw, but withdrawal is optional and not mandatory.

D. No, the lawyer may not withdraw once litigation is underway, regardless of the conflict of interest.

ANALYSIS. Rule 1.16(a)(1) requires a lawyer to decline or withdraw from representation if "the representation will result in violation of the rules of professional conduct or other law," even if the representation is already underway. This problem presents a relatively commonplace scenario—conflicts of interest are not always evident at first glance, so sometimes lawyers take on a client without realizing that another client will turn out to be the adverse party in the matter. Sometimes, completely new conflicts arise during the course of representation due to a corporate merger or acquisition of another client of the lawyer. New conflicts also develop through property transfers or an impleader/joinder of an additional party. When a lawyer becomes aware of a conflict of interest or other violation of the Model Rules, there is a duty to withdraw. Remember that even where the Model Rules require a lawyer to withdraw, if litigation is underway, the lawyer will have to request (and will probably obtain) permission from the court.

A is the best answer. Rule 1.16(a) requires lawyers to decline or withdraw from representation whenever continuation of the representation would result in a rule violation. A conflict of interest, especially between two parties in the same litigation, is a serious violation of the Model Rules, so the lawyer cannot continue.

B is incorrect because the two clients are adverse parties in the same litigation, which makes this conflict nonconsentable.

C is incorrect because in this case, withdrawal is mandatory under Rule 1.16, not optional. There are many other situations in which withdrawal would be optional (as when a client refuses to pay their bills), but this is not one of those cases.

D is most likely incorrect as well. Lawyers may withdraw from representation after litigation is underway, at least in cases like this, as long as the court approves the withdrawal. It is indeed true that a court might forbid withdrawal once a trial is underway, but that is extremely unlikely when the same lawyer would have to represent both parties in litigation.

QUESTION 16. You're fired! A client hired an attorney to represent her in a litigation matter. At the end of the first day of trial, the client is unhappy with her lawyer's performance in the courtroom and informs the attorney that she is firing him and will find another lawyer. The attorney wants to continue representing this client until the end of the trial. May the client discharge the attorney after a trial has begun?

A. Yes, as long as a client obtains permission from the court to discharge an attorney, it is permissible.
B. Yes, a client has a right to discharge a lawyer at any time, with or without cause, subject to liability for payment for the lawyer's services.
C. No, a client may not discharge a lawyer once a trial is underway, because the disruption could be prejudicial to the opposing party.
D. No, a client cannot discharge a lawyer once the lawyer has received confidential information about the client's case.

ANALYSIS. As a rule, a client may discharge a lawyer at any time, for any reason (including a silly reason). The policy rationale behind this rule is that we should not force anyone to use a lawyer whom he or she finds unacceptable. There is one minor exception and one important caveat to this rule. There are rare instances in which a judge may forbid a client to drop a lawyer in the middle of trial, as when it appears that a (losing) party is merely firing their lawyer to disrupt or delay the proceedings or to vie for a mistrial/retrial. Normally, a judge would not interfere with a party's decision to find a new lawyer. Note that lawyers sometimes try to insist on continuing with the representation, especially if the lawyer is desperate for clients and the case is potentially lucrative. It is surprisingly easy to find state disciplinary actions involving lawyers who continued working on (and billing for) a client's case after the client had explicitly discharged the attorney.

The important caveat is that the client who fires a lawyer will probably still have to pay any legal fees the lawyer has earned up to that point, and could be liable (that is, could be sued) if the client refuses to pay for the time the lawyer has already spent on the matter. This can become complicated if the lawyer has been working on a contingent fee basis and there is no verdict or award yet at the time of discharge. A court may either order that the discharged lawyer receive a pro-rata share of the eventual award (meaning a subsequent lawyer will have to split the normal contingent fee with the original lawyer), or the court may order that the discharged lawyer receive reasonable hourly fees for the time spent on the case, under a theory of quantum meruit.

For purposes of a multiple-choice question on the MPRE, begin your analysis by assuming the client will be free to discharge the lawyer at any time, even for a seemingly terrible reason (such as the client learning that the lawyer is a fan of a rival sports team).

A is not correct—the default rule is that a party does not have to obtain court permission to discharge its lawyer, although a lawyer would have to request court permission to withdraw from the case.

B is correct—clients have a nearly absolute right to discharge their attorneys at any time, for any reason. Usually, this can occur even in the middle of a trial, although in very rare instances a judge may forbid the discharge if it seems calculated merely to disrupt and delay the proceedings.

C is also incorrect. Normally, clients can discharge a lawyer in the midst of a trial, despite the inevitable disruption and inconvenience that result (and that affects everyone involved).

D is incorrect regarding clients discharging lawyers (as in this problem), but learning confidential information *can* be a reason that a lawyer might not be able to withdraw from representing one client and switch to representing the other client instead.

QUESTION 17. **Withholding client documents.** A client fired an attorney after the attorney had completed 80 percent of the work involved in the representation. The client refuses to pay any of the fees that were in the original agreement at the beginning of representation. The client also demands that the attorney turn over all papers and documents relating to the representation. Must the attorney immediately return the client's documents regardless of the fees owed?

A. Yes, a lawyer must surrender all papers and property to the client as soon as representation ends, even if it ends with an untimely discharge of the lawyer.

B. Yes, because the client has not received what she bargained for if she wants to discharge the lawyer before the representation is complete.
C. No, because a client forfeits any right to papers and documents related to the representation if she discharges the lawyer without cause before the representation is complete.
D. No, because a lawyer may retain papers relating to the client to the extent permitted by law.

ANALYSIS. Comment 9 to Rule 1.16 says, "The lawyer may retain papers as security for a fee only to the extent permitted by law." Normally, a lawyer must return all of the client's documents promptly at the end of representation, even if the client has discharged the lawyer prematurely. The only exception is when the client has refused to pay fees that the lawyer clearly has earned. This does not apply to unearned fees that the lawyer may still hold in a trust account—discharged lawyers must return unused or unearned fees to the client immediately. This issue has appeared on the MPRE in recent years.

A is incorrect, although it accurately states the normal rule. Under normal circumstances, attorneys must surrender all papers and property to a client as soon as the representation terminates. The sole exception is the one described in this fact pattern—when the client discharges a lawyer after the lawyer has performed substantial work and then refuses to pay for the work already performed.

B is also incorrect, because even a dissatisfied client must pay the agreed-upon fees for work already performed by a discharged attorney, and the lawyer may hold on to client papers as security for the unpaid fees.

C is incorrect under any scenario—even in a case when the attorney has a right to hold onto client papers as security for unpaid legal fees, the client has not forfeited all rights to the papers or property. Instead, as soon as the client pays the fees that the lawyer has already earned, the attorney must return the client's papers and property. When no fee dispute is involved, discharged lawyers must immediately return all client papers, property, and unused funds.

D is correct—unless state law provides otherwise, a lawyer may hold on to client documents as security until the client pays the fees that the client actually owes to the lawyer for work already performed.

QUESTION 18. **Returning unused funds to the client after discharge.** A client fired an attorney after two weeks of representation, long before the matter was complete. Client had prepaid a large refundable retainer, against which the attorney was to draw his fees as the representation went on. The client therefore has fully paid her fees up to that point to the attorney. The attorney is very upset about the client discharging him without cause and believes it is unfair and wrongful. The attorney refuses to return the remainder of the fees, and refuses to turn over any documents from the representation to the client. Is it proper for the attorney to take this course of action, if indeed the client had no good reason to discharge him?

A. Yes, because a client must obtain court permission to discharge a lawyer before the representation is complete.
B. Yes, it is proper for an attorney to retain the remaining funds and the documents.
C. No, it is improper for an attorney to retain the unused funds, but an attorney may withhold the documents.
D. No, it is improper for an attorney to retain either the unused funds or the documents.

ANALYSIS. Rule 1.16(d) states:

> Upon termination of representation, a lawyer shall take steps to the extent reasonably practicable to protect a client's interests, such as giving reasonable notice to the client, allowing time for employment of other counsel, surrendering papers and property to which the client is entitled and refunding any advance payment of fee or expense that has not been earned or incurred.

It is normal for a lawyer to feel upset when discharged wrongfully by a client, but clients have a nearly absolute right to discharge lawyers (that is, to terminate the representation). Some lawyers in this situation may feel tempted by spite to be uncooperative with the client or the next lawyer that takes over the matter. Except where a lawyer legally holds client papers as security for unpaid legal fees, lawyers must promptly return all documents, personal property, and unused funds to the client. Failure to do so is a violation of the Model Rules, and a common cause for disciplinary actions (reprimand, suspension, or disbarment) against attorneys.

A is incorrect, because clients normally do not have to obtain court permission to discharge a lawyer, and even if they did, the lawyer would still have to surrender client papers and property at the end of the representation.

B is also incorrect, because Rule 1.16(d) states that it is not proper for lawyers to retain remaining client funds or documents. Lawyers should promptly surrender everything that belongs to the client.

C is partly incorrect—lawyers indeed must return unused client funds, but they may not withhold client documents except as a legal security for unpaid fees.

D is correct—it is generally improper for a lawyer to retain either unused client funds or client documents, no matter how unfair it was for the client to discharge the lawyer.

QUESTION 19. The nonpaying client. A client, who happened to be a judge, hired an attorney to represent her in her divorce proceeding against her husband, who is guilty of marital infidelity. Their fee agreement stipulates that the attorney would bill the client every month for the work performed in the previous thirty days. After two months of representation, the attorney has sent the client two bills, and has received no payments. Is it proper for the attorney to seek to withdraw from the case on the basis of unpaid fees?

A. Yes, because otherwise the attorney will develop a conflict of interest with his own client, as the share of the marital assets will impact the client's ability to pay all the outstanding fees at the end of the proceeding.

B. Yes, because a lawyer may withdraw if the client fails substantially to fulfill an obligation to the lawyer regarding the lawyer's services and has been given reasonable warning that the lawyer will withdraw unless the obligation is fulfilled.

C. No, because a lawyer representing a judge may not withdraw without the judge's approval or permission.

D. No, because withdrawing over unpaid fees turns the representation into a contingent fee arrangement, which is impermissible in a divorce case.

ANALYSIS. Rule 1.16(b)(5) permits "optional withdrawal" (the moniker used in the comments) for instances when the client is delinquent on paying the lawyer's bills: ". . . the client fails substantially to fulfill an obligation to the lawyer regarding the lawyer's services and has been given reasonable warning that the lawyer will withdraw unless the obligation is fulfilled." Note that an attorney does not *have* to withdraw, and in practice, many lawyers continue the representation in hopes that the client will eventually pay.

A is incorrect for purposes of the Model Rules, although it accurately hints at what often happens in legal practice—a nonpaying client is more likely to pay the outstanding legal fees if the outcome of the matter is sufficiently remunerative. Even so, the Model Rules do not include this as a true "conflict of interest" (in a sense, this type of theoretical potential conflict would apply to almost every client).

B is the correct answer, as it accurately states the rule in 1.16(b)(5). Forcing lawyers to continue to represent delinquent clients would be an undue hardship for many, and could create a perverse incentive to decline representation for many needy clients.

C is incorrect because the fact that a client happens to be a judge does not change the lawyer's duties or options regarding withdrawal from representation. This answer might fool a hasty reader because lawyers generally do have to obtain permission from the presiding judge in a litigation matter in order to withdraw from a case. In this problem, even though the client is a judge, she is not serving as the presiding judge in the present matter.

D is partly incorrect—even though it is true that contingent fees are impermissible in divorce actions, the option of withdrawal does not automatically make the representation a contingent fee arrangement, at least for purposes of the Model Rules.

E. The Closer

While many of the Model Rules pertain to some aspect of representing a client, one set of rules covers the formalities of the client-lawyer relationship (formation, termination, retainer contracts, fees, and so on) as well as the essential nature of the relationship. Some of the rules are very specific, such as the requirement that contingent fee agreements be in writing, while others are more open ended, like the rules about communicating regularly with the client. In legal practice, the specific rules come up less frequently in disciplinary actions than the open-ended rules, probably because it is easier for lawyers to follow clear-cut, specific requirements. In contrast, for purposes of test questions (MPRE or law school final exam), the specific rules are more likely to appear in questions because they fit easily into short hypotheticals.

QUESTION 20. **Firing the lawyer before the big win.** An attorney agreed over the phone to represent a client, and began working on the case immediately. The client came into the office two weeks later to sign the representation agreement. At the same time, the attorney gave the client a written statement of the hours worked so far and requested immediate payment for that portion of the fee, plus a $10,000 retainer up front against which the lawyer would draw fees as the representation proceeded.

The fee arrangement was complicated. In addition to the hourly fee for the time he had already worked, the agreement called for an hourly rate of $150 per hour for any work done before trial. If the case were to go to trial, the hourly fee would be $250 per hour for the entire trial phase and any appeals. The agreement also stipulated that it incorporated by reference any oral agreements regarding additional fees and expenses. The client signed the agreement. Then the lawyer explained orally that in addition to the hourly fees and the non-refundable retainer, he would take a 25 percent contingent fee of any money that the other side had to pay the client as a result of the representation, whether in damages, as there were claims and cross-claims in the case, or in court-ordered attorneys' fees. The client agreed, and they shook hands to confirm their oral agreement. Finally, the agreement authorized the lawyer to have full discretion to accept or reject any settlement offers without prior approval from the client, although no such offers occurred.

The case proceeded through the discovery phase and went to trial. On the last day of the trial, before closing arguments, it appeared that the client might win a large verdict. The client became resentful about the prospect of sharing this with the lawyer, and fired the lawyer during a recess before closing arguments. The client returned to the courtroom alone, waived his right to closing argument, and still won a significant verdict. The client now refuses to pay the lawyer the contingent fee or even the hourly fees for the last day of trial, because the client claims the attorney performed incompetently that day. The attorney has threatened to sue the client to obtain the fees. Could the attorney be subject to discipline?

A. Yes, because the lawyer made an agreement that removed the client from the decisions about accepting or rejecting settlement offers.
B. Yes, because all contingent fee agreements must be in writing, not merely oral agreements incorporated by reference.
C. No, because the client terminated the representation before the lawyer could collect a contingent fee, which made the prior agreement irrelevant.
D. No, because the written fee agreement explicitly incorporated by reference the subsequent oral contingent fee agreement.

ANALYSIS. This question ties together various rules regarding the lawyer-client relationship—its formation, termination, allocation of authority, and fees. Students should have spotted some potential violations immediately, such as the lawyer excluding the client from settlement decisions, the lawyer working under an oral agreement for two weeks without facts indicating whether the client understood the rates or fees that would accrue, and the oral agreement for a contingent fee.

A is incorrect, but highlights an ambiguity in the rules. Rule 1.4 requires lawyers to communicate settlement offers to clients, but Rule 1.2 permits lawyers to take actions specifically authorized by the client. Yet a blanket authorization to accept any settlement is probably not specific enough to satisfy the rule. Even so, it is not clear that the lawyer violated the rules merely by asking for or obtaining such authorization from the client, if the situation never arose.

B is correct. The clearest violation here is that the attorney did not put the terms of the contingent fee in a writing signed by the client, as required by Rule 1.5(c). Incorporating an oral agreement by reference in a prior written agreement is clever but it does not satisfy the stated purposes or provisions of the rule, such as making clear to the client beforehand what percentages accrue to the lawyer, what litigation expenses the client must cover, and so on.

C incorrectly assumes that termination by the client erases the lawyer's violations. Rule 1.5's provisions about fees, such as the requirement that contingent fee arrangements be in writing, apply to the agreement at the beginning of the representation, regardless of whether the lawyer actually collects a fee in the end. A client may terminate a lawyer, as in this question, or may lose the case, in which case there is no award from which to deduct a percentage for the lawyer. Nevertheless, the arrangement itself violates Rule 1.5.

D is also incorrect, because the purported incorporation by reference of a subsequent oral agreement could not possibly satisfy the specificity requirements of Rule 1.5(c), which demands detailed written explanations of the terms of a contingent-fee agreement.

Stevenson's Picks

1.	Waiving the right to a jury trial	C
2.	"Don't even call me"	C
3.	Insurers and attorneys	A
4.	Client Uses Lawyer's Advice to Commit Fraud	A
5.	Discussing negotiation strategies with the client	A
6.	Several ways to structure a large donation	B
7.	What he doesn't know can't hurt him	D
8.	Waiting for the second offer	B
9.	Contingent fees in criminal cases	A
10.	Enforcing child support orders	B
11.	After it's over	C
12.	It all worked out in the end	A
13.	Written agreements not always required	C
14.	A share of the divorce proceeds	D
15.	A conflict of interest discovered during representation	A
16.	You're fired!	B
17.	Withholding client documents	D
18.	Returning unused funds to the client after discharge	D
19.	The nonpaying client	B
20.	Firing the lawyer before the big win	B

3

Litigation and Other Forms of Advocacy

A. Rule 3.1—Meritorious Claims and Contentions

Even though lawyers have a duty to provide zealous advocacy for their clients, this does not mean that they may assert ridiculous or frivolous claims in the process. Some students will see Rule 3.1 as providing balance to the previous rules requiring zealous advocacy and diligence; others may see the rules as being in tension. Model Rule 3.1 begins with the basic prohibition: "A lawyer shall not bring or defend a proceeding, or assert or controvert an issue therein, unless there is a basis in law and fact for doing so that is not frivolous . . ." Several important caveats or exceptions follow this basic rule against frivolous claims and arguments, but before moving on to discuss those exceptions, students should note some quick rules of thumb for applying this rule on the Multistate Professional Responsibility Examination (MPRE) or on a Professional Responsibility exam:

- Even though many people associate "frivolous claims" with plaintiffs' lawyers, the rule forbids bringing *or* defending a claim without a non-frivolous basis in law and fact. In other words, *defending* a client in a lawsuit in which the defendant is undeniably at fault (and liable under relevant law) could violate this rule. Keep in mind that this rule applies equally to plaintiffs' and defendants' lawyers.
- The rule applies not only to bringing frivolous lawsuits, but also to making frivolous *arguments* or *assertions* within an otherwise valid lawsuit.
- The rule requires some non-frivolous basis in law *and* fact—in test questions, watch out for a lawsuit or argument that has great supporting evidence (factual basis) but no legal basis, or vice-versa (strong legal rule, but zero evidence).
- A "weak" argument or claim is *not* necessarily "frivolous"—even though litigators may refer to opponents' arguments as frivolous merely because they are unconvincing, the Model Rules use the term narrowly. Comment 3 for Rule 3.1 explains, "[An] action is not frivolous even though the lawyer believes that the client's position ultimately will not prevail. The action is frivolous, however, if the lawyer is unable either to make a good faith argument on the merits of the action taken or to support the action taken by a good faith argument for an extension, modification, or reversal of existing law." The operative phrase here is "good faith argument." Ask yourself if the lawyer in the problem is making the argument or claim in bad faith.
- For multiple-choice questions on final exams or the MPRE, a hypothetical claim or argument "without basis in law" will probably be an extreme example—a lawyer who knows that the statute of limitations has passed, or who tries to deny blameworthiness where the law imposes strict liability, and so on.

Rule 3.1 includes some important caveats and exceptions. The first is a phrase that modifies "not frivolous"— "which includes a good faith argument for an extension, modification, or reversal of existing law." Consider, for example, the plaintiffs in the famous case *Brown v. Board of Ed.*, who argued that the state laws requiring racially segregated schools were unconstitutional. Prior to that point—indeed, at the time they brought the case—one could have said that there was no basis in law for their assertion, because segregation was a deeply entrenched part of the regional culture and the legal system. Rule 3.1 allows lawyers to bring a *good-faith* claim that the current law is invalid, outdated, or applied too narrowly, to ask courts to broaden a law's scope, to change the longstanding judicial interpretation of a statute, or even to invalidate a piece of legislation or regulation. The operative phrase, again, is "good faith." It is hard to imagine, for example, that a lawyer could argue in good faith that all traffic laws are unconstitutional or that murder should always be legal. On the other hand, a lawyer *could* argue in good faith for a narrowing or abandonment of the felony murder rule (some courts have done this already), or that traffic violations should not carry unreasonable punishments. As Comment 1 to Rule 3.1 observes, "[T]he law is not always clear and never is static."

The second main exception in Rule 3.1 applies only to criminal proceedings. Even in a prosecution where the evidence against the defendant seems overwhelming (say, there is a videotape of the entire crime and the defendant gave a full, voluntary confession), a criminal defense lawyer "may nevertheless so defend the proceeding as to require that every element of the case be established." In other words, the Model Rules recognize the value of providing a defendant with a fair trial and making the prosecution do its job—proving every element beyond a reasonable doubt—even if a guilty verdict appears nearly certain from the beginning. Watch out, therefore, for test questions that present a defendant whose guilt seems undeniable—it is still *not* frivolous for the defense attorney to demand a trial and make the prosecutor prove his case to a jury.

Another important caveat appears in the official comment to Rule 3.1. Comment 2 explains that it is permissible—that is, *not frivolous*—for a lawyer to file a lawsuit even though the evidence necessary to prove his case will (he hopes) come out during pretrial discovery. A lawyer does not have to fully substantiate a claim before filing the lawsuit or have sufficient evidence to meet the burden of proof in that case. Instead, the lawyer must be familiar with the facts of the case and applicable law enough to make good-faith arguments for the client's positions. Again, if the lawyer cannot make a good-faith argument on the merits (fact or law) or for a change in the law, then the claim *is* frivolous.

As mentioned above, a weak case or weak argument is not necessarily frivolous. In fact, a lawyer can bring a case that she knows is a "long shot"—say, a case that has only a 30 percent chance of succeeding, and is 70 percent likely to result in an adverse outcome, if the client is aware of these chances and insists on proceeding. The Model Rules do not provide a bright-line cutoff for when a claim is so unlikely to prevail that it becomes frivolous, but as the chances of prevailing become more remote, the chances of appearing frivolous commensurately increase.

The final exception to Rule 3.1 is in Comment 3—"The lawyer's obligations under this Rule are subordinate to federal or state constitutional law that entitles a defendant in a criminal matter to the assistance of counsel in presenting a claim or contention that otherwise would be prohibited by this Rule." This is a poorly drafted sentence, but the gist of it seems to be that criminal defendants have certain constitutional trial rights—including an automatic right to appeal a death sentence—and these constitutional rights trump Rule 3.1's prohibition on frivolous claims or arguments. For example, the Supreme Court has held that most criminal defendants in felony cases have a right to counsel for their first appeal, even if the lawyer is certain that there are no good arguments to make on appeal for reversing the guilty verdict. *Anders v. California*, 386 U.S. 738 (1967). In such a case, the lawyer should review the trial transcript, write a brief mentioning any possible non-frivolous grounds for appeal or reversal (even if they are extremely weak), file the brief, and seek to withdraw from further representation. The Supreme Court has explicitly authorized such representation (and other similar procedural and appellate rights), and Rule 3.1 should not encroach on these rulings.

QUESTION 1. Leverage. An attorney represents Conglomerate Corporation in a lawsuit against the company brought by an individual plaintiff. The lawsuit could bring very bad publicity to Conglomerate Corporation and could adversely affect its stock share price. Conglomerate offers to settle the matter quietly, but the plaintiff rejects the settlement offer. The attorney then files a counterclaim against plaintiff, alleging libel and slander of Conglomerate Corporation, vexatious litigation, and tortious interference with contract, for which he demands millions of dollars in damages. The attorney and plaintiff's counsel both know these counterclaims lack any real basis in fact, but will be costly for plaintiff to defend. The attorney uses the counterclaims as leverage in reopening the settlement negotiations, offering to withdraw the counterclaims if plaintiff will accept a new, slightly higher settlement offer. The plaintiff calculates the cost of defending against the counterclaims and the difference between the settlement offer and the expected damages if plaintiff wins at trial, and reluctantly agrees to accept the terms of the offer. Could the attorney be subject to discipline for filing the counterclaims?

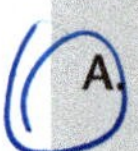

A. Yes, because there is no factual basis for the claims, and the lawyer did not bring them in good faith.
B. Yes, because the lawyer used the counterclaims as leverage to induce the opposing party into accepting an unfavorable settlement.
C. No, because an advocate has a duty to use legal procedure for the fullest benefit of the client's cause.
D. No, because the claims and counterclaims settled before going to trial, so the lawyer did not violate his duty of candor to the court.

ANALYSIS. This question illustrates the basic rule set forth in Rule 3.1, prohibiting frivolous claims and assertions by lawyers. Such claims are an abuse of the legal system and attorneys have an ethical duty to avoid such behavior. In this case, the lawyer on the losing side is using frivolous counterclaims to extort a more favorable settlement agreement from the other party. Such behavior is unfair, and it tarnishes the reputation of the legal profession as a whole, and clogs the court system with unmeritorious claims and motions.

A is correct, because the lawyer knows that the counterclaims are bogus and is merely using them to drive up the opposing party's potential litigation costs (even frivolous claims impose some litigation costs on the parties, after all) in order to obtain an *in terrorem* bargaining chip during settlement negotiations. This is exactly the type of behavior that the drafters intended to prevent with Rule 3.1—the lawyer here is not acting in good faith, as the Model Rules use that phrase. Note that Rule 3.1 applies to defendants' counterclaims as well as to the original complaint filed by a plaintiff.

B is incorrect because seeking a strategic advantage or an improved bargaining position would not be a valid justification for an otherwise frivolous claim. As Comment 1 to Rule 3.1 explains, "The advocate has a duty to use legal procedure for the fullest benefit of the client's cause, but also a duty not to abuse legal procedure." Answer **B** illustrates zealous advocacy taken too far, to the point where it constitutes an abuse.

C is incorrect because Rule 3.1 cabins the lawyer's duty for zealous advocacy. Even the rule requiring diligence on behalf of clients, Rule 1.3, contains this caveat in its comment: "A lawyer is not bound, however, to press for every advantage that might be realized for a client." The duty to advocate for the client does not entail abusing the process or bringing frivolous claims—much less using frivolous claims to extort a settlement out of the other party.

D is incorrect because the duty to bring meritorious claims extends to the entire process of litigation ("a proceeding") and not merely to the trial itself. Candor to the court is a separate rule (Rule 3.3); this rule is about fairness to the other party and trying to prevent frivolous claims from overwhelming the court system overall. Even if a case settles before trial, a lawyer may be in violation of Rule 3.1 and could be subject to discipline.

QUESTION 2. **Against the odds.** A client asked an attorney to represent him in a lawsuit. The attorney conducts some preliminary research and quickly discovers that the lawsuit is a very long shot. In fact, based on the attorney's survey of the existing judicial decisions in very similar cases, the attorney estimates that they have only a 15 percent chance of winning, and it will depend on an extraordinarily lopsided jury, a strongly partisan judge whose political leanings go in their favor, as well as a mediocre lawyer representing the other side. Otherwise, all things being equal, the attorney advises the client that he is about 85 percent certain that they will not prevail. The client is willing to take risks, however, and urges the attorney to take the matter. The attorney reluctantly agrees, on the condition that he can charge a somewhat higher fee than usual, and files the lawsuit. Could the attorney be subject to discipline for bringing a frivolous claim?

A. Yes, because the attorney knows from his research that the claim is very unlikely to prevail, and is therefore wasting the court's time.
B. Yes, because he should not have charged a higher fee in a case where the client is already facing unfavorable odds of winning, as this puts the client into an even worse position.

C. No, because an action is not frivolous even though the lawyer believes that the client's position ultimately will not prevail.

D. No, because the client should control the overall objectives of the representation, even if the lawyer controls the specific strategies, methods, and tactics.

ANALYSIS. Comment 2 for Rule 3.1 says that a lawsuit "is not frivolous even though the lawyer believes that the client's position ultimately will not prevail. The action is frivolous, however, if the lawyer is unable either to make a good faith argument on the merits of the action taken or to support the action taken by a good faith argument for an extension, modification, or reversal of existing law." The mere fact that a potential lawsuit is a "long shot" does not mean that it is frivolous. For many clients, bringing or defending a case that has a small chance of winning might still be worthwhile, if the potential payoffs (discounted for the probabilities) outweigh the expected costs.

A is incorrect. It does not necessarily waste a court's time to raise a tenuous argument or bring an action that has slim chances of winning. Such unlikely winners have sometimes turned out to be turning points in our legal history. In any case, even if the judge considers the claim to be a "waste of time," this is not the standard in the Model Rules for determining whether an action is frivolous.

B is also incorrect—indeed, Rule 1.5 permits lawyers to charge higher fees in cases that involve more risk. It is important to communicate the risk to the client, as the attorney did in this problem, but if the client chooses to proceed, the lawyer's fee may reflect the fact that the case is unlikely to turn out well.

C is correct. The rule against "frivolous claims and actions" does not automatically apply to any case with a less than 50 percent probability of winning. A lawyer may argue for a court to embrace the "minority view" among other jurisdictions on a question for which there is a split of authority, even though most courts will decline to do so. Similarly, a lawyer could argue in good faith for a court to apply or extend a narrow legal exception to the relevant statute in the case—again, unlikely, but sometimes worth asking. Alternatively, a lawyer may realize that his own client will make a bad impression on a jury, despite the merits of a claim, or that the opposing party's lawyer is "undefeated" in litigation until now.

D is true, but is not a good answer for this question. A client should indeed control the overall objectives of the representation, as occurred here. Even so, client input or control is not relevant to the question of whether a claim was frivolous enough to constitute a violation of the Model Rules. A lawyer must not bring frivolous claims or actions even when the client urges the lawyer to do so.

QUESTION 3. Time for a change. A client, age eighteen, is facing criminal charges of sex with a minor, based on his sexual relationship with his thirteen-year-old girlfriend, who lives in the same tenement building. The relevant statute has strict liability for perpetrators—that is, no mens rea or scienter element—and places the victim's age cutoff for the most serious grade of felony at age fourteen. It is indisputable in the case that the defendant had a sexual relationship with the victim when she was thirteen, but the victim claims she wanted the relationship and willingly consented to the sexual contact with her boyfriend. A state psychologist examined the victim and included in his report that she was emotionally mature for her age and was making relationship decisions in the same way as an adult. Even though the attorney is certain that the trial court will convict the client, he believes there is a slight chance that he could convince an appellate court to take a loose view of the age-of-consent provision in the statute, either on substantive due process grounds or simply as a matter of progressive statutory construction. Attorney believes that many thirteen-year-olds, and even younger, are sexually active nowadays and that the criminal laws should reflect the changing values of society. The attorney agrees, therefore, to take the client's case and to use it as a test case to try to change the law of sexual consent in the appellate courts. Is it proper for the attorney to make a defense in a criminal case that goes against the clear statutory verbiage and established case precedent?

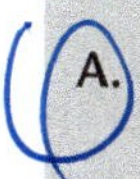

A. Yes, because a claim or argument is not frivolous if the lawyer is making a good-faith argument for modification or reversal of existing law.

B. Yes, because the statute has no mens rea requirement, but is a strict liability crime.

C. No, because a lawyer shall not bring or defend a proceeding, or assert or controvert an issue therein, unless there is a basis in law and fact for doing so that is not frivolous.

D. No, because the unlikelihood that the lawyer will win on appeal, in contradiction to the plain language of the statute, makes the lawyer's fee in the case a contingent fee, which is not permissible in a criminal case.

ANALYSIS. Rule 3.1 says that a "good faith basis in law or fact" should include "a good faith argument for an extension, modification, or reversal of existing law." A number of landmark decisions in our legal history began with a lawyer asking a court to declare an existing statute unconstitutional, or to overturn prior precedent on a particular question. Asking the court to break with precedent or invalidate a statute is certainly an uphill battle, but it does not make a claim "frivolous" for purposes of the Model Rules.

A is correct. Rule 3.1 specifically provides that a lawyer can make a good-faith argument for a modification or reversal of existing law (whether statutory law or judicial precedent). Statutory rape laws have been increasingly controversial for the last several decades because of the unusual combination of strict liability with a serious penalty for those convicted. It is reasonable for a lawyer to believe that some courts would consider changing the law in this area.

B is incorrect, as it merely states the existing law relevant to this case, which does not automatically make the defendant's argument frivolous.

C correctly states the first part of Rule 3.1, but omits the provision that specifically allows lawyers to argue to a modification or reversal of existing law. A good-faith argument for a change or reversal of existing law is, according to the Model Rules, a non-frivolous argument with a basis in law or fact.

D is incorrect, because the Model Rules do not deem a fee to be "contingent" merely because the case is inherently risky or unlikely to prevail.

QUESTION 4. **Make the prosecutor do his job.** An attorney is a criminal defense lawyer. The court has appointed him to represent a defendant who has already given a full confession of the burglary to the police, after receiving proper *Miranda* warnings, and the prosecution has several witnesses who either saw the crime or heard the defendant discussing his plans to commit the crime beforehand. The police properly obtained all necessary warrants during their investigation and arrest, and the defendant's actions clearly meet the elements in the statute. The lawyer explains to the defendant that he has almost zero chance of an acquittal, given the evidence against him and the fact that the Supreme Court has repeatedly upheld the penal code provision that furnished the basis of the charges in the case. In fact, the attorney cannot imagine any viable defense to raise at trial. Does the attorney have an obligation to ask the court for permission to withdraw from the representation?

A. Yes, because if an attorney is already that fatalistic about the outcome of the trial, he will not be able to provide the diligent, zealous advocacy that every defendant deserves.

B. Yes, because the defense is frivolous if the lawyer is unable either to make a good-faith argument on the merits or to support the defense taken by a good-faith argument for an extension, modification, or reversal of existing law.

C. No, because a lawyer for the defendant in a criminal proceeding may nevertheless so defend the proceeding as to require that every element of the case be established.

D. No, because the court appointed the lawyer to represent the defendant, so it would be futile to petition the same judge for permission to withdraw from the case.

ANALYSIS. Rule 3.1 concludes its prohibition against frivolous claims by stating, "A lawyer for the defendant in a criminal proceeding, or the respondent in a proceeding that could result in incarceration, may nevertheless so defend the proceeding as to require that every element of the case be established." This qualification does not mean that the rule against frivolous claims does not apply in criminal proceedings, of course—a defense lawyer should not attempt to argue that murder is not really a crime, for example. At the same time, the American legal system has always placed a high burden of proof on prosecutors in criminal cases, in order to avoid wrongful convictions of the innocent and to provide even the guilty with a fair trial, as due process bolsters the moral legitimacy of administering punishment (fines, incarceration) to those properly convicted. Even when the guilt of a defendant seems clear to everyone involved—including the defendant's attorney—it is still appropriate to make the prosecutor do his or her job and prove the case beyond reasonable doubt. In practical terms, this means that defense counsel may still object to inadmissible evidence (hearsay, irrelevant material, fruits of unconstitutional seizures, and so on), may cross-examine the prosecution's witnesses, and may offer closing arguments reminding the jury that they should acquit the defendant unless the prosecutor has proven the defendant guilty beyond a reasonable doubt.

Of course, in reality, around 95 percent of criminal cases end in plea bargains before trial, and this presumably includes nearly all the cases in which the defendant has already given a full, admissible confession and has no alibi or affirmative defenses. Even so, some defendants still want a trial, and they have a constitutional right to a trial—and sometimes surprises occur at trial, such as an eyewitness retracting his account of the crime, or the jury reacting against what it perceives as overcharging by the prosecutor (unnecessarily multiplying counts or overstating the grade of the offense).

A is incorrect even though it states a valid pragmatic concern (in practice, a thoroughly demoralized lawyer might want to consider transferring the case to another attorney), as the Model Rules do not require a lawyer to withdraw from a case merely because the lawyer predicts the outcome will be unfavorable.

B is incorrect in that it incompletely quotes Rule 3.1, omitting the provision that explicitly permits representation in scenarios like this one.

C is correct, as it essentially quotes the provision from Rule 3.1 permitting criminal defense lawyers to require the prosecution to prove every element of the crime. Even when a case seems hopeless, it is appropriate for lawyers to represent defendants in order to safeguard the legal protections offered by the burdens of proof.

D is both incorrect in fact and incorrect as an answer to the question—judges usually do allow appointed lawyers to withdraw from representation if the representation would involve a violation of the lawyer's ethical duties (as when the lawyer has a conflict of interest).

B. Rule 3.2 — Expediting Litigation

Model Rule 3.2 is just one sentence: "A lawyer shall make reasonable efforts to expedite litigation consistent with the interests of the client." The accompanying comment is just one paragraph, but adds some helpful clarification — the ABA drafters were primarily concerned with unnecessary, protracted delays in litigation. The old adage, "Justice delayed is justice denied" is the guiding policy concern for Rule 3.2. Of course, delays are still commonplace, despite the rule, and many delays are perfectly appropriate — lawyers and judges must manage busy schedules, and often it is mutually beneficial to both parties to have more time to negotiate a settlement or develop the evidence for the case. Note that "postponements" (the term in the Model Rules) can go by other names in daily legal practice — "extension of time," "continuance," "continuation," and so on, depending on the jurisdiction.

Dilatory practices can arise from lawyers' self-interest, such as laziness, procrastination, or leisure pursuits. Worse, some delays arise from strategic opportunism, as when a lawyer attempts to slow down litigation in the expectation that the opposing party will give up or run out of funds to litigate. In legal practice, sanctions for inappropriate delays can take the form of either disciplinary actions by the bar (reprimand or suspension) or adverse judicial action in the case at hand (dismissal, contempt).

QUESTION 5. **Constant accommodation demanded.** Attorney Adams is a busy litigator, but she is also a single mother of two young children. She has to pick her children up from daycare every weekday by 4 P.M. As a result, whenever she is scheduling hearings, conferences, settlement negotiations, or trial dates, she simply refuses to schedule anything in the late afternoon, as that could easily run into the time when she must pick up her children. The result is that her cases tend to stretch out over a long period, as she is available for hearings, trials, and other litigation-related meetings only in the mornings and early afternoons, and otherwise must seek postponements. Could Attorney Adams be subject to sanctions for managing her schedule in this way?

A. Yes, because it is always improper for an Attorney to seek postponement for personal reasons, rather than the needs of the client or the court.

B. Yes, because it is not proper for a lawyer to fail routinely to expedite litigation solely for the convenience of the advocates.

C. No, because there are occasions when a lawyer may properly seek a postponement for personal reasons.

D. No, because a failure to accommodate a lawyer who is a single mother regarding her childcare schedule would constitute a form of gender bias or even discrimination.

ANALYSIS. The comment for Rule 3.2 states, "Although there will be occasions when a lawyer may properly seek a postponement for personal reasons, it is not proper for a lawyer to routinely fail to expedite litigation solely for the convenience of the advocates." Watch out for test questions at each extreme—those that seem to suggest a lawyer can *never* ask for a postponement (or continuance, extension of time, etc.) for personal or scheduling reasons, and those that involve a lawyer who constantly delays everything and inconveniences others regularly. It is appropriate for attorneys to ask for scheduling accommodations from time to time in order to take a vacation, attend a family event, or due to scheduling conflicts with other courtroom appearances. Every lawyer has such things come up. The problem is when one lawyer makes a habit of inconveniencing others, so that it becomes a routine.

A is incorrect because it overstates the prohibition—it is not *always* improper to seek a postponement for personal reasons, as the comment to Rule 3.2 says.

B is correct, as it restates the provision from the comment to Rule 3.2. The attorney in this problem is imposing unreasonable burdens on the other individuals involved in her cases.

C is also incorrect, though it correctly states the first part of the provision in the comment to Rule 3.2. Indeed, there are occasions when it is proper for lawyers to request a scheduling accommodation from the others involved in a case. Yet **C** omits the remainder of the sentence from the comment, which qualifies this provision by saying that this should not become a routine practice.

D is incorrect because it does not reflect the provisions of the Model Rules. The Model Rules do prohibit gender discrimination or bias, but the professionalism expected of lawyers includes high demands on lawyers' time, especially for litigators.

QUESTION 6. **Waging a war of attrition.** An attorney represents a client in a commercial litigation matter against a small independent bookstore. It is known in the local business community that the opposing party (the bookstore) has been on the verge of bankruptcy for the last two or three years. The facts and law of the present litigation, however, make it a close case—the attorney believes, accurately, that his client has at best a 50 percent chance of winning at trial. At the client's urging, the attorney files frequent motions asking for more time in discovery, more time to respond to the opposing party's motions, and a postponement of the trial date to allow more time to prepare and locate the necessary expert witnesses. The attorney thinks that the opposing party may have to close down and file for bankruptcy soon, which would make the opposing party's claims moot. The judge has an overcrowded docket, and is always glad to grant postponements or more time on various responses.

Is it proper for the attorney to take this "time is on our side" approach to litigation?

A. Yes, because regarding the ethical duty to expedite litigation, it constitutes a justification that similar conduct is often tolerated by the bench and bar.

B. Yes, because the attorney is acting in the best interests of his own client, and the opposing party's financial fragility is not his fault or responsibility.

C. No, because an attorney has a duty to seek the best result possible for both sides in a case, under the "lawyer for the case" approach.

D. No, because realizing financial or other benefit from otherwise improper delay in litigation is not a legitimate interest of the client.

ANALYSIS. Comment 1 for Rule 3.2 concludes by saying, "Realizing financial or other benefit from otherwise improper delay in litigation is not a legitimate interest of the client." It is often appropriate to seek postponements for the sake of the client's interests—for example, to schedule a trial for a time when the client will be available to attend the proceedings, or to request more time to respond to discovery requests so that the client can prepare complete answers to the interrogatories. At the same time, it is inappropriate to delay proceedings "for the purpose of frustrating an opposing party's attempt to obtain rightful redress or repose," according to the comment. Using a strategy of attrition in litigation—delaying the proceedings solely to drain the opposing party's resources or capacity to continue with the case—is improper, and can subject a lawyer to disciplinary action.

A is incorrect—in fact, the comment to Rule 3.2 says the exact opposite: "It is *not* a justification that similar conduct is often tolerated by the bench and bar." (emphasis added)

B is partly incorrect. Rule 3.2 says that lawyers should expedite "consistent with the interests of the client," that is, the lawyer must try to serve the client's interests, which sometimes involves requesting postponements, but should also generally try to expedite matters. The comment to Rule 3.2 explicitly states that the type of client interest here—exhausting the opposing party's capacity to continue with the litigation—is *not* a legitimate interest of the client for purposes of the Model Rules.

C is also incorrect—the Model Rules have abandoned the "lawyer for the case" idea that was popular several decades ago. The lawyer has a duty to the client and to the integrity of the court/legal system, but not to seek the best interest of the opposing party.

D is correct. The lawyer and the client in this problem have a case of ambiguous merit (50 percent at best), and they are using delays merely in hopes that the other party will dissolve in bankruptcy and they will win by attrition.

QUESTION 7. European vacation. Attorney is a busy litigator. During one scheduling conference with the judge and opposing counsel, Attorney asked for a continuance (postponement) of a particular hearing until a later date because she planned to be on vacation in Europe during that time. The judge and the opposing counsel agreed. On another occasion, three months later, Attorney asks another judge to reschedule a hearing so that it will not fall on her anniversary, when she has dinner plans in the early evening. In that instance, which was not the same matter or client as the first instance, the lawyer for the other party complained about rescheduling for such a trivial reason, but the judge agreed to reschedule the hearing for a month later. Was it improper for Attorney to seek these postponements?

A. Yes, because a lawyer shall make reasonable efforts to expedite litigation consistent with the interests of the client.
B. Yes, because it is not proper for a lawyer to fail to expedite litigation solely for the convenience of the advocates.
C. No, because there are occasions when a lawyer may properly seek a postponement for personal reasons.
D. No, it was not improper to seek a postponement for a scheduled vacation, but the postponement merely for an anniversary dinner was improper.

ANALYSIS. The previous questions illustrated the duty to expedite matters under Rule 3.2, but this question illustrates the other side of the rule—occasional requests for postponement, even for personal reasons, can be proper. The most common reason for requesting extensions of time are directly work-related—the lawyer has to avoid scheduling two trials or depositions for the same day and time, or the lawyer and client need more time to complete a responsive brief or to fulfill a discovery request. On the other hand, most lawyers take vacations from time to time, or must attend family events such as weddings and other important ceremonies. This problem illustrates a proper request for a postponement.

A is incorrect even though it correctly states the default rule—lawyers do have a general duty to expedite, but this question presents the explicit caveat or exception in the comment.

B is an overstatement of the rule, and therefore incorrect—it is occasionally proper for attorneys to seek postponements for personal reasons, as long as this is an exception occurrence and not a habit.

C is correct—this is the type of scenario contemplated by the Model Rules for a proper postponement.

D is incorrect, because the Model Rules do not distinguish between different types of personal reasons, for example, vacations versus anniversaries. As long as rescheduling for personal reasons is occasional rather than a frequent occurrence, it is proper.

C. Rule 3.3—Candor Toward the Tribunal

Rule 3.3 is a truthfulness rule—it forbids lawyers to lie to a tribunal (i.e., a judge) about facts or the law. This prohibition on lying includes the lawyer's clients and witnesses—a lawyer cannot intentionally ("knowingly") have someone else lie to a judge, as when testifying in court.

The "requirement of candor" also includes three affirmative obligations, that is, instances in which the lawyer must actually volunteer information against his side's interest. First, lawyers must "disclose to the tribunal legal authority in the controlling jurisdiction known to the lawyer to be directly adverse to the position of the client and not disclosed by opposing counsel." (See Rule 3.3(a)(2).) This is a favorite point for multiple-choice questions, so students should be clear on the parameters of this provision. If there is controlling judicial precedent (or, perhaps, a controlling statute) that the other side has overlooked, even if it is unfavorable or devastating to the lawyer's position, the lawyer has a duty to volunteer it to the judge. Note that this does *not* apply to "persuasive authority" from lower courts or sister jurisdictions, and it does *not* apply to authority that the other side has already brought up in their briefs. It does *not* apply outside the context of litigation or tribunals—for example, there is no duty to inform the other party during transactional negotiations (such as the sale of a business) about controlling legal authority for the transaction. Watch for questions in which a litigator, while conducting legal research, finds a very unfavorable judicial decision that the other side seems to have overlooked for some reason. The lawyer naturally does not want to disclose it, but if it is controlling law in that jurisdiction, Rule 3.3 requires the disclosure.

The second "affirmative duty" of truth-telling for lawyers under Rule 3.3 is the obligation to correct false statements that the lawyer or his client has inadvertently made to the court. Note that this does not include a duty to correct inaccurate statements by the opposing party. Of course, if a judge were to ask a lawyer whether the opposing counsel's inaccurate statement is correct, the lawyer then has an obligation to tell the truth and correct the other lawyer's mistake.

The third affirmative obligation under the duty of candor pertains to a very specific, narrow circumstance (but this has appeared on the MPRE nonetheless)—an *ex parte* hearing at which only one lawyer appears before a judge (opposing counsel is absent). The most common such hearing is a preliminary hearing for a temporary restraining order—often one side appears before the judge asking for an emergency restraining order or injunction that the other side can dispute at a full hearing at a later scheduled date. In such a situation, the lawyer appearing alone before the judge has a special duty to present *all the relevant facts*, favorable and unfavorable to the client—in other words, to mention the facts that the opposing counsel would certainly bring up if both lawyers were there. If you see a question about this on the MPRE or a law school exam, the problem will almost certainly specify that this is an "*ex parte* proceeding" or perhaps an "application for a temporary restraining order." In such an instance, remember that the lawyer has a duty to reveal all the facts, including those that normally the duty of confidentiality would protect from disclosure.

QUESTION 8. The lying client. An attorney represented a client in a criminal prosecution. The client agreed to a plea bargain, and the case moved on to a sentencing hearing. The prosecution's pre-sentencing report to the judge erroneously indicates that the client has no prior convictions, and the trial judge asked the client directly whether that is true. The client affirmed that he had no prior criminal record, and the judge sentenced him leniently, giving his six months' probation. Yet the attorney had represented the client previously in another jurisdiction in a criminal matter, and he knew that the pre-sentencing report was erroneous. Before adjourning, the judge asked the attorney if he had anything else to say. Could the attorney be subject to discipline if he does not correct the judge's misperception about the client's criminal record?

A. Yes, because the attorney must not allow his client to offer evidence that he knows to be false to a tribunal.
B. Yes, because the client committed perjury when he answered the judge's question in the courtroom, once the court was in session for the sentencing hearing.
C. No, because a lawyer cannot violate his ethical duty of confidentiality to his client.
D. No, because the attorney did not make the false statement, and has no duty to correct the false statements of others.

ANALYSIS. Rule 3.3(a)(3) provides, "If a lawyer, the lawyer's client, or a witness called by the lawyer, has offered material evidence and the lawyer comes to know of its falsity, the lawyer shall take reasonable remedial measures, including, if necessary, disclosure to the tribunal." We assume that the client's statement on the record during a sentencing hearing constitutes "material evidence," given that it is the crucial information influencing the leniency or severity of the sentence in this case, and in most sentencing cases—and in such a case, the lawyer has a duty to correct his client's false statement to the judge. As Comment 2 to Rule 3.3 explains, "Consequently, although a lawyer in an adversary proceeding is not required to present an impartial exposition of the law or to vouch for the evidence submitted in a cause, the lawyer must not allow the tribunal to be misled by false statements of law or fact or evidence that the lawyer knows to be false."

A is correct. A lawyer must not allow his client to offer evidence the lawyer knows to be false, and if the client does so, the lawyer either must persuade the client to correct the misstatement, or must do it herself.

B is incorrect, because it overstates what actually occurred—it is not entirely clear that the client was under oath giving testimony at this time (the usual scenario when we speak of "perjury"), but the client nonetheless has made a definitive statement to the judge that is likely to affect the outcome of the proceeding.

C is incorrect because a lawyer has a duty of candor to the tribunal that overrides the duty of confidentiality, at least when it comes to statements the lawyer actually knows are false.

D is also incorrect, because Rule 3.3 requires lawyers to correct false statements made to a tribunal by their own client or witness.

QUESTION 9. **Flight risk.** An attorney was representing a client in a criminal matter. At the bail hearing, the prosecutor told the court that the defendant was a flight risk, and asked the court either to confine the defendant until trial or to set bail at $15,000. When it was the attorney's turn to speak, he assured the judge that the client had a medical condition that would prevent him from leaving the area, and that the client did not intend to flee the jurisdiction, but was confident that he could stand trial and clear his name of all charges. The attorney knew, however, that the client already had plane tickets to Venezuela, a non-extradition country, and that the client had already fully recovered from his serious medical condition. Is the attorney subject to discipline for making these statements to the court?

A. Yes, because there is no constitutional right to have bail in state court.
B. Yes, because a lawyer may not knowingly make a false statement of fact or law to a tribunal.
C. No, because the statements made at a bail hearing would not affect the merits or outcome of the case.
D. No, because the lawyer does not know for a fact that the client will actually flee the jurisdiction, and he cannot say with medical certainty that the client's medical condition will not relapse.

ANALYSIS. Rule 3.3(a)(1) says that a lawyer must not knowingly "make a false statement of fact or law to a tribunal or fail to correct a false statement of material fact or law previously made to the tribunal by the lawyer." This rule applies in bail hearings, sentencing hearings, and administrative hearings, in addition to the normal trial context. Note that Comment 8 to Rule 3.3 clarifies this to actual knowledge: "The prohibition against offering false evidence only applies if the lawyer knows that the evidence is false. A lawyer's reasonable belief that evidence is false does not preclude its presentation to the trier of fact. A lawyer's knowledge that evidence is false, however, can be inferred from the circumstances." (See also Rule 1.0(f).) In this problem, the lawyer has actual knowledge that the client is planning to flee the jurisdiction in order to avoid trial and punishment.

A is the wrong answer, even though the statement is legally correct. Even though the Supreme Court has never incorporated the right to bail against the states under the Fourteenth Amendment, the lawyer still has a duty to tell the truth to the judge.

B is correct. Lawyers must not knowingly make a false statement to the tribunal, even when doing so would be advantageous to the client or would fulfill the client's wishes.

C is incorrect because the bail hearing can indeed affect the outcome of the matter if the client flees the jurisdiction and becomes a fugitive from the law without facing trial. Even if a statement during a pretrial hearing did not affect the merits or outcome of the case, the lawyer cannot knowingly make false statements to the court.

D is also incorrect because the facts given state that the lawyer "knew" enough facts that a reasonable person would assume that the client intended to flee, and he knew that the client had already recovered from his medical condition.

QUESTION 10. **The witness.** A witness testified on a client's behalf at trial. That evening, when the attorney was reviewing exhibits and documents to prepare for the next day of trial, he noticed a document that completely negated the witness' testimony from earlier that day. The testimony was material evidence in the case. The witnesses left the jurisdiction after his testimony concluded, and he is no longer available to correct the false statements. The opposing party's lawyer waived his opportunity to cross-examine the witness, because the testimony was unfavorable to his side and he was eager to move on to a more favorable witness. Does the attorney have a duty to take remedial measures to correct the false testimony, such as disclosing the falsehood to the court?

A. Yes, because no proper cross-examination occurred, which violated the other party's constitutional rights.

B. Yes, because if a witness called by the lawyer has offered material evidence, and the lawyer comes to know of its falsity, the lawyer shall take reasonable remedial measures, including, if necessary, disclosure to the tribunal.

C. No, if a witness called by the lawyer has offered material evidence and the lawyer comes to know of its falsity, the lawyer has no duty to correct the information if the opposing counsel waived his right to cross-examination.

D. No, because the lawyer did not realize at the time of the testimony that it was false, and therefore did not knowingly offer any false statements to the tribunal.

ANALYSIS. Rule 3.3(a)(3) says that when "a witness called by the lawyer, has offered material evidence and the lawyer comes to know of its falsity, the lawyer shall take reasonable remedial measures, including, if necessary, disclosure to the tribunal." Of course, the first recourse should be to try to get the witness to correct the false statement and tell the truth, but they are not always willing to do so. Even though the lawyer has a general duty of loyalty to the client, which includes a duty of zealous advocacy, the duty of candor to the court overrides it, out of concerns for the integrity of the legal system. This problem illustrates that the duty to correct falsehoods also applies when a lawyer "comes to know" of the falsity of the statement only after it is already in evidence.

A is incorrect, both as a statement of legal principle and as an answer to this question. Parties indeed have a right to cross-examination, but parties often waive the right (i.e., waive their opportunity for cross-examination) when they believe it would be a waste of time or counterproductive.

B is correct—the lawyer in this problem has a duty to correct the false statements made by a witness, even though the statements were favorable to his client, and even though the lawyer came to know of the falsehood only later.

C is incorrect, even though the first clause incorporates verbiage from Rule 3.3, because the second clause is incorrect—a waiver of cross-examination by opposing counsel does not remove a lawyer's duty to correct false statements to a tribunal by the lawyer's own witness.

D is incorrect because Rule 3.3(a)(3) imposes a duty of candor on lawyers even when the lawyer "comes to know" of the falsehood after the statement is already in evidence.

QUESTION 11. **Disclosing adverse legal authority.** While conducting research on a litigation matter, an attorney finds a very new case from the highest court in his jurisdiction that is directly adverse to his client's legal position in the case. The opposing party did not mention the case in its briefs, and the attorney realizes that the opposing party's lawyer has been recycling his firm's briefs for this type of case for several years without updating his research. Does the attorney have an ethical duty to disclose the unfavorable binding precedent to the court?

A. No, because it is the other lawyer's duty to find the cases favorable to his own side, and providing the research to the opposing side is facilitating the other lawyer's neglect of diligent representation.

B. No, because it would be a breach of the attorney's duty of loyalty to his own client to disclose a case unnecessarily that undermines their position.

C. Yes, because it is very common for litigators to recycle their briefs for years at a time, and everyone should help each other out with updating their legal research on issues that arise frequently in that area of litigation.

D. Yes, because a lawyer must disclose to the tribunal legal authority in the controlling jurisdiction known to the lawyer to be directly adverse to the position of the client and not disclosed by opposing counsel.

ANALYSIS. Rule 3.3(a)(2) says that a lawyer must "disclose to the tribunal legal authority in the controlling jurisdiction known to the lawyer to be directly adverse to the position of the client and not disclosed by opposing counsel." This rule may be more counterintuitive to law students than the other portions of Rule 3.3 (which prohibit outright lying about facts). For purposes of multiple-choice test questions, remember that this rule applies *only* to controlling precedent, *not* to persuasive authority from lower courts or sister jurisdictions. For purposes of legal practice, it may be possible for lawyers to distinguish a seemingly relevant case due to factual differences, even when the case would otherwise be controlling precedent from that jurisdiction. The situation here is sadly commonplace—a number of legal practitioners fail to update their research when reusing arguments from previous briefs.

A is incorrect, even though each lawyer does have a duty of competence and diligence to his or her own client. The other lawyer's incompetence does not excuse an attorney from the duty of candor to the court.

B is also incorrect because the duty of candor, when it actually applies, outweighs the duty of loyalty to one's client.

C is the wrong answer even though the statement is mostly true—many lawyers do recycle their briefs, but there is no duty to "help out" the opposing counsel—rather, Rule 3.3 is a duty of candor to the *court*.

D is correct. The lawyer in this case has a duty to disclose unfavorable controlling precedent that the opposing party has overlooked or neglected.

QUESTION 12. Ex parte hearings. An attorney represented a client in her divorce and custody case. The client's husband had been abusive, so she asked the attorney to obtain a temporary restraining order against her ex-husband. The application for the temporary restraining order is an ex parte proceeding, so opposing counsel is not present. The attorney knows that the ex-husband has not been physically abusive to the client in over two years, and that he has been faithfully attending an anger-management support group during that time that appears to have produced genuine results. At the same time, the client is fearful that the ongoing custody battle will push her ex-husband over the edge, and that the abuse she endured in the past will resume. At the hearing for the temporary restraining order application, does the attorney have an affirmative duty to disclose the length of time since the last abuse occurred and the ex-husband's faithful participation in an anger management program?

A. Yes, but only if the judge asks the attorney if there are any countervailing facts or considerations in the matter.
B. Yes, in an ex parte proceeding, a lawyer shall inform the tribunal of all material facts known to the lawyer that will enable the tribunal to make an informed decision, whether or not the facts are adverse.
C. No, in an ex parte proceeding, a lawyer has no affirmative duty to inform the tribunal of all material facts known to the lawyer that will enable the tribunal to make an informed decision, if the facts are adverse.
D. No, because disclosing those facts would violate the lawyer's duty of loyalty to his own client, because the client feels fearful and requested the restraining order.

ANALYSIS. Rule 3.3(d) succinctly provides, "In an ex parte proceeding, a lawyer shall inform the tribunal of all material facts known to the lawyer that will enable the tribunal to make an informed decision, whether or not the facts are adverse." Comment 14 to Rule 3.3 clarifies this terse provision:

> However, in any ex parte proceeding, such as an application for a temporary restraining order, there is no balance of presentation by opposing advocates. The object of an ex parte proceeding is nevertheless to yield a substantially just result. The judge has an affirmative responsibility to accord the absent party just consideration. The lawyer for the represented party has the correlative duty to make disclosures of material facts known to the lawyer and that the lawyer reasonably believes are necessary to an informed decision.

Thus, a lawyer at an ex parte proceeding must present facts for both sides of the issue. The facts in this problem are similar to the example offered in Comment 14—an application for a temporary restraining order. Rule 3.3(d) is a very narrow rule, but as such it is appealing for those drafting multiple-choice exam questions.

A is incorrect, though this would be the right answer in a regular proceeding (not an ex parte hearing). Rule 3.3(d) imposes an affirmative duty on lawyers to volunteer unfavorable facts that are material to the judge's decision, regardless of whether the judge asks questions or requests more information. If it were not an ex parte proceeding, the lawyer would *not* have a duty to volunteer unfavorable information, but the lawyer would have to answer truthfully if the judge asked a question, unless he could invoke privilege in that instance.

B is correct. The lawyer in this case indeed has a duty to disclose the length of time since the last abuse occurred and the husband's faithful participation in an anger management program.

C is also incorrect—Rule 3.3 states that lawyers *do* have an affirmative duty to inform an ex parte tribunal of all material facts, including those unfavorable to the lawyer's own client.

D would be correct outside the setting of ex parte hearings, but Rule 3.3(d) imposes a special duty on lawyers in ex parte hearings (with no opposing counsel present before the tribunal) to disclose all material facts, and this duty outweighs the normal duty of loyalty to one's own client.

D. Rule 3.4—Fairness to Opposing Party and Counsel

For purposes of the MPRE, Rule 3.4 is part of the category the examiners call "Litigation and Other Forms of Advocacy," which as a category makes up 10 to 16 percent of the sixty test questions (the category includes other rules as well, primarily 3.1 through 3.7). Recent MPRE tests have consistently included at least two questions each time based on Rule 3.4.

The American trial system is adversarial—lawyers (and parties through their lawyers) compete with each other to win the case. Rule 3.4 sets some boundaries for how far one may go for the sake of winning a case. Its provisions include prohibiting forging or destruction of evidence, abuse of discovery procedures, witness tampering, and so on. Most of these provisions resonate with nearly universal moral sentiments about cheating, and students often find questions about these provisions to be rather intuitive.

On the other hand, students may find the provisions in Rule 3.4(e) more surprising, as this section prohibits behaviors regularly depicted in television dramas about lawyers. Lawyers must not:

> in trial, allude to any matter that the lawyer does not reasonably believe is relevant or that will not be supported by admissible evidence, assert personal knowledge of facts in issue except when testifying as a witness, or state a personal opinion as to the justness of a cause, the credibility of a witness, the culpability of a civil litigant or the guilt or innocence of an accused

Unfortunately, the comment to Rule 3.4 does not offer any clarification of Subsection (e.) Obviously, a lawyer giving a closing argument for his own client will necessarily imply (even if it is unstated) that the opposing party's witnesses, evidence, or experts are unreliable or somehow deficient. For purposes of test questions, an examiner is likely to make the violation explicit: a lawyer begins an argument to the jury saying, "In my opinion, ______" or "We all know that ________ [some fact not formally in evidence]." If a lawyer wants to use facts from personal knowledge in the courtroom, the lawyer must either ask the judge to take judicial notice of a fact (if it is common knowledge), or take the stand as a witness. The latter, however, will instantly trigger the conflict of interest rules and Rule 3.7, which generally forbids lawyers from serving as a witness and as counsel in the same case.

The MPRE has recently included questions about this subsection (Rule 3.4(e)). Watch for questions in which one of the lawyers tells the jury that in his opinion, no intelligent person would believe a certain witness, or that no intelligent person would vote for a verdict for the other party, or something similar.

Far more significant for purposes of the MPRE are the provisions about witness tampering in Rule 3.4(b) and (f). Lawyers cannot bribe or intimidate potential witnesses to testify favorably or to keep silent. MPRE questions usually focus on the technical rules in Comment 3 about paying witnesses versus covering expenses. Students should begin by thinking of all witnesses as fitting into one of two categories—expert witnesses and regular witnesses. The Model Rules call non-expert witnesses "occurrence witnesses." This category includes eyewitnesses, employees of one of the parties, character witnesses, and so on. Expert witnesses review some evidence in the case file, but have no personal knowledge of the parties or the events in question. Grouping witnesses into the right category is important, because the rules about compensating a witness differ for each group. Paying contingent fees is impermissible for *any* type of witness—no lawyer can offer to compensate a witness, or to pay more, if the outcome of the trial is ultimately favorable for the lawyer's client.

Lawyers can pay expert witnesses, but only on an hourly basis or a flat fee for the case. Contingent fees are never permissible for expert witnesses.

In contrast, lawyers cannot offer to pay an occurrence witness (such as an eyewitness or character witness) except for reimbursing the travel, lodging, and other out-of-pocket expenses associated with testifying at a deposition or trial. A lawyer can offer to pay airfare (even from overseas), can put the witness up in a nice hotel during the trial, and in most jurisdictions, can compensate witnesses for their time, especially lost wages due to time away from work.

Lawyers cannot ask a potential witness for the other party not to testify, except for relatives and employees of the lawyer's client—and even then, only if the witness' personal interests will not be in jeopardy by not testifying (as when a witness could end up being held responsible instead of the client and needs to testify in self-defense). Watch for MPRE questions about lawyers who try to deter potential witnesses (say, by threatening to expose the person's deep, dark secrets) or lawyers who simply offer to pay a hostile witness to refrain from testifying.

QUESTION 13. **I know it in my heart.** During opening arguments in a criminal trial before a jury, an attorney, who was representing the defendant, closed his statements by declaring, "My client is innocent; I know it in my heart. By the end of the trial, I am confident that you will agree with me that this is an innocent man." Are such comments proper for a defense lawyer to make during trial?

A. Yes, because we presume that every defendant is innocent until proven guilty.
B. Yes, because the fact that the defendant has pleaded not guilty has already put that assertion before the jury.
C. No, because such comments could manipulate and prejudice a jury, even though the comments would be acceptable in a bench trial.
D. No, because at trial, a lawyer shall not state a personal opinion as to the guilt or innocence of an accused.

ANALYSIS. Rule 3.4(e) states that during a trial, a lawyer must not "state a personal opinion as to the justness of a cause, the credibility of a witness, the culpability of a civil litigant or the guilt or innocence of an accused." This rule surprises many students, as television and movie courtroom scenes nearly always include the lawyers asserting their own opinions and beliefs on behalf of their client. A lawyer may argue that the opposing party has not met their burden of proof, or that the evidence points conclusively in the lawyer's direction, but it is improper for the lawyer to assert mere opinions, personal convictions, or feelings about a matter. It is improper for a prosecutor to claim a personal opinion about the guilt of the accused, and it is improper for a defense attorney to assert a personal conviction about the defendant's innocence. The MPRE has recently included similar questions on this point.

A is incorrect. Even though there is a presumption of innocence in criminal cases, the presumption refers to the prosecutor's burden of proof, not to the lawyer's subjective convictions.

B is also incorrect. Even though it is appropriate for the client to assert his innocence, and for the lawyer to refer to that fact, the lawyer cannot properly make this assertion from his own knowledge. The defendant's original plea of "not guilty" at a preliminary hearing is part of the record of the case, and counts as admitted evidence. It is proper for the lawyer to refer to the defendant's plea, which is part of the record, but not for the lawyer to claim that the innocence is a known fact.

C is partly correct and may state an underlying policy rationale for Rule 3.4(e)—lawyers' assertions of personal opinions could be unduly prejudicial—but this answer is incorrect because the prohibition applies to both jury trials and bench trials.

D is correct. The lawyer in this case led his argument with a reference to his personal opinion or convictions—"I know it in my heart." Such feeling-based statements belong in the closing scene of a romantic comedy, not in a courtroom. It would be perfectly appropriate to claim, "By the end of the trial, we will have shown that there is no more than weak, circumstantial evidence to support the charges against the accused, and that he steadfastly maintains that he is innocent." The problem here in the question is that the lawyer is asking the jury to accept the lawyer's own subjective beliefs, rather than the evidence in the case.

QUESTION 14. **I've known him for years.** During his closing argument at a bench trial, an attorney makes the following statement to the judge: "Your Honor, I know this client, because we grew up together and I have represented him in various legal matters for years. I know that he is an honest person who would never lie or try to take advantage of another person unfairly. In fact, I am doing this case on a pro bono basis because I feel so strongly about the justness of his cause." All of these statements were truthful—the attorney had known the client since childhood and had represented him many times, the attorney admired the client's integrity, and the attorney had offered to handle this case without charging any fee because he believed so strongly that the client was on the right side. Was it proper for the attorney to make these comments during closing arguments?

A. Yes, because it was a bench trial so there was no danger of manipulating or prejudicing a jury in this case.
B. Yes, because a lawyer has a duty to be a zealous advocate for his client, and lawyers merely represent the assertions of their clients, rather than vouching for the accuracy of all the claims.
C. No, because at trial, a lawyer shall not assert personal knowledge of facts in issue except when testifying as a witness, or state a personal opinion as to the justness of a cause, or the credibility of a witness.
D. No, because it is improper to disclose during a trial how much, if anything, a lawyer is charging to represent a client.

ANALYSIS. This question highlights another clause of Rule 3.4(e), which forbids assertions of personal knowledge of the matter or the parties, unless the lawyer is going to take the stand and testify under oath (in which case he probably cannot serve as the trial lawyer in the case). Whereas the previous question highlighted the problem with lawyers asserting opinions and personal convictions, this problem presents a lawyer speaking from his personal first-hand knowledge—actually, these are facts to which a witness could testify (under oath, and subject to cross-examination). Note that it is inappropriate for the lawyer to assert personal knowledge even in a bench trial, when there is no risk of prejudicing a jury.

A is incorrect. Even though courts are often more relaxed about certain evidentiary rules during bench trials (as there is no risk of prejudicing a jury), Rule 3.4 applies to lawyer courtroom conduct equally in either situation.

B does not accurately reflect the facts given in the problem, even though the statements in this answer are correct in the abstract. The lawyer in the problem went beyond advocacy for the client or representing the client's assertions, and instead asserted personal knowledge of the client's character and intentions.

C is correct. The lawyer in this case has personal experience and first-hand knowledge about the client's character and previous legal matters. If the lawyer wishes to have the things he knows considered as factors in the adjudication of the case, the lawyer should transfer the case to another attorney and take the stand as a character witness. He could then make his assertions under oath and subject to cross-examination, which is the right of the opposing party.

D overstates a rule and thus gives an incorrect reason for the lawyer's actions being improper. Of course, statements about how much the lawyer is charging (if anything) would often fall under the prohibition in Rule 3.4(e), as it is a fact not in evidence and probably not relevant to the merits of the case. Comments about the lawyer's fees or lack thereof are also usually in bad taste. Even so, there are many instances where a party is seeking attorney's fees at the end of the trial, during which statements about the lawyer's fee are entirely appropriate (but usually submitted under oath). In addition, in rare cases, a lawyer might need to declare that his representation is pro bono in order to defend against a motion for disqualification (due to certain types of conflicts of interest) at the beginning of the trial.

QUESTION 15. A clean slate. A client is aware that he is under investigation for student loan fraud. A friend who works at the courthouse tips off the client that a magistrate issued a warrant to search the client's home for evidence the next day in the early morning. In a panic, the client calls his attorney, whom he has retained to represent him during the investigation and any prosecution that follows, and asks what he should do. The attorney informs him that the agents executing the warrant will surely seize any computers and hard drives that they find, and that the client should probably wipe and reformat all his drives or dispose of his computers, that he should probably smash his cell phone, and that he might want to go on a long vacation immediately. Is the attorney subject to discipline for this advice?

A. Yes, because the Sixth Amendment right to counsel does not arise until formal adjudicatory proceedings begin.

B. Yes, because a lawyer shall not counsel or assist another person to destroy or conceal a document or other material having potential evidentiary value.

C. No, because the traditional rules against destroying documentary evidence apply only to printed copies, not to electronic files stored on a computer hard drive.

D. No, because until the police execute the warrant and legally seize the computers, they are the client's private property and he can do whatever he wants with them.

ANALYSIS. Rule 3.4(a) says that a lawyer must not "unlawfully alter, destroy or conceal a document or other material having potential evidentiary value. A lawyer shall not counsel or assist another person to do any such act." This type of question should be relatively intuitive for students, as the rule about destruction of evidence resonates with popular morality about cheating. Nevertheless, it is useful for students to clarify their thinking about the rules, as the MPRE can offer a confusing selection of answers that echo other procedural or ethical rules that seem familiar to students.

A states an irrelevant, but valid, precept from the area of criminal procedure. The Model Rules apply to lawyer activities even if a constitutional right to counsel for the defendant has not yet attached.

B is correct. The lawyer in this problem encouraged his client to destroy evidence and flee the jurisdiction, all of which are usually illegal. Rule 3.4 not only forbids the lawyer to destroy evidence, but also to counsel a client to do so.

C is also incorrect—although there was some uncertainty when digital documents first appeared about whether they had the same legal status as printed documents, the ABA has amended the Model Rules in recent years to make explicit that electronic documents come under the purview of the rules.

D is legally incorrect—even though the computers and phone are the client's private property, and will remain the client's property even after a police seizure (unless formal asset forfeiture proceedings have concluded), a number of statutes limit what property owners may do with items that are likely to be evidence in upcoming litigation.

QUESTION 16. **The $10,000 witness.** After much effort, an attorney located a witness who could fully corroborate his client's story and could impeach the testimony of the opposing party's star witness. The witness, however, was afraid of retaliation from others if she testified, and did not want to be involved. The attorney offered the witness $10,000 to appear at the trial for one afternoon and testify for an hour or two. The witness reluctantly agreed. Was it proper for the attorney to offer to pay a favorable witness to undergo the trouble of testifying at the trial?

A. Yes, because expert witnesses routinely charge large sums to testify at trial, so it is proper for a non-expert to receive a modest amount of compensation, especially if she is fearful of adverse consequences from testifying.

B. Yes, because the goal of the trial is to determine the facts of what happened, and it is important to have every material witness testify in order to corroborate the truth and impeach the false statements of others.

C. No, because the lawyer offered the witness an unreasonably large amount of money.

D. No, because the common law rule in most jurisdictions is that it is improper to pay an occurrence witness any fee for testifying apart from expenses.

ANALYSIS. Lawyers can pay experts to testify (as long as it is not a contingent fee), but paying non-expert witnesses, such as an eyewitness to the events that triggered the case, is improper, except for reimbursing a witness for the costs of testifying. The traditional rule is that lawyers can compensate a witness's travel expenses (including airfare), lodging, food, lost wages, if any, for the time away from work, and possibly for the time it takes to prepare for testimony, such as reviewing old e-mails or corporate records. Reimbursing or compensating a witness can apply to testifying at trial or at a deposition. It is never proper to pay a witness a contingent fee—that is, to offer to pay the witness only if the case goes well, or to pay more if the case goes well. Nor is it proper to pay the witness a large sum that appears to be an inducement to testify rather than reimbursement for costs, as the lawyer did in this problem. As Comment 3 for Rule 3.4 says, "... [I]t is not improper to pay a witness's expenses or to compensate an expert witness on terms permitted by law. The common law rule in most jurisdictions is that it is improper to pay an occurrence witness any fee for testifying ...."

A is incorrect—the Model Rules make a significant distinction between expert witnesses and non-expert witnesses—it is not proper for a lawyer to compensate an occurrence witness in a way that is merely a discounted version of what the lawyer might pay an expert.

B is also incorrect—even though it is important to reach accurate results in trials, and it is generally a good thing to call witnesses, it is still a violation of the ethical rules for a lawyer to pay a regular witness to testify. Such payments are likely to bias the witnesses and reduce the reliability—or at least the perceived reliability—of their testimony.

C is partly correct but offers the wrong reason. It is true that the lawyer's conduct was improper, and that $10,000 seems like an unreasonable sum to pay a witness merely for impeachment testimony and corroboration of the client's story. Even so, paying witnesses to testify is improper under the Model Rules regardless of the sum (not counting reimbursement for expenses incurred when testifying, like travel and lodging).

D is correct. The attorney offered an inducement, or at least an outlandish fee, to a witness to testify on one occasion. This violates Rule 3.4(b).

QUESTION 17. Everything is covered. An attorney located a witness who could corroborate his client's story. The witness, however, was afraid of retaliation from others if she testified, and did not want to be involved. The witness also lives 1,000 miles away and works as a waitress, so she cannot afford the travel expenses and lodging, and cannot afford to miss work, because she receives no wages if she does not work. The attorney offers to pay all the witness's expenses. The attorney then pays for airfare and pays to put the witness in one of the nicest hotels in the city, and pays for all of the witness's dining bills at expensive downtown restaurants. The witness reluctantly agrees. Was it proper for the attorney to offer to pay the expenses for a favorable witness to undergo the trouble of testifying at the trial?

A. Yes, because expert witnesses routinely charge large sums to testify at trial, so it is proper for a non-expert to receive a modest amount of compensation, especially if she is fearful of adverse consequences from testifying.

B. Yes, because it is proper to pay a witness's expenses, as long as the attorney does not offer to pay the witness an inducement to provide favorable testimony.

C. No, because it is improper to pay an occurrence witness any fee for testifying.

D. No, because it is proper to compensate a witness only if the lawyer will also compensate a witness for the opposing party.

ANALYSIS. This problem begins in a very similar way to the previous problem, but the attorney here takes a different approach—instead of offering a lump sum to a witness to testify, the attorney offers to cover travel (airfare), lodging, expensive meals, and possibly lost wages from missing work. Compensating an occurrence witness for costs related to testifying is proper, according to Comment 3 for Rule 3.4, but offering to pay the witness to testify is *not* proper. Of course, in some cases, the distinction is mostly semantic—an attorney may end up (properly) spending thousands of dollars for a witness' travel, lodging, food, and so on—the same amount that would have been *improper* to offer the witness as an inducement to testify. The difference is that compensating the witness leaves the person no better or worse off than if the person had not testified, so it is not a true inducement. Note also that "reasonable" reimbursement or compensation for costs includes nice hotels and nice restaurants—perhaps nicer than what the witness could normally afford personally. There is no requirement that lawyers put witnesses in the cheapest hotel in town or force them to eat cheap fast food. Of course, it is conceivable that compensating for "costs" could become too excessive and unreasonable—perhaps a luxury hotel or restaurant that normally caters only to the super-wealthy. Courthouses are typically in downtown locations, and the nearby restaurants and hotels typically have downtown prices.

A is incorrect—Comment 3 to Rule 3.4 reflects the traditional view that there are different rules for expert witnesses and occurrence witnesses, so there is no basis in the Model Rules to try to bring the two into parity.

B is correct—Comment 3 to Rule 3.4 explicitly allows a lawyer to compensate occurrence witnesses (the type of witness described here) for the costs incurred from testifying. It is not proper to offer an outright financial inducement to testify.

C is also incorrect because it overstates the prohibition on compensating occurrence witnesses—a witness cannot receive an inducement to testify, but a lawyer *can* properly offer to make the witness whole if he or she testifies, so that the witness has no direct financial impediment to appearing at the trial or deposition.

D is wrong because there is no duty of reciprocity when it comes to compensating occurrence witnesses—lawyers absolutely do not have to compensate witnesses who will testify on behalf of the other party.

QUESTION 18. **If you don't win, you don't pay.** An attorney interviewed an expert witness whom he thought he might hire to testify at a client's trial. The attorney explained he was meeting with several expert witnesses and would hire the one who he thought would seem most persuasive to the jury. The expert witness offered to work on a contingent fee basis; if the attorney did not win the case at which the expert testified, no fee would be due. The attorney would have to pay the expert witness only if his testimony was compelling enough to produce a favorable outcome in the case. The attorney thought that this would give the expert an incentive to prepare more thoroughly for trial, and that it would be fairer to the client, who would be left bankrupt if they lost at trial and would have trouble paying the expert's fee anyway. Would it be proper for the attorney to hire the expert witness under such terms?

A. Yes, it is permissible to pay an expert witness a large fee.

B. Yes, because if the client loses the case and would be unable to pay the fees to the lawyer and the expert, the same type of contingency would result either way.

C. No, because it is improper to pay the expert witness a contingent fee.

D. No, because a lawyer cannot offer any inducement to a witness to testify.

ANALYSIS. Comment 3 for Rule 3.4 permits lawyers to pay experts to testify (customary fees), as long as it is not a contingent fee, i.e., the fee or the amount of the fee depends on whether the case outcome is favorable. This includes the "if-you-don't-win-you-don't-pay type of contingent fee described here, as well as tiered fees that pay more if the outcome is favorable, or pay a percentage of the total award at trial. The concern is that we do not want experts to have a perverse incentive to distort their findings or conclusions. Of course, experts are aware that they are more likely to have repeat business if their testimony is both favorable and convincing.

A is the wrong answer, even though it includes a true statement. The Model Rules do not set caps on the fees that lawyers may pay expert witnesses, and some experts are quite pricey. The answer is incorrect because the lawyer paid a contingent fee, which is not proper—it does not matter if the contingent fee is large or small.

B is also incorrect, though it may describe the realities of legal practice. The answer does not reflect the provisions of the Model Rules, which simply forbid contingent fees for expert witnesses. It does not matter that in practice, many things are contingent on the client being able to pay. The client would still have a contractual obligation to pay the expert, even if the client turned out to be judgment-proof after the ordeal.

C is correct—it is improper to pay an expert witness a contingent fee. It would be fine for the lawyer to pay an hourly rate or a flat fee for the service, but a lawyer cannot properly make the expert's fee dependent on the outcome of the trial.

D is incorrect in that it overstates the rule—while it is impermissible to pay a contingent fee to expert witnesses (as happened in this problem), it is appropriate to pay an expert an hourly or flat fee for testifying.

QUESTION 19. **Don't even talk to them.** An attorney represents a small business in a contract dispute with one of its suppliers. The attorney meets with the employees of his client, in groups of four or five at a time, and explains that there is litigation pending, that Big Firm is representing the supplier, and that they should simply decline to discuss the case with anyone, especially lawyers from Big Firm. Was it proper for the attorney to ask the employees not to talk to the other party?

A. Yes, the Rules of Professional Conduct permit a lawyer to advise employees of a client to refrain from giving information to another party, for the employees may identify their interests with those of the client.

B. Yes, because each of those individuals is still free to ignore the lawyer and talk to whomever they want about the case or about the company.

C. No, because the Rules of Professional Conduct do not permit a lawyer to advise employees of a client to refrain from giving information to another party, for the employees may identify their interests with those of the opposing party.

D. No, because a lawyer shall not request a person other than a client to refrain from voluntarily giving relevant information to another party.

ANALYSIS. Rule 3.4(f) complements 3.4(b)—the latter prohibits offering potential witnesses an inducement to testify, and the former prohibits asking potential unfavorable witnesses *not* to testify. Presumably, this would include a prohibition against threatening a potential witness (not only with physical injury, which would be illegal, but also with a lawsuit, embarrassing disclosure of the witnesses' secrets, and so on). Like other sections of Rule 3.4, the last subsection may surprise students who are used to seeing characters in lawyer dramas on television routinely ask people not to testify against their clients. The MPRE has recently included questions about lawyers threatening to embarrass potential witnesses. At the same time, Rule 3.4(f) carves out a set of exceptions to the rule against asking witnesses not to testify: relatives and employees of the client, as long as the witness' own legal interests will not suffer if they refrain from testifying. For example, if a group of employees is suing their employer for unsafe working conditions or violating a collective bargaining agreement, the employer's attorney cannot ask the employees not to testify in that case, as refraining would be adverse to their legal interest in the lawsuit. Similarly, it is normally proper for a lawyer to ask his client's relatives not to testify against the client, even if the relatives are estranged from the client or harbor a grudge against the person. Nevertheless, if the case is a dispute about a family inheritance or parental visitation rights, the relatives may have interests in the case directly adverse to the client (even if the relatives are not parties to the litigation). In such a case, the lawyer cannot ask the relatives to refrain from testifying.

A is correct, as it reflects one of the exceptions delineated in Rule 3.4(f). Comment 4 to Rule 3.4(f) extends the exception to asking employees not to speak with the opposing party or counsel about the matter as well. A lawyer may ask employees of the client to refrain from testifying, or from talking to the opposing party or opposing counsel.

B is wrong, though it includes a true statement—employees may indeed be free, from a legal standpoint, to ignore the employer's lawyer and talk to the opposing side (or to testify). Even so, this is not the best answer, as it does not reflect the provisions in the Model Rules.

C is incorrect because it does not reflect the facts in the problem. It is true that the "exception to the exception" in Rule 3.4(f) is that a lawyer cannot ask employees of the client to refrain from testifying if doing so would be adverse to the employees' interest, as in a case where the litigation involves a dispute between the employer and the employees. In contrast, this problem involves a dispute with the client's supplier, so the employees have no clear adverse interest.

D incorrectly overstates the rule because it ignores the exception for employees of the client.

E. Rule 3.5 — Impartiality and Decorum of the Tribunal

Rule 3.5 prohibits attempts to undermine the fairness of a tribunal or to disrupt it. This includes improper influence of judges, jurors, and officials (such as bribery or threats), ex parte communications with judges, conversations with jurors before a verdict, and disruptive conduct in the courtroom. For whatever reason, questions based on this rule have appeared infrequently on recent MPRE tests, compared to Rules 3.3 and 3.4. Even so, the examiners include it in the published list of subjects tested, so it is important for students to know the basic rules.

Rule 3.5(a) contains the prohibition against "improper influence" of judges, jurors, or other government officials. Bribery and extortion are clearly in view here, but the comment to Rule 3.5 does not elaborate except to refer readers to state penal codes and the Code of Judicial Conduct (CJC). The implication seems to be that a transaction between a judge and a lawyer would place the judge in violation of the CJC (some provisions of which are rather subtle), and the lawyer would simultaneously be in violation of Rule 3.5.

Subsection (b) contains the prohibition on ex parte contacts with a judge or jurors that is familiar to most law students. Obvious exceptions for judges are routine scheduling calls (i.e., the judge's staff calls each lawyer in a case separately to see if they are willing to reschedule a certain hearing) and genuine emergencies. Any official court order or statute that permits communication between the lawyer and a judge would also fit under the rule — for example, the parties may agree to have the judge attempt mediation between them, and explicitly authorize the judge to talk to each party separately to see if they can reach an agreement. Such an approach to a case would obviously be in the trial record and would presumably include a court order from the judge authorizing each party to speak with the judge privately for the purposes of mediation.

The rule against talking to jurors during the trial is *very* strict — the rule not only applies to actual discussions of a case with a juror, but also could apply to attempts to charm a juror through idle chitchat (about the weather, or sports, or whatever), for example, in the elevator on the way to the courtroom. Note that the rule applies even if a juror initiates the conversation with the attorney — a lawyer must refuse to talk to the juror.

Rule 3.5(c) covers lawyers communicating with jurors *after* the trial. Many lawyers want to talk to jurors after the trial to glean constructive criticism about their performance (or the opposing counsel's performance) during the trial. This is generally permitted, but Rule 3.5(c) prohibits posttrial communications with a juror who has asked to be left alone, or where a court has ordered there to be no communication with jurors (a rare event), or where the lawyer is harassing, coercing, or lying to the juror.

Subsection (d) is a general ban on disruptive behavior at trial — emotional outbursts by a lawyer, storming out of the courtroom while a hearing is still in progress, and so on. It is important to note that this also applies to *depositions*—trying to disrupt the opposing counsel's deposition with constant unwarranted objections, for example, might violate this rule.

QUESTION 20. **The innocent lunch at the diner.** During a personal injury trial, the court took a lunchtime recess for an hour. The plaintiff's lawyer from the case walked across the street from the courthouse to a familiar diner to buy lunch. The diner was very crowded, so it was difficult for patrons to find a table to sit and eat. After ordering his sandwich at the counter, the attorney noticed two jurors from his own trial standing with their food, waiting for a free table. One of the jurors asked the attorney if they could share a table with him when one became available. The attorney agreed, but reminded them that they could not talk about the case. The three sat together and ate their sandwiches. The two jurors talked most of the time, getting to know each other—discussing their children, their jobs, and their pets. The attorney did not participate in the conversation except to answer their questions about how many children he had, and whether he owned any pets. Another juror from the trial was at the diner, and noticed the attorney sitting with the other two jurors, which he reported to the judge when court reconvened. Could the attorney be subject to discipline for sharing a table with the jurors during a lunch break?

A. Yes, because a lawyer should not have any ex parte social contact with jurors during a proceeding, even if they do not discuss the case.

B. Yes, because he allowed the two jurors to sit with each other and get to know each other, which makes it more likely they will influence each other during deliberations.

C. No, because this is a civil trial rather than a criminal trial.

D. No, because the lawyer did not discuss the case with the jurors at all and barely participated in their socializing.

ANALYSIS. Rule 3.5(b) prohibits all ex parte communications between lawyers and jurors during a proceeding. Courts have held that lawyers should be subject to discipline on facts very similar to these—sharing a table with jurors at a restaurant during a trial recess, even without ulterior motives. The lawyer in this case should have politely explained that he could not share a table with them or talk to them at all until the case was over—and should probably have left the restaurant, if several jurors were there.

A is correct. A lawyer must not communicate ex parte (that is, without the other lawyer and the judge present) at all during a proceeding, even if they are not discussing the case itself. Bonding with jurors through even superficial social contact can create a suspicion of undue influence, and undermine the integrity of the proceedings.

B is not correct. The lawyer did not have an obligation to prevent the two jurors from sitting together or talking to each other (although the judge probably instructed the jurors before the recess not to discuss the case with each other until formal deliberations began at the end of the trial). The reason the lawyer would be subject to discipline is that the lawyer himself sat with the jurors.

C is also incorrect, as the Model Rules make no distinction between civil and criminal trials when it comes to the prohibition on ex parte contacts.

D is incorrect, because Rule 3.5(b) does not merely prohibit talking about the case with jurors, but communicating with them at all outside of the courtroom.

QUESTION 21. **Concerned criticism for the judge.** During a trial, the judge overruled an objection by one of the attorneys. The attorney felt that the judge had made a fundamental error and had ignored a clear provision of the official Rules of Evidence. Court adjourned for the day a few minutes later, and the judge retreated to his chambers. The attorney approached the judge's clerk, who was still in the courtroom, and gave him a handwritten note, folded into a square, to pass along to the judge. The clerk gave the note to the judge. The note thanked the judge for recently inviting the attorney to the judge's home, along with sixty other people from the legal community, for a holiday party. It also said that the judge had made a mistaken ruling on the attorney's objection that day, and referred the judge to the relevant provision of the Rules of Evidence. Could the attorney be subject to discipline for his actions?

A. Yes, because the lawyer was mixing personal matters with his representation of a client.

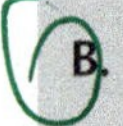

B. Yes, because the lawyer communicated ex parte with a judge during the proceeding, without being authorized to do so by law or court order.

C. No, because the note did not directly ask the judge to take a position on the merits of the case.

D. No, because the lawyer did not speak to the judge directly, but instead gave a note to the clerk, who is not a judicial officer.

ANALYSIS. Rule 3.5(b) prohibits all ex parte communications with a judge during a proceeding. Assuming the objection and the judge's ruling are part of the trial record or transcript, the lawyer can appeal this decision (usually as part of an appeal of an unfavorable verdict after the trial). The purpose of this question is to highlight for students that lawyers cannot communicate ex parte with a judge even indirectly. Ex parte communications do not have to be in-person conversations between a lawyer and a judge—using a neutral intermediary is a violation of the rules as well.

A includes an incorrect reason for the lawyer to face disciplinary charges—the problem was not that the lawyer included a reference to a recent social event in a note about an evidentiary ruling in the client's case. Instead, the problem was that the lawyer attempted an ex parte communication with the judge during a proceeding. It is common for lawyers to think a judge is mistaken about an evidentiary ruling, but arguments about this should occur inside the courtroom, on the record, with the other lawyer present.

B is correct—the lawyer's note constitutes an ex parte communication with the judge during a proceeding. It does not matter that the note begins with an innocent-sounding reference to a social event. The MPRE will often include extraneous facts like this to make the questions more confusing.

C is also incorrect. An ex parte communication violates Rule 3.5(b) regardless of whether it includes a request or petition. If a lawyer sends a note to a judge pointing out an error by the judge during the trial, presumably the lawyer hopes the judge will correct the mistake, or find some way to make up for it in a subsequent ruling.

D is incorrect because ex parte communications violate the Model Rules even if they do not involve direct, "live" communication (such as a phone call or in-person conversation). Indirect communications, as through a neutral intermediary, also violate the rule.

QUESTION 22. **Have your secretary make a visit.** An attorney represented a client in a prosecution for murder, and the prosecutor was seeking the death penalty. The trial was not going well, and the judge had not sequestered the jury, so the attorney sent his secretary to visit some of the jurors in their homes one evening, bringing them cookies and talking to them about the seriousness of sentencing a fellow human being to death. The secretary did not say she worked for the attorney, but instead introduced herself as a member of an advocacy group that seeks to abolish the death penalty, and she left pamphlets about abolishing the death penalty in each juror's home. Could the attorney be subject to discipline for this activity?

A. No, because the attorney did not actually speak to any of the jurors directly and therefore had no ex parte contact with them.

B. No, because the attorney did not have the secretary discuss the merits of the case or the evidence, but only the morality of the death penalty, which is a serious public policy issue.

C. Yes, because he was communicating ex parte with the jurors through the secretary during the proceeding.

D. Yes, because the secretary did not inform the jurors that she worked for the attorney.

ANALYSIS. Rule 3.5(b) prohibits communicating ex parte with jurors during a proceeding, and this includes indirect communication, as well as communications that the juror may not realize have come from the attorney. The point of this problem is to emphasize that the prohibition of ex parte communications does not depend on the juror's subjective impressions or knowledge, but on the actions of the lawyer.

A is incorrect because indirect communications (such as through another person) still constitute a violation of Rule 3.5(b).

B is also incorrect because the rule against ex parte communications with jurors applies to *all* communication, not only to discussions of the case or its merits.

C is correct—even though the secretary went instead of the lawyer, the secretary was acting as an agent of the lawyer. This was an attempt to influence the jurors outside the courtroom. It does not matter that the jurors did not know the secretary worked for the lawyer or that the content of the communication related to the morality of the death penalty generally rather than the merits of the case.

D is partly incorrect—while it is true that it was probably also unethical for the secretary to conceal the fact that she worked for the attorney in the case, the fact that she visited the jurors at all constitutes a violation of Rule 3.5(b).

QUESTION 23. **Post-game interview.** Attorney is a litigator and finds it helpful to talk to jurors after a trial concludes to see what they thought about the performance of the lawyers in the case. Assuming the judge has not forbiden talking to jurors and the jurors are willing to talk to him, is it proper for Attorney to have conversations with jurors in their homes, a week after the trial?

A. Yes, because a lawyer may communicate with a juror after the discharge of the jury, but must respect the desire of the juror not to talk with the lawyer.
B. Yes, as long as the lawyer does not talk about the merits of the case, the evidence, or the credibility of the witnesses.
C. No, because a lawyer may talk to jurors after discharge only with opposing counsel present and while they are still at the courthouse.
D. No, because a lawyer may not communicate ex parte with a juror, without an express authorization by the judge.

ANALYSIS. Comment 3 for Rule 3.5 contemplates that lawyers will often take the opportunity to talk to jurors after the conclusion of a case, which is normally permissible. The prohibition against talking to jurors applies during the proceedings; after the discharge of the jury, it is usually proper for the lawyers in the case to interview them or chat with them. Some lawyers hope to receive constructive feedback about the trial—what arguments or witnesses seemed most convincing, what the lawyers could have done better, and so on. This can help lawyers improve their own courtroom performance, but also understand how jurors think. Other lawyers see it as a public relations opportunity—jurors who liked one of the lawyers may refer that lawyer to their friends or relatives later on. Still others are hoping to discover information that would furnish the basis for an appeal.

As mentioned above, Rule 3.5(b) imposes some restraints on lawyers during this posttrial discussion with jurors. First, judges can order the lawyers to refrain from talking to the jurors in a particular case, and it is possible that some state statute could bar such conversations, at least in specific types of cases. Second, jurors never have any obligation to talk to the lawyers, and if a juror does not wish to talk to a lawyer (and says as much), the lawyer must refrain from pursuing any further contact. Some jurors feel uncomfortable talking with lawyers (especially the lawyer whom they ruled against), and others may be in a hurry to get home after the inconvenience of having jury duty. Finally, a lawyer may not harass, coerce, threaten, or lie to a juror. "Harass" includes pestering the juror with repeated phone calls or home visits, and "coerce" includes threatening to "tell the judge" something the lawyer learned about the juror's background or conduct during the trial.

A is correct. Normally, these conversations with jurors occur at the courthouse, before everyone disperses after the conclusion of the trial. Even so, there is no prohibition against lawyers visiting jurors at their homes, if the jurors are willing to talk to them, after the trial is over.

B gives an incorrect limitation on the lawyer—the Model Rules do not forbid lawyers from discussing the merits of the case, the persuasiveness of various items of evidence, or the credibility of witnesses with jurors after the case.

C is incorrect because the Model Rules do not require a lawyer to have the opposing counsel present during posttrial interviews with jurors, nor to have the conversations at the courthouse, although it is usually more convenient for everyone to talk while they are still at the courthouse.

D is also incorrect in that the prohibition on ex parte contacts applies only during the proceedings.

QUESTION 24. Just a clerk. An attorney represented a client in an action for replevin. After the filing of the case, but before the court had sent any notices about the docket number, the attorney spoke to a clerk at the courthouse, and inquired whether the case had received an assignment yet to a judge. The clerk said it was still unassigned. The attorney then asked the clerk to mention to the Director of Judicial Administration, who was also the Chief Presiding Judge, that they should not assign the case to a particular judge, who was notorious for having a bias against parties like the attorney's client, and who had an extraordinarily high reversal rate from the appellate courts in replevin cases. The clerk said he would mention the conversation to the Director, which he did. The Director said she could not accommodate special requests from lawyers regarding case assignments, but when it came time to assign the case, she assigned the case to another judge merely to avoid another embarrassing reversal from the appellate courts. Was it improper for the attorney to ask the clerk to pass his concerns along to the Director?

A. Yes, because he should have waited until the case was assigned before asking the administrator to reassign it to another judge.

B. Yes, because during a proceeding a lawyer may not communicate ex parte with persons serving in an official capacity in the proceeding, such as judges, masters, or jurors, unless authorized to do so by law or court order.

C. No, because Attorney did not actually speak ex parte with the judicial officer, but instead spoke with a front-counter clerk.

D. No, because the case had not yet been assigned to any judge.

ANALYSIS. Rule 3.5(a) prohibits lawyers from having ex parte contact with anyone serving in an official capacity in a case. The purpose of this problem is to emphasize for students that the prohibition applies to more individuals than the judge who actually presides at a trial. It can apply to hearing officers or commissioners in administrative proceedings, court administrators (as in this case), bailiffs, and judicial clerks. Note that it does not matter if the ex parte communication actually produces the result that the attorney had sought—an attorney can be subject to discipline even if the official or judge ignores the communication. Similarly, it does not matter that the official or judge *does* do what the attorney wanted, but for another (perfectly legitimate) reason—that is, whether the judge or official would have done it anyway, even without the ex parte communication. What matters is the action taken by the lawyer.

A is incorrect. The timing of the request was not the problem—it was the fact that the lawyer is privately asking a court administrator to use her discretion to give the lawyer an advantage (or remove a disadvantage).

B is correct. The Director of Judicial Administration has an official capacity in the proceeding at this stage—assigning the case to a judge. As evidenced by the lawyer's request, the assignment of a particular judge to a case can have an impact on the outcome—some judges have reputations for being pro-defendant or pro-plaintiff.

C is the wrong answer because ex parte communications do not require direct, in-person conversation—sending a note can constitute a violation of the Model Rules.

D is also incorrect; the proceeding is underway already, at least for purposes of the Model Rules, even if it is still at the pretrial stage and is still waiting for a judicial assignment.

QUESTION 25. Making a scene. A client is struggling through a deposition, during which opposing counsel is subjecting him to intense questioning. The attorney, who represents the client, tries objecting a few times in order to break the opposing counsel's momentum, but it was to no avail. The attorney then stood up, shouted, and with a heave overturned the conference table around which the lawyers, court reporter, and deponent were sitting. Notes, cell phones, and open briefcases flew across the room, and the stenographer's equipment tumbled to the floor. The attorney and the client gathered their things and stormed out of the room. A few days later, the attorney called opposing counsel and halfheartedly apologized, and agreed to reschedule the deposition if opposing counsel would agree to behave himself this time. Opposing counsel reported the attorney to the state bar disciplinary authority. Could the attorney be subject to discipline for the way in which he disrupted the deposition?

A. No, because the disruption was merely at a deposition, which is not as formal as a trial or hearing.
B. No, because his response was appropriate given the aggressiveness of opposing counsel in the deposition.
C. Yes, because the attorney did not properly apologize for his own conduct or take responsibility for his actions.
D. Yes, because the duty to refrain from disruptive conduct applies to any proceeding of a tribunal, including a deposition.

ANALYSIS. Comment 5 for Rule 3.5(d) says, "The duty to refrain from disruptive conduct applies to any proceeding of a tribunal, including a deposition." Movies and television dramas often feature lawyers "making a scene" in a trial or in a deposition, but the Model Rules prohibit this, and the lawyer could be subject to discipline for being disruptive. Note that even provocation—such as annoying behavior by opposing counsel—does not justify a disruptive outburst from an attorney.

A is incorrect. Rule 3.5(d) applies to depositions (see Comment 5) as well as trials.

B is also incorrect because aggressive advocacy by opposing counsel does not provide a justification for disruptive retaliatory behavior. It can be frustrating—sometimes even infuriating—when opposing counsel comes on too strong to a client during a deposition, but the lawyer should behave as if they were in a courtroom with the judge present.

C is incorrect, as it focuses on the apology rather than the underlying conduct that violated Rule 3.5. Even if the apology had been sincere and obsequious, and even if the other lawyer had graciously accepted the apology, it would not have changed the fact that the attorney violated a rule. Apologies are certainly appropriate when lawyers have been rude, but they do not necessarily undo the ethical violation involved.

D is correct. The lawyer in this case created an ugly disruption that terminated the deposition. Depositions are an important part of pretrial discovery. The apparent motivation here is exactly what Rule 3.5 seeks to prevent—strategic behavior by the lawyer designed to undermine the integrity of the process and to force a more favorable outcome.

F. Rule 3.6—Trial Publicity

Rule 3.6 limits the comments lawyers may permissibly make to the media about pending litigation. The ABA has amended this rule (twice, first in 1994 and again in 2002) in response to a landmark United States Supreme Court decision holding that the original version of the rule was void for vagueness and therefore unconstitutional. The result, rather predictably, has been to expand the rule in order to provide more clarity and less vagueness—hence, the rule is somewhat longer than the surrounding sections of the Model Rules.

In recent years, the MPRE has included one question about Rule 3.6 on each exam, and the questions tend to be tricky, focusing on the less-obvious provisions of the rule and its official comment. It is important, though, for students to keep clear the basic rule, set forth in Rule 3.6(a), before mastering its exceptions and extensions: litigators in a case must not make statements to or through the media that could materially prejudice the adjudication, such as turning public opinion in the client's favor before jury selection. Practitioners sometimes refer to this phenomenon as "trying the case in the press," and the Model Rules strongly disfavor such behavior. Note that the last section, Rule 3.6(d), extends the rule to all lawyers in the litigator's firm or government agency. In other words, a lawyer cannot circumvent the rule simply by asking a partner or associate to talk to the press about the case instead, or even to talk to someone the lawyer knows will pass the statement along to a reporter. The MPRE has tested on this specific point about other lawyers in the same firm talking to the press about a case.

On the other hand, Comment 3 to Rule 3.6 says that the rule does *not* apply to lawyers at other firms not involved in the case: " . . . [T]he rule applies only to lawyers who are, or who have been involved in the investigation or litigation of a case, and their associates."

Most of the verbiage of Rule 3.6 pertains to the exceptions rather than extensions of the rule. A lawyer may permissibly talk to the media about the nature of the claim, the identity of the persons involved, information already contained in a public record, that an investigation of a matter is in progress, and scheduling or results of any step in litigation. Lawyers may request assistance in obtaining evidence and information about the case, and may warn the public of danger concerning the behavior of a person involved. In criminal cases, prosecutors or defense lawyers can reveal the identity, residence, occupation, and family status of the accused; information necessary to aid in apprehension of a fleeing fugitive; the fact, time, and place of arrest; and the identity of investigating and arresting officers or agencies and the length of the investigation.

Comment 5 to Rule 3.6 is very lengthy and contains a list of "presumably prejudicial" statements—a list that was part of Rule 3.6 itself in an earlier version, but which the ABA decided to move to the comment in a recent amendment. Lawyers must not comment to the media about the character or credibility of any party or witness in the case. Prosecutors and defense lawyers in criminal cases must not discuss the possibility of a plea bargain or the defendant's refusal to accept a plea deal. Lawyers must not discuss the results of tests such as polygraphs, DNA testing, and so on, nor may they comment on a party's refusal to submit to such a test. Perhaps most significantly, neither lawyer in a criminal case may offer an opinion in the media about the guilt or innocence of the accused. A prosecutor may say what charges a defendant faces, but not that he is "guilty," and the defense counsel can say that the defendant has raised a particular defense or maintains his own innocence, but the lawyer himself cannot assert the defendant's innocence. Finally, a lawyer may not talk to the media about information that the lawyer knows would be inadmissible at trial (such as items illegally seized by police, or hearsay evidence, or a criminal defendant's previous conviction record).

Another exception that the MPRE has tested recently is Rule 3.6(c), the so-called "self-defense clause." The ABA carefully rephrased this section to comport with the Supreme Court's decision about it, so it is best to look at the actual wording:

> . . . a lawyer may make a statement that a reasonable lawyer would believe is required to protect a client from the substantial undue prejudicial effect of recent publicity not initiated by the lawyer or the lawyer's client. A statement made pursuant to this paragraph shall be limited to such information as is necessary to mitigate the recent adverse publicity.

In other words, a lawyer *can* hold a press conference to rebut negative publicity about a client in litigation, as long as the lawyer did not initiate the negative publicity, and as long as the comments address only the points that are already receiving media attention. Lawyers cannot start the media war with opposing counsel and then avail themselves of the self-defense provision for a later round, and lawyers cannot use self-defense as an opportunity to escalate the public mudslinging with the opposing party.

QUESTION 26. **The pundit on the courthouse steps.** A lawyer is engaged in civil litigation. On his way into the courthouse on the day of jury selection, reporters gather around the lawyer hoping for comments. The lawyer explains that the (unrelated) criminal trial happening at the courthouse that day is far more important, and he expresses regret that he is not involved in that case at all. He states that he believes the criminal case should result in an acquittal because the police (who are testifying as witnesses in the case) violated the defendant's civil liberties, and because the relevant penal statute itself, which furnished the basis for charges in the case, violates the Bill of Rights. His own civil case, he says, is a brief matter scheduled for a one-day trial, so he hopes to observe the closing arguments tomorrow in the important criminal case in the other courtroom. Were the lawyer's statements proper?

A. Yes, because the rule limiting trial publicity applies only to lawyers who are, or who have been involved in the investigation or litigation of a case.

B. Yes, because the lawyer is expressing opinions about the constitutionality of a law and of the state's actions, and such statements receive special protection under the First Amendment.

C. No, because the lawyer is commenting on the character or reputation of police who will be witnesses in the case.

D. No, because the lawyer's arguments would be inadmissible at trial, if the courts have already upheld the constitutionality of the statute and the police actions in this circumstance.

ANALYSIS. Rule 3.6(d) extends the prohibition on media discussions about pending litigation to other lawyers in the same firm or government agency as the lawyer handling the case. At the same time, Comment 3 to Rule 3.6 provides, "Recognizing that the public value of informed commentary is great and the likelihood of prejudice to a proceeding by the commentary of a lawyer who is not involved in the proceeding is small, the rule applies only to lawyers who are, or who have been involved in the investigation or litigation of a case, and their associates." The MPRE recently included a question based on this provision in the comment.

A is correct. Lawyers can give public commentary about cases in which they are not involved—in fact, the Model Rules appear to encourage this as a way of keeping the public informed.

B is incorrect—even though it is true that the lawyer's actions were proper, the reasoning offered in this answer is wrong. There may be normal First Amendment protections for the lawyer's speech, but there are not "special protections" under the First Amendment for lawyers—in fact, the Supreme Court has held that restrictions on lawyer speech such as those found in the current version of Rule 3.6 do not violate the First Amendment.

C is incorrect. It is improper for a lawyer involved in a case to comment on the character or reputation of witnesses in the case—but the lawyer in this problem is not involved with the case. The prohibition does not apply to lawyers with no involvement in the case.

D is also incorrect because the lawyer is not involved with the case. If the lawyer were involved with the case (or even if someone from his firm were involved in it), then it would be improper for him to discuss inadmissible evidence. Even in that case, however, it is not clear that a legally erroneous or weak constitutional argument is "inadmissible" in the sense that lawyers normally use that term. Rather, lawyers often raise legal arguments that the opposing party refutes by citing recent case law.

QUESTION 27. But he started it. A lawyer is representing the defendant in a highly publicized criminal trial. On his way into the courthouse on the day of jury selection, reporters gather around the lawyer hoping for comments. The lawyer explains that the prosecutor already held a press conference in which she shared that the defendant had refused to take a polygraph test, that DNA tests had confirmed the defendant's guilt, and that the defendant had refused several offers of guilty pleas. To set the record straight before trial, the defense lawyer explains that his client had actually agreed to take a polygraph test but that none had occurred. He adds that defense experts would testify about problems with the DNA tests, and that the plea offers had all been the same (a life sentence instead of the death penalty) and were unacceptable to the client. Were the defense lawyer's statements proper?

A. Yes, because the First Amendment and Sixth Amendment protect a defendant's right to defend himself publicly through his attorney against false accusations.
B. Yes, when prejudicial statements have been publicly made by others, responsive statements may have the salutary effect of lessening any resulting adverse impact on the adjudicative proceeding.
C. No, because there is a presumption of prejudicial effect on the proceedings when a lawyer comments publicly about the possibility of a guilty plea, or a party's refusal to confess to a crime.
D. No, because there is a presumption of prejudicial effect on the proceedings when a lawyer comments publicly about the performance or results of any examination or test or the refusal or failure of a person to submit to an examination or test.

ANALYSIS. Comment 7 for Rule 3.6 says, "When prejudicial statements have been publicly made by others, responsive statements may have the salutary effect of lessening any resulting adverse impact on the adjudicative proceeding." Rule 3.6(c) specifically permits lawyers to engage in "self-defense" disclosures to the media. Even statements that would have been impermissible for the lawyer to make to the media could be proper if offered solely to offset negative publicity (especially negative or false information improperly disseminated by the opposing side); the other side has opened the door, so to speak. The MPRE has tested on this provision recently, so it is valuable for students to understand it. In this problem, the prosecutor has supposedly violated several of the provisions of Comment 5 to Rule 3.6. It is proper, therefore, for the lawyer to give reporters specific denials in response.

A is partly incorrect. First, the Sixth Amendment does not apply directly to media publicity—it merely gives criminal defendants a right to representation by a lawyer during the adjudication. Second, even though the Supreme Court has held that the First Amendment does give litigants some rights to make public statements, the Court also recognized that this right does not include a right to prejudice adjudicatory proceedings in one's own favor through the public media. In other words, a state bar can indeed place restrictions on a lawyer's media commentary about pending litigation, if the restrictions serve the purpose of protecting the fairness and integrity of adjudication.

B is correct, as it reflects the self-defense exception in Rule 3.6(c). Lawyers normally have to be very cautious about what they say to the media (or have others tell the media), but if there is already enough media coverage to prejudice the proceedings against one's client, a lawyer may take corrective measures.

C is incorrect. Comment 5 to Rule 3.6 says that there is indeed a presumption of prejudicial effect on proceedings when lawyers give statements to the media about guilty pleas or refusals to confess to a crime.

D is also partly incorrect. It is correct about the presumption, but incorrect about the lawyer in this case. If the lawyer were initiating the media coverage of the case with statements about test results, it would be improper. Nevertheless, the lawyer in this problem is availing himself of the self-defense exception to Rule 3.6.

QUESTION 28. **He started it, but you took it too far.** A lawyer is representing the defendant in a highly publicized trial. On his way into the courthouse on the day of jury selection, reporters gather around the lawyer hoping for comments. The lawyer explains that the prosecutor already held a press conference in which she shared that the defendant had refused to take a polygraph test, and that DNA tests had confirmed the defendant's guilt. The lawyer explains that polygraph tests are inadmissible due to their unreliability, and that the DNA results are in dispute and will be the subject of expert testimony at trial. He adds that the sleazy prosecutor has a habit of holding such press conferences to prejudice the proceedings before every criminal trial, and that it merely reveals that the prosecutor's cases are too weak to win on the merits without such stunts. His client, he says, is now guilty until proven innocent, which is a shame considering the serious criminal charges in the case. He also mentions that the state's star witness is a dangerous convicted felon who is testifying in exchange for early release from prison. Were the defense lawyer's statements proper?

A. Yes, when prejudicial statements have been publicly made by others, responsive statements may have the salutary effect of lessening any resulting adverse impact on the adjudicative proceeding.

B. Yes, because the First Amendment and Sixth Amendment protect a defendant's right to defend himself publicly through his attorney against false accusations.

C. No, because there is a presumption of prejudicial effect on the proceedings when a lawyer comments publicly about the performance or results of any examination or test or the refusal or failure of a person to submit to an examination or test.

D. No, such responsive statements should be limited to contain only such information as is necessary to mitigate undue prejudice created by the statements made by others.

ANALYSIS. This problem deliberately extends the facts of the previous problem to highlight the limits on the self-defense exception to Rule 3.6. Rule 3.6(c) concludes its provision about the exception with the following caveat: "A statement made pursuant to this paragraph shall be limited to such information as is necessary to mitigate the recent adverse publicity." Comment 7 for Rule 3.6 expresses it this way: "Such responsive statements should be limited to contain only such information as is necessary to mitigate undue prejudice created by the statements made by others." Students should watch for test questions in which the responsive lawyer (the one availing herself of the self-defense exception) goes beyond refuting the existing negative publicity and goes on the offensive, escalating the level of attacks between the lawyers or parties.

A is incorrect. While this answer correctly states the substance of the self-defense exception to Rule 3.6, it omits the limitation placed in Rule 3.6(c) and Comment 7 to Rule 3.6—the lawyer must limit such public comments to information necessary to mitigate the negative publicity.

B is also incorrect—The Sixth Amendment does not apply directly to trial publicity, but rather to the defendant's right to counsel during the proceedings. The First Amendment does apply, but it does not protect statements by lawyers designed to prejudice an upcoming adjudicatory proceeding.

C is incorrect. There is indeed a presumption of prejudicial effect from such comments, but the problem here is that the lawyer went beyond giving the information necessary to refute the prejudicial effect of the prosecutor's statements.

D is correct. In this problem, the lawyer went far beyond the information necessary to refute the unfair or inaccurate media coverage, and attacked the prosecutor's reputation, as well as the character of one of the witnesses in the upcoming case. As tempting as it may be for lawyers to push back aggressively against poor behavior by opposing counsel, the Model Rules do not permit a lawyer to escalate the prejudicial effect on the case by taking the attacks to a new level.

QUESTION 29. **Get all the facts out in the open.** A lawyer is representing the defendant in a personal injury trial between a celebrity plaintiff and a famous hotel, where the plaintiff claims to have suffered injuries due to unsafe conditions. On his way into the courthouse on the day of jury selection, reporters gather around the lawyer hoping for comments. The lawyer explains that his client has already made renovations to the hotel to ensure that no accidents happen in the future, even though they do not admit liability in the present case. He also explains that if his client loses, his insurance company will simply pay the damages, and lawsuits like this make everyone's insurance premiums go up. The lawyer has his client's permission to talk to the media. Opposing counsel is standing nearby waiting for his turn to talk, and he expresses no objection to the first lawyer giving interviews like this, or to the lawyer's comments. Were the lawyer's statements proper?

A. No, it violates the Model Rules for a lawyer to make public statements about information that the lawyer knows or reasonably should know is likely to be inadmissible as evidence in a trial and that would, if disclosed, create a substantial risk of prejudicing an impartial trial.
B. Yes, because the other lawyer is present and did not object to the comments at the time, and the client has consented to the lawyer's media communications.
C. No, because in civil trials a defendant's lawyer should not tell the press that his client denies liability in the case.
D. Yes, the rules about trial publicity explicitly permit lawyers to talk about defenses in the case, and the client's mitigation efforts and public policy concerns over skyrocketing insurance rates could be the defendant's main arguments to the jury.

ANALYSIS. Comment 5 to Rule 3.6 delineates several types of statements that "are more likely than not to have a material prejudicial effect on a proceeding, particularly when they refer to a civil matter triable to a jury, a criminal matter, or any other proceeding that could result in incarceration." In other words, these subjects are presumptively prejudicial for purposes of Rule 3.6

and the prohibition on media statements about litigation. The subjects are specific enough to be especially well-suited for multiple-choice questions, meaning they are good to study in preparation for the MPRE. The fifth subsection in Comment 5 specifies, "[I]nformation that the lawyer knows or reasonably should know is likely to be inadmissible as evidence in trial and that would, if disclosed, create a substantial risk of prejudicing an impartial trial." In the facts above, the lawyer is discussing information (remedial measures taken after an accident) that would normally be inadmissible in a personal injury trial. The fact that the other lawyer does not object does not change the fact that this constitutes a violation of the rule. It undermines the rules about admissible evidence if lawyers can simply disseminate inadmissible evidence through the media before trial.

A is correct. The defendant's insurance and post-accident renovations would clearly be inadmissible at trial due to their potential for prejudicial effect. A lawyer should not disseminate through the public media information that would be inadmissible at trial—its inadmissibility is due to its prejudicial effect.

B is incorrect. Rule 3.6 contains no exception for instances where the opposing counsel is present and acquiesces to improper comments. The comments still constitute a violation. Similarly, the client's consent is irrelevant to the propriety of public media comments by lawyers—on the contrary, we would assume that many clients would want their lawyers to engage in strategically prejudicial behavior in order to gain an advantage in litigation.

C is also incorrect. It is permissible to tell the media in a civil trial that a client denies the allegations of negligence or other tortious conduct.

D is partly incorrect—while it is true that Rule 3.6 permits lawyers to talk about defenses in the case, in Rule 3.6(b)(1), the remedial measures after the accident are not relevant to the defendant's conduct prior to the accident, and would be inadmissible.

QUESTION 30. Just the basics. An attorney represented a newspaper publisher in a defamation case brought by a popular actor. A radio talk show invited the attorney to participate in their afternoon program and respond to calls from the radio listeners. The first caller asked the attorney to explain the case involving the superhero that the popular actor had played in a recent film. The attorney explained that the actor (using the actor's legal name as it appeared in the pleadings, rather than his stage name or the character for which the actor was most famous), and the legal name of the publisher the attorney represented. He also explained that the lawsuit was over alleged defamation by the newspaper, and that the newspaper planned to raise an affirmative defense of truth, that is, it would attempt to show that the stories it printed about the actor were factually accurate, even if they were unflattering. The attorney also mentioned that the actor owns a home and a business in the state, which is a matter of public record, and this is why the case is in the courts in that state. Did the attorney violate the Rules of Professional conduct by making these statements on a radio talk show program?

A. Yes, because a lawyer who is participating or has participated in litigation shall not make an extrajudicial statement that the lawyer knows or reasonably should know will be disseminated by means of public communication.

B. Yes, because he explained that his side would assert the truth of the unflattering stories it published, which could prejudice the upcoming proceedings, and revealed where the actor lives.

C. No, because a lawyer may state the claim, the defense involved, the identity of the persons involved, and matters in the public record.

D. No, because a lawyer has a right to explain his client's side of the story and defend his client in public when the client has been subjected to the stigma of a lawsuit.

ANALYSIS. Rule 3.6(b)(1) and (2) allow a lawyer to make statements to the media about "the claim, offense or defense involved and, except when prohibited by law, the identity of the persons involved" and "information contained in a public record." In this problem, all of the information the lawyer shares during the radio interview comes under these provisions—the claims, defenses, identities of the parties, and matters already in the public record (the real property owned in that state). Watch for questions on the MPRE that test the specific exceptions to the general rules.

A is incorrect, though it accurately states the general rule about trial publicity. It overlooks the provisions in Rule 3.6(b) that create several exceptions, including the information disclosed by the lawyer in this problem.

B is also incorrect, because Rule 3.6(b) specifically allows discussing litigation defenses in the media, including the standard defense to libel and slander, namely that the statements were true. Most litigation defenses, if proved, could be somewhat unflattering to the opposing side, but this information falls under the protection of a specific provision in Rule 3.6.

C is correct. Rule 3.6(b)(1) and (2) specifically allow disclosure through the mass media of information in this problem.

D is incorrect—a lawyer does not actually have an unqualified right to tell his client's side of the story in public when litigation is pending. Some information contained in "the client's side of the story" could be highly prejudicial to the proceedings and possibly inadmissible in court.

QUESTION 31. See you next summer. A prosecutor in a felony drug case addressed a group of reporters outside the District Attorney's office. In response to questions about the specific case underway, the prosecutor explained that the judge had consolidated the trials of three co-defendants into a single proceeding and had postponed the proceeding until the next summer, four months away. Was it proper for the prosecutor to disclose such details about the case to reporters?

A. Yes, because the public has a right to know how the details of a criminal prosecution, as the taxpayers are paying the prosecutor's salary.
B. Yes, because a lawyer may tell reporters the scheduling or result of any step in litigation.
C. No, because no lawyer associated in a firm or government agency subject to the Rules of Professional Conduct shall make a statement prohibited by the rules.
D. No, because criminal jury trials will be most sensitive to extrajudicial speech.

ANALYSIS. Rule 3.6(a)(4) permits lawyers to make extrajudicial statements in the public media regarding "the scheduling or result of any step in litigation." The various provisions of Rule 3.6 are the ABA's attempt to balance the public's need to know about court proceedings with the need to avoid prejudicing the outcome of a pending adjudication. An example of information that is not too prejudicial, and therefore permissible to disclose to the media, is the expected trial date or other scheduling information about a proceeding.

A gives the wrong reason for the otherwise right answer. It was indeed proper for the prosecutor to share the information, but not because of concerns about taxpayer dollars paying the prosecutor's salary. Rather the correct reason is that Rule 3.6(b) specifically allows for lawyers to share this information about proceedings in which they are involved.

B is correct. The prosecutor in this case appropriately told the media about the consolidation of the proceedings and the postponement of the trial until the following summer.

C is also incorrect, though it is true that government lawyers are subject to the Rules of Professional Conduct just like private-sector lawyers. This answer is incorrect because the statement is not improper under Rule 3.6.

D is the wrong answer, even though it includes a correct statement. Comment 6 to Rule 3.6 states flatly, "Criminal jury trials will be most sensitive to extrajudicial speech. Civil trials may be less sensitive. Non-jury hearings and arbitration proceedings may be even less affected." Nevertheless, **D**

is not a correct answer, because even though this is a criminal proceeding, the prosecutor's statements were permissible under the specific exception in Rule 3.6(b)(4).

G. Rule 3.7—Lawyer as Witness

The "advocate-witness rule" embodied in Rule 3.7 covers situations when a lawyer must testify as a witness. In practice, this occurs more often in certain areas of practice—patent litigation, labor arbitration, child advocacy, and criminal prosecutions. In post-verdict hearings to determine attorneys' fees in a case, lawyers may have to testify in order to authenticate (and justify) their billing records for the matter. Of course, legal malpractice cases usually require testimony by a lawyer about the actions taken during the representation in question. In commercial litigation contexts, a lawyer may be the only person who was in the room when parties negotiated a contract term (or a provision in a will), and thus becomes a necessary witness when a dispute arises. Occasionally, a prosecutor (and rarely a defense attorney) may have to testify about the chain of custody for an important piece of evidence. Note that the advocate-witness rule can also apply to lawyer affidavits (even if the lawyer does not take the stand during the trial), if the affidavit pertains to material facts in the case. Courts generally do not apply the rule to routine sworn "verifications" or affidavits by lawyers regarding compliance with regular procedural rules (service on other parties, etc.).

Recent administrations of the MPRE have averaged one question each time about this rule, often about imputation to the rest of the firm. The advocate-witness rule underwent a significant amendment in the 1980s, allowing other lawyers in the same firm to continue representing a client even when a lawyer must testify. This newer provision, which appears in Rule 3.7(b), seems to be of special concern to the MPRE examiners: "A lawyer may act as advocate in a trial in which another lawyer in the lawyer's firm is likely to be called as a witness unless precluded from doing so by Rule 1.7 or Rule 1.9."

From a functional standpoint, in practice the rule primarily operates as a screening factor for whether a lawyer can undertake representation, usually included in the conflicts check for a new potential client. Lawyers should, and usually do, decline to handle a case if it is foreseeable that the lawyer will have to testify at trial as a witness. In terms of enforcement, disqualification motions from opposing counsel are by far the most common punishment for violations of the rule, even though courts consider disqualification for this reason to be rather drastic. Disciplinary actions for violating the advocate-witness rule are far less common, but they do occur. Section (b) of Rule 3.7 appears to contemplate the reality that disqualification would be the primary enforcement mechanism.

Note that the rule applies only to advocacy "at trial." Most courts and ethics opinions have taken the view that the rule does not apply to pretrial and posttrial advocacy—but this approach is not yet universal. Given that around 95 percent of cases settle before trial, and a significant number of the remainder end with a dismissal or summary judgment, the rule's applicability to practice is rather limited. Nevertheless, the rule is important enough to the MPRE examiners that students are very likely to encounter it on the test.

Rule 3.7(a) contains three important exceptions to the basic advocate-witness rule. It does not apply if "the testimony pertains to an uncontested issue"—that is, both parties stipulate a particular fact, but a lawyer may need to take the stand to put something on the record (such as authenticating a document or chain of custody for a piece of evidence). The rule also does not apply when "the testimony relates to the nature and value of legal services rendered in the case," as when a lawyer must verify his or her bills in a case during the hearing about attorneys' fees.

The third exception is less specific. The rule does not apply when "disqualification of the lawyer would work substantial hardship on the client." Comment 4 to Rule 3.7 encourages courts to treat this as a balancing test, weighing factors such as the importance of the lawyer's testimony; the situation of the client; and whether the need to testify was foreseeable. "Hardship on the client" refers to the fact that the client who loses a lawyer through disqualification must scramble to find a new lawyer on the eve of trial. A recent MPRE question presented just this scenario—a lawyer who was present when his client and the opposing party made a business agreement, who realized on the eve of trial that he will have to testify in the matter, and who now faces a motion to disqualify.

QUESTION 32. Sole witness to a crime. As he left work one evening, an attorney was approaching his car in the parking garage when he noticed two men arguing near a car at the far end of that floor of the garage. He could not hear what they were arguing about, but could hear occasional profanities and insults, and one of them shouting, "I warned you!" Then he saw that the men began to fistfight. A few other people by this point had stopped to watch in the parking garage and someone called the police, who arrived within five minutes. By that point, one of the men who had been fighting was bloody and could not walk away from the fight on his own. The police took the men into custody and the other witnesses quickly dispersed, so the police took a statement from the attorney, the only witness who remained. The officer turned to his partner, who was standing near the squad car with its driver door open, and shouted that one of the witnesses was actually a lawyer, which prompted a snide remark from the other officer. One of the arrestees in the car overheard this exchange and asked the officer to get the attorney's business card so that he could hire him. May the attorney represent the arrestee in the criminal or civil proceedings that follow?

A. Yes, because only one of the arrestees asked the attorney to represent him and the attorney owed no ethical duty to the other man who had been fighting.
B. Yes, because the attorney did not engage in solicitation of a client at the scene of an incident, but instead the prospective client requested his representation.
C. No, because a lawyer should not represent a client who was referred to him by a police officer, even if the referral was in the context of a casual exchange between police in the client's presence.
D. No, because a lawyer shall not act as advocate at a trial in which the lawyer is likely to be a necessary witness.

ANALYSIS. Rule 3.7(a) states, "A lawyer shall not act as advocate at a trial in which the lawyer is likely to be a necessary witness . . ." The remainder of the section contains three exceptions, none of which applies here. The lawyer in this problem should know at the time he gives his statement to the police that he will probably be a witness in any prosecution that follows, so the lawyer should decline to represent either of the arrestees from the start. The lawyer-advocate rule is supposed to be self-executing—that is, lawyers are supposed to avoid putting themselves into this situation, even if that means turning away a potential client.

A is incorrect. The fact that there is no potential conflict of interest with the other arrestee does not mean the lawyer can represent the man, although potential conflicts of interest are a significant factor to keep in mind when analyzing advocate-witness problems, discussed at length in Comments 4, 5, and 6 to Rule 3.7. From the standpoint of potential conflicts, the lawyer could still end up with a conflict regarding his own client, were he to represent the man. For example, while testifying under oath, he has a duty to be completely truthful, and might have to give information that would be unfavorable to his own client. Even if his testimony were entirely favorable, it would lack credibility because of his relationship to the client.

B is incorrect. If the problem were about solicitation, it would be significant that the lawyer did not solicit the client at the scene. For purposes of the advocate-witness rule, this is not relevant.

C is also incorrect—there is no rule against representing a client referred by a police officer, and even if there were, it would not be relevant to the advocate-witness rule.

D is correct. Rule 3.7 directs lawyers to refrain from representing clients at trial if the lawyer is likely to be a necessary witness. Given that the lawyer in this problem was the only eyewitness who remained to give a statement to the police about the incident, it is likely that he will have to serve as a witness if one or both of the arrestees face prosecution.

QUESTION 33. Passing the client to a partner. An attorney works in a partnership with one other lawyer. A client wants the attorney to represent her in litigation over a contract dispute, because the attorney helped negotiate the contract. In fact, the attorney was the only other party in the room when the client and the other party reached a final agreement on the terms and signed the contract. The attorney explains that he will probably have to testify as a witness at the client's trial, as the dispute involves the parties' intention regarding a certain ambiguous provision of the contract. The attorney said he would truthfully corroborate the client's version of the events. As a result, the attorney explains, he cannot represent the client at the trial, but his partner at the firm (a two-lawyer partnership) could represent the client instead. The client retained the attorney's partner to represent her in the litigation. Is this arrangement proper?

A. Yes, because the client has agreed to it and there is no conflict of interest.
B. Yes, because lawyer may act as advocate in a trial in which another lawyer in the lawyer's firm is likely to be called as a witness.
C. No, because the firm had only two partners and the relationship is too close for one to be objective while conducting direct examination of the other.
D. No, because a lawyer may not act as advocate in a trial in which another lawyer in the lawyer's firm is likely to be called as a witness.

ANALYSIS. Rule 3.7(b) was a significant amendment to the advocate-witness rule, which traditionally could result in the disqualification of an entire law firm from representing a client on the eve of trial. The current rule allows a lawyer to transfer the case to another lawyer in the firm (who will handle the trial) so that the original lawyer can testify as a witness. The MPRE has tested on this particular amendment in recent years.

A is incorrect. Client consent can waive a conflict of interest (in most cases), but it does not necessarily waive the advocate-witness rule. The advocate-witness rule in Rule 3.7 does include concerns about conflicts of interest in its rationale, but there are other concerns as well—for example, that the lawyer will either have too much impact as a witness due to his position in the case, or that the lawyer's testimony will seem too biased to the jury. In either case, the effect would be prejudicial, and would undermine the integrity of the process.

B is the right answer. Rule 3.7(b) specifically permits another lawyer in the firm to serve as advocate in a trial when an attorney at the firm is likely to testify as a witness. Of course, the conflicts of interest rules still apply—if, for example, a junior associate would have to cross-examine the managing partner at his own firm, who supervises the associate's work, the associate might hesitate to engage in vigorous cross-examination. Assuming that such a conflict is not present in this problem (the facts given do not suggest it), one partner can testify and the other can serve as advocate.

C is also incorrect, although it raises a concern that the lawyers should consider—it depends on the relationship between to the two partners. In some cases, lawyers may conclude that it would be more prudent to have a lawyer from another firm handle the courtroom proceedings. For purposes of Rule 3.7, however, Section (b) specifically allows another partner at the same firm to handle the case, as in this problem, and does not specify a limit on the minimum number of lawyers in the firm.

D incorrectly states the rule without its qualification. Rule 3.7 generally proscribes advocates at trial testifying as witnesses in the same proceeding, but Section (b) specifically allows for another lawyer from the firm to handle the case when one lawyer must testify.

QUESTION 34. **Partners covering for each other.** An attorney, an associate at Big Firm, applied for a patent for a client and successfully obtained the patent. Three years later, another party sued the client for allegedly infringing on one of their patents. The attorney was a necessary witness in the patent infringement matter, and planned to testify on behalf of the client that the client had successfully obtained a patent to the invention in dispute. Two partners at Big Firm, where the attorney worked, handled the representation of the client in the infringement case, pursuant to the client's written consent. Will the two partners at Big Firm be subject to disqualification from representing the client in the patent infringement case, if the attorney will be a witness about the original patent application?

A. Yes, because a lawyer shall not act as advocate at a trial in which the lawyer is likely to be a necessary witness, and this restriction applies by imputation to the other lawyers in the same firm.
B. Yes, because a lawyer cannot serve as an advocate if a lawyer with whom the lawyer is associated in a firm is precluded from doing so.
C. No, because the client provided written consent.
D. No, because a lawyer may act as advocate in a trial in which another lawyer in the lawyer's firm is likely to be called as a witness.

ANALYSIS. This problem is similar to the previous one, but the MPRE seems to test this particular provision of Rule 3.7 most frequently, so it is worthwhile for students to see it applied in a few hypothetical situations. Patent law cases are one of the areas in which the advocate-witness scenario arises most often. Rule 3.7(b) allows a lawyer to act as advocate in a trial in which another lawyer in the lawyer's firm is likely to testify as a witness, unless there is a conflict of interest that would violate Rule 1.7 or Rule 1.9 (as when a lawyer must testify against one client and in favor of another).

A is incorrect. The statement in this answer actually represents the old version of the rule, before the ABA's most recent amendments to Rule 3.7—an entire firm could face disqualification if one of the lawyers testified in a case. Note that in some jurisdictions, the old rule may still apply, or may have been changed only recently.

B is also incorrect for the same reason. This answer merely reiterates the statement in **A**, using different terminology. This reflects the old rule, but the ABA changed Rule 3.7 to allow other lawyers in the firm to handle a case when an attorney at the firm must testify at trial.

C incorrectly applies client consent to the advocate-witness rule. Client consent or written waiver can sufficiently address the conflict of interest problem in a case, but that is only one of the concerns motivating the advocate-witness rule. There is also the concern about the prejudicial effect of the lawyer's status as advocate on his testimony (which could cut either way), and the perceived integrity of the proceedings.

D is correct. Note that any other lawyer (or lawyers) in the firm can handle the trial. It is proper for the lawyer who handled the initial patent application to pass the case to another lawyer, as it is very likely that he will have to testify at the infringement trial. Of course, the lawyer who will testify can still work on the case in the pretrial stage—discovery, motions, and so on.

QUESTION 35. **Verifying attorneys' fees.** After obtaining a favorable verdict at trial, a client asked the court to award attorneys' fees, which was permissible under relevant law. An attorney had represented the client throughout the litigation and now had to testify as a witness about the fees he had charged during the representing, authenticating, explaining, and justifying both the billable hours recorded on the timesheets and the lodestar rate for his legal services. Was it improper for the attorney to testify as a witness in the same proceeding in which he had represented a party as trial counsel?

A. Yes, because combining the roles of advocate and witness can prejudice the tribunal and the opposing party and can also involve a conflict of interest between the lawyer and client.
B. Yes, because a lawyer shall not act as advocate at a trial in which the lawyer is likely to be a necessary witness.
C. No, because the fact-finder has already rendered a verdict in the case.
D. No, because the testimony relates to the nature and value of legal services rendered in the case.

ANALYSIS. Rule 3.7(a)(2) specifically exempts testimony about billing (the fees and the activities that earned them) from the advocate-witness rule. This is a relatively routine scenario in litigation, when the victorious party requests attorneys' fees, although verifications of fees usually can happen through affidavits rather than oral testimony.

A is incorrect. This verbiage actually comes from the comment to Rule 3.7, but it pertains to the general advocate-witness rule (it describes the primary policy rationales for the underlying rule). Yet this problem implicates one of the specific exceptions to the general rule—testimony about fees earned or time spent on a matter. In fact, testimony about fees does not run a serious risk of prejudicing a tribunal or opposing party, and it is very unlikely to involve a conflict with the client. In other words, the primary rationales for the general rule seem inapplicable to testimony about fees, which is one reason that there is an exception to the rule for such testimony.

B is also incorrect. This answer merely states the basic rule of Rule 3.7 without the necessary exceptions. Even though lawyers generally must not agree to represent clients in matters in which the lawyer is likely to be a necessary witness, testimony about fees for seeking reimbursement from the losing party is an exception.

C is the wrong answer—even though a verdict has issued in the case already, it is common for awards of attorneys' fees (and hearings about the appropriate amount of such fees) to occur after the verdict.

D is correct. Rule 3.7 specifically allows for the type of testimony described here (regarding fees).

QUESTION 36. **He was there.** Three years into the litigation in a complex antitrust lawsuit, it became necessary to have the attorney, who alone represented the defendant corporation, testify as a witness at the trial. The attorney had been present at a private meeting between his client and an industry rival, at which they allegedly discussed a price-fixing scheme, and the testimony of the two rivals (the only ones besides the attorney at the meeting) contradicted each other. The question of what occurred at the meeting was a hotly contested issue in the case, but was only one of many issues in the protracted, extremely complex litigation. The opposing party moved to disqualify the attorney from representing his client after the attorney took the stand to testify. Should the court disqualify the attorney from representation, or from testifying as a witness?

A. Yes, because a lawyer shall not act as advocate at a trial in which the lawyer is likely to be a necessary witness.
B. Yes, because the testimony relates to a contested issue.
C. No, because disqualification of the lawyer would work substantial hardship on the client.
D. No, because testifying allows the lawyer to promote the truth and integrity of the proceedings when it is clear that one of the witnesses is lying about the conversation.

ANALYSIS. Rule 3.7(a)(3) identifies an exception to the advocate-witness rule for situations in which disqualification of the lawyer-witness from the case would result in substantial hardship on the client. Disqualification is the primary enforcement mechanism for the advocate-witness rule—it means that a judge issues an order forbidding the lawyer who will testify from serving as an advocate in the trial. The client then has to find another lawyer, typically on the eve of trial. This can be very difficult—it takes time to find another lawyer willing to take a case that would allow so little notice or preparation time before the trial begins, and the new lawyer may charge a substantially higher fee due to the timing and urgency of the matter. In addition, the new lawyer is simply at a disadvantage to an opposing counsel who has had months or years to become familiar with the case and to prepare for trial. It is also a significant loss for an attorney (financially and psychologically) to lose a lucrative client in this way. The disadvantage to the client is so predictable that many litigators will file motions to disqualify the opposing counsel (assuming some possible grounds for disqualification are present) simply to gain a strategic advantage. For this reason, judges view disqualification as a drastic remedy. In some cases, finding a replacement lawyer can be nearly impossible, if the other litigators in that locale all have conflicts of interest that would preclude them from taking the case (that is, the client's interests are adverse to interests of some of their existing clients).

In this problem, the trial is already underway—in its third year of complex antitrust litigation—meaning that changing lawyers in the midst of it would be very difficult and disadvantageous for the client. In addition, the facts suggest that the need for the lawyer to testify may not have been apparent at the outset of the litigation, but emerged only after the testimony of the parties turned out to be contradictory, and the issue became an important point in the case. Judges are less sympathetic to lawyers (and their clients) when it was apparent at the beginning of the representation that the lawyer would be a necessary witness, and in such cases, disqualification is more likely. On the other hand, when the need to testify arises somewhat as a surprise after the trial has begun, a judge should seriously consider how forcing one party to find a new lawyer for the remainder of the trial could prejudice the outcome of the proceedings.

A is incorrect, though it states the basic rule of Rule 3.7. It omits the important exception in Rule 3.7(a)(3), which covers scenarios like the one in this problem.

B is also incorrect, although the fact that the testimony relates to a contested issue is certainly a factor in deciding whether to disqualify the lawyer. If the testimony were about an uncontested issue, it would fall under an earlier specific exception—Rule3.7(a)(1)—and the hardship to the client would not be dispositive.

C is correct. This is exactly the type of scenario the drafters of the Model Rules had in mind when they added the exception in Rule 3.7(a)(3) for hardship to the client. In this problem, the potential hardship to the client is evident, and the chance of prejudicing the tribunal if the advocate testifies on this one point is relatively small.

D offers an incorrect rationale to the right answer about applying an exception to the advocate-witness rule. Normally, allowing an advocate to testify does just the opposite—it undermines the truth and integrity of the proceedings.

H. The Closer

Rules 3.1 through 3.7 impose a variety of truthfulness requirements on lawyers during litigation—candor to the court, avoiding frivolous claims and arguments, refraining from dilatory tactics, and modest restrictions on using media publicity to influence the outcome of a case. While these are distinct issues in the abstract, violations of several of the provisions often arise out of the same case—either because a single action by the lawyer violates multiple rules at once, or because a lawyer who becomes desperate in a case may resort to a variety of dishonest tricks in order to avoid losing.

QUESTION 37. **At this point, I will try anything.** Unable to find a convincing defense for his criminal client, the defense lawyer began to think about desperate measures. He felt an overwhelming duty to rescue his client from a long prison sentence, no matter what.

Just before the close of evidence, the lawyer raised a defense of entrapment. The defendant had not been the target of a sting operation, and there was no evidence that the police had offered any inducement to commit the crime, which was an aggravated assault on a family member. The prosecutors immediately objected that the defense counsel should have raised this earlier, and the judge quickly dismissed the claim as unfounded and told the lawyer to move on.

He next tried stalling, and told the judge he could prove someone else committed the crime if there could be more time. This was a complete fabrication, and the judge asked several searching questions, but the lawyer was insistent. The judge denied the request for more time. Then the lawyer claimed that he also wanted to challenge the constitutionality of the assault statute itself, claiming the Second Amendment's right to bear arms implied a right to assault people with a weapon under a wide range of circumstances. The judge laughed and agreed to give him two weeks to brief the issue in order to preserve it for appeal. The next day, the lawyer held a press conference, in which he claimed the judge was biased and that it was clear that someone else had committed the crime and had framed his client.

A. The lawyer could not be subject to discipline because his claims did not affect the outcome of the case—the court rejected two of them, and the third is nearly certain to fail as well.

B. The lawyer could not face discipline for requesting more time, regardless of the reason, nor for raising a constitutional challenge, which is a protected liberty interest, but could face discipline for the frivolous and untimely attempt to claim entrapment, as well as the comments at the press conference.

C. The lawyer could face discipline for the fabricated attempt to delay the proceedings and for the frivolous constitutional argument, but not for the comments at the press conference or for raising the entrapment defense, which does not require a showing of supporting facts.

D. The lawyer could face discipline for the press conference, for raising the entrapment defense, for the request to have additional time, and for raising the constitutional claim.

ANALYSIS. While it is good for lawyers to feel a duty toward their client, this duty is not absolute—a lawyer must provide zealous advocacy within the confines of the rules about meritorious claims and candor to the court. Here, the lawyer raised three claims or arguments for which there was no support, whether in fact or law. The entrapment defense could not apply if there had been no police inducement or some kind of sting operation. The Second Amendment claim (that statutes criminalizing aggravated assault are unconstitutional) is laughable, and the request for a delay rested upon a fabrication.

A is incorrect. The duties to the tribunal (candor, meritorious contentions, and expediting litigation) apply regardless of the effectiveness of the lawyer's attempts. The lawyer still violated the rules even if his actions were unsuccessful in achieving his goals.

B is partly correct and partly incorrect. The lawyer could face discipline for stalling tactics and for raising a frivolous constitutional claim. As Comment 1 for Rule 3.2 says, "The question is whether a competent lawyer acting in good faith would regard the course of action as having some substantial purpose other than delay." It is correct, however, that the lawyer would be subject to discipline for claiming entrapment and for the press conference.

C is similarly partly correct and partly incorrect. The dilatory measures clearly violate Rule 3.2, as the answer suggests, and Rule 3.1 applies to the ridiculous claim that the Second Amendment provides a constitutional right to assault one's relatives with weapons. The same applies to the other issues—the press conference violated the rules about trial publicity, and the entrapment defense does indeed require a showing of supporting facts.

D is correct. All three of the claims or arguments by the lawyer that are described in this question have no basis, whether in fact or law, and therefore violate Rule 3.1. The inflammatory press conference violates Rule 3.6, and the lawyer's lies to the judge about an alternate perpetrator violate Rule 3.3. Finally, the attempt to delay the proceedings, merely to stall or postpone the inevitable, violates Rule 3.2.

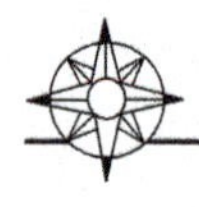

Stevenson's Picks

1. Leverage	A
2. Against the odds	C
3. Time for a change	A
4. Make the prosecutor do his job	C
5. Constant accommodation demanded	B
6. Waging a war of attrition	D
7. European vacation	C
8. The lying client	A
9. Flight risk	B
10. The witness	B
11. Disclosing adverse legal authority	D
12. Ex parte hearings	B
13. I know it in my heart	D
14. I've known him for years	C
15. A clean slate	B
16. The $10,000 witness	D
17. Everything is covered	B
18. If you don't win, you don't pay	C
19. Don't even talk to them	A
20. The innocent lunch at the diner	A
21. Concerned criticism for the judge	B
22. Have your secretary make a visit	C
23. Post-game interview	A
24. Just a clerk	B
25. Making a scene	D
26. The pundit on the courthouse steps	A
27. But he started it	B
28. He started it, but you took it too far	D
29. Get all the facts out in the open	A
30. Just the basics	C
31. See you next summer	B
32. Sole witness to a crime	D
33. Passing the client to a partner	B
34. Partners covering for each other	D
35. Verifying attorneys' fees	D
36. He was there	C
37. At this point, I will try anything	D

4

Competence, Legal Malpractice, and Other Civil Liability

CHAPTER OVERVIEW

The MPRE examiners use this heading to describe a cluster of subjects that together constitute 6 to 12 percent of each test—that is, three to seven questions. The subjects included in this group are as follows:

- Maintaining competence—Rule 1.1
- Competence necessary to undertake representation—Rule 1.1
- Exercising diligence and care—Rule 1.3
- Civil liability to client, including malpractice—Rule 1.8
- Civil liability to non-clients—Rule 2.3
- Limiting liability for malpractice—Rule 1.8
- Malpractice insurance and risk prevention— Common Law

A. Rule 1.1—Competence

The "competence rule" in the Model Rules of Professional Conduct (MRPC) Rule 1.1 is just two sentences: "A lawyer shall provide competent representation to a client. Competent representation requires the legal knowledge, skill, thoroughness and preparation reasonably necessary for the representation." This is a rudimentary (and rather commonsensical) rule, but a number of other rules and comments throughout the MRPC refer back to attorney competence.

The comment to Rule 1.1 adds some flesh to this bare bones competency requirement. First, Comment 1 states that the level of competency required is that of a general practitioner, not necessarily an expert or specialist in the area of law that applies to the client's needs. On the other hand, Comment 1 concludes saying that some (unusual) circumstances may require expertise or specialization.

Comment 2 adds that lawyers can take cases in areas of law that are new or unfamiliar: "A lawyer can provide adequate representation in a wholly novel field through necessary study." A lawyer unfamiliar with the area of law applicable to a new client can also seek help from another lawyer with more experience or knowledge on the subject (with informed consent from the client, if the other lawyer will actually participate in the representation). In other words, it is permissible for a personal injury lawyer to take a criminal case for the first time, and vice versa.

Of all the subtopics included by the Multistate Professional Responsibilty Examination (MPRE) examiners under "Competence, Legal Malpractice, and Civil Liability," this is the least-tested rule, except that each recent MPRE has included a question about the authority of the courts or state legislature to require continuing legal education courses (CLE). Comment 8 for Rule 1.1 concludes by saying that competency means lawyers must "engage in continuing study and education and comply with all continuing legal education requirements to which the lawyer is subject." A number of lawyers over the years have challenged their states' continuing legal education requirements as a violation of the First Amendment, Equal Protection, or some other civil liberty, always unsuccessfully. Courts have universally held that the state judiciary has inherent power to require lawyers to complete a certain number of CLE credits, to report their compliance with CLE requirements, and to suspend or disbar lawyers who fail to fulfill their CLE requirements. A majority of courts considering the issue have also held that courts have exclusive power to regulate lawyers—that is, the legislature can enact eligibility requirements for lawyers' initial bar admission, but not for ongoing license retention.

A number of courts have considered challenges to criminal convictions based on ineffective-assistance claims due to appointed counsel for the defendant being under suspension due to a failure to fulfill CLE requirements. Most courts have held that the lawyer's suspension does not constitute ineffective assistance of counsel, but a few have ruled to the contrary.

CLE requirements vary significantly across states. Several states have no CLE requirements; most require ten to fifteen hours of CLE per year. Colorado, Minnesota, North Dakota, Oregon, and Washington top the list with forty-five hours of required CLE per year. A number of states have additional requirements for lawyers who receive state funding as appointed counsel (indigent criminal defense, etc.).

QUESTION 1. **Doubling the CLE requirements.** The Supreme Court in a state adopted a new rule that doubled the number of continuing legal education hours each lawyer must complete every year in order to maintain a license to practice law in the state. The fifty-hour annual CLE requirement was the highest of any state in the nation. A legal aid lawyer challenged the new rule on constitutional grounds, claiming that it was unduly burdensome to poverty lawyers, given the high cost of the CLE courses, and therefore could leave more poor citizens without representation. Is the legal aid lawyer likely to prevail in this challenge?

A. Yes, because heavy CLE requirements create an undue burden on poverty lawyers, which violates the Equal Protection Clause of the Constitution.
B. Yes, because forcing lawyers to attend classes on subjects that may not pertain to their area of practice, and which may espouse views that they find politically objectionable, violates the First Amendment of the Constitution.
C. No, as state courts have inherent authority to impose reasonable regulations on the lawyers practicing in their jurisdiction.
D. No, because the state courts have absolute authority to impose any requirements they want on lawyers in their state.

ANALYSIS. Rule 1.1 says that lawyers must "engage in continuing study and education and comply with all continuing legal education requirements to which the lawyer is subject." Numerous constitutional challenges to CLE requirements have proved unsuccessful, as long as the rules come from the judiciary instead of another branch of government. Challenges very similar to the one described in this problem have consistently failed in the courts. Questions similar to this have appeared on the MPRE in recent years.

A is incorrect. Courts have held that CLE requirements do not violate the Equal Protection Clause even though they may be particularly burdensome for lawyers representing the poor, such as indigent criminal defense.

B is also incorrect. Courts have held that CLE requirements do not violate lawyers' First Amendment rights.

C is correct. The judiciary has inherent power to regulate the lawyers who practice before it. While this power has outer boundaries, every case that has considered the state judiciary's requirement of continuing legal education hours every year has upheld the regulation.

D incorrectly overstates the power of courts. The United States Supreme Court has actually held that certain state judicial rules about lawyers (especially those pertaining to lawyer advertising) violated the Constitution. To date, the inherent power of courts to impose CLE requirements on lawyers has withstood constitutional challenges in the state appellate courts.

QUESTION 2. Legislative intervention. A state legislature enacted a statute that doubled the number of continuing legal education hours each lawyer must complete every year in order to maintain a license to practice law in the state. The fifty-hour annual CLE requirement was the highest of any state in the nation. A legal aid lawyer challenged the new rule on constitutional grounds, claiming that it was unduly burdensome to poverty lawyers, given the high cost of the CLE courses, and therefore could leave more poor citizens without representation. In the alternative, the lawyer claimed that it violated the separation of powers. Is the legal aid lawyer likely to prevail in this challenge?

A. Yes, because heavy CLE requirements create an undue burden on poverty lawyers, which violates the Equal Protection Clause of the Constitution.

B. Yes, because the legislature has inherent power to enact legislation to protect the public, who need competent legal representation.

C. No, the state courts have exclusive inherent authority to regulate the lawyers practicing in their jurisdiction.

D. No, because continuing legal education is strictly voluntary, and the government cannot force lawyers to take courses.

ANALYSIS. All states have some statutes that apply to lawyers (especially the minimum eligibility requirements for seeking admission to the bar initially), but they normally do not relate to maintaining competence on an ongoing basis. The regulation of practicing lawyers is generally the exclusive domain of the courts. State ethical codes or disciplinary codes (most of which resemble the Model Rules) produced by the state bar will normally receive official adoption by the state supreme court. Courts that have addressed legislative attempts to regulate lawyer competence (for those already practicing) have concluded that such statutes violate the separation of powers doctrine. Similar questions to this one have appeared on the MPRE in recent years.

A is incorrect. Courts that have addressed constitutional challenges to the state CLE requirements have rejected claims that such rules violate Equal Protection principles.

B is also incorrect. The common law rule is that the judiciary has exclusive authority to regulate the legal profession, and courts have held that legislative intrusions into this domain violate the separation of powers doctrine.

C is correct. The common law rule is that the judiciary has authority (usually exclusive authority) to regulate lawyers.

D does not reflect the facts. Most states have rules requiring lawyers to complete continuing legal education hours every year. Courts routinely uphold license suspensions and disbarments for lawyers who fail to fulfill the CLE requirements.

QUESTION 3. **An unfamiliar area of law.** A client consults with an attorney, a solo practitioner, about a family law issue. The attorney has never practiced family law, but has spent his years as an attorney practicing strictly construction litigation issues. The attorney accepts the case, as he is only handling a few construction litigation cases at this time and could use the money this case will bring to his practice. The attorney believes he can get advice on how to handle the case from attorneys in the area who practice family law, and with whom he has good relationships. Is the attorney subject to discipline?

A. Yes, because attorneys are required to have experience in an area of law before accepting a case to ensure the attorney is competent to represent the client.
B. Yes, because attorneys are required to have assistance of other counsel when handling a case in an area of law in which the attorney is unfamiliar.
C. No, because an attorney who is authorized to practice in a state may practice regardless of his or her legal knowledge and skill.
D. No, even when a lawyer does not have to have prior experience to practice in a specific area of law, a lawyer can represent clients as long as they are able to provide competent representation.

ANALYSIS. Rule 1.1 requires that lawyers provide competent representation, but Comment 2 clarifies that this does not mean that a lawyer needs expertise, specialization, or even prior experience in a given matter. Lawyers can take cases that involve an unfamiliar area of law, because most lawyers could acquire the knowledge necessary for the representation with some research and conversations with more experienced practitioners. Note that some matters may be so complex that a novice should not attempt them, and certain areas of law, such as patent litigation, require admission to the patent bar. As Comment 2 explains, "A lawyer need not necessarily have special training or prior experience to handle legal problems of a type with which the lawyer is unfamiliar. A newly admitted lawyer can be as competent as a practitioner with long experience." Comment 4 adds, "A lawyer may accept representation where the requisite level of competence can be achieved by reasonable preparation. This applies as well to a lawyer who is appointed as counsel for an unrepresented person."

A is incorrect. The comment for Rule 1.1 explicitly says the opposite—an attorney does not have to possess experience in an area in order to provide competent representation to a client, although that could be true in some exceptionally complex matters or areas of law.

B is also incorrect. Lawyers do not have to have assistance of other counsel when handling a case in a new area of law, although Comment 2 offers this as a permissible option for the lawyer: "Competent representation can also be provided through the association of a lawyer of established competence in the field in question." This is a permissive rule, not mandatory.

C incorrectly overstates the lawyer's latitude in providing representation. As Comment 1 for Rule 1.1 provides, "Expertise in a particular field of law may be required in some circumstances."

D is correct. A lawyer can provide representation in a subject area that is new or unfamiliar to the lawyer. Comment 2 for Rule 1.1 says, "A lawyer can provide adequate representation in a wholly novel field through necessary study."

QUESTION 4. **A very complicated problem.** A client asks an attorney to represent him in a complex corporate taxation matter regarding the taxable earnings of an overseas corporate subsidiary that pays its American employees by direct deposits to bank accounts in the United States. All of the overseas subsidiary's sales occur in the United States, but all its products and supplies it purchases overseas, and half the employees are foreigners. A dispute with the IRS over the matter has been going on for several years. The attorney never took a tax course in law school and has no practice experience in the area. The attorney needs more clients, so he agrees to take the case and to conduct the necessary study to provide adequate representation. The client agrees to those terms, and the attorney undertakes the representation. A few months later, due to a change in which political party controlled the White House, the IRS abruptly dropped the case against the client, so the client receives a satisfactory resolution to the matter. Would the attorney be subject to discipline for undertaking this representation?

A. Yes, because another change in the political climate could put the client back into the same position as before.
B. Yes, because expertise in a particular field of law is a requirement in circumstances where the nature of the matter is complex and specialized, and the lawyer has no training or experience in the field.
C. No, because a lawyer can provide adequate representation in a wholly novel field through necessary study.
D. No, because the client obtained a satisfactory resolution to the matter, so the attorney's competence, or lack thereof, did not harm the client in any way.

ANALYSIS. Comment 2 for Rule 1.1 ends with a cautionary note: "Expertise in a particular field of law may be required in some circumstances." Earlier in the same comment, it explained the factors for identifying such instances:

> In determining whether a lawyer employs the requisite knowledge and skill in a particular matter, relevant factors include the relative complexity and specialized nature of the matter, the lawyer's general experience, the lawyer's training and experience in the field in question, the preparation and study the lawyer is able to give the matter and whether it is feasible to refer the matter to, or associate or consult with, a lawyer of established competence in the field in question.

Watch for MPRE questions involving remarkably complex matters and a completely inexperienced lawyer—multiple-choice questions lend themselves best to clear-cut scenarios, which often means extreme examples if the rule itself is ambiguous. The client in this question has an extremely complex situation, at least from a legal standpoint—international corporation taxation, something that does not lend itself to a quick research project. Note that a lawyer can be subject to discipline for incompetence even if a client was satisfied with the representation and the outcome was favorable from the client's standpoint. Of course, happy clients rarely file grievances against their lawyers, but another lawyer, judge, or government official familiar with the situation could do so.

A gives an incorrect reason, even though it could be a realistic scenario. The fact that the regulations or enforcement policies of a federal agency could change back to an earlier approach is not the reason the lawyer should be subject to discipline. The Model Rules do not focus on the actual consequences of the lawyer's behavior as much as the lawyer's compliance with the relevant rules. In this case, the lawyer could be subject to discipline for providing incompetent representation, even though the matter resolved in the client's favor (unrelated to the lawyer's representation), and regardless of the fact that the client could later face a problem with the same agency.

B is correct. The lawyer in this case is too inexperienced to take on a case involving corporate taxation of international entities.

C is incorrect, even though it states part of the rule. Even though Comments 2 and 4 to Rule 1.1 permit a lawyer under normal circumstances to take a case in a wholly novel field of law, the facts in this question present an unusually complex matter. It fits better with the warning in Comment 1, which refers to some circumstance in which expertise may be necessary.

D is incorrect. A lawyer can be subject to discipline regardless of whether the client is satisfied with the representation and regardless of the favorability of the outcome.

B. Rule 1.3—Diligence

Rule 1.3 is the shortest rule in the MRPC—it contains just one sentence: "A lawyer shall act with reasonable diligence and promptness in representing a client." The official comment adds a bit more material (five paragraphs), with some specific clarifications. First, Comment 1 adds an important limitation to the "zealous advocacy" of lawyers: "A lawyer is not bound, however, to press for every advantage that might be realized for a client. For example, a lawyer may have authority to exercise professional discretion in determining the means by which a matter should be pursued."

Second, lawyers have a duty to control their own workload so that they can give proper attention (competent representation) to each client's matters. It is a violation of Rule 1.3 to take on so many cases at once that the lawyer has to shortchange the representation of one or more matter. This is a special problem in public defenders' offices and legal aid clinics, which seem chronically understaffed (due to inadequate funding) for the need. Supervisors may assign an unreasonable number of cases to each lawyer in the office, and each lawyer has a duty to refuse to take cases that would make it impossible to provide competent representation for every client. Recent MPRE questions have tested this specific provision.

In addition, Comment 4 directs lawyers to let a client know in writing if the lawyer is not handling the appeal after the initial phase of a case has concluded. Watch for problems involving a genuine misunderstanding between the client and lawyer about whether the representation has concluded—the lawyer in such a case has usually failed to inform the client properly.

Finally, Comment 5 requires sole practitioners to have a plan "that designates another competent lawyer to review client files, notify each client of the lawyer's death or disability, and determine whether there is a need for immediate protective action." The latter provision (the requirement of a death-or-disability plan to transfer cases) has appeared in questions on the MPRE in recent years.

Despite the brevity of the rule, it turns out to be one of the most important rules for lawyers and law students alike. For lawyers, "neglect of a client matter" (the term for a violation of the diligence rule) is tied with "failure to communicate with the client" as the most common basis for state bar grievances or disciplinary actions against practitioners. For law students, it is important to remember that every MPRE contains at least one or two questions about Rule 1.3—it appears on each test. Neglect of a client matter can constitute a violation (and make the lawyer subject to discipline) even if the client suffered no injury, and even if the client obtained the desired outcome in the matter. Of course, a satisfied client is unlikely to complain to the bar, making disciplinary actions improbable, but it is certainly possible for the judge in a case or the opposing counsel to notify the bar of the lawyer's neglect.

QUESTION 5. **All's well that ends well.** A lawyer received a court appointment to represent an indigent criminal defendant in a complex case involving felony money laundering, counterfeiting, tax fraud, and other aspects of organized crime. The lawyer tried to refuse the appointment, explaining to the judge that she was handling too many other cases right then, and that she had never before handled a complex criminal case. The judge ignored her concerns and ordered her to take the case. The lawyer reluctantly took the case and did a minimal amount of work on it—no more than she would normally do for a simple misdemeanor matter, apparently as a type of protest. Ultimately, the prosecutor needed her client to agree to testify against another more important member of the same criminal conspiracy, and offered her client a surprisingly favorable (lenient) plea deal. The client was very pleased with the outcome of the matter and grateful to the lawyer who represented him. Could the lawyer be subject to discipline, based on these facts?

A. Yes, because she tried to refuse to accept a court appointment to represent an indigent defendant.
B. Yes, because she did not act with reasonable diligence in representing the client.
C. No, because the client obtained a favorable outcome and was satisfied with her representation.
D. No, because the judge forced her to take a case after she raised a reasonable objection to accepting the appointment.

ANALYSIS. Rule 1.3 says, "A lawyer shall act with reasonable diligence and promptness in representing a client." The lawyer in this problem intentionally gave her client's matter less attention than she should have, in order to protest having a burdensome court appointment foisted on her. Problems similar to this appeared on recent MPRE tests.

A is incorrect, though it can be a violation to refuse to accept court appointments without a valid reason. Her reason in this case was legitimate—she was concerned that her current caseload would prevent her from providing adequate attention to the matter.

B is correct. The lawyer in this case did not act with reasonable diligence in representing her client. It was proper for her to try to decline the case if she did not have time to handle it, given her other cases. Once the court forced the case on her, though, she had a duty to give it full, diligent representation. She should have asked for reasonable postponements in some of her other matters, or asked another lawyer to handle one or more of her other cases, at least temporarily.

C is incorrect—diligent representation is not dependent on client satisfaction or outcomes—a terribly neglectful lawyer might still win a case due to fortuitous mishaps befalling the opposing party. In such a case, the neglectful lawyer prevails despite her lack of diligence, not because of it. Even though a satisfied client is unlikely to file a grievance against the lawyer, the judge in the case, or another lawyer, could do so.

D is incorrect, though the judge should not have forced the case on a lawyer who is truly overwhelmed already with her caseload. Keep in mind that the judge may not have believed the lawyer (some lawyers will claim to be too busy even when they are not), or it may have been that she was the only lawyer on the court appointments list in that courthouse who did not have a conflict of interest preventing her from accepting the case.

QUESTION 6. **As many as possible, whatever the cost.** An attorney works as a public defender. The office is always underfunded, meaning they cannot afford to hire enough staff attorneys, and the current attorneys all carry an overload of cases. The attorney feels that she is unable to provide full representation to each client, as she must conduct about seven plea bargaining sessions for different clients per weekday, and usually meets the clients for the first time about fifteen minutes before each plea bargain session. Each plea bargain takes about an hour, with short breaks in between. The attorney strongly encourages nearly all of her clients to accept a plea bargain, because taking one case to trial will mean that the public defender's office must turn away about two dozen indigent clients. The attorney and her colleagues believe that it is better for defendants to have a little representation rather than none at all, and that most defendants would lose at trial anyway. Does the attorney have an ethical problem, under the Rules of Professional Conduct?

A. Yes, because a lawyer must control her workload so that each matter can be handled competently.
B. Yes, because it would be better for clients to have no lawyer at all than to rely upon a lawyer who is providing minimal or inadequate representation.
C. No, if most of the clients would, in fact, fare worse if they went to trial, then the attorney's representation is their best option.
D. No, because there is a special exception for public defenders in the Rules of Professional Conduct regarding diligence.

ANALYSIS. Comment 2 for Rule 1.3 says, "A lawyer's work load must be controlled so that each matter can be handled competently." This means that a lawyer with a full caseload must turn away some prospective new clients, or must transfer existing clients to another lawyer in order to accept a new case. This question illustrates an unfortunately common situation in legal aid clinics and public defenders' offices—funding is inadequate, and too few lawyers are on staff trying to meet an overwhelming demand for legal assistance of indigent clients. Managers at these offices may assign too many cases to each lawyer (this is an ethical violation on the manager's part), and the lawyers may take the cases out of a sense of obligation, but even good intentions can lead to ethical violations. In this case, the lawyer is not controlling her workload properly, and this illustrates what inevitably happens in such circumstances—the lawyer must shortchange her representation of some or all of her clients in order to maximize the number of people she represents. See also ABA Formal Op. 06-441, which addresses this subject in detail. Similar questions have appeared on the MPRE in recent years.

A is correct. Comment 2 for Rule 1.3 requires lawyers to manage their workload so that they can give adequate attention and diligence (competent representation) to each client. The lawyer has settled on the idea of minimizing her effort in each case in order to help more indigent clients—but some of these clients could accept pleas that they would have been better off refusing. In addition, hurried lawyers will usually have less leverage in plea bargaining negotiations—not only because they are desperate to avoid a trial, but also because they do not have enough time to develop possible defenses, check if the prosecutor's evidence is truly admissible, and so on. An experienced prosecutor can spot this uneven bargaining situation and exploit it by offering a less favorable plea, knowing the overworked defense lawyer will probably pressure the defendant to accept it.

B is incorrect, though it reflects the rationale that gives rise to many of these situations. Even though it is deplorable to have so many individuals in our legal system left without the legal representation they need, those who have lawyers must receive diligent, competent representation. This is an ethical duty for every attorney.

C is incorrect, as it relies on averaging the outcomes of these clients' cases rather than on the requirements of the Model Rules. Even if it is true that many defendants would fare worse at trial than they would if they accepted a plea offer, every lawyer owed each client a duty of diligent, competent representation. Pressuring every client to accept a plea offer overlooks the fact that some clients would actually fare better at trial, or at least would fare better if they held out longer for a better offer from the prosecutor.

D is incorrect, as there is no exception for public defenders in the rules about diligence. If anything, the client's stakes in a criminal case are higher than in a civil trial (if the client faces possible incarceration and other long-term penalties), making the lawyer's duty of diligence seem even greater.

QUESTION 7. **Strategic procrastination.** An attorney is representing the plaintiffs in a class action lawsuit over a mass tort, and the case has become surprisingly complex and time-consuming. The federal court has scheduled a five-week trial for the case, and the trial is coming up next week, meaning that the attorney must work long hours on trial preparation from now until then. The attorney has about twenty other open cases with other clients, but none of them have motions due until after the upcoming class action trial, so the attorney has been focusing exclusively on the class action suit and has been temporarily ignoring the other cases. The attorney has not commenced discovery on the other cases or responded to recent discovery requests, because they do not even have scheduled trial dates yet, and there is nothing new to report to the clients about the other cases, so the attorney has not been in touch with them for the last two or three months. Could the attorney be subject to discipline for procrastinating about these other cases?

A. Yes, because one class action lawsuit does not equal the individual cases of twenty other clients, and a lawyer has a duty to apportion time evenly across open cases.
B. Yes, because a client's interests can be adversely affected by the passage of time, and unreasonable delay can cause a client needless anxiety.
C. No, unless the lawyer has actually missed a deadline or statute of limitations, there is no rule violation in this instance.
D. No, as long as the class action lawsuit involves more clients in the class than the twenty individual clients who comprise the remainder of the lawyer's caseload.

ANALYSIS. Comment 3 for Rule 1.3 has harsh words about procrastination:

> A client's interests often can be adversely affected by the passage of time or the change of conditions; in extreme instances, as when a lawyer overlooks a statute of limitations, the client's legal position may be destroyed. Even when the client's interests are not affected in substance, however, unreasonable delay can cause a client needless anxiety and undermine confidence in the lawyer's trustworthiness.

Watch for MPRE questions in which the lawyer procrastinates or delays working on the client's matter for months (perhaps after agreeing to do it quickly), but the client suffers no harm and is still satisfied with the lawyer's performance. Even if the client is satisfied and the outcome is desirable, a lawyer can be subject to discipline for unreasonable delays or procrastination. Even if the client is pleased and does not file a grievance against the lawyer, others involved—a judge, judicial clerk, or a lawyer for another party involved in the matter could report the attorney.

A is incorrect, because a lawyer does not have a duty to allocate time evenly between cases. Some cases require far more time than others due to their relative complexity, and some cases are more urgent than others. The duty of the lawyer is to give each case the time it needs, and to do so as promptly as is necessary.

B is correct. The lawyer in this problem neglected the other matters unreasonably. Every lawyer must manage a caseload and decide which cases to work first, but ignoring some matters for an unreasonable amount of time can be a violation.

C is incorrect, because Rule 1.3 does not depend on outcomes or consequences—a lawyer has a duty of diligence even if no injury befalls the client.

D is also the wrong answer. The Model Rules do not allocate a lawyer's duties based on an even division of the number of clients. Some matters are simple and others very complex; some are urgent and others have no particular deadline. A lawyer cannot weigh one group of clients against another group and neglect the representation of the group that has fewer clients in it. A lawyer has a duty of diligence to each client that relies on the lawyer for representation.

QUESTION 8. **Preparing for the worst-case scenario.** An attorney has her own firm and works as a sole practitioner. She has been practicing law for about twenty years, and is now in her mid-40s. Recently, though, a routine visit to her doctor revealed indications of multiple sclerosis, and she has scheduled appointments with specialists for more testing. She has been struggling with several symptoms that usually result from this condition. Does the attorney have any ethical obligations toward her clients, at least related to her possible condition?

A. Yes, because each sole practitioner must prepare a plan that designates another lawyer to review client files, notify each client of the lawyer's death or disability, and determine whether there is a need for immediate protective action.
B. Yes, because every lawyer has an obligation to make sure that a medical condition or disability does not in any way influence her actions, decisions, or plans regarding client representation.
C. No, because lawyer medical information is strictly confidential and should not influence a lawyer's actions, decisions, or plans regarding client representation.
D. No, because clients need to feel that they can rely fully upon their lawyer's ongoing representation, and any planning or decisions based around potential disability or death could undermine the trust that is so essential to the attorney-client relationship.

ANALYSIS. Comment 5 for Rule 1.3 says that "each sole practitioner prepare a plan, in conformity with applicable rules, that designates another competent lawyer to review client files, notify each client of the lawyer's death or disability, and determine whether there is a need for immediate protective action." Note that the provision applies only to sole practitioners, not lawyers in firms with partners or multiple associates; presumably, the other lawyers in the firm can cover the cases of the lawyer who has died or who became disabled. Sole practitioners, of course, have no one else in their firm, so they must have a contingency plan to transfer cases to another lawyer in case the unthinkable happens. The MPRE has tested on this provision in recent years.

A is the correct answer. The lawyer in this problem is a sole practitioner. Even if she did not have a diagnosed condition, a sole practitioner must have an arrangement with another lawyer to take over their cases and contact their clients should they become disabled or they die suddenly. The onset of a debilitating disease illustrates the need for sole practitioners to have this type of contingency plan—she has a degenerative disease that is already symptomatic, and will probably become too disabled to manage her caseload at some point.

B is incorrect. The fact that the lawyer has a medical condition or disability is not what triggers the provision in Comment 5 of Rule 1.3—rather, it is the fact that the lawyer is a sole practitioner.

C is also incorrect. The confidentiality of medical information does not matter in this case—the rule is about sole practitioners, not sick lawyers, although the possibility of a medical disability is part of the rationale behind the rule.

D incorrectly brings the client's subjective needs into the sole practitioner rule. Clients do not even need to know who the backup person is with whom their lawyer has made such a contingency arrangement, unless perhaps the lawyer's withdrawal or demise is imminent.

QUESTION 9. **Every possible angle.** A client hired a lawyer to represent her in bringing a lawsuit against a manufacturer over a defective product that was very expensive. The attorney regularly represents plaintiffs in product liability cases. The client believes that the manufacturer has knowingly sold defective products to other customers as well, and wants the attorney to include a claim for "civil RICO" (accusing the manufacturer of racketeering) as part of the lawsuit. In addition, the client discussed reporting the manufacturer to various government regulatory agencies to try to get the company in trouble with them, as this might overwhelm the defendant with simultaneous litigation on several fronts, and might even bring out otherwise undiscoverable information about the manufacturer's wrongdoing. The attorney reluctantly adds the civil-RICO claim to the complaint and is not surprised when the judge strikes that claim at the request of the defendant. The attorney declines to notify government agencies about the manufacturer, and suggests that the client do that on her own, writing complaint letters to whatever agencies she has in mind. The attorney proceeds with the tort litigation and prevails, winning a favorable verdict for the plaintiff. Was it proper for the attorney to decline to pursue the regulatory attack against the manufacturer?

A. No, because a lawyer must act with commitment and dedication to the interests of the client and with zeal in advocacy upon the client's behalf.

B. No, because a lawyer is bound to press for every advantage that might be realized for a client.

C. Yes, because a lawyer is not bound to press for every advantage that might be realized for a client.

D. Yes, because the lawyer acquiesced to the client about the civil RICO claim, and a lawyer should not have to defer to the client on more than one unusual request in the same representation.

ANALYSIS. Comment 1 for Rule 1.3 says that the duty of diligence and zealous representation has boundaries: "A lawyer is not bound, however, to press for every advantage that might be realized for a client. For example, a lawyer may have authority to exercise professional discretion in determining the means by which a matter should be pursued." Misguided clients may sometimes request that lawyers use every conceivable angle or strategy to gain an advantage over the other party in a matter, but lawyers must preserve a semblance of civility and decorum, and often the lawyer feels it would be more advantageous to pick one strategy and stay with it. Here, the lawyer declines to file complaints against the other party with various regulatory agencies—something the client could do without legal representation, and that could distract from the complex litigation work at hand.

A is incorrect. Even though it is true that a lawyer must "act with commitment and dedication to the interests of the client and with zeal in advocacy upon the client's behalf," this does not mean that a lawyer has to use every tactic or method the client suggests.

B is also incorrect. The rule in Comment 1 of Rule 1.3 says the exact opposite—a lawyer is *not* bound to press for every possible advantage.

C is correct. The lawyer in this case does not have an obligation to do every spiteful thing the client suggests, especially if the primary task of the representation is labor-intensive, such as commencing litigation. Complaining to numerous government agencies is something the client can do alone. In addition, such acrimonious actions could negatively affect the lawyer's position in the eventual settlement negotiations.

D is partly correct but gives an incorrect reason. Even if a lawyer reluctantly agrees to carry out some of the client's misguided suggestions or requests, doing so would not trigger an obligation to do *everything* the client thought up from then on. Lawyers should be faithful to accomplishing the client's objectives (within the bounds of reason and legality), but should exercise their professional judgment about the details of how to arrive at those ends.

C. Rule 1.8 and Common Law—Malpractice

The MPRE usually contains at least one or two questions about legal malpractice actions, malpractice insurance, malpractice waivers, and so on. The examiners include these subjects under the heading "Competence, Legal Malpractice, and Other Civil Liability," and malpractice seems to be the most consistently tested topic under this heading. Unlike most of the delineated subjects tested, malpractice does not really have its own rule within the Model Rules. Rule 1.8(h) is perhaps the only section within any of the Model Rules that pertains directly to malpractice liability for lawyers, and MPRE questions about malpractice often focus on this provision and its associated comment. Other MPRE questions about malpractice appear to have their basis in common law or the Restatement of the Law Governing Lawyers.

Rule 1.8(h), which is part of the conflicts of interest rules, has two provisions. First, a lawyer shall not "make an agreement prospectively limiting the lawyer's liability to a client for malpractice unless the client is independently represented in making the agreement." Watch for questions on the MPRE about lawyers who include in their retainer agreement with clients a waiver of liability for malpractice. Do not overlook the clause that follows the word "unless." If a potential client actually has retained another lawyer who advises the client about the agreement with the new lawyer, then a waiver of malpractice liability is permissible. For example, a corporation may have in-house counsel that outsources litigation work for the corporation to one or more law firms in the area. In such a case, the client-corporation already has a lawyer representing it (that is, its in-house counsel) when it hires an outside lawyer to handle a lawsuit. In such a case, the in-house counsel can review the retainer and advise the corporate directors about the pros and cons of waiving malpractice liability for the litigator that it hires. Similarly, some litigation attorneys specialize in trial work but never handle appeals. If the trial lawyer's client has an appeal of the trial verdict, the client must find another lawyer to do the appeal. In such a case, the client may have the trial lawyer who has been representing here review the retainer agreement with the prospective appellate lawyer—and in this scenario, the appellate lawyer may include a waiver of potential malpractice liability.

On the other hand, it is not sufficient for the lawyer merely to advise the client about seeking independent legal advice before signing the malpractice waiver (unlike other provisions of Rule 1.8, or even the second provision of Rule 1.8(h)). The client must actually have another lawyer providing representation. Otherwise, the agreement limiting liability is improper, and the lawyer could be subject to discipline.

The second provision of Rule 1.8(h) says that a lawyer cannot "settle a claim or potential claim for such liability with an unrepresented client or former client unless that person is advised in writing of the desirability of seeking and is given a reasonable opportunity to seek the advice of independent legal counsel in connection therewith." This refers to situations when the malpractice has already occurred, and the lawyer wants to settle the matter quietly with the client (perhaps even before the client files a malpractice lawsuit). Unlike the first provision of Rule 1.8(h), this one does not require that the client actually have representation by another lawyer, but only that the attorney advise the client in writing of the desirability of retaining other counsel, and give a reasonable opportunity for the client to do so.

Comment 14 for Rule 1.8 adds some additional clarification, and the MPRE has included questions on each significant provision in the comment as well as the clauses in Rule 1.8(h). For example, Comment 14 says that Rule 1.8(h) does not "prohibit a lawyer from entering into an agreement with the client to arbitrate legal malpractice claims, provided such agreements are enforceable and the client is fully informed of the scope and effect of the agreement." Binding arbitration agreements within a client retainer contract are permissible.

Comment 14 goes on to provide, "Nor does this paragraph limit the ability of lawyers to practice in the form of a limited-liability entity, where permitted by law, provided that each lawyer remains personally liable to the client for his or her own conduct and the firm complies with any conditions required by law, such as provisions requiring client notification or maintenance of adequate liability insurance." Modern corporate forms such as LLCs and LLPs are permissible for law firms, even though the effect (and purpose) of such organizational forms is to limit the personal liability of the partners for malpractice.

Regarding legal malpractice insurance, it is important to remember two points for the MPRE. First, most states (49 states at the time of this writing) do *not* require attorneys to carry malpractice insurance, although several states require uninsured lawyers to provide notice to their prospective clients that they do not carry malpractice insurance. Second, many states (perhaps most) require LLCs and LLPs generally (not just law firms) to have a reasonable amount of liability insurance.

Third, Comment 14 allows lawyers to limit the scope of the representation at the outset (for example, transactional lawyers stating that they will not do litigation work if a dispute arises, trial lawyers refusing to handle appeals, and appellate lawyers refusing to handle the trial if there is a remand). Rule 1.2 specifically allows lawyers to restrict their representation to certain tasks, within reason. When a lawyer limits the representation to one phase of the legal work, he thereby escapes liability for malpractice that occurs in the other phases (done by other lawyers). At the same time, a lawyer cannot use a retainer that limits the scope of representation so much that a lawyer has no real obligations, as a backdoor way to evade possible liability down the road. As Comment 14 states, "[A] definition of scope that makes the obligations of representation illusory will amount to an attempt to limit liability."

Violations of the Model Rules do not necessarily constitute legal malpractice. The Preamble to the Model Rules flatly states, "They are not designed to be a basis for civil liability." Of course, rule violations could be evidence of negligence on the part of the lawyer—for example, failure to conduct a reasonable check for conflicts of interest could be the basis for a legal malpractice claim. Even so, a violation of the Model Rules does not necessarily mean that a lawyer would be liable in tort for malpractice. Malpractice actions, like most torts, require a showing of a duty of care to the client, causation, and damages, and a violation of the lawyer's ethical duties would be only one component of these three elements. Various affirmative defenses may be available, and contributory negligence by the plaintiff could negate the claim. From an evidentiary standpoint, students should remember that disciplinary proceedings by the state bar are administrative hearings, which have relaxed rules of evidence (especially hearsay) and procedure compared to civil trials. This means that the evidence forming the basis of the decision for a disciplinary tribunal may be inadmissible in court during a trial for malpractice. This principle has been the subject of questions on two recent MPRE tests. Note that there is an additional element for clients who suffer a wrongful criminal conviction due to a lawyer's malpractice—the client must first succeed in having the conviction set aside before asserting a claim for malpractice against the lawyer.

QUESTION 10. **Convicted due to the lawyer's malpractice.** A criminal defense lawyer represented a defendant in a criminal prosecution. The defendant had given an incriminating confession to the police during his first interrogation, but the police had never given him *Miranda* warnings. At the beginning of questioning, the defendant had stated that he wanted his lawyer and did not want to answer any questions without his lawyer present. The police said they would let him talk to his lawyer later, but for now, he had to answer some questions. The interrogators even threatened him with physical injury if he refused to confess, so he confessed under coercion. The confession should have been inadmissible at trial due to the lack of *Miranda* warnings, the questioning without his lawyer present, and the physical coercion. Nevertheless, the lawyer did not inquire about the circumstances of the confession and did not bother objecting to its admission at trial. The jury convicted the defendant, largely on the evidence of the illegal confession. The defendant retained a different lawyer on appeal, who raised the problem with the confession, but the appellate courts affirmed the conviction, until he had exhausted his remedies. The defendant then sued his original lawyer from prison for legal malpractice, claiming that he suffered significant damages due to the lawyer's negligence, given that he was unsuccessful in having his conviction overturned. Assuming the jurisdiction follows the majority rule and the Restatement of the Law Governing Lawyers, could the lawyer be liable for legal malpractice?

A. Yes, because his negligence in failing to object to the admission of the illegally obtained confession fell far below the standard for a reasonable lawyer in the profession.

B. Yes, because the lawyer negligently caused the conviction of the client, and the client suffered serious injury in the form of incarceration, which he could not overturn on appeal.
C. No, because the client was unable to convince an appellate court to overturn his conviction.
D. No, because the defendant was probably not actually innocent of the crime if he gave a full confession to the police during his first interrogation.

ANALYSIS. The Restatement of the Law Governing Lawyers says that a client who faced a wrongful conviction due to his lawyer's malpractice could indeed sue the lawyer for malpractice, even without the client proving his innocence. At the same time, the rule in most jurisdictions (and the Restatement) is that the client must have had that conviction set aside before bringing a malpractice claim. A defendant does not necessarily have to prove his innocence in order to win a reversal of his conviction on appeal—the burden to prove guilt is always on the government. In this problem, the client was unable to have his conviction overturned on appeal, so a malpractice remedy against the lawyer would not be available.

A is incorrect. The minimal standards of professional competence are part of the analysis for ineffective assistance of counsel claims, but are not enough to assert a legal malpractice claim against a lawyer.

B is incorrect, even though it contains the three essential elements for most tort actions. It is missing the additional requirement, found in most jurisdictions, that criminal defendants have their wrongful conviction set aside in order to have grounds for a malpractice action against the lawyer.

C is correct, because the rule in most jurisdictions is that a convicted defendant, when seeking damages for malpractice causing a wrongful conviction, must have had that conviction set aside in order for a tort remedy (malpractice) to be available.

D is the wrong answer because a wrongfully convicted client does not have to prove his innocence in order to bring a malpractice claim against the lawyer. Instead, he merely has to have the conviction overturned (set aside, reversed, etc.), which is a lower threshold than proving his innocence, and the burden is always on the government in criminal proceedings to prove the guilt of the accused.

QUESTION 11. **Automatic liability?** An attorney is a partner in a newer law firm that has no effective measures in place to ensure that lawyers in the firm conform to the Rules of Professional Conduct. An associate at the firm violates the rules, and the state bar investigates the policies and procedures in place at the firm. The state disciplinary authority has determined that the attorney is subject to discipline for his failure to take reasonable measures to ensure conformity with the rules. Because of this determination and the subsequent sanction, which of the following is true?

A. The determination of an ethical violation does not automatically mean that the attorney would be civilly or criminally liable.
B. The fact that the state bar found the attorney guilty of a violation of the rules, and imposed a sanction, means that the attorney is automatically liable in any legal malpractice action related to the violation.
C. The fact that the state bar found the attorney guilty of a violation of the rules, and imposed a sanction, means the attorney is automatically guilty in any criminal prosecution related to the violation.
D. The fact that the state bar already imposed a sanction for the violation precludes being subject to damages in a malpractice action or criminal sanctions in a criminal prosecution related to the same violation, due to the double jeopardy rules.

ANALYSIS. The Preamble to the Model Rules flatly states, "They are not designed to be a basis for civil liability." The Restatement takes the same position. Both acknowledge, of course, that a violation could be relevant for deciding whether a lawyer should be liable in tort, but it is not automatic. The conduct in this problem clearly violates the Rules of Professional Conduct, but that in itself does not guarantee that the violators will face tort liability. There are important differences between a civil suit and an enforcement action that could produce different results even when analyzing the same activity. A malpractice action includes showing damages (actual injury), causation, and must address various affirmative defenses, mitigating factors, contributory negligence by the plaintiff, and so on. In addition, hearsay evidence is admissible in an administrative hearing (like most disciplinary proceedings), but not in court, so the strongest evidence of the lawyer's violation could be inadmissible in a malpractice case, even though it is admissible at the disciplinary hearing.

A is correct. A determination by a state disciplinary authority that a lawyer violated the ethical rules does not necessarily trigger tort liability (that is, does not necessarily constitute legal malpractice). Of course, such a finding would be relevant evidence in a malpractice lawsuit, and a court could give it substantial weight. Even so, this is the best answer to this question.

B is incorrect, as it contradicts the Preamble to the Model Rules, as well as the Restatement. There is no automatic tort liability that results from an administrative decision (like a disciplinary hearing).

C also contradicts the Preamble of the Model Rules, and is therefore incorrect—a violation of the MRPC, even when established by a disciplinary tribunal, does not necessarily mean that the lawyer will have a criminal conviction. First, most of the ethical rules do not constitute "crimes" under state statutes or penal codes. Second, the burdens of proof and evidentiary rules are very different in criminal trials, compared to an administrative proceeding.

D is also incorrect. Double jeopardy rules pertain only to criminal prosecutions, not to civil lawsuits or administrative enforcement actions. An acquitted criminal defendant can still face a civil lawsuit and a separate administrative enforcement proceeding over the same incident that was the basis of the criminal prosecution.

QUESTION 12. **The uninsured lawyer who commits malpractice.** What is currently the requirement under the Rules of Professional Conduct regarding lawyers having liability insurance for legal malpractice claims?

A. The Model Rules require every practicing lawyer in the private sector to carry at least minimal liability insurance, but not government lawyers.
B. The Model Rules require lawyers practicing in certain areas, like real estate and family law, to carry malpractice insurance, but not lawyers doing criminal defense work.
C. The Model Rules do not require lawyers to have malpractice insurance, but many states require disclosure to clients if the lawyer is uninsured.
D. The Model Rules forbid lawyers to carry malpractice insurance because of the moral hazard problem—insurance provides a perverse incentive to take more risks or to be less careful.

ANALYSIS. Malpractice insurance is very common today for law firms, especially the larger firms. Insurance is a prudent way to manage risk, especially in an era when malpractice verdicts against firms have grown significantly in size and frequency. Nevertheless, most states do not require lawyers to have malpractice insurance, though several require uninsured lawyers to provide notice of their lack of insurance to prospective clients (or to the bar, in some jurisdictions). Of course, most lawyers have firms incorporated in some form (LLC, LLP, PC, etc.), which can provide some protection against personal liability. The MPRE has tested students' knowledge of this point on several recent exams.

A is incorrect, as the Model Rules do not have any requirement that law firms have malpractice insurance.

B is also incorrect—there is no requirement whatsoever in the Model Rules that lawyers carry liability insurance, regardless of the field of specialty or area of practice.

C is correct. The Model Rules do not require lawyers to carry malpractice insurance, and most states do not have such a requirement. Many (especially single-lawyer firms) are uninsured.

D wrongly states that it is impermissible for lawyers to carry malpractice insurance. Larger firms normally have malpractice insurance. It is true that insurance inherently presents moral hazard problems—all forms of insurance do—and insurance providers try to offset the moral hazard through deductibles, coverage limits, premium increases after claims occur, contractual obligations for the insured to refrain from certain high-risk activities, and so on.

QUESTION 13. **Settling a claim after committing malpractice.** A client retained an attorney to represent him in a car accident case. The client sought to recover $5,000 for damage to his vehicle and a few medical expenses the client incurred because of the accident. The attorney failed to timely file a lawsuit for the client before the statute of limitations ran. After realizing that the suit was barred because the attorney failed to timely file, the attorney sent the client a letter with a check for $20,000 and an agreement for the client to sign and return. The agreement stated that keeping the $20,000 check constituted acceptance of the agreement and that acceptance of the agreement included releasing the attorney for any malpractice claims against the attorney. Is the attorney's conduct proper?

A. Yes, attorneys can settle claims or potential claims for malpractice as long as the settlement amount is reasonable.

B. Yes, attorneys can settle claims or potential claims for malpractice as long as the agreement terms are provided to the client in writing and the settlement amount is reasonable in relation to what the client would expect to receive.

C. No, attorneys must advise the client of the importance of obtaining advice of independent counsel and provide reasonable time for the client to obtain such counsel prior to settling a claim or potential claim for malpractice.

D. No, attorneys cannot settle claims or potential claims for malpractice with clients.

ANALYSIS. Rule 1.8(h)(2) requires lawyers, when settling a claim (or potential claim) for legal malpractice with a former client or an unrepresented person, to advise the person in writing to seek independent legal counsel in connection with settling the claim, and to give the person a reasonable opportunity (that is, enough time) to do so. The attorney in this case did not advise the former client to seek independent legal counsel, and did not provide a reasonable opportunity to do so.

A is incorrect. Attorneys can indeed settle claims for reasonable amounts, but the Model Rules also require attorneys to advise the person in writing of the desirability of obtaining independent legal counsel. Note that if the lawyer had advised the person about this in writing, and had given the person a reasonable time to do so, the lawyer could have settled the claim, even if the person elected not to seek independent counsel.

B is also incorrect, due to what it omits. Rule 1.8(h)(2) prohibits a lawyer from settling a claim with a disgruntled client "unless that person is advised in writing of the desirability of seeking and is given a reasonable opportunity to seek the advice of independent legal counsel in connection therewith." It is not enough that the agreement terms are in writing and reasonable – they must also include verbiage exhorting the client to seek independent representation before settling the potential claim.

C is correct, reflecting the wording of Rule 1.8(h). The lawyer's conduct was improper because he did not advise the client to consult with another lawyer first, and the terms of acceptance did not provide a reasonable opportunity for the client to do so.

D is incorrect, as there is no prohibition against settling malpractice claims. Our legal system today encourages settlement of claims—over 90 percent of civil claims settle before trial.

QUESTION 14. The imaginary client. A patient of a well-known doctor suffers complications after her surgery, and believes she is the victim of medical malpractice. The patient writes to a lawyer, describing a medical-malpractice suit that the patient is contemplating, and she inquires about retaining the lawyer to represent her in the lawsuit. The lawyer never responds. Eventually, many months later, the statute of limitations expires for her claim. The patient then files a legal malpractice lawsuit against the attorney due to the failure to file a claim on the original case on time. Could the lawyer be liable for malpractice to the patient?

A. Yes, because lawyers have some duties even to potential clients, and it was reasonably foreseeable to the lawyer that if he did not respond, eventually the statute of limitations would expire on her claim.

B. Yes, because a lawyer can be liable for malpractice even to a non-client, if the lawyer violated the ethical rules in his interactions with the person.

C. No, because the lawyer has no duties to a person if there is no client-lawyer relationship explicitly in place.

D. No, because it was not reasonable for the patient to have relied upon the lawyer, as the lawyer never communicated to the patient.

ANALYSIS. This problem is intentionally similar to one of the examples in Section 14 of the Restatement of the Law Governing Lawyers. A lawyer can be liable in malpractice to a non-client—either a prospective client or a third-party beneficiary of one of the lawyer's clients—if the person reasonably relied upon the lawyer and then suffered an injury as a result.

A is incorrect, even though the statement is mostly true. It probably was reasonably foreseeable to the lawyer that a potential client could have the statute of limitations expire on a contemplated claim if the lawyer never responds to an initial inquiry. It is also true that the Model Rules impose some ethical duties on lawyers toward potential clients, such as a duty of confidentiality. Nevertheless, a crucial question for malpractice liability to non-clients (as opposed to disciplinary actions) is whether the non-client reasonably relied upon the lawyer, which is not the case here.

B is partly true and partly incorrect. A lawyer can be liable in malpractice to a non-client under certain circumstances, but ethical violations do not automatically trigger malpractice liability, as stated explicitly in the Preamble to the Model Rules.

C is untrue and therefore incorrect. Lawyers can have duties, such as the duty of confidentiality, to potential clients, or to third parties the lawyer knows will rely upon work the lawyer performs for a client.

D is correct. No client-lawyer relationship arose here, because the lawyer simply did not respond to the person's inquiry. It was unreasonable for the patient to rely upon a lawyer who never responded at all.

QUESTION 15. The disgruntled heir. An attorney agreed to draft a will for a new client who wanted to leave his entire estate to his children, but wanted to disinherit his estranged wife entirely. The will stated that the entire estate would pass to the children. After the client died, the wife claimed her statutory share, which in that jurisdiction was 50 percent of the estate, in spite of the instructions in the will. It should have been foreseeable to the attorney at the time of drafting that the will would not be sufficient to overcome the wife's claim to her statutory share, but he did not explain this to the client or recommend measures to circumvent the problem. Could the frustrated children have a viable claim against the attorney for legal malpractice?

A. Yes, because the heirs under a will always have privity to sue the lawyer who drafted the will.

B. Yes, because the client's intention was clear on the face of the will, and the lawyer therefore could be liable to the heirs even though they are not clients.

C. No, as there is no client-lawyer relationship between the attorney and the children.

D. No, because the lawyer did not violate any ethical or fiduciary duty in this case.

ANALYSIS. This is similar to a recent question that appeared on the MPRE and an example from the Restatement. A lawyer can be liable to the intended heirs under a will drafted by the lawyer, even though the heirs were not the lawyer's clients, if the client's intent was clear on the face of the document. The lawyer here did not exercise due competence or diligence, and failed to communicate to the client sufficiently enough for the client to make proper decisions.

A is incorrect. Even though heirs traditionally lacked privity with lawyers, and therefore often could not bring claims, modern law recognizes some circumstances under which non-clients, such as a third-party beneficiary, may hold the lawyer liable for legal malpractice.

B is correct. As the Restatement says, "When the claim is that the lawyer failed to exercise care in preparing a document, such as a will, for which the law imposes formal or evidentiary requirements, the third person must prove the client's intent by evidence that would satisfy the burden of proof applicable to construction or reformation (as the case may be) of the document." The will here clearly showed the client's intent, which the lawyer frustrated through his own malpractice.

C is partly incorrect. It is true that there was no client-lawyer relationship between the children and the attorney, but there are some circumstances under which lawyers may be liable to third-party beneficiaries of the work they perform for clients, such as drafting a will.

D is incorrect. The lawyer violated the duty of diligence and/or competence, as well as the duty to communicate adequately to the client.

D. Rule 2.3—Evaluation for Use by Third Persons

Continuing with the sections on malpractice, Rule 2.3 covers a special subset of potential malpractice actions—non-clients for whom the lawyer prepares an evaluation (an audit or report about outstanding legal liabilities, and so on) at the behest of one of the lawyer's clients. This Rule is almost never the subject of disciplinary actions against practitioners—case law and ethics opinions about this rule are rare or nonexistent. Nevertheless, the MPRE tests on this rule—especially with regard to duties toward third parties—on almost every test, and the questions are tricky.

Lawyers often must prepare written reports, analyses, memoranda, and other informational documents at the behest of clients, which the client will then turn over to a third party for review, who may rely on the lawyer's representations or opinions. In some cases, the client may even ask or authorize the lawyer to send the report directly to the other party. This is a common scenario in transactional work, in which a prospective buyer of a business or parcel of property may review (and rely upon) title opinions, reports, or legal appraisals by the seller's lawyer regarding potential liabilities, issues with the ownership interests, and so on. Similarly, some clients need lawyers to prepare reports or filings for institutional lenders (banks), insurers, outside auditors, or even government agencies. In addition, sometimes the third parties forward the lawyer's written assessments to yet other parties—say, their own lawyer or an institutional lender, who in turn forwards the report yet again to the bank's lawyer. An attorney cannot always predict who will eventually end up with the attorney's report, or how much they will rely on it.

The problem is that the lawyer must balance two types of duties in these situations—a duty not to deceive or mislead other parties (or assist the client in perpetrating fraud), and a duty to protect the client's interests and confidentiality. The client's interests come first, but do not cancel out the duties to the other party entirely—if a report will be unfavorable to a client, the lawyer must obtain the client's informed consent before delivering it to a third party. Even if the client already directed the lawyer to prepare an objective report and deliver it directly to the other party, if the lawyer realizes the report contains some unfavorable information, he must inform the client of this and obtain consent again before sending it on. At the same time, if the report/appraisal/title opinion has nothing damaging to the client's interests, a lawyer might prepare it and send it with only implied authorization from the client (that is, without the client's explicitly authorizing the delivery of the report directly to the other party).

Rule 2.3 itself mostly addresses the lawyer's duty to the client in this situation—that is, the duty to obtain the client's informed consent before providing a report to a third party. Comment 4 for Rule 2.3, on the other hand, contemplates some duties of the lawyer to third parties who will foreseeably rely on the report. In some cases, the comment says lawyers have an affirmative duty to make a disclosure: "For example, certain issues or sources may be categorically excluded, or the scope of search may be limited by time constraints or the noncooperation of persons having relevant information. Any such limitations that are material to the evaluation should be described in the report." On the other hand, lawyers also have a duty to refrain from making fraudulent statements (of law or fact) in evaluations covered under Rule 2.3, even if the client instructs the lawyer to include false information. In addition, Comment 2 requires that a lawyer's evaluation for use by third parties should identify the person who retained the lawyer to prepare the report.

As mentioned above, Rule 2.3 is rarely the subject of disciplinary actions, but the duties to non-clients delineated in the comment do come up regularly in legal malpractice lawsuits. This is one of the main areas of non-client malpractice actions against lawyers. MPRE questions about this rule generally ask if the lawyer's behavior was proper rather than if the lawyer could be liable.

QUESTION 16. Who is behind this report? A client wants to sell a parcel of commercial real estate, and he hired an attorney to represent him in the matter. As part of the representation, the client asked his attorney to prepare a thoroughly researched opinion memorandum concerning the title of the property, for the information of a prospective purchaser and the purchaser's prospective lender. The attorney gave the title opinion to the client, who gave it to the prospective purchaser, who in turn submitted it to the prospective lender. The prospective lender received and reviewed the attorney's title opinion, but was not aware that the lawyer who prepared the title opinion represented the seller of the property rather than the buyer. Could the attorney be subject to discipline for failing to disclose explicitly in the memorandum what party he represents and that he has a duty of loyalty and confidentiality to the seller?

A. Yes, because when a lawyer knows that third parties may rely on his written legal opinions, he has a diminished duty of loyalty or confidentiality to the original client.

B. Yes, because the title opinion should identify the person by whom the lawyer is retained, and should make this clear not only to the client under examination, but also to others to whom the results are to be made available.

C. No, because the lawyer's duty of loyalty, confidentiality, and candor runs only to the client who retained the lawyer.

D. No, because everyone in a commercial real estate transaction presumes that title opinion letters from lawyers represent the best interest of the seller of the property.

ANALYSIS. Comment 2 for Rule 2.3 requires that lawyers identify the client who retained the lawyer within the report or evaluation that third parties might rely on. The comment leads into this requirement by explaining that in some cases (as when there is a single prospective purchaser of a business or a parcel of real estate) the other party might misunderstand that the lawyer has a duty of loyalty to the seller instead. A lawyer may not disclose information to the non-client if the client has forbidden it, but the lawyer must disclose the identity of the client, to avoid misleading the other party in the transaction. In some situations, the other party may have been the first to request the report or evaluation (from the client), so it can become confusing for non-lawyers to see that the lawyer actually prepared the report for someone else, in the sense of the lawyer's duty of loyalty.

A is incorrect. The lawyer does not have a diminished duty of loyalty or confidentiality to the original client—in fact, if the client tells the lawyer to omit certain information from a report, the lawyer must do so. Even so, in order to prevent situations where a client would use a lawyer to perpetrate a fraud, lawyers must disclose within the report the identity of the lawyer's actual client who retained the lawyer.

B is correct and uses the verbiage from Comment 2. The lawyer in this case must disclose the identity of the client who hired the lawyer to prepare the report, to avoid misleading the third party that might rely upon the lawyer's evaluation.

C is incorrect. Comment 2 to Rule 2.3 says that whether there are legal duties to third parties is outside the scope of the Model Rules—that is, it is a matter of tort law, and specifically malpractice law. Other statutory mandates may also create duties for the lawyer (as those that apply to filing tax returns). At the same time, Comments 2 and 4 impose both affirmative duties and a negative duty on lawyers with regard to third parties, even if it is not a duty *to* the third party. First, the lawyer has an affirmative duty to disclose the identity of the client who retained the lawyer, and an affirmative duty to disclose any limitations on the scope of coverage in the report (that is, an indication of what the lawyer did not include). A lawyer has a negative duty to refrain from outright misrepresentations of law or fact.

D is also incorrect, as the Comment imposes an affirmative duty for the lawyer to identify the client, regardless of what conventional practice or presumed procedures in a particular industry may be.

QUESTION 17. **What's missing here?** An attorney represents a client before a government agency that enforces securities regulations. As part of the representation, the attorney must prepare an opinion concerning the legality of the securities registered for sale under the securities laws, for submission to the government agency, which requires such reporting. The client authorizes the attorney to prepare the written opinion, but insists that the attorney exclude any mention of a particular business loss the client's company incurred recently, in order to avoid upsetting the shareholders. In order to preserve the client's confidential information, the attorney prepares the written opinion without the information the client asked him to withhold. The report does not mention that it excludes some unfavorable information. The attorney prepares the written opinion and gives it to the client, who submits it to the agency. Is it proper for the attorney to follow the client's instructions in preparing this report?

A. Yes, because when the lawyer is retained by the person whose affairs are under examination, the general rules concerning loyalty to client and preservation of confidences apply.

B. Yes, because it is the client's decision what to disclose to the agency; and the client alone will bear the consequences if the agency concludes later that the client submitted a misleading report.

C. No, because when a lawyer's report categorically excludes certain issues or sources, then the lawyer must describe in the report any such limitations that are material to the evaluation in the report.

D. No, because an attorney has a duty to include in the report whatever information the government agency requested, as the agency will rely upon the report in making its decisions.

ANALYSIS. Comment 4 for Rule 2.3 says that when lawyers prepare a report or evaluation for use by non-client third parties, "certain issues or sources may be categorically excluded, or the scope of search may be limited by time constraints or the noncooperation of persons having relevant information." The report must describe "any such limitations that are material to the evaluation." A lawyer must honor the client's wishes to limit the coverage of a report or evaluation, but the limitation must receive mention in the report, so that third parties relying upon the report will not find it misleading.

A is partly true, but incorrect. The general rule is that the duties of confidentiality and loyalty to the client still apply when a client retains a lawyer to prepare an evaluation for use by a third party. Nevertheless, Comment 4 to Rule 2.3 requires that limitations on the scope of the evaluation must receive mention within the report, to avoid misleading the reader.

B is incorrect. There are statutory requirements about what must be in a report to a federal agency, and a lawyer cannot assist a client in illegality. Lawyers can face liability—in tort (malpractice) and under some federal reporting statutes—for misleading evaluations that the lawyer prepared according to the client's instructions.

C is correct. The lawyer in this case must mention such limitations that the client imposed on the lawyer in preparing the report. Otherwise, the lawyer would be assisting the client in perpetrating a fraud.

D is incorrect for this problem, although this may be correct for certain reports and certain agencies. For example, one SEC regulation permits lawyers to disclose information without the client's consent to rectify violations of federal securities laws for which the lawyer's services were involved. (17 C.F.R. 205.3(d)(2)(iii)). Normally, however, a lawyer should either follow the client's instructions about the scope of the evaluation, or withdraw from the representation in order to avoid participating in illegal conduct.

QUESTION 18. They will find out eventually. A government agency contacts an attorney, who works as in-house counsel for Corporation, and requests a report about some of Corporation's activities that come under the agency's regulatory jurisdiction. As the attorney begins to investigate the matter to prepare the report, he learns that the information requested by the agency will subject Corporation to significant regulatory enforcement sanctions, and if the information became public, would adversely affect Corporation's share price. At this point, the agency has not issued a subpoena and compliance with the request is voluntary, although the agency could compel the disclosure eventually. The managers and directors of Corporation instruct the attorney not to submit the report until the agency issues a subpoena, in order to buy some time to mitigate their regulatory violations. May the attorney prepare the report and submit it to the agency at this time?

A. Yes, because a lawyer should have whatever latitude of investigation seems necessary as a matter of professional judgment.
B. Yes, because the agency will inevitably subpoena the information anyway, and delaying merely provides the managers with an opportunity to conceal their wrongdoing.
C. No, because even if the managers and directors consented to the disclosures, the attorney should not disclose information that will adversely affect the shareholders.
D. No, because when a lawyer knows or reasonably should know that the evaluation is likely to affect the client's interests materially and adversely, the lawyer shall not provide the evaluation unless the client gives informed consent.

ANALYSIS. Rule 2.3(b) instructs a lawyer to withhold an evaluation (or postpone performing it) if the lawyer realizes that it necessarily include disclosures that will have material adverse consequence on the client. In this case, the lawyer has done the investigation at the behest of the client (the management), and has discovered information that will subject the client to a regulatory enforcement action. The client asked the lawyer to withhold the report, and the lawyer should do so. The situation might be different if an investigation were already underway and a subpoena had been issued, but at this point, that has not occurred—the lawyer can wait until the agency begins demanding information, and then revisit the issue. As the subsection says, "When the lawyer knows or reasonably should know that the evaluation is likely to affect the client's interests materially and adversely, the lawyer shall not provide the evaluation unless the client gives informed consent."

A is incorrect. Rule 2.3(b) is clear that a lawyer does not have absolute discretion about what to do with a report—the primary duty is still to the client.

B is irrelevant to the Model Rules and therefore is incorrect. It does not matter that the information presently undisclosed will eventually become public—the Model Rules require the lawyer to avoid disclosures that would be adverse to the client without the client's informed consent.

C is partly correct, but partly incorrect. It is true that under Rule 1.13, the lawyer has a duty to the corporation client (which could be the same as the shareholders in many contexts), but for purposes of reports prepared for third parties at the behest of a corporate client, the attorney should acquiesce to the wishes of the management that directs the representation.

D is correct. Clients sometimes ask lawyers to prepare evaluations or reports for use by third parties, a common instance of which are government regulators. Even though lawyers may have some legal duties to third parties who might rely upon the report (and there may be special statutory or regulatory duties when the recipient is a government agency), the lawyer retains a primary duty to the client. If the client instructs the lawyer to stop preparing an unfavorable report or to withhold it, the lawyer should comply, as in this case.

QUESTION 19. Seller beware. A client intends to purchase a parcel of real estate, and retained an attorney to analyze the seller's title to the property. The attorney requests information from the seller regarding the seller's original acquisition of the property, and obtains additional information from the local tax assessors and title registry. The attorney concludes that the seller does not have clear title to the property, and informs the seller of this opinion when the seller asks him about it. The seller forbids the attorney to disclose the information to the prospective purchaser of the property and insists that he showed the attorney his documents about the original acquisition of the parcel with the understanding that the attorney would not say anything unfavorable. May the attorney inform the prospective purchaser of his opinion about the title?

A. Yes, because remaining silent or withdrawing from representation at this point would make it easier for the seller to perpetrate a fraud on the purchaser.
B. Yes, because the seller does not have a client-lawyer relationship with the attorney.
C. No, because the attorney is bound by the duty of confidentiality to keep the information private.
D. No, because the seller did not provide informed consent.

ANALYSIS. Comment 2 for Rule 2.3 warns readers to pay special attention to which party is actually the lawyer's client:

> The question is whether the lawyer is retained by the person whose affairs are being examined. When the lawyer is retained by that person, the general rules concerning loyalty to client and preservation of confidences apply, which is not the case if the lawyer is retained by someone else. For this reason, it is essential to identify the person by whom the lawyer is retained.

In this problem, the purchaser retained the lawyer, not the seller. The seller is the one whose property the lawyer is examining, and the seller made some disclosures to the lawyer. For purposes of answering MPRE questions on Rule 2.3, it is important to pay close attention to which party retained the lawyer—sometimes it is the party under examination, but sometimes it is not. The lawyer does not have a duty of confidentiality to the seller. Of course, the lawyer should make clear to a non-client under examination that he represents the other party, so that the person does not make disclosures against their own interest under the misimpression that the lawyer has a duty to protect the information. Comment 2 adds, "This should be made clear not only to the person under examination, but also to others to whom the results are to be made available." The facts given in this problem are silent as to whether the lawyer made this clear to the seller.

A is partly true but partly incorrect. It is true that a lawyer cannot assist another party (such as a seller when the lawyer represents a buyer) in defrauding one of the lawyer's clients. The immediate problem, though, is that the lawyer has no client-lawyer relationship with the seller, and probably has no reason to acquiesce to the seller's wishes on this point.

B is correct. The lawyer is not representing the seller and does not owe the seller any particular duties regarding the information about the title examination. The attorney should have warned the seller when asking for the information that the attorney represented the buyer, but it is not clear that he did not do that. Even if the lawyer failed to make this point clear to the seller, the seller probably cannot control what the lawyer does with the information the seller disclosed, though he may be able to file a grievance against the lawyer if the lawyer misled him in order to obtain the information. In addition, the lawyer obtained further information from the local government offices about the property, and the seller would have no right whatsoever to control what the lawyer does with that information.

C is incorrect—the lawyer does not have a duty of confidentiality toward the seller, because the seller is not the lawyer's client. Of course, the lawyer does have a duty of confidentiality to the client, which covers even the information that the lawyer obtains from other sources, such as the seller or the government office—so the client (the purchaser) could forbid the lawyer from telling anyone else the information in the future.

D is incorrect because the lawyer did not need to obtain informed consent from the seller. The seller assented to divulging some information as part of moving forward with a real estate transaction. The lawyer represents the other party, and did not need to obtain informed consent from the seller in this case. Of course, Comment 2 to Rule 2.3 does require the lawyer to inform the seller that the lawyer represents the buyer instead, and the facts are silent about whether that occurred. This is not a duty to obtain informed consent, however—it is merely a duty to avoid misleading a non-client third party

QUESTION 20. Just go with it. An attorney represents a client, who wants to sell his business. A prospective purchaser has required from the client an evaluation of the business' solvency, detailing its current liabilities, potential liabilities, revenue, and assets. The client provides the attorney with documents pertaining to each of these issues, and explains to the attorney in confidence that he has often understated the earnings of the business in order to avoid paying taxes on the business profits. Now he is concerned that the prospective purchaser will undervalue the profitability of the business and refuse to pay an appropriate price to purchase it. He asks the attorney to adjust the earnings figures upward by 25 percent, the same amount by which the client falsely lowered them in the corporate records, in order to portray the business accurately to the potential purchaser. The attorney finds this objectionable and prepares a report based on what the records actually say regarding the earnings, and gives the evaluation directly to the purchaser. When the client learns about this, he explains to the prospective purchaser over the phone what happened. Despite the low reported earnings, the purchaser pays the client's asking price for the business, because of the client's truthful representations over the phone. Could the attorney be subject to discipline for his conduct in this matter?

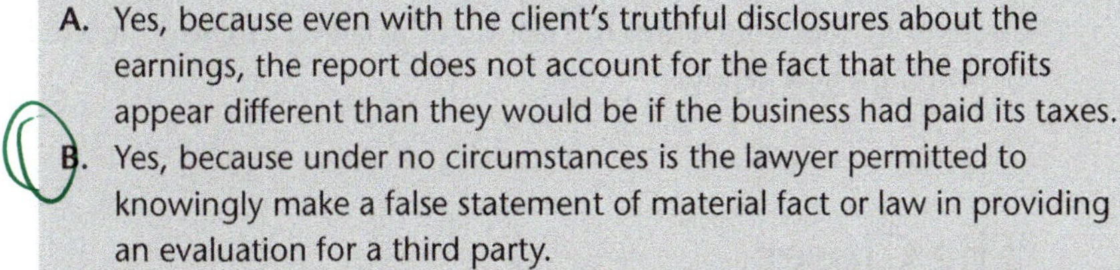

A. Yes, because even with the client's truthful disclosures about the earnings, the report does not account for the fact that the profits appear different than they would be if the business had paid its taxes.

B. Yes, because under no circumstances is the lawyer permitted to knowingly make a false statement of material fact or law in providing an evaluation for a third party.

C. No, because the lawyer's evaluation accurately represented the earnings reported in the corporate records.

D. No, because the client's phone conversation with the purchaser ensured that the purchaser was not relying on false information when he made his decision.

ANALYSIS. Comment 4 for Rule 2.3 strictly prohibits knowingly providing false information in a report to a non-client third party. This rule applies to false statements of law or statements of fact. The lawyer in this problem learned from the client that the business records had understated the earnings of the business—in other words, the client had falsified the records that formed the basis of the attorney's report. The attorney prepared a report based on records that he knew were misleading and gave the report directly to the other party. Even though the lawyer may appear scrupulous or honest at first, the lawyer violated the rule nonetheless and gave the seller a false report - he refused to adjust the numbers upward somewhat arbitrarily solely to make the business more appealing to the potential buyer. It also does not matter that the client explained the entire situation to the buyer after the fact and that the buyer was agreeable.

A is partly incorrect. It is true that the report the client requested, with the earnings corrected to their actual amount, overstates the value of the business because it does not account for the unpaid taxes due to the prior years of false recordkeeping. If the IRS were to uncover the fraud at some point in the future, the client could be liable for back taxes with interest—a significant liability. Even so, the fact that the client's proposal would also have been materially false does not justify the lawyer's action of providing the other party with a report based on records the lawyer knew to be false.

B is correct. Under no circumstances may a lawyer make a false statement of material fact in a report for a non-client third party. This broad rule applies even when the client urges the lawyer to submit the false report, and even when the other party endorses the false report after becoming fully aware of the matter.

C is incorrect. Even though the lawyer's evaluation accurately represented the earnings reported in the corporate records, the client had informed the lawyer that the records understated the earnings—that is, that the information was false. A lawyer cannot knowingly incorporate false information into an evaluation for a non-client third party.

D is also incorrect. The buyer's acceptance of the situation, after becoming aware of it, does not change the fact that the lawyer violated the Model Rules by sending a false report.

E. The Closer

Competence, diligence, and malpractice liability overlap conceptually—all pertain to lawyers' mistakes or the duty to avoid such mistakes. Yet the adverse consequences of practitioner error can come from three different sources—malpractice actions by the client or third parties, disciplinary actions by the state bar, and sometimes sanctions from a federal agency. Of course, lawyers can also face liability for other types of torts and breaches of contract. Often a single representation involving one or more mistakes can subject the lawyer to more than one type of these adverse actions.

QUESTION 21. **Estate planning.** A lawyer who has previously done only residential real estate closings agreed to represent a new client in a complex estate planning matter for a client who owns numerous residential and commercial properties. The estate assets also include numerous securities (stocks, bonds, and commodity shares), and an art collection. The elderly client has had children with each of his three wives over the years. Concerned about being responsible for a case with such high stakes and conceptual difficulty, the lawyer includes in the representation agreement a provision that limits his liability for any tax consequences or contested inheritance issues, which are unfamiliar to him. At the same time, he does not try to limit his liability for the portions of the representation that pertain to the real estate, as he knows that area well—the limitations on liability apply only to specific areas. The lawyer informed the client in writing of the advisability of "seeking a second opinion" before signing the representation agreement, but the client consulted with no other lawyers and signed the document, along with giving oral consent to the provisions limiting liability on certain points. The client added a codicil to the will explaining that under no circumstances should the executor of the estate (the client's eldest son) or any heirs sue the lawyer for malpractice.

The lawyer competently handled the disposition of all the real property within the client's estate except for one small parcel of commercial property, for which he made a mistake with recording the transfer. He also surprised himself by dealing with the tax issues (estate and capital gains tax) properly, after a few weeks of research and consultations with other attorneys. Unfortunately, the lawyer made some serious errors with the federal reporting and notification requirements that applied to some of the client's securities, which later resulted in penalties assessed on the estate. In addition, the lawyer arranged for temporary storage of the art collection in a storage rental facility, without climate controls, and the most valuable paintings sustained damage. What adverse consequences could the lawyer face for his mistakes?

A. None, because he attained competence on the tax issues, which were previously unfamiliar to him, and he shielded himself effectively from liability with the provision in the representation agreement, for which he advised the client to seek a second opinion.

B. The lawyer could face disciplinary action for taking a matter beyond his competence or ability to acquire competence, but not malpractice liability, due to the codicil and to the provision in the representation agreement.

C. The lawyer could face both disciplinary action (for taking a matter for which he lacked competence and for neglect) and could be liable in tort under a bailment theory for the damaged artwork, and could face personal sanctions from the government for his erroneous reporting about the securities.

D. The lawyer could not be subject to discipline for the provision in the representation agreement, because he advised the client to seek independent representation, and would not face disciplinary actions for incompetence, as he was familiar with real estate transactions, which were an important part of the estate.

ANALYSIS. Rule 1.1 requires competent representation—and by implication, that lawyers do not take cases beyond their acquirable competence. Lawyers have a duty to exercise diligence and care (the opposite of negligence) under Rule 1.3. Violations of these duties can trigger disciplinary actions but also could furnish the basis for a malpractice (negligence) action. Attempts to limit one's own malpractice liability prospectively with waiver-like provisions in a representation agreement violate Rule 1.8(h), unless the client actually has representation by independent counsel (not merely advised to seek independent representation). Presumably, the provisions would not only violate the Model Rules, but would be ineffective in shielding the lawyer, although there is little case law on this point.

A is incorrect. Even though the lawyer obtained competence on the tax issues, other components of the representation, such as the securities and handling the art collection, were outside his competence. Worse, the lawyer was evidently aware of this fact, as he tried to limit his liability on those points. Advising a client to seek independent representation before signing a malpractice waiver is insufficient under Rule 1.8(h).

B is partly correct and partly incorrect. It is correct that the lawyer may face disciplinary action for taking complex matters beyond his reasonably acquirable competence. The provision in the representation agreement violates Rule 1.8(h), and the codicil appears to be merely precatory, with no binding legal force on the addressees or the courts.

C is correct. It is insufficient that the lawyer warned the client to seek a second opinion—Rule 1.8(h) requires that the client actually have independent representation in order to waive legal malpractice liability prospectively. The lawyer could probably face tort liability for the damaged art, and probably for the securities violations as well (less clear), but could certainly face personal penalties from the government for reporting violations.

D is completely incorrect. Rule 1.8(h) requires that the client actually have independent representation if a lawyer attempts to limit liability prospectively—warnings are not enough. In addition, even though the client was competent to handle part or perhaps most of the representation, his incompetence in the other areas would subject him to disciplinary action.

Stevenson's Picks

1. Doubling the CLE requirements	C
2. Legislative intervention	C
3. An unfamiliar area of law	D
4. A very complicated problem	B
5. All's well that ends well	B
6. As many as possible, whatever the cost	A
7. Strategic procrastination	B

8.	Preparing for the worst-case scenario	A
9.	Every possible angle	C
10.	Convicted due to the lawyer's malpractice	C
11.	Automatic liability?	A
12.	The uninsured lawyer who commits malpractice	C
13.	Settling a claim after committing malpractice	C
14.	The imaginary client	D
15.	The disgruntled heir	B
16.	Who is behind this report?	B
17.	What's missing here?	C
18.	They will find out eventually	D
19.	Seller beware	B
20.	Just go with it	B
21.	Estate planning	C

5

Client Confidentiality—Rule 1.6

CHAPTER OVERVIEW

A. The Closer

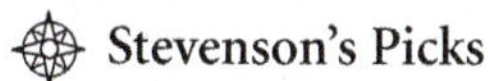
Stevenson's Picks

Model 1.6 covers the duty of confidentiality that lawyers owe to their clients. The Multistate Professional Responsibility Examination (MPRE) examiners have announced that confidentiality questions constitute 6 to 12 percent of the MPRE, which means there are between three and seven confidentiality questions on each test, in the second tier of subjects in terms of their importance for the exam. The examiners claim that they also test common law doctrines of attorney-client privilege and attorney work product, but of the two, only the former has appeared on the MPRE in recent years. The MPRE typically includes one question about whether a client waived privilege inadvertently by some specific action. The remaining questions under this category are always from Model Rule 1.6 and its delineated exceptions.

The basic confidentiality rule is straightforward enough, but there are numerous specific exceptions. Such exceptions lend themselves easily to the multiple-choice question format, so most of the questions are about the exceptions rather than the basic rule. The underlying rule is in Rule 1.6(a): "A lawyer shall not reveal information relating to the representation of a client unless the client gives informed consent, the disclosure is impliedly authorized in order to carry out the representation or the disclosure is permitted by paragraph (b)." Section (b) lists seven exceptions, and a final section (c) imposes an affirmative duty on lawyers to ensure that even inadvertent disclosures do not occur (e.g., through lack of security on a computer network, etc.). The official comment for Rule 1.6 is extensive—twenty enumerated paragraphs—making it one of the longest comment sections anywhere in the Model Rules.

Before moving to the exceptions, it is important to note the parameters of the basic confidentiality rule: it applies to all information the lawyer obtains relating to the representation of a client, regardless of the source. Unlike the doctrine of privilege, which covers only communication by a client to a lawyer, the duty of confidentiality covers information from any source—potential witnesses, the opposing party, private investigators who work for the lawyer, the lawyer's other clients, the lawyer's own research (including Internet research), anonymous tips, and so on. In fact, the duty of confidentiality can apply to information that the client does not even know—the lawyer has a duty to tell no one but the client about information learned from these other sources. "Disclosure" applies even to indirect disclosures, that is, a lawyer disclosing information that in turn "could reasonably lead to the discovery of such information by a third person." (See Comment 4 to Rule 1.6.) It also includes lawyers using the information to benefit themselves at the client's expense.

In addition, confidential information can include even the name of the client or the fact that the lawyer represents the client. Of course, the identity of the client and the fact that the lawyer represents the client are usually necessary disclosures to carry out the objectives of the representation (filing a lawsuit, incorporating a business, filing documents with government agencies, and so on), so normally these are "impliedly authorized" disclosures. Nevertheless, a client may consult (on one occasion or many times) with a lawyer merely for legal advice, without asking the lawyer to take any action on behalf of the client; and in such a case, the lawyer may not disclose the fact that the client has consulted with him, unless the client authorizes the disclosure.

Client authorization is another important parameter of the basic rule. Rule 1.6 forbids *unauthorized* disclosures. If a client authorizes the lawyer to disclose certain information—either explicitly or impliedly—the prohibition of Rule 1.6 does not apply. Comment 4 to Rule 1.6 discusses the implications of client authorization—for example, a lawyer presumably has implied authorization to talk to other lawyers in the same firm about the client's case, unless the client actually forbids it. "Lawyers in a firm may, in the course of the firm's practice, disclose to each other information relating to a client of the firm, unless the client has instructed that particular information be confined to specified lawyers."

The duty of confidentiality is also permanent—it does not end when the representation concludes. Years later, even after a client's eventual death, the lawyer cannot permissibly disclose confidential information related to the representation.

The duty under Rule 1.6 runs only to the client. As long as a client authorizes a particular disclosure, a lawyer does not necessarily have to protect the confidentiality of other sources who provide information to the lawyer, if they are not the lawyer's clients. "Client" includes current clients, former clients, and prospective clients. For example, if a prospective client comes to the lawyer for an initial consultation and the lawyer declines to take the case (whether due to a possible conflict of interest or because the lawyer does not handle that type of case), the lawyer cannot disclose the information that the individual shared during the interview.

Moving on to the exceptions in Rule 1.6(b), the first three are to prevent clients from doing serious harm to themselves or to third parties—death or serious bodily harm (to anyone), serious financial harm (or property damage) to others through crime or fraud using the lawyer's services, and to prevent harms already caused from continuing. The remaining four exceptions relate more to the lawyer's interests, starting with disclosures to secure legal advice about how to comply with the Model Rules. Exceptions also include disclosures to establish a claim against a client (usually for unpaid fees) or to defend against a claim or prosecution (for malpractice or illegal activity), disclosures to comply with a court order, and the minimal disclosures needed to screen or conflicts of interest. The exceptions to prevent harm to others are the most recent additions and the most controversial.

The ethical duty of confidentiality, which is relatively new to our legal system (appearing in the early 1970s), overlaps somewhat with longstanding common law doctrines of privilege and attorney work product, but there are important distinctions. All three protections can, and often do, apply to the same information. Privilege is primarily an evidentiary-exclusionary rule—a basis for objection to official requests for information, as from a court or enforcement agency. Confidentiality forbids disclosures made even in informal, social settings. Privilege, once breached even by the lawyer, is no longer available to the client—breach of privilege constitutes waiver and makes the information admissible (the client may subsequently have a malpractice action against the lawyer, but cannot re-invoke privilege in the current matter). Confidentiality, in contrast, does not disappear merely because the lawyer wrongfully disclosed the information on a previous occasion—and the lawyer could be subject to discipline, not just malpractice liability. Courts generally cannot order disclosure of privileged information, but they can order the disclosure of otherwise confidential information. Finally, note that privilege applies only to information disclosed by the client herself to the attorney (for seeking legal advice or representation), whereas confidentiality can apply to information from any source.

The privilege questions are few in number and usually relate to waiver. A client (or the client's lawyer) can waive privilege inadvertently by revealing the information to another party—for example, someone who overhears a chat in an elevator, or documents filed with another government entity, or even a failure to make a timely objection to the demand for information. In addition, note that privilege applies to information, but not to underlying facts. At the same time, a lawyer's observations that are the *product* of a privileged conversation with a client—such as a lawyer's observation of a criminal defendant's secret money cache as a result of a client telling the lawyer where to find it—would come under the protection of privilege.

QUESTION 1. What's in a name? A government entity provides grants to a legal aid office that represents indigent individuals. The government entity requires reporting of the names of clients, brief factual summaries, and the type of representation involved for all matters where the government entity's funds provided the financial support for the representation. An attorney works for the legal aid office. The government entity uses this information to ensure that the funding is going to its intended purposes and complies with various statutory requirements. Most of his clients are uneducated and unsophisticated, so he does not explain to them how the finances work for the legal aid office or that he must disclose their information. Is it proper for the attorney to represent legal aid clients without obtaining their informed consent to the disclosures required by the funding agency?

A. Yes, because the information is going to a government entity, not to a private party, so the disclosure does not violate the Rules of Professional Conduct.

B. Yes, because the client names, basic facts, and type of case do not constitute confidential information that would require client authorization for disclosure.

C. No, because the client names, basic facts, and types of cases are confidential information, and require client authorization for disclosure.

D. No, because information disclosed by a lawyer about a client to the government automatically constitutes a breach of the duty of confidentiality.

ANALYSIS. Basic facts, including names and types of cases (the type of information that may fill database entries), are confidential information. Furthermore, sending information from one government entity to another constitutes disclosure, regardless of intended use, and such disclosure requires informed consent. The attorney needed to explain to the client where the information was going and how it would be used in order to obtain informed consent. *See* ABA Formal Op. 96-399.

A is incorrect because disclosure requiring client authorization includes communications or transmissions from one government entity to another. Just because the attorney works for the government does not mean that they may share clients' confidential information with any other government employee.

B is incorrect. Basic facts, including names and types of cases, are confidential information, and they require informed consent and client authorization for disclosure.

C is correct because even facts as basic as these listed are protected as confidential under the Rules of Professional Conduct, and they would require informed client authorization for disclosure.

D is incorrect because not all disclosures of confidential information to the government constitute a breach of the duty of confidentiality. If the client authorizes the disclosure, the attorney may disclose confidential information to the government without breaching their duty.

QUESTION 2. **Third-party billing.** An attorney uses an outside billing service to track client billing and send bills to clients each month. The attorney keeps track of his time, and submits computerized reports by e-mail to the billing company at the end of each workday about how much time he spent on which tasks for which clients. The billing company calculates the monthly totals and sends detailed bills to clients on the attorney's behalf. The attorney found this outside billing company online, visited their website, downloaded their app, and used their online lawyer registration form to create an account with the company. At one point in setting up the account and downloading the app, the attorney had to click on an "I accept the terms and conditions" of a long user agreement that the attorney scrolled through quickly, without reading. Clients are not aware that the attorney uses an outside billing service until they receive their bills. Has the attorney violated his ethical duties to his clients?

A. Yes, because a lawyer must not outsource components of the representation, including billing, to non-lawyers.

B. Yes, because submitting the client names, time worked, and tasks involved constitutes a disclosure of confidential information for which clients must provide informed consent beforehand.

C. No, because a lawyer may outsource administrative tasks to non-lawyers for a reasonable fee.

D. No, because a lawyer entitled to a fee is permitted to prove the services rendered in an action to collect it.

ANALYSIS. Basic facts, including client names, times worked, and tasks involved—the type of information that may fill database entries—are confidential information. Furthermore, sending information to a contracted billing company (or any private third party) constitutes disclosure, regardless of intended use, and such disclosure requires informed consent. The attorney needed to explain to the client where the information was going, and how others would use the information, in order for the lawyer to obtain proper informed consent. *See* ABA Formal Op. 08-451.

A is incorrect. A lawyer may outsource components of their representation, but only if they inform their client where the information is going and how it is being used, and only if the client authorizes such a disclosure beforehand.

B is correct because even facts as basic as these listed are protected as confidential under the Rules of Professional Conduct, and they would require informed client authorization for disclosure.

C is incorrect. Basic facts (including names and billing lines) are confidential information, and they require informed consent and client authorization for disclosure.

D is incorrect because the lawyer's discretion in the use of third-party services does not supersede the duty of confidentiality.

QUESTION 3. **Discussing a case with the partners.** An attorney is a partner in a seven-lawyer firm. A client retained the attorney to handle his workers' compensation matter. The attorney did discuss with the client that he would normally disclose to the other partners in the firm some of the details about his cases and clients, and the client expressly forbade the attorney from telling anyone in his firm anything about his case. Nevertheless, at the weekly meeting of the partners, as everyone discussed their pending cases, the attorney explained the client's case and solicited input from the partners. One partner had an ingenious suggestion that would have been very helpful to the client's case. The attorney mentioned to the client in their next phone call that one of his partners had made a brilliant suggestion that could turn the case in the client's favor. The client was upset that the attorney had discussed the case with anyone else. Was it proper for the attorney to discuss the case with the others at the firm?

A. Yes, because a lawyer is impliedly authorized to disclose client information to other partners in his firm merely from the fact that the representation has been undertaken, regardless of client attempts to limit such necessary disclosures.

B. Yes, because the routine check for potential conflicts of interest presumably already eliminated any potential injury to client that could result from the disclosure.

C. No, because lawyers in a firm may not disclose to each other information relating to a client of the firm if the client has instructed that particular information be confined to specified lawyers.

D. No, because a lawyer is never permitted to discuss client matters with other lawyers in the firm without express client authorization.

ANALYSIS. The client must consent to any disclosure of confidential information, which includes any information pertaining to their representation. The client may also restrict disclosure further by specifying certain people with whom the lawyer may not disclose information, or they may specify that the lawyer may not share certain information with anyone (including fellow attorneys at their firm). In this case, the lawyer would breach his duty of confidentiality by disclosing the information outside of the bounds his client has specified. *See* Rule 1.6, Comment 5.

A is incorrect. The client may restrict disclosure of his information as narrowly as he chooses, including prohibiting the lawyer from discussing it with his own partners.

B is incorrect. Regardless of whether there may be conflicts of interest, the client has narrowed and re-established the bounds of confidentiality of his information, and the lawyer must abide by his restrictions.

C is correct because it was not proper for the attorney to disclose information about his client's case after the client had requested that the information not be disclosed.

D is incorrect because the lawyer (in most cases) may disclose information to other lawyers in his firm; the firm itself is bound to a duty of confidentiality. Unless otherwise specified, lawyers may discuss their clients and cases with other lawyers in their firm.

QUESTION 4. **Test results.** A client was with three friends in a car when a police officer stopped the vehicle. During the stop, the police officer found cocaine and marijuana in the vehicle. The prosecutor charged the client for possession of a controlled substance. The prosecutor did not charge anyone for possessing marijuana, though it was illegal to possess such a substance in the jurisdiction where the vehicle was stopped. The attorney knows the client uses marijuana. The client has expressed that he has never used cocaine but that he knows a friend that was in the car uses it. The client takes a drug test at the attorney's recommendation. The drug test shows the client negative for controlled substances, but positive for marijuana. The attorney wants to use the drug test to show it was unlikely that the cocaine found in the car belonged to the client. Nevertheless, providing the drug test to the prosecutor would reveal that the client tested positive for marijuana and might lead to charges based on the marijuana found in the vehicle at the time of the stop. The attorney asks his client if he can show the prosecutor the drug test as evidence that the client did not use cocaine around the time of the finding and that the cocaine likely did not belong to the client. The client tells the attorney he can share the results with the prosecutor. Did the attorney act properly?

A. Yes, because an attorney is impliedly authorized to carry out the representation of a client, including revealing confidential information.
B. Yes, because an attorney can disclose confidential information if the client permits the attorney to do so.
C. No, because attorneys shall not reveal any confidential information despite what the client requests or authorizes.
D. No, because the client must give informed consent and the attorney did not make the client aware of the risks and reasonable alternatives.

ANALYSIS. Rule 1.6(a) states: "A lawyer shall not reveal information relating to the representation of a client unless the client gives informed consent, the disclosure is impliedly authorized in order to carry out the representation or the disclosure is permitted by paragraph (b) [a list of exceptions]." Except for the cases listed in (b), an attorney should not disclose information about a client or their case unless the client gives the attorney permission. Additionally, the permission which the client gives must be "informed consent," which requires the attorney to explain the material risks of the course of action in question (in this case, disclosure) as well as denote any relevant reasonable alternatives to that course of action. In this case, the attorney explained only part of the consequences of disclosure (namely, the positive consequences) without explaining potential risks or alternative courses of action. The consent is therefore not informed consent, and the attorney acted improperly.

A is incorrect because an attorney may not disclose a client's confidential information without the informed consent of the client, and the attorney's implied authorizations do not include the disclosure of confidential information.

B is incorrect. Although the attorney informed the client of the purpose of disclosing the information, the attorney did not inform the client of the risks of, or reasonable alternatives to, such a disclosure. The consent that the client gave the attorney, therefore, does not constitute informed consent.

C is incorrect because it is too broad; if the client authorizes the attorney to disclose confidential information, the attorney may make the disclosure.

D is correct because the attorney neglected to inform the client of the potential risks of disclosure, including marijuana-related charges, or alternatives to disclosure before obtaining consent. The consent was therefore not "informed consent" as set forth in Rule 1.6.

QUESTION 5. **Asking for advice.** An attorney is representing a client who is a notorious celebrity-turned-criminal. The attorney is confused about whether he may publicly disclose information that he learned in confidence from his client if the information is already a matter of public record, and his research indicates there is a split of authority on this question. The attorney calls another lawyer who specializes in lawyer malpractice and lawyer disciplinary matters to seek advice about what course of action would comply with the Rules of Professional Conduct. The other lawyer, an expert in legal ethics, agrees to provide an opinion and to keep the conversation a secret. The attorney tries to use a hypothetical to explain the problem, but given the client's national reputation and celebrity status, the other lawyer knows immediately who the client is, and can easily surmise the nature of the confidential information. Is the attorney subject to discipline for disclosing confidential information about his client?

A. Yes, because the attorney used a hypothetical that was obvious enough that the other lawyer immediately knew the identity of the client and the client's information that the attorney was supposed to protect.

B. Yes, because a lawyer's confidentiality obligations generally preclude a lawyer from securing confidential legal advice about the lawyer's personal responsibility to comply with the rules.

C. No, because a lawyer may reveal information relating to the representation of a client to the extent the lawyer reasonably believes necessary to secure legal advice about the lawyer's compliance with the Rules of Professional Conduct, even when the lawyer lacks implied authorization to make the disclosure.

D. No, because a lawyer may generally disclose confidential information to another lawyer as long as the other lawyer promises to keep the conversation secret, and the other lawyer has a reputation for complying with the ethical rules.

seeking advice abt complying w/ MRPC

ANALYSIS. One of the exceptions to the unauthorized-disclosure restriction allows lawyers to disclose (even without implied authorization) client-representation information to secure legal advice for compliance with the Rules of Professional Conduct, to the extent that the attorney reasonably believes is necessary in order to secure the advice. This provision can be found in Rule 1.6(b)(4), with further clarification in Comment 9. In this case, the attorney used a hypothetical and did not directly identify his client, which would be a reasonable disclosure in order to obtain advice, even if the attorney's ethics expert could surmise the client's identity and circumstances due to factors outside of the attorney's control.

A is incorrect because, although the other lawyer was able to surmise the nature of the information, the attorney did not directly identify the client or directly address the circumstances of the case and only disclosed information to the extent the attorney reasonably believed was necessary to obtain legal advice about compliance with the Rules of Professional Conduct.

B is incorrect because the attorney's personal responsibility to comply with the rules generally precludes confidentiality obligations, which themselves are obligations to comply with the rules.

C is correct because the attorney only revealed information relating to the client's representation to the extent reasonably believed necessary to obtain legal advice about compliance with the Rules of Professional Conduct.

D is incorrect because the other lawyer's reputation is irrelevant to confidentiality obligations, and the attorney must only disclose information reasonably believed necessary to obtain legal advice about compliance with the rules.

QUESTION 6. **Under orders.** An attorney represents a client before an Administrative Law Judge in a regulatory enforcement matter. The Administrative Law Judge orders the attorney to disclose whether the client was informed by counsel about the regulatory requirements in question before the violation occurred. The client forbids the attorney to answer the question. The attorney initially objects, but the Administrative Law Judge insists. Could the attorney be subject to discipline for disclosing such confidential client information to the Administrative Law Judge?

A. Yes, because an Administrative Law Judge is not a court or tribunal for purposes of the exceptions to the confidentiality rules that might permit disclosures in response to a court order.

B. Yes, because a lawyer shall not reveal information relating to the representation of a client unless the client gives informed consent.

C. No, because a lawyer may comply with an order to reveal information relating to the representation of a client by a court or by another tribunal or government entity claiming authority pursuant to other law to compel the disclosure.

D. No, because the information relates only to what the lawyer told the client, not to what the client told the lawyer, so the duty of confidentiality does not apply.

ANALYSIS. Rule 1.6(b)(6) allows a lawyer to disclose confidential information "to comply with other law or a court order," which settles the apparent conflict here between complying with the duty of confidentiality and meeting the demands of the Administrative Law Judge. A lawyer may comply with any court order or authority pursuant to other law, which compels the disclosure.

A is incorrect. The Administrative Law Judge here fits the requirements of an authority pursuant to other law as described in Comment 15.

B is incorrect because it was proper for the attorney to disclose the information in compliance with the Judge's order pursuant to other law.

C is correct because it was proper for the attorney to disclose the information in compliance with the Judge's order pursuant to other law.

D is incorrect because the duty of confidentiality applies to all communications relating to representation (lawyer-to-client and client-to-lawyer).

QUESTION 7. The victim's story. An attorney represented a client in a misdemeanor criminal matter involving minor vandalism. The attorney interviewed the victim, who incurred the property damage, hoping to learn more about the value of the damage and how frequently vandalism occurs in that neighborhood. The property owner explained to the attorney that the client had been demanding "protection money" from him and other business owners in the neighborhood for a long time, and that the vandalism followed his refusal to continue paying the protection money. The amount involved was substantial, and the attorney realized that the client could face much more serious charges for extortion. The attorney never discussed this with the client, and the client gladly accepted a plea bargain offer for a few months' probation on the misdemeanor vandalism charge. Several years later, the client died in a car accident, and the property owner became a business-world celebrity when he published a book about how businesses transform neighborhoods. A reporter eventually found the attorney and interviewed him about the vandalism incident, several years prior, that had damaged the property owner's building at the time. The attorney explained that the incident was actually part of a larger extortion operation and that the business owner had handled the matter nobly. Should the attorney be subject to discipline for this disclosure?

A. Yes, because the confidentiality rule applies not only to matters communicated in confidence by the client but also to all information relating to the representation, whatever its source.

B. Yes, because the disclosure violated the attorney-client privilege.

C. No, because the attorney did not receive the confidential information from his own client, but rather from the client's victim, whom he did not represent.

D. No, because the disclosure occurred after the client was dead, so it could no longer harm the client.

ANALYSIS. Comment 3 for Rule 1.6 distinguishes between the overlapping areas of attorney-client privilege (which applies only in judicial and other proceedings in which the lawyer may have to produce evidence obtained directly from a client), and the duty of confidentiality, which is much broader. "The confidentiality rule, for example, applies not only to matters communicated in confidence by the client but also to all information relating to the representation, whatever its source." Here, the lawyer publicly disclosed information that he obtained from another source—not the client—and made the disclosure after the client's death. This disclosure violated the duty of confidentiality, but not the attorney-client privilege.

A is correct. Even though the attorney obtained the information from a source independent of the client—and even if the client did not know the attorney had the information—it comes under the duty of confidentiality and the disclosure was impermissible.

B is incorrect. Attorney-client privilege does not apply to information a lawyer obtains from an independent source (not the client) during a representation. In addition, normally the client is the holder of the privilege, that is, the one who must assert it in a proceeding to block a requested disclosure, and the client is deceased.

C is also incorrect. It does not matter that the lawyer obtained the information from a party that he did not represent—in fact, the victim of his client—because the duty of confidentiality applies to "*all* information relating to the representation, whatever its source." (Emphasis added.)

D is irrelevant. Unlike some of the other duties of lawyers under the Model Rules, the duty of confidentiality continues after the representation and after the client's death. Note that if the client authorized the lawyer to make disclosures after the client's death, then disclosures would be permissible.

QUESTION 8. **Fighting over the fees.** A client met with an attorney for a free consultation, and explained that she had met with two other lawyers for consultations and that she planned to hire one of the three to provide the legal services necessary to set up her professional business. The attorney needed to make a good impression on the client, so he mentioned a few prominent accountants and physicians in town whom the attorney had represented and helped with incorporating their partnerships or practice groups. These former clients had never explicitly authorized the attorney to disclose his representation of them in these matters. The client hired the attorney, and the attorney provided the legal services necessary to set up her business. Unfortunately, a dispute arose between the client and the attorney over the fees, and this fee dispute turned into litigation between the attorney and the client. In order to support his claims and defenses in the fee dispute, the attorney had to disclose to the tribunal exactly what he did for the client and the complexity of the issues involved, which necessarily involved the disclosure of confidential information. Was it proper for the attorney to disclose this confidential information about the client merely to prevail in a fee dispute?

A. Yes, because the representation of the client ended when the fee dispute began, so the attorney has no remaining duty of confidentiality to the client.
B. Yes, the lawyer may reveal information relating to the representation to establish a claim in a fee dispute between the lawyer and the client.
C. No, because the former clients did not authorize the attorney to disclose that he had represented them or the nature of the matters involved in the representation.
D. No, because the duty of confidentiality continues after the client-lawyer relationship has terminated, including the prohibition against using such information to the disadvantage of the former client.

ANALYSIS. Rule 1.6(b)(5) provides an important exception to the duty of confidentiality: situations in which the lawyer needs "to establish a claim or defense on behalf of the lawyer in a controversy between the lawyer and the client." Typical examples are fee disputes, such as the one described here, or legal malpractice actions by a client against the lawyer. The fact that the client refused to pay an agreed-upon fee, and forced the lawyer to litigate against his own client in order to obtain payment, has opened the door to the lawyer disclosing any information necessary to prevail in his claim.

A is incorrect. The duty of confidentiality does not end when the representation ends—it is permanent. The only reason the lawyer can make the disclosures is that the lawyer must do so in order to establish a claim, and defend against various accusations, to overcome the client's refusal to pay the fees.

B is correct. Lawyers have a right to receive reasonable payment for their services, and clients who force a lawyer to litigate over the fees trigger this important exception to the duty of confidentiality.

C is incorrect. Even though the client did not authorize the disclosures (normally a prerequisite if the regular duty of confidentiality applies), the fee dispute comes under the exception in Rule 1.6(b)(5).

D is partly true but partly incorrect. It is true that the duty of confidentiality applies after the end of the representation, but there is an exception to the duty when the lawyer must establish claims or defenses in a legal dispute with the client.

QUESTION 9. **Stories over drinks with friends.** An attorney represented a client, who was a defendant in a criminal prosecution. The client's trial ended in a conviction and a life sentence. After all possible appeals were complete, the attorney's representation of the client ended. The attorney sent the client a letter, which the client received in prison, explaining that his representation was now ending and providing a detailed accounting of all billing matters. No outstanding bills remained. Several years later, the attorney met with some former law school classmates at an alumni event, and they swapped stories over drinks about some of their cases over the years. The attorney mentioned the client, but only by first name, and explained how the guilty verdict felt like a failure on his part even though he knew the client was guilty because the client's friends and family members had all witnessed the crime and told the attorney privately what they had seen. Could the attorney be subject to discipline for disclosing confidential client information?

A. Yes, because the information the attorney disclosed did not come from the client, but from friends and family members who had betrayed the client by telling the attorney that they saw the client commit the crime.

B. Yes, because the duty of confidentiality continues after the client-lawyer relationship has terminated.

C. No, because the defendant was no longer his client, as the representation had ended several years before.

D. No, because the client is already serving a life sentence for the crime in question, so the disclosure could not possibly be prejudicial to the client.

ANALYSIS. Comment 20 for Rule 1.6 states tersely, "The duty of confidentiality continues after the client-lawyer relationship has terminated." The lawyer had an ongoing duty to safeguard the client's information permanently unless the client authorized otherwise. The fact that the lawyer omitted the client's last name from the story is insufficient to protect the client, as other lawyers present might be familiar with the case. Life sentences usually apply only to serious crimes, such as murder, and such crimes receive attention in the media and legal community.

A is incorrect. Comment 3 for Rule 1.6 clarifies that the duty of confidentiality applies to all information gleaned during the representation, whatever the source. It does not matter that the information did not come from the client (although this *would* matter for purposes of the separate attorney-client privilege rule). It also does not matter whether the sources of the information were unsympathetic, treacherous, or otherwise blameworthy.

B is correct. The duty of confidentiality does not end when the representation terminates. The lawyer should not have disclosed that the client's family witnessed the crime and told the lawyer privately what they had seen.

C is incorrect. It does not matter that the defendant is no longer a client of the attorney, because the duty of confidentiality is permanent—it does not end when the representation ends.

D is irrelevant. The duty of confidentiality does not depend on how damaging or harmless the disclosure might be—any disclosure of confidential information, obtained from any source, could be a violation of Rule 1.6. Besides, even if the disclosure could not result in any additional legal sanctions or punishment against the defendant, it could damage the reputations of the family members involved, as well as intangible interests of the former client (such as his relationship with his family members, his memories of them, and so on).

QUESTION 10. **The prospective client.** An attorney has been practicing law for two years, and has represented some law school graduates in their appeals before the bar when the Board of Law Examiners had denied the applications for licenses on character or fitness grounds. A former law school classmate who was a first-year student when the attorney was a third-year student visits the attorney in his office. The former classmate was on law review and graduated near the top of the class, but now he expresses concern about the character portion of the bar application. "I need you to represent me before the Board of Law Examiners," the former classmate said. The attorney asks the classmate to explain the problem. The classmate then explains a history of heroin addiction in college, which led to a criminal conviction and a period of incarceration; but a successful rehabilitation program enabled the student to beat this addiction and live drug-free throughout law school. The classmate does not want to disclose this on the bar application. The attorney declines to represent the former student, and later receives a call from the bar examiners inquiring about this former classmate's character and fitness. The attorney then recounts everything the classmate said about the past addiction and criminal conviction. Was the attorney's conduct proper in this situation?

A. Yes, as bar admission is a delineated exception to the usual attorney-client relationship, so confidentiality and privilege do not apply.

B. Yes, because no attorney-client relationship exists until the parties sign a retainer, so the confidentiality rules do not apply here.

C. No, as the student did not actually ask the attorney to write a recommendation letter or get involved in the matter, but was just seeking advice.

D. No, the former classmate here was a prospective client, and the attorney owed a duty of confidentiality, even though no representation occurred.

ANALYSIS. Comment 1 to Rule 1.6 says that the duty of confidentiality may apply even to prospective clients (including those whom the lawyer declines to represent), and incorporates by reference Rule 1.18(b). That provision says, "Even when no client-lawyer relationship ensues, a lawyer who has learned information from a prospective client shall not use or reveal that information. . . ." In other words, Rule 1.18 extends Rule 1.6's duty of confidentiality to prospective clients who come to the lawyer for an initial consultation.

A is incorrect. There is no exception in the Model Rules for bar applications under which the duty of confidentiality would not apply to a prospective client, as here.

B is also incorrect. Rule 1.18 creates a duty of confidentiality to prospective clients who have not yet—and may never—sign a retainer agreement, and Rule 1.6 incorporates this provision by reference in Comment 1.

C does not reflect the facts in the question. The former classmate said, "I need you to represent me," which is sufficient to make the person a prospective client for purposes of Rule 1.18 and Rule 1.6.

D is correct. Lawyers often learn some confidential information during consultations with prospective clients, including those whom the lawyer declines to represent (due to conflicts of interest, lack of time or expertise, etc.). Here, the lawyer should not have disclosed the information, because the individual had approached the lawyer and made the disclosures in the course of seeking representation.

A. The Closer

The duty of confidentiality compels lawyers to limit the information they share with others to whatever the client expressly or implicitly authorized the attorney to disclose. There are some important exceptions for preventing harm to others or to the lawyer himself, whether to avoid personal liability for the client's actions, to defend against claims by the client, or to obtain fees a client refuses to pay. Under the Model Rules, these exceptions are permissive rather than mandatory—a lawyer may properly preserve a client's confidences even when that results in serious harm or even death to another person. It is also important to remember how the duty of confidentiality overlaps partly—but only partly—with the evidentiary rules about privilege and attorney work product.

QUESTION 11. **Too much information.** In anticipation of a round of settlement negotiations over a business partnership breakup, a client authorized his lawyer to disclose that the client was having personal financial troubles, but added that the lawyer should "leave it at that—don't elaborate too much." The lawyer was to attend the settlement conference without the client.

At the settlement conference, when the other parties pressed the lawyer about why his client seemed so inflexible about a settlement amount for dissolving the partnership, the lawyer said that his client was having personal financial problems. Counsel for one of the other partners asked, "Like what? Perhaps the other partners could do something to help, and it would make it easier to resolve the partnership breakup." The lawyer then explained that everyone in the room must keep the following information completely confidential, and went on to explain that his client was on the verge of bankruptcy due to a gambling problem. He also explained, in a hushed tone, that the client had even assigned his equity share in the partnership to a business rival of the partnership in order to pay off a personal loan. The others were shocked, with a mixture of sympathy for their partner's gambling problem, and alarm at the implications of their main market rival owning a significant share of the existing partnership. One of the other attorneys, however, checked the terms of the original partnership agreement, and informed the rest that equity interests in the company were unassignable without a majority vote of the other partners, making the assignment legally void. Could the lawyer be subject to discipline for the disclosures he made at the settlement conference?

A. Yes, because the lawyer asked the other lawyers to keep the information completely confidential, which would force them to violate their duty of loyalty to their own clients.

B. Yes, because he went beyond what the client had authorized him to disclose, thus breaching his duty of confidentiality to the client.

C. No, as the client impliedly authorized the disclosure before the settlement conference.

D. No, because the disclosure was necessary to prevent, mitigate, or rectify substantial injury to the financial interests of the other partners.

ANALYSIS. The client in this question explicitly authorized the lawyer to disclose the existence of the client's personal financial problems, but instructed the lawyer not to elaborate. Instead, the lawyer told the other parties about the client's gambling problems, impending bankruptcy, and even the assignment of his equity interest. Merely asking his hearers to keep the information confidential does not mitigate the violation in this case.

A is incorrect. The fact that the lawyer asked the others to keep the information secret is irrelevant—they have no obligation to heed him on this point, and presumably would inform their clients about it. The duty of confidentiality is only between a lawyer and his own client—opposing counsel cannot have a duty of confidentiality to the client in this case.

B is correct. The lawyer went far beyond what the client authorized him to say, and disclosed information to the opposing parties that could be highly prejudicial in the settlement negotiations for dissolving the partnership.

C is incorrect. The client authorized the lawyer to disclose only the existence of the client's personal financial trouble, and asked the lawyer not to say more about it. The client did not impliedly authorize the lawyer to share the details that he divulged in the meeting.

D is the wrong answer. Admittedly, there is an exception to Rule 1.6 for unauthorized disclosures "to prevent, mitigate or rectify substantial injury to the financial interests or property of another that is reasonably certain to result or has resulted from the client's commission of a crime or fraud in furtherance of which the client has used the lawyer's services." That might (the point is arguable) have applied to a valid assignment of a partnership equity interest to a rival of the business. Nevertheless, the fact that the assignment was legally void means that the client's action posed no direct threat to the financial interests of the other partners. Therefore, the exception does not apply. The disclosure is prejudicial to the client because it is likely to make them less sympathetic toward the client as the negotiations proceed.

Stevenson's Picks

1.	What's in a name?	C
2.	Third-party billing	B
3.	Discussing a case with the partners	C
4.	Test results	D
5.	Asking for advice	C
6.	Under orders	C
7.	The victim's story	A
8.	Fighting over the fees	B
9.	Stories over drinks with friends	B
10.	The prospective client	D
11.	Too much information	B

PART II

Lightly Tested Topics

6

Regulation of the Legal Profession

CHAPTER OVERVIEW

A. Rule 5.1 — Responsibilities of a Partner or Supervisory Lawyer

Law Firms and Associations: Introduction

Rule 5 and its subparts address the responsibilities of lawyers in various roles in a firm, from supervisors, managers, and partners (Rules 5.1 and 5.3), to subordinate lawyers (Rule 5.2). Rule 5.4 mandates professional independence of a lawyer, prohibiting fee sharing and relinquishment of a lawyer's professional judgment to a non-lawyer. At the same time, the rules carve out several important exceptions or circumstances that are not considered "fee sharing," such as: to an estate of a deceased lawyer for a reasonable time; non-lawyer participation in a profit-sharing plan; purchasing a practice from a deceased lawyer's estate; or sharing court-awarded legal fees with a non-profit which hired the lawyer. In any case, a lawyer is not permitted to allow a non-lawyer to direct the lawyer's professional decisions. Rule 5.5 prohibits a lawyer from engaging in the unauthorized practice of law, or assisting another in so doing, and Rule 5.6 forbids a lawyer to agree to or require the restriction of a lawyer's practice of law as a condition of employment or settlement. Finally, Rule 5.7 provides that a lawyer is still subject to the rules for "law related" activities unless the lawyer makes clear that the services are not legal services subject to the rules.

The professional responsibility of a lawyer extends not only to her individual conduct, but also to the conduct of those lawyers and assistants under her direct supervision, to "make reasonable efforts" to ensure that the subordinate lawyer or assistant abides by the rules. The rules do not specifically define "reasonable efforts," but the rules forbid a supervisory lawyer from directing a subordinate to break the rules or to ratify such behavior after the fact. Further, if either the supervisory lawyer or any partner or one with "comparable managerial authority" in the firm knows or discovers that the subordinate has failed to comply with the rules, both the supervisor and/or the partner, and the subordinate lawyer have the responsibility to try to mitigate the consequences of that misconduct by taking remedial action promptly. A person need not qualify as a partner in order to trigger responsibility for a subordinate; the language in the rule includes lawyers who have "direct supervisory authority" over the lawyer whose conduct is at issue.

Partners, shareholders, or those lawyers in the firm with "comparable managerial authority" must also make reasonable efforts to ensure that the firm has measures in place to assure compliance with the rules. Thus, the direct supervisor may exert more direct control over the individual associate, but all those with managerial responsibilities in the firm bear the consonant responsibility to make reasonable efforts to have procedures or policies in place to help younger associates comply with the rules. According to the comments, some of these internal measures may include Continuing Legal Education (CLE) courses in ethics, procedures for identifying conflicts, informal supervision, or a referral system for vetting more difficult ethical questions in more complex cases.

In analyzing the questions regarding supervisory responsibility, test takers should distinguish between those lawyers who are partners with those who are direct supervisors. A more senior associate may serve as a direct supervisor without qualifying for being a partner. Both must make reasonable efforts to ensure that others abide by the rules, but in the case of the partners, they have a general responsibility to the firm and its policies whereas the senior associate in a supervisory capacity's duty is more specifically directed toward her subordinates rather than the firm in general. The following questions illustrate these principles.

QUESTION 1. Responsibility versus liability. An attorney is a partner in a newer law firm that has no effective measures in place to ensure that lawyers in the firm conform to the Rules of Professional Conduct. An associate at the firm violates the rules, and the state bar investigates the policies and procedures in place at the firm. The state disciplinary authority has determined that the first attorney is subject to discipline for his failure to take reasonable measures to ensure conformity with the rules. Because of this determination and the subsequent sanction, which of the following is true?

A. Whether a lawyer may be liable civilly or criminally for another lawyer's conduct is a question of law beyond the scope of the rules; the determination of a violation does not automatically mean that the partner attorney would be civilly or criminally liable.
B. The fact that the state bar found the partner attorney guilty of a violation of the rules, and imposed a sanction, means the attorney is automatically liable in any legal malpractice action related to the violation.
C. The fact that the state bar found the partner attorney guilty of a violation of the rules, and imposed a sanction, means the attorney is automatically guilty in any criminal prosecution related to the violation.
D. The fact that the state bar already imposed a sanction for the violation precludes being subject to damages in a malpractice action or criminal sanctions in a criminal prosecution related to the same violation, due to the double jeopardy rules.

ANALYSIS. This question illustrates the scope of the rules and the impact a violation has on a lawyer's civil and criminal liability. The rules provide a framework for the ethical practice of law, guidance for lawyers, and structure for disciplinary agencies in regulating lawyers' conduct. A violation of a rule by itself is not sufficient to create a cause of action against a lawyer. Additionally, it does not create a presumption that the lawyer has breached a duty imposed by law. A lawyer's failure to abide by the rules invokes the disciplinary process and is not a basis for criminal or civil liability.

A is correct because the comments to Rule 5.1 specifically provide that a lawyer's civil or criminal liability for another lawyer's conduct is a question of law outside the scope of the rules.

B is wrong because a violation of the rules alone does not give rise to a cause of action or create a presumption that a lawyer breached a legal duty. Although the attorney is not automatically liable for malpractice, his violation may evidence a breach of the applicable standard of conduct for lawyers as established by the rules.

C is wrong because a lawyer's criminal liability for another lawyer's violation is a question of law outside the scope of the rules. The attorney's failure to comply with the rules is a basis for a disciplinary action by the state bar and does not automatically give rise to criminal liability.

D is incorrect. The rules are not a basis for liability, criminal or otherwise. Since the rules cannot establish liability, the rules cannot preclude liability either. Double jeopardy is a procedural defense that prohibits duplicative prosecution for the same crime. The disciplinary process and sanctions imposed by the state bar are not criminal proceedings or punishments and will not bar subsequent criminal or civil action related to the violation.

QUESTION 2. **Not my brother's keeper.** An attorney is a second-year associate at a law firm with no supervisory responsibilities. He learns that another second-year associate is working on a case in which the client is suing a company that the other associate used to represent at his previous firm, and the attorney suspects it is a substantially related matter. The firm has done nothing to screen the other associate from the matter. No one ever discusses it with the attorney, and the attorney does not know all the facts of the situation. Later, the client sues the firm for malpractice due to the conflict of interest, and reports the matter to the state disciplinary authority. Which of the following is true regarding the attorney's involvement in the situation?

A. The attorney does not have disciplinary liability for the conduct of the other associate, because he is neither a partner nor in a supervisory position, and did not participate in the violations directly.

B. The attorney is subject to discipline because he had an affirmative duty to inquire about the potential conflict and the lack of screening of this other associate.

C. The attorney is subject to discipline because the Rules of Professional Conduct impute violations of any lawyer in the firm to all other lawyers in the firm.

D. The attorney does not have disciplinary liability in this matter because the Rules of Professional Conduct do not impute conflicts of interest to other lawyers in the same firm just because the firm failed to screen one associate with a possible conflict with former clients.

ANALYSIS. Partners, managers, and supervisors are required to make reasonable efforts to ensure a firm's compliance with the Rules of Professional Conduct. These individuals must establish internal policies and procedures, such as those used to detect and resolve conflicts of interest, to ensure compliance. As you may recall, Rule 1.9 specifically prohibits a lawyer who has formerly represented a client in a matter from representing another person in the same or a substantially related matter in which the new client's interests are materially adverse to the interests of the former client without informed consent, confirmed in writing. In this question, the associate's conflict of interest with his former client imputes to all lawyers in the same firm, unless the firm screened him from representation and received written informed consent from the former client. Otherwise, the firm's representation of the client would result in a violation of the rules. The partners, managers, and supervisors who failed to establish policies and procedures to avoid the conflict of interest would be subject to disciplinary action.

A is correct. Given that the attorney is neither a partner nor the other associate's supervisor, the attorney is not subject to disciplinary liability for the associate's conduct. Additionally, the attorney is not subject to disciplinary liability for violating the rules regarding conflicts of interest because he did not directly participate in the case.

B is wrong because the attorney has no affirmative duty to inquire about the potential conflict, or lack of screening, because he is not a partner or supervising the attorney. It is the responsibility of the managing lawyers to establish internal policies and procedures to ensure all lawyers in the firm comply with the rules, including those "designed to detect and resolve conflicts of interest."

C is incorrect because the rules do not impute violations of a lawyer to all lawyers in the firm. Under certain circumstances, partners, managers, or supervisors may be responsible for violations committed by other lawyers as described in Rule 5.1.

D is also incorrect. The answer correctly states that the attorney does not have disciplinary liability, but the reason for his exclusion is incorrect. He is not subject to disciplinary liability because he did not personally participate in the case. In this matter, the associate's conflict of interest with his former client is imputed to all the attorneys in the same firm, including the attorney.

QUESTION 3. **Respondeat superior.** An attorney is a fifth-year associate at a large firm, and is responsible for supervising the work of a first-year associate. The attorney, however, now spends most of his time in Singapore, trying to open a satellite office for the firm there to service one of its major corporate clients. He has not inquired into the associate's compliance with the Rules of Professional Conduct in over eighteen months, as they mostly communicate by e-mail regarding pending cases and assignments. To the best of his knowledge, though, the attorney believes the associate is following the rules, and he knows that the associate has attended two Legal Ethics CLE courses in the last year. Unbeknownst to the attorney, the new associate has been overbilling hours and has been neglecting certain client matters. Which of the following is true regarding the attorney's situation?

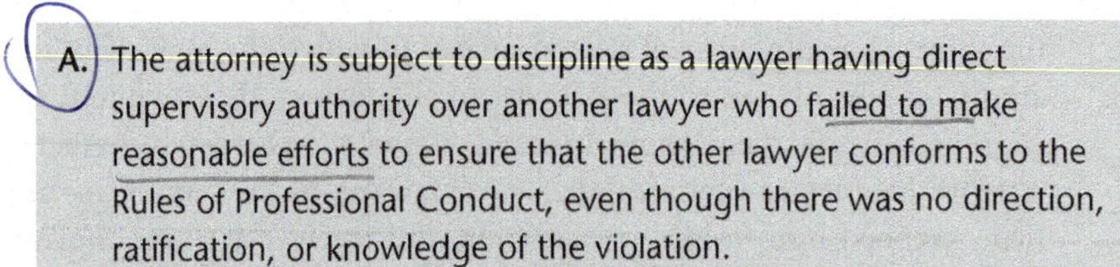

A. The attorney is subject to discipline as a lawyer having direct supervisory authority over another lawyer who failed to make reasonable efforts to ensure that the other lawyer conforms to the Rules of Professional Conduct, even though there was no direction, ratification, or knowledge of the violation.

B. The attorney is subject to discipline for effectively ratifying the associate's violations through his neglect of his supervisory role.

C. The attorney is not subject to discipline because there was no direction, ratification, or knowledge of the violation.

D. The attorney is subject to discipline because the Rules of Professional Conduct impute violations of any lawyer in the firm to all other lawyers in the firm.

ANALYSIS. Under Rule 5.1(b), supervising attorneys must make reasonable efforts to ensure the lawyers under their supervision comply with the Rules of Professional Conduct. A supervising attorney may be subject to discipline for neglecting his responsibilities if a lawyer under his supervision violates the rules. Additionally under Rule 5.1(c), the supervising attorney would be responsible for the other lawyer's violation if the supervisor ordered or, with knowledge, ratified the misconduct. The two potential violations for supervising lawyers are not mutually exclusive. The adequacy of a supervisor's efforts may depend on the firm's size, structure, and the nature of its practice. Periodic review and informal supervision may suffice in a smaller firm, but larger firms typically require supervision that is more formal. Any size firm may supplement its own ethics training with Continuing Legal Education courses.

A is correct because the attorney must make reasonable efforts to ensure the associate's compliance with the rules because he is the associate's direct supervisor. It is irrelevant that the attorney did not provide direction, ratification, or have knowledge of the associate's misconduct, as those are elements of a separate violation.

B is wrong because the attorney must have knowledge of the specific conduct to ratify the associate's misconduct. The facts indicate that the attorney had no knowledge that the associate was overbilling and neglecting client matters.

C is wrong because the attorney remains subject to discipline for a violation of Rule 5.1(b) for failing to make reasonable efforts to ensure an associate under his supervision conformed to the rules. A supervising attorney may be subject to discipline without direction, ratification, or knowledge of the violation.

D is wrong because the rules do not impute violations of any lawyer in the firm to all other lawyers in the firm. Under specific circumstances, partners, managers, or supervisors may be responsible for violations committed by other lawyers as described in Rule 5.1.

QUESTION 4. Protocols in place. An attorney is a partner in a medium-size firm. Another partner at the firm, the managing partner, is responsible for implementing policies and procedures to detect and resolve conflicts of interest, to account for client funds and property, to identify dates by which actions must occur in pending matters, and to ensure that inexperienced lawyers receive proper supervision. The managing partner, however, now spends most of his time in Singapore, trying to open a satellite office for the firm there to service one of its major corporate clients. The managing partner is rarely at the home office and has completely neglected the implementation of ethical policies in the firm, so that minimal safeguards or procedures are in place. One of the new associates has committed several serious violations of professional responsibilities in the last few months, including an egregious conflict-of-interest problem and several missed deadlines for filing responsive pleadings. The attorney knew nothing about the violations and was not directly supervising the associate, and tries not to meddle in any of the managing partner's responsibilities, including the implementation of ethical policies and procedures. Which of the following is correct?

A. The attorney is subject to discipline as a partner in the firm for failing to make reasonable efforts to ensure that the firm has in effect measures giving reasonable assurance that all lawyers in the firm conform to the Rules of Professional Conduct.

B. The attorney is not subject to discipline because it was the managing partner's job to implement measures giving reasonable assurance that all lawyers in the firm conform to the Rules of Professional Conduct.

C. The attorney is not subject to discipline because he did not directly supervise the associate who violated the Rules of Professional Conduct.

D. The attorney is subject to discipline because the Rules of Professional Conduct impute violations of any lawyer in the firm to all other lawyers in the firm.

ANALYSIS. Rule 5.1(a) delegates responsibility to the lawyers in the firm who have managerial authority over the professional work of the firm such as partners, shareholders, and members of other associations authorized to practice law. All partners share the responsibility for establishing internal procedures and policies to detect and resolve conflicts of interest, to account for client funds and property, to identify dates by which actions must occur in pending matters, and to ensure that inexperienced lawyers receive proper supervision. Additionally, all partners must make reasonable efforts to ensure the entire firm's compliance with the rules. The rules do not distinguish between managing partners and regular partners for purposes of compliance with Rule 5.1.

A is correct because the attorney, as a partner in the firm, is responsible for making reasonable efforts to ensure the firm has measures in effect to prevent violations by all lawyers in the firm.

B is wrong because all partners, managing or otherwise, must comply with Rule 5.1(a). Since the attorney is a partner and has managerial authority over the professional work of the firm, he must make reasonable efforts to ensure the firm's compliance with the rules, even if the managing partner was primarily responsible for ensuring the firm's compliance with the rules.

C is wrong. Although the attorney was not the associate's direct supervisor, he remains subject to discipline as a partner for failing to make reasonable efforts to ensure that the firm had measures in effect to prevent violations of the rules by the other lawyers in the firm.

D is wrong because the rules do not impute violations of any lawyer in the firm to all other lawyers in the firm. The rules impose disciplinary liability only on partners, managers, and supervisors for other lawyers' conduct in particular circumstances.

QUESTION 5. Let's fix this. An attorney is a fifth-year associate at a large firm, hoping to make partner in the next two or three years. She supervises the first-year associates at the firm. She learns that the most recently hired associate recently shredded some evidence that would have undermined a client's case, and then told the judge and opposing party that the missing documents had been in a briefcase that went missing when a burglar broke into the associate's car. The attorney knows this is not true and discusses it with the senior litigation partner, who finds the story amusing. Neither reports the associate's deception to the judge or opposing party. Which of the following statements is true regarding this situation?

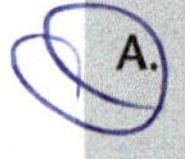

A. Both the attorney and the litigation partner are subject to discipline for not taking action to correct the associate's false statements and misconduct.

B. The attorney is subject to sanctions, as she was directly supervising the associate, but the senior litigation partner was not involved, did not know about it at the time, and has no responsibility in the matter.

C. The associate is subject to discipline, but neither the attorney nor the senior litigation partner would be subject to discipline, as they were not aware of the misconduct until after the fact.

D. The senior litigation partner is subject to discipline because he has a responsibility to take reasonable measures to ensure that everyone in the firm complies with their ethical duties, but the attorney is not subject to discipline, as she is merely an associate at the firm.

ANALYSIS. Direct supervisors and managing lawyers have a duty to intervene if they acquire knowledge about an associate's misconduct when the consequences are avoidable. Although partners have indirect responsibility for all work in the firm, the partners who manage a particular area, like the litigation partner in this question, would have a greater supervisory responsibility for the other lawyers in that practice group. The supervisor or managing partner will be subject to discipline if he fails to take reasonable remedial action, such as notifying opposing counsel or the judge, after learning of the misconduct when the consequences are avoidable.

A is correct because both the attorney and the litigation partner had knowledge of the associate's misconduct at a time when its consequences could have been avoided or mitigated and failed to take reasonable remedial action. The attorney is subject to discipline because she is the associate's direct supervisor; the litigation partner is subject to discipline under the same rule because he had knowledge of the misconduct at a time when its consequences could have been avoided or mitigated and failed to take reasonable action. Additionally, the litigation partner has managerial authority in the law firm and specifically in the litigation practice group where the associate likely practices.

B is wrong because the litigation partner is subject to discipline for failing to take appropriate remedial action. The litigation partner has a duty to intervene to prevent the avoidable consequences of the associate's misconduct, even though he acquired knowledge of the misconduct after the fact and was not personally involved in the misconduct.

C is wrong. Even though they acquired their knowledge of the misconduct after the fact, both the attorney and the litigation partner are subject to discipline because they failed to take reasonable remedial action at a time when the consequences of the associate's misconduct were avoidable.

D is wrong because the attorney is subject to discipline as a supervising attorney for failing to take remedial action after learning of the associate's misconduct. Since she is subject to discipline as the associate's supervising the attorney, it is irrelevant that the attorney is merely an associate and not a partner.

QUESTION 6. **Dumping on the associates.** An attorney works at the state Public Defender office. Due to their insufficient funding and the overwhelming number of indigent defendants in her city, her caseload is so great that she cannot do adequate investigation into any of her client's cases or conduct legal research about possible defenses. Nevertheless, 95 percent of the cases end in plea bargains without going to trial, so the attorney tells herself that her neglect of case development makes no difference. Her supervisor at the Public Defender office is aware of the unreasonable caseloads of all the attorneys who work there, but the supervisor wants the attorneys to increase their caseloads in order to provide representation to more indigent defendants, even if that means doing minimal work on each case. Which of the following is true regarding the ethical situation facing the attorney and her supervisor?

A. The supervisor could be subject to discipline for not ensuring that a subordinate attorney can manage her workload, even if that means not assigning the lawyer any more cases for now.

B. The attorney's supervisor is not subject to discipline because it is a valid policy decision to provide minimal representation to as many defendants as possible, as even minimal representation is better than having no representation at all.

C. The normal duty of diligence does not apply to public defenders, as everyone recognizes that the priority should be to provide representation for every defendant.

D. For purposes of professional discipline or sanctions, the supervisor is the one responsible for the case overload, not the attorneys who work there. Both

ANALYSIS. Rule 1.3 provides that a lawyer must act with reasonable diligence and promptness in representing clients. Lawyers are responsible for managing their caseload so that each client has competent representation. Although a lawyer is ultimately responsible for managing his or her own caseload, the lawyer's supervisors may be responsible for the lawyer's violation of Rule 1.3. If the supervisor orders the lawyer to represent additional clients knowing that the lawyer's caseload is unmanageable, the supervisor violates Rule 5.1(c)(1). Additionally, the supervisor is subject to discipline if he ratifies the lawyer's acceptance of additional clients when he knows the lawyer's ability to represent his clients will suffer. A direct supervisor has a duty to make reasonable efforts to ensure the lawyers under his supervision comply with the rules, which may include overseeing the lawyer's assignments to ensure compliance with Rule 1.3. Note that another related question drawn from this situation appears in the chapter on malpractice liability in this volume.

This question illustrates how both a lawyer and supervisor can be subject to disciplinary liability for poor caseload management. Under Rule 5.1(b), the supervisor has a duty to ensure that the attorney conforms to the rules, including her duty to represent her clients with reasonable diligence. Since he wants her to continue accepting new clients, even if it means providing minimal representation, his efforts to ensure the attorney's compliance with Rule 1.3 are unreasonable and may subject him to disciplinary liability. Additionally, he is responsible for her violation of Rule 1.3 because he ordered, and ratified, the attorney's neglectful representation of her clients. Even though the attorney is following her supervisor's orders to continue accepting new clients, she is responsible for managing her own caseload and must provide diligent representation to each client. Her failure to provide competent representation to her clients would subject her to disciplinary sanctions for a violation of Rule 1.3.

A is correct. The supervisor must refrain from assigning so many cases to subordinates that the lawyers cannot provide competent, thorough representation to each client.

B is incorrect. It is never a valid policy decision to provide minimal representation. The rules require lawyers to provide each client with diligent and competent representation. The supervisor is subject to discipline because he continues to increase the attorney's caseload even though he knows that it is unreasonable and her clients are receiving insufficient representation.

C is wrong because lawyers, public defenders or otherwise, have a duty to act with reasonable diligence in representing their clients. A lawyer should not strive to represent as many clients as possible. Rather, a lawyer must strive to provide diligent representation to as many clients as he or she can represent competently.

D is wrong because both the attorney and her supervisor are subject to discipline for mismanaging the attorney's caseload. The duties imposed on the attorney's supervisor under Rule 5.1 do not relieve the attorney of her duty to provide diligent and competent representation to her clients.

B. Rule 5.2—Responsibilities of Subordinate Lawyers

Unquestioningly following orders is not an excuse to act in an unethical manner. Rule 5.2 addresses the responsibilities of a subordinate when she is directed to do something that she thinks may be a violation of the rules. If there is no arguable support for the course of action directed by the supervisor, the subordinate is still required to act in an ethical manner in conformity with the rules. Even so, if the supervisor resolves the ethical question in favor of a certain course of action that reasonably may be within the confines of the rules, then the subordinate does not violate the rules to follow that course of conduct, and only the supervisor bears the responsibility for the chosen course of conduct.

Thus, even when a lawyer is acting under the direction of a supervisor, he may be subject to disciplinary liability for violating the Rules of Professional Conduct. The determinative factor is whether the subordinate lawyer knew the conduct would result in a violation of the rules. If the lawyer knew his conduct would result in a violation, he is subject to disciplinary liability for his actions. If the lawyer was following the instructions of his supervisor and was unaware of the potential violation, the state disciplinary authority will consider the lawyer's lack of knowledge as a relevant factor when it decides whether to impose sanctions or other disciplinary actions.

Possible exam pitfalls may involve situations where there is no reasonable or arguable support for a course of action directed by a supervisor. If the question presents facts that show that the subordinate knows that the action would unquestioningly violate the rules (the comments use the example of knowing that a pleading is frivolous but filing it anyway at the direction of the supervisor), then the answer stating that both the supervisor and the subordinate are responsible for the violation would be correct. The following questions illustrate the contours of the rule.

QUESTION 7. **Just following orders.** The attorney is an associate at a small firm, and her supervising partner instructs her to draft pleadings in a case for a client. The supervising partner knows that the statute of limitations has already run on the claim, and that the client had virtually no factual evidence to support the claim in any case. The partner believes the opposing party will want to settle the claim quickly for a modest sum, and will not bother to investigate issues such as the statute of limitations or the factual support for either side. The attorney follows the partner's instructions and drafts the pleadings, without checking the statute of limitations for this particular claim or conducting her own investigation into the facts of the case. Opposing counsel, however, is upset over the frivolous claim and reports the attorney to the state bar. Which of the following is correct regarding the attorney's situation?

A. The attorney is probably not responsible for asserting a frivolous claim, and the fact that she was just following orders could support her defense that she was unaware that the claim was frivolous.
B. The attorney is responsible for asserting a frivolous claim, despite the fact that her supervising partner insisted that she do it.
C. Neither the attorney nor the partner would be subject to discipline as long as the case settles before trial.
D. If the partner had terminated the attorney for refusing to assert the frivolous claim, the state bar disciplinary authority would have compelled the firm to reinstate her.

ANALYSIS. Before filing an action, all lawyers should inform themselves of the facts of the case and applicable law. Rule 3.1 prohibits a lawyer from bringing a frivolous claim, which is one with no basis in law or fact. While a lawyer should use the law for the client's full benefit, he should never abuse legal procedures to motivate the opposing party to settle like the partner in this question. The state disciplinary authority considers the lawyer's knowledge, or lack thereof, in determining whether to impose disciplinary liability. Since the partner knew the claim was frivolous, he will be subject to discipline actions or sanctions. On the other hand, the attorney did not know the claim was frivolous and was following the partner's orders so she is probably not responsible.

A is correct because the attorney may not have the requisite knowledge to render her conduct a violation of Rule 3.1. Since the attorney was following her supervisor's instructions, the attorney may be relieved of responsibility for asserting the frivolous claim. Her lack of knowledge is a relevant consideration for the state disciplinary authority.

B is wrong because the attorney may be relieved of responsibility since she did not know the claim was frivolous and was simply following the partner's orders.

C is incorrect. Both the attorney and the partner may be subject to discipline for bringing the frivolous claim, even if the case settles before trial. The partner knew the statute of limitations had run and that there was no factual evidence to support the claim in any case. The attorney may be subject to discipline for failing to learn of the facts of the case and applicable law before filing the pleadings.

D is wrong because the state disciplinary authority does not have the power to compel the firm to reinstate the attorney. The attorney's remedies for wrongful termination are created by state law and can only be enforced by the courts.

QUESTION 8. **Reasonable resolution.** An attorney is a new associate at a law firm, and the managing partner assigns her a new case, in which the firm will represent two co-plaintiffs in a personal injury case. The attorney is concerned that a conflict of interest could arise between the two plaintiffs, and suggests that the firm should represent only one of them. When she discusses this with the managing partner, the managing partner disagrees, because the interests of the two plaintiffs seem perfectly aligned, and they can have each sign an informed consent form waiving the conflict up front. Both admit the question is a close one in terms of the ethical rules for conflicts of interest, but the managing partner insists that they proceed. Which of the following is true regarding this situation?

A. The supervisor's reasonable resolution of the question should protect the subordinate professionally if the resolution subsequently faces a challenge.

B. The attorney has a duty to follow her own judgment about her ethical obligations to clients under the Rules of Professional Conduct, even if that means ignoring the managing partner's instructions.

C. The fact that the two discussed the potential conflict at length will help shield both of them from any professional repercussions if they turn out to be wrong later.

D. The answer depends on whether the firm will receive a contingent fee if they prevail, as there is a strict prohibition on representing co-plaintiffs in a contingent fee case.

ANALYSIS. Under Rule 5.2(b), a subordinate lawyer does not violate the rules if he acts in accordance with a supervisory lawyer's reasonable resolution of an arguable question of a professional duty. This rule allows the lawyers to take a position and consistent course of action. Both the supervisor and subordinate lawyer are responsible for an ethical violation when the resolution is certain. When the ethical dilemma creates ambiguity, the supervisor assumes the responsibility for the decision if the resolution is challenged.

This question illustrates the disciplinary liability of a supervisor and subordinate lawyer when faced with an arguable question of a professional duty. The ethical dilemma that the attorney and managing partner need to resolve involves a concurrent conflict of interest. The relevant rule, Rule 1.7, permits the attorney's representation of both co-plaintiffs if she believes that she can provide competent and diligent representation to both; the law does not prohibit the representation; the clients' interests are aligned; and each client gives informed consent in writing. While both lawyers admit the representation is questionable, the managing partner reasonably believes the attorney's representation of the co-plaintiffs is acceptable and the attorney may act upon his decision. The managing partner assumes the responsibility of making the decision because the resolution is uncertain. Meanwhile, the attorney is relieved of responsibility for the decision by Rule 5.2 if the decision is subsequently challenged.

A is correct. The attorney is protected from disciplinary liability because she acted in accordance with her managing partner's reasonable resolution of an arguable question of a professional duty regarding concurrent conflicts of interest. The managing partner's belief that there is not a violation of Rule 1.7 is reasonable because the co-plaintiffs' interests appear to be aligned and each gave informed consent in writing.

B is incorrect. The attorney's deference to the managing partner's judgment, rather than her own, is reasonable since she is a new associate and the ethical implications of the representation are far from certain.

C is wrong because the managing partner remains responsible for an ethical violation despite the fact they discussed the matter at length.

D is wrong because the attorney is representing the two co-plaintiffs in a personal injury case so it is proper for her to receive a contingent fee if they prevail. Lawyers cannot receive contingent fees in domestic relations matters or when representing a criminal defendant.

Clear Question of Professional Duty

Because every lawyer is responsible for observance of the rules, a lawyer who commits a violation while acting under the direction of a supervisor remains subject to discipline for his conduct. A lawyer must stand firm in his ethical obligations and refuse to follow directions that he knows would render his conduct a violation of the rules. Even if the lawyer was induced by threats, the state disciplinary authority can impose sanctions on the lawyer if he knew of the potential violation. The following illustrates this principle.

QUESTION 9. Nuremburg defense. An attorney is an associate in a litigation firm representing plaintiffs. In her current case, her supervising partner instructs her to assert that the defendant had an affirmative statutory duty to protect the plaintiff's interests, even though the attorney can find no statute to support this assertion. The attorney has brought this to the attention of her supervising partner, who rebuked her for questioning his authority and insisted that she do as he said. He assures her that the defendants will settle before trial anyway, so the bogus claim merely gives some psychological leverage during settlement negotiations, and cannot do any harm. Moreover, the partner says that the attorney may not last long at the firm if she cannot follow instructions, which seemed to be a threat of termination. At a preliminary hearing, however, the judge confronts the attorney about the unsupportable claim, and she concedes that no statutory duty exists. The judge is irate and considers reporting the attorney to the state bar disciplinary authority. Which of the following is correct regarding the attorney's situation?

A. The attorney is responsible for asserting a frivolous claim, despite the fact that her supervising partner insisted that she do it and threatened her with termination.

B. The attorney is not responsible for asserting a frivolous claim, because her supervising partner insisted that she do it and threatened her with termination.

C. Neither the attorney nor the partner would be subject to discipline as long as the case settles before trial and the bogus claim about statutory duties was not the sole basis for their complaint.

D. If the partner had terminated the attorney for refusing to assert the frivolous claim, the state bar disciplinary authority would have compelled the firm to reinstate her.

ANALYSIS. Although the attorney is acting under the supervising partner's directions and is induced by his threats, she can be held responsible for asserting the claim because she knows it is frivolous. Rule 3.1 prohibits a lawyer from asserting a claim that has no basis in law and fact. The attorney and the supervising partner know that the defendant has no legal duty to protect the plaintiff's interests. The supervising partner's tactics are an abuse of legal process and violation of Rule 3.1. The attorney is not relieved of responsibility for complying with the rules because she is following the supervising partner's orders. Therefore, the attorney remains subject to discipline for asserting a claim that has no basis in law or fact.

A is correct because the attorney is not relieved of responsibility for knowingly violating the rules, even though her supervising partner ordered the conduct and threatened to terminate her if she did not proceed as directed. Since she has a duty to comply with the rules, the attorney should refuse to follow orders that she knows would result in a violation.

B is wrong because the attorney knows the defendant did not have a statutory duty to protect the plaintiff's interests. She is therefore responsible for asserting the frivolous claim. It is irrelevant that the partner attorney insisted she do it and threatened her with termination.

C is wrong because both the attorney and partner attorney are subject to discipline for making the bogus claim. Even if the case settled before trial, both the attorney and partner attorney knowingly violated Rule 3.1. Since the partner attorney directed a subordinate lawyer to violate the rules, he is also subject to discipline under Rule 5.1 for failing to make reasonable efforts to ensure other lawyers in the firm conform to the rules.

D is incorrect. The state disciplinary authority does not have the power to compel the firm to reinstate the attorney. The attorney's remedies for wrongful termination are created by state law and can only be enforced by the courts.

Knowledge of a Violation: Opportunity to Verify Facts

The state disciplinary authority considers a lawyer's knowledge of the violation, or lack thereof, when deciding whether to impose disciplinary sanctions. If the lawyer is acting under a supervisor's directions, the state disciplinary authority considers whether the lawyer had the opportunity to investigate or verify the facts of the case or applicable law. A lawyer's reliance on a supervisor's instructions and information is relevant in determining whether the lawyer had the knowledge required to render the conduct of a violation of the rules.

QUESTION 10. **Relevant factors.** A partner gives an associate the typed notes from a previous client interview conducted by the partner, and the associate has the task of drafting a complaint for a personal injury lawsuit based on the allegations in the notes. The associate has no direct contact with the client, and does not really have any way to verify whether the notes represent everything discussed in the interview (the notes are not a transcript) or whether the allegations are factually accurate, truthful, or tell the complete story. The associate completes the task as assigned, drafting the pleadings based on the notes. The associate then submits the drafted complaint to the partner for review. Later, the pleadings turn out to be frivolous, based on complete falsehoods. Which of the following is true regarding the associate attorney's role in drafting the complaint?

A. The lack of opportunity for the associate to investigate or verify facts on her own will be a relevant factor for the state disciplinary authority in deciding whether to discipline the associate.

B. The lack of opportunity for the associate to investigate or verify facts on her own will not be a relevant factor for the state disciplinary authority in deciding whether to discipline the associate.
C. The client will be subject to discipline, but not her lawyers, who merely took her at her word and filed complaints based on what she told the lawyers.
D. The associate will be subject to discipline for drafting a complaint based on interview notes rather than a transcript of the interview or a notarized affidavit.

ANALYSIS. Rule 3.1 prohibits a lawyer from asserting a claim that has no basis in fact or law. Before asserting a claim, a lawyer must be informed of the facts of the case and applicable law to prevent a frivolous lawsuit and violation of Rule 3.1. Since the associate did not have contact with the client, she is relying upon the partner's information to draft the pleadings. The format of the information, note or transcript, is not determinative. Rather, the associate attorney's lack of opportunity to verify the facts has greater relevance. Since the associate did not have the opportunity to verify the facts, she may not have the knowledge required to render her conduct a violation of the rules.

A is correct. The associate may be relieved of liability for filing a frivolous claim because she relied on the partner's information and did not have the opportunity to conduct her own investigation into the facts of the case. Because she did not have any way to verify the facts and she acted at the partner's direction, the state disciplinary authority would consider her lack of personal knowledge in deciding whether to impose disciplinary sanctions.

B is wrong because the associate is not relieved of responsibility for a violation merely because she acted at the partner's direction. The state disciplinary authority will consider the associate's own knowledge and opportunity to investigate when determining whether to impose sanctions for a violation of the rules.

C is wrong because only lawyers, not their clients, are subject to discipline under the rules. Although the client may be subject to other claims by the opposing party for her falsehoods, she will not be subject to discipline by the state disciplinary authority.

D is incorrect. The format of the interview notes is not a determinative factor in deciding whether to subject the associate to disciplinary liability. The state disciplinary authority, however, may consider the casual nature of the client interview process when it determines whether the attorney and the partner had the knowledge required to render their conduct a violation of the rules.

C. Rule 5.3—Responsibilities for Conduct of Non-Lawyer Assistants in a Firm

Lawyers commonly hire non-lawyer employees and service providers from outside the firm to aid in their rendition of legal services. Non-lawyer services outside the firm may include investigative or paraprofessional services, document management services, third-party scanning and printing services, and online client information storage services. Lawyers must make reasonable efforts to ensure the non-lawyers provide services in a manner compatible with the lawyers' professional obligations. In doing so, the lawyer should communicate directions and expectations to give reasonable assurance that the non-lawyer's services are consistent with the lawyer's professional obligations.

QUESTION 11. **Duties in the cloud.** The attorney has switched to cloud computing, meaning that their firm pays a monthly fee to store all their spreadsheets and documents in an Internet-based database or archive. This protects client information and case documents from being lost whenever a computer at the firm crashes; the cloud service automatically creates an online backup for every file. According to the Rules of Professional Conduct, which of the following is true?

A. The attorney and his firm have an affirmative duty to make reasonable efforts to ensure that the cloud service is secure against computer hacking or other invasive access to clients' confidential information.

B. The attorney and his firm were correct in prioritizing the protection of documents against loss from failed hard drives over the protection of client confidentiality, as the chances of a security breach on the cloud server are extremely low.

C. If the cloud storage company advertised that its online servers were super-secure, the lawyers have no duty to make additional inquiries about the risk of disclosing clients' confidential information.

D. It is not a violation of the rules if the employees at the cloud storage company can access the information stored on their servers.

ANALYSIS. In this question, the attorney and his firm hired the cloud storage company, a non-lawyer service provider outside the firm, to store client information on their Internet-based servers. Under Rule 5.3, the attorney and his firm must make reasonable efforts to ensure the company's services do not conflict with their professional obligations. One such obligation is the duty to prevent the inadvertent and unauthorized disclosure of client information under Rule 1.6. Since confidential client information will be stored on the cloud, the attorney and his firm must make reasonable efforts to ensure the cloud storage company's services are secure to prevent a violation of Rule 1.6.

A is correct because the attorney and his firm have a duty to make reasonable efforts to ensure the cloud service safeguards the confidentiality of their clients' information.

B is wrong. Although the chances of a security breach are low, the attorney and his firm have an affirmative duty under the rules to guard against the disclosure of protected client information. The attorney and his firm should prioritize the protection of client confidentiality over the protection of documents against loss because they are subject to disciplinary liability for the improper disclosure of client information.

C is wrong because it would be unreasonable for the attorney and his firm to rely solely upon the cloud storage company's promises of security in their advertisements. Since the attorney and the firm must make reasonable efforts to ensure the cloud storage company's services are compatible with their professional obligations, they should communicate with the company to ensure the company's services are consistent with their duty to safeguard client confidentiality.

D is incorrect. It would be a violation of Rule 1.6 if the cloud service's employees accessed the clients' information without informed consent. The attorney and the firm should confer with the company to establish policies and procedures to guard against the inadvertent and unauthorized access to their clients' information.

Client Choice of Non-Lawyer Assistants

Rule 5.3 requires lawyers to make reasonable efforts to ensure non-lawyer services are provided in a manner compatible with their professional obligations. The extent of this obligation depends on a variety of factors such as the non-lawyer's experience and reputation. Regardless of this duty, a lawyer should ordinarily allow their clients to select their own non-lawyer service providers and share in the responsibility of monitoring. The reasoning is supported by Rule 1.2, which provides that a lawyer should abide by a client's decisions concerning the objectives of representation.

QUESTION 12. **Have it your way.** The attorney represents a sophisticated business client in a litigation matter. The attorney wants to hire an outside non-lawyer investigator/paraprofessional to help find and develop evidence and witnesses for the case. Client agrees, but wants the attorney to hire a particular outside company with whom Client has close business dealings and a long history. The attorney would normally have used a different firm that is more familiar to him. Which of the following is correct, according to the Model Rules and the accompanying comments?

A. Where the client directs the selection of a particular non-lawyer service provider outside the firm, the lawyer ordinarily should agree with the client concerning the allocation of responsibility for monitoring as between the client and the lawyer.

B. Where the client suggests the selection of a particular non-lawyer service provider outside the firm, the lawyer ordinarily should make the selection and override the client's suggestion, given that the lawyer bears responsibility for monitoring the ethical behavior of the service provider.

C. Where the client directs the selection of a particular non-lawyer service provider outside the firm, the client bears the responsibility for monitoring the behavior of the service provider he selected.

D. Where the client directs the selection of a particular non-lawyer service provider outside the firm, the lawyer will be subject to discipline for allowing the client to engage in the unauthorized practice of law.

ANALYSIS. In this question, the attorney should be amenable to Client's selection of an outside investigator/paraprofessional. Although the attorney is not familiar with the investigative firm, Client, a sophisticated businessperson, has had close business dealings and a lengthy history with them. By sharing in the responsibility of monitoring the investigator with Client, the attorney can satisfy his obligation to make reasonable efforts to ensure the investigative firm's compliance with his professional obligations.

A is correct because Comment 4 to Rule 5.3 provides that a lawyer should ordinarily agree with a client's selection of an outside non-lawyer service provider and the allocation of monitoring responsibilities.

B is wrong because a lawyer should not override a client's selection of an outside service provider. The lawyer should ordinarily follow the client's suggestion and share in the responsibility of monitoring the service provider with the client.

C is wrong because the client does not bear the entire responsibility of monitoring the outside service provider. Rather, the lawyer and client share the responsibility. The lawyer must fulfill his duty to make reasonable efforts to ensure the non-lawyer's services are compatible with the lawyer's professional obligations.

D is wrong because the lawyer is not subject to discipline for allowing the client to select the outside service provider. Since the client has the ultimate authority to determine the purposes to be served by legal representation, the client does not engage in the unauthorized practice of law by selecting the non-lawyer service provider. The attorney should ordinarily agree to his decision so long as it is within the limits imposed by law and his professional obligations.

D. Rule 5.4 — Fee Division with a Non-Lawyer

Model Rule 5.4 addresses the independence of lawyers — that is, it prohibits partnerships or fee-sharing arrangements in which a non-lawyer could control decisions about how to handle matters for the lawyer's clients. The rule has four sections, each pertaining to a different problematic situation for lawyers: (a) splitting fees in a case with non-lawyers; (b) legal partnerships (a firm) with non-lawyer partners; (c) recommenders or payors of lawyers to direct or regulate the lawyer; and (d) non-lawyers having ownership shares in a lawyer's firm. The MPRE tests Rule 5.4 relatively lightly compared to other rules in this chapter, and when it does, the questions usually pertain to fee sharing or control of litigation by insurers (the latter also falling under Rule 1.8).

Students should be aware that European countries generally allow the very type of "multidisciplinary firms" forbidden by Rule 5.4 — that is, publicly traded corporations can offer legal representation through staff attorneys to customers, and accounting firms can employ lawyers who provide legal representation for the firm's clients. In the 1990s, a number of law professors and influential lawyers sought to bring the rule in the United States into line with other industrialized countries (some American firms wanted to merge with European multidisciplinary firms, in fact), and this led to a protracted debate at the American Bar Association meeting. To the surprise of many, the vote on this issue favored the retention of Rule 5.4, but the topic is still a favorite for many law professors, so students may have spent considerable class time discussing the issue. The ABA seems to have abandoned the idea. Washington, D.C. permits non-lawyers to be partners in law firms, so the ABA added a provision to Rule 5.4 specifically allowing for lawyers in other states to work on cases with lawyers from D.C. firms, even if they share fees.

The next two questions are intentionally very similar, in order to highlight the crucial difference between the two scenarios.

QUESTION 13. **Profit sharing for paralegals.** An attorney practices personal injury law, representing plaintiffs on a contingent fee basis. The attorney employs a paralegal to assist with preparing documents for litigation. The paralegal's salary arrangement is 10 percent of the firm's total net revenue each year. In years when the attorney wins several large cases, the paralegal receives higher wages, and in years when the attorney has no big wins, the paralegal receives almost nothing. The paralegal does not bring clients to the firm, and does not participate in judgments about which clients to represent, or about how to handle the cases. Is the attorney subject to discipline for this arrangement?

A. Yes, unless the paralegal has a law degree and has obtained a law license in another state.

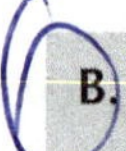

B. No, because non-lawyers may participate in a firm compensation plan based on overall profit sharing.
C. Yes, because the paralegal here is engaged in the unauthorized practice of law.
D. No, because the rules treat paralegals the same as lawyers for purposes of sharing fees or profits.

ANALYSIS. Rule 5.4(a)(3) allows that "a lawyer or law firm may include nonlawyer employees in a compensation or retirement plan, even though the plan is based in whole or in part on a profit-sharing arrangement." Lawyers cannot pay a non-lawyer a direct contingent fee related to a particular case, but they can share profits with non-lawyer employees based on the firm's total revenue, even though that revenue comes (at least partly) from contingent fees earned by the lawyer.

A is incorrect. An employee of a firm does not have to be a lawyer—or have a law degree—in order to share in a firm's profit-sharing plan.

B is correct. Non-lawyers, such as paralegals, legal assistants, receptionists, and secretaries may participate in a law firm's profit-sharing plan, even though the profits derive partly (or even mostly) from contingent fees that the lawyer(s) earned from client matters.

C is incorrect. There is no indication here that the paralegal engaged in the unauthorized practice of law.

D is partly correct, but also partly incorrect. The Model Rules do require that lawyers ensure their staff (paralegals or others) comply with the MRPC's duties to clients and courts—protecting client confidentiality, avoiding conflicts of interest, and so on. For purposes of sharing fees, however, paralegals are not the same as lawyers. A lawyer cannot pay a paralegal a contingent fee (or a percentage of the lawyer's contingent fee) for a particular case or client, because the paralegal is not a lawyer. Nevertheless, a paralegal may participate in a profit-sharing plan that includes the combined contingent fees earned by the lawyer(s) in the firm.

QUESTION 14. **Profit sharing and votes for paralegals.** An attorney practices personal injury law, representing plaintiffs on a contingent fee basis. The attorney employs a paralegal to assist with preparing documents for litigation. The paralegal's salary arrangement is 10 percent of the firm's total net revenue each year. In years when the attorney wins several large cases, the paralegal receives higher wages, and in years when the attorney has no big wins, the paralegal receives almost nothing.

The paralegal does not bring clients to the firm, but does participate in judgments about which clients to represent, how to structure contingent fee arrangements, and how much to seek in damages after a verdict, as these matters directly affect the paralegal's income as well as the attorney's. Is the attorney subject to discipline for this arrangement?

A. Yes, unless the paralegal has a law degree and is admitted in another state.

B. No, because non-lawyers may participate in a firm compensation plan based on overall profit sharing.

C. Yes, because a non-lawyer has a right to influence the professional judgment of the lawyer under this arrangement.

D. No, because the rules treat paralegals the same as lawyers for purposes of sharing fees or profits.

ANALYSIS. Rule 5.4(d)(3) forbids situations in which "a nonlawyer [not the client] has the right to direct or control the professional judgment of a lawyer." This question is nearly identical to the last one, except that in this question, the paralegal participates in decisions about representing clients. That makes all the difference—this situation clearly violates the Model Rules. This question also highlights the hazard of profit-sharing plans with law firm staff—eventually, those whose compensation depends on the firm's profits may want to voice opinions about decisions that will affect the firm's profitability. The MPRE has included questions in recent years similar to this, or highlighting the same point.

A is incorrect. Even if a paralegal has a law degree in another state, if the individual is unauthorized to practice law in this jurisdiction, the lawyer cannot allow the paralegal to participate in decisions that affect the representation and could interfere with the lawyer's independent judgment.

B is incorrect. Even though a non-lawyer may participate in a profit-sharing plan that incorporates the firm's aggregate contingent fees, a non-lawyer may not participate in decisions that implicate the lawyer's judgment concerning representation of clients.

C is correct. The paralegal in this problem participates in decisions about which clients to represent, how to structure contingent fee arrangements, and how much to seek in damages after a verdict, and this violates the Model Rules.

D is partly correct and partly incorrect. Some of the Model Rules apply equally to paralegals (or require lawyers to ensure that their paralegals comply with the rules as agents of the lawyer), but paralegals cannot influence the judgment of the lawyer(s) in the firm regarding representation.

QUESTION 15. **Working with Washington lawyers.** An attorney in a state that has adopted the Model Rules in their current form enters into a fee-sharing agreement with a lawyer admitted in Washington, D.C., which permits fee sharing with non-lawyers and multidisciplinary practices. They collaborate on a case and divide the fees as agreed. The attorney from the Model Rules state is aware that the other attorney will share his part of the fees with non-lawyers in the D.C. office; in fact, the D.C. lawyer's firm has accountants who hold an ownership share in that firm. Is the non-D.C. attorney subject to discipline for indirectly sharing legal fees with non-lawyers, given that he practices in a state that forbids fee sharing with non-lawyers?

A. Yes, the attorneys have a duty to uphold the rules in their own jurisdiction, and given that the attorney knows that the other lawyer will share some of the fees with non-lawyers, he has violated the rule in his own state.

B. Yes, but only because the lawyer had actual knowledge of the fee-sharing arrangement.

C. No, as long as the first attorney shares fees only with another attorney, it does not matter if the other attorney shares fees with non-lawyers as permitted by his home jurisdiction.

D. No, because the rule in the attorney's own state, prohibiting fee sharing with non-lawyers, is unconstitutional, according to the Supreme Court.

ANALYSIS. Traditionally, the American legal system absolutely forbade law firms (or firms providing legal representation) having non-lawyer owners (partners or shareholders). Washington, D.C. is the one jurisdiction in the country that permits this in a limited way. This presents problems when lawyers from a D.C. firm collaborate on a case with lawyers from another state (Virginia, Maryland, etc.) and share fees. Thus, the ABA addressed this problem in Formal Opinion 13-464, saying that lawyers from other states may share fees with a lawyer in D.C., even if that lawyer will in turn share them with a non-lawyer partner—as long as the lawyer from the other state does not pay the non-lawyer directly.

A is incorrect. The lawyer has a duty to share fees only with other lawyers, but does not have a duty to control what those lawyers do with their fees.

B is also incorrect. The ABA decided not to make the rule dependent on the lawyer's actual knowledge, but rather on whether the payments to a non-lawyer were direct or indirect (that is, through another lawyer).

C is correct. The ABA has decided that it is proper for a lawyer in one state (following the Model Rules) to share fees with a lawyer from a jurisdiction that allows fee sharing with non-lawyers (note there is only one such jurisdiction—Washington, D.C.).

D is simply false. The Supreme Court has not addressed this issue.

QUESTION 16. The marketing guru and his contract. The attorney hires a nationally known Internet-marketing specialist, a tech guru, to help develop the firm's reputation and attract new clients. The Internet specialist has made millions on previous tech startups, while the attorney is relatively unknown and has been practicing for only two years. The tech guru demands certain terms in the contract that require the attorney to confer with the tech guru about accepting clients that were former clients of the tech guru, in order to avoid conflicts of interest. The attorney must also clear any litigation positions, approaches, or strategies that pertain to intellectual property or Internet marketing liability with the tech guru, to avoid positions that would jeopardize the guru's other business. Is the attorney subject to discipline for this arrangement?

A. No, because the attorney is merely hiring an advertising specialist and can pay normal rates for such services.

B. No, because the contract merely reflects the lawyer's duty under the Model Rules to avoid conflicts of interest between current clients.

C. Yes, because a non-lawyer has a contractual right to direct or control the professional judgment of the lawyer.

D. Yes, because the attorney is advertising online, which means Internet users in other states can see the firm's advertisements and offers of representation, even though the attorney does not have a license to practice in most of those jurisdictions.

ANALYSIS. This problem is another example of a non-lawyer having too much control over a lawyer's judgment. Note that this individual is not a client—the client should have control over the objectives of the representation, and may have some input about the methods for achieving those goals (especially if some methods will be much more costly or risky for the client). The non-lawyer in this question is a consultant that the lawyer hired to help attract more clients to his firm. Practitioners must be watchful for contracts with publicists and consultants that could interfere with the decisions about representation.

A is incorrect because it does not matter that the person merely hired this individual for a particular purpose. The problem is that a lawyer here has a contractual obligation to let a non-lawyer control the representation that the lawyer provides to clients.

B is also incorrect, because it misstates the rules about conflicts. The lawyer has a duty to avoid conflicts of interest between clients, but not necessarily between clients and independent service providers who do contract work for the lawyer.

C is correct. The fact that the non-lawyer has a contractual right to influence the judgment of the lawyer regarding the representation of clients violates the requirement that lawyers exercise independent judgment.

D wrongly states that advertising online violates the rules. Lawyers can advertise online as long as they do not offer through the website to represent clients in states where the lawyer is unlicensed.

E. Rule 5.5—Unauthorized Practice of Law by Lawyers and Nonlawyers; Multijurisdictional Practice

Every MPRE includes at least one question about the unauthorized practice of law—usually a licensed lawyer from a neighboring state practicing in a state where he is unlicensed. Also included are questions about the Supreme Court's line of cases holding that states may not impose protectionist residency requirements on lawyers—in other words, a lawyer who resides in Vermont can seek bar admission in neighboring New Hampshire. The Supreme Court has also held that federal statutes permitting non-lawyers to serve as advocates before certain important agencies (the Patent and Trademark Office, the Social Security Administration, the Veteran's Administration, and Immigration agencies) have supremacy over state rules about the unauthorized practice of law. This means that a patent lawyer who practices exclusively before the USPTO can live and have an office in a state where the lawyer is unlicensed.

Rule 5.5 is lengthy and complex, and its associated comment is extensive and tedious (twenty-one paragraphs). The default rule is that lawyers cannot practice in a jurisdiction where they are unlicensed. The rest of the rule covers important exceptions—pro hac vice appearances for litigation, in-house counsel for corporations traveling to the corporation's offices in other states, lawyers doing legal work related to a matter in their home state that happens to occur in another jurisdiction, and lawyers doing temporary work in another jurisdiction that somehow arises from their work in their home state. Lawyers cannot open offices or solicit clients in states where they are unlicensed.

Law firms cannot employ individuals engaged in the unauthorized practice of law, including disbarred attorneys. Assisting or facilitating the unauthorized practice of law by other individuals is itself a violation of Rule 5.5.

QUESTION 17. **The disbarred lawyer-agent.** A firm specializing in sports law represented several professional athletes as clients. The state disciplinary authorities suspended and eventually disbarred one of the associates at the firm, but the disciplinary action did not implicate the rest of the firm (the lawyer's misconduct had occurred completely outside the scope of his duties there). The firm retained the disbarred lawyer as a sports agent for some of the athletes who were clients of the firm. The disbarred lawyer would draft contracts for the athletes and negotiate deals for the firm's clients with their sports teams or with companies seeking the athlete's product endorsement. Could the partners at the firm be subject to discipline for facilitating the disbarred lawyer in the unauthorized practice of law?

A. Yes, because a firm may never have any business dealings with a disbarred attorney.
B. Yes, because the disbarred lawyer is engaging in the unauthorized practice of law by drafting and negotiating contracts for the firm's clients.
C. No, because the firm is not representing that the disbarred lawyer is an attorney and the agent does not have his own clients.
D. No, because the disbarred attorney is working under the supervision of licensed attorneys.

ANALYSIS. Rule 5.5(a) says, "A lawyer shall not practice law in a jurisdiction in violation of the regulation of the legal profession in that jurisdiction, or assist another in doing so." Jurisdictions vary in what they allow disbarred lawyers to do. Some states, such as Indiana, forbid a disbarred or suspended lawyer from "maintaining a presence or occupying an office where the practice of law is conducted." Others, like New York, allow law firms to employ disbarred attorneys as legal assistants, investigators, or paralegals, as long as the individual has no contact with clients. No state would permit a disbarred lawyer to continue drafting contracts and negotiating deals for a law firm's clients. The disbarred lawyer is therefore engaging in the unauthorized practice of law, and the firm is facilitating it, which is also a violation. A recent MPRE tested on this issue.

A incorrectly overstates the prohibition. Even in states where a firm cannot employ a disbarred attorney, the firm could represent the individual as a client, or could purchase the disbarred lawyer's law library, law offices, and so forth.

B is correct. The disbarred lawyer should not be negotiating and drafting contracts, or having any contact with clients (and in some states, should not be working at the firm at all). The partners at the firm are assisting him in the unauthorized practice of law, which violates Rule 5.5(a).

C is incorrect. A firm or lawyer can be guilty of assisting another in the unauthorized practice of law even without representing to others that the person is a lawyer.

D is also incorrect. Merely working under another lawyer's supervision is something that most associates do—for an attorney subject to disbarment, this constitutes the unauthorized practice of law.

QUESTION 18. One time thing. In anticipation of a hearing before a federal agency in Washington, D.C., an attorney travels to a Washington suburb in Virginia from her own state to meet with her client (from her home state), interview witnesses, and review relevant documents. The attorney makes weekly trips there over the course of a year, and spends most of her workweek there each time (four or five days), as the agency hearing pertains to a complex antitrust matter. The attorney solicits no new clients there, but works only on the matter for the client from her home state, but is nonetheless unlicensed in Virginia. Is the attorney's conduct proper?

A. Yes, the rules pertaining to unauthorized practice of law do not apply to any federal agency hearings.
B. No, because her activity there continued for a full year, and therefore is not "temporary," so she is engaged in the unauthorized practice of law.
C. No, because she is spending more time there than in her home state where she holds a license, despite this being a temporary arrangement.
D. Yes, because a lawyer rendering services in a foreign jurisdiction on a temporary basis does not violate the rules merely by engaging in conduct in anticipation of a proceeding or hearing in a jurisdiction in which the lawyer is authorized to practice law.

ANALYSIS. Rule 5.5(c)(2) allows lawyers to practice in another jurisdiction temporarily if they "are in or reasonably related to a pending or potential proceeding before a tribunal in this or another jurisdiction, if the lawyer, or a person the lawyer is assisting, is authorized by law or order to appear in such proceeding or reasonably expects to be so authorized." Similarly, 5.5(c)(4) permits it for instances that "arise out of or are reasonably related to the lawyer's practice in a jurisdiction in which the lawyer is admitted to practice." Both of these provisions could be applicable here. Further, Comment 10 to Rule 5.5 says, "A lawyer rendering services in this jurisdiction on a temporary basis does not violate this Rule when the lawyer engages in conduct in anticipation of a proceeding or hearing in a jurisdiction in which the lawyer is authorized to practice law or in which the lawyer reasonably expects to be admitted pro hac vice."

A is incorrect as it overstates the rule about federal preemption. Some federal statutes preempt state rules about the unauthorized practice of law by allowing non-licensed advocates to appear before the agency (such as the Social Security Administration or the Patent and Trademark Office). Not all agencies have such a statutory provision, though, and preemption must be clear in the statute.

B is incorrect. Rule 5.5 does not define "temporary" for purposes of the exceptions, but Comment 6 offers some guidelines: "Services may be 'temporary' even though the lawyer provides services in this jurisdiction on a recurring basis, or for an extended period of time, as when the lawyer is representing a client in a single lengthy negotiation or litigation."

C is also incorrect. Any lawyer spending time in another jurisdiction is, at least temporarily, there more than in the home state. Rule 5.5 does not delineate a clear threshold as to how much time would no longer constitute a "temporary" endeavor.

D is correct. The lawyer in this case traveled to the other jurisdiction only temporarily to handle tasks in anticipation of an upcoming proceeding. The lawyer does not solicit clients there or have an office open to the public.

QUESTION 19. **Recent graduates awaiting their bar results.** An attorney hires three new associates upon their graduation from law school in a neighboring state. The associates passed the bar in the neighboring state, but they are still unlicensed in the attorney's state. The associates confine their work to conducting research, reviewing documents, and attending meetings with witnesses in support of the attorney, who is responsible for all the litigation. The research done by the associates, however, is far beyond the capabilities of a paralegal or a typical law student associate. Is the attorney subject to discipline for this arrangement?

A. Yes, because the attorney has facilitated the unauthorized practice of law by the associates.

B. No, because the associates are licensed in a neighboring state, which presumably has similar laws and precedents.

C. Yes, because the attorney is relying on research done by lawyers unlicensed in that jurisdiction.

D. No, because the associates merely conduct delegated work under the attorney's supervision, for which the attorney is ultimately responsible.

ANALYSIS. Comment 2 for Rule 5.5 says, "This Rule does not prohibit a lawyer from employing the services of paraprofessionals and delegating functions to them, so long as the lawyer supervises the delegated work and retains responsibility for their work." The MPRE has included questions about law students and recent law graduates. Until a law school graduate has received formal bar admission (that is, not only passing the bar, but also the swearing-in admission process), they cannot provide legal services without engaging in the unauthorized practice of law.

A is incorrect. It is true that the attorney would be subject to discipline were he to assist another in the unauthorized practice of law, but the law school graduates here are working within the parameters set forth in Comment 2 to Rule 5.5, so there is no violation.

B is incorrect, because having a license in a neighboring state does not give an individual authorization to practice law in this state, even if their laws were identical in every respect.

C is also incorrect, because the test for "unauthorized practice of law" is not whether an attorney relies on the legal research, but whether the unlicensed associates are providing direct representation to clients.

D is correct. The associates are working under the supervision of a licensed attorney, not offering to represent clients on their own. This is proper, unless the attorney begins to refer to them as "lawyers" or "attorneys."

QUESTION 20. **Exclusively federal practice.** Attorney has a firm in a state in which the attorney lacks a license to practice law. Attorney's legal work, however, consists entirely of representing local inventors before the United States Patent and Trademark Office in Washington, D.C., either by correspondence or by traveling to appear there in patent proceedings. A relevant federal statute states that non-lawyers may represent patent applicants before the USPTO. The attorney does no other legal work for clients—if clients need representation for family law matters, employment matters, incorporating businesses, or personal injury suits, Attorney refers them to outside counsel. All of Attorney's clients, however, are located in the state where the firm has its office, and Attorney is unlicensed there. Is Attorney subject to discipline?

A. Yes, because Attorney is regularly engaged in the unauthorized practice of law in that state.
B. Yes, because all of the clients reside in a state where Attorney is unlicensed.
C. No, because Attorney is providing services authorized by federal law, which preempts state licensing requirements.
D. No, because Attorney has specialized in a single area of law, and refers all other matters to outside counsel.

ANALYSIS. Rule 5.5(d)(2) allows a licensed lawyer from another jurisdiction to offer legal representation if it includes only "services that the lawyer is authorized by federal or other law or rule to provide in this jurisdiction." This provision was the ABA's response to a landmark U.S. Supreme Court holding that federal law preempts state regulations about lawyer licensing. The seminal case was *Sperry v. Fla. ex rel. Fla. Bar*, 373 U.S. 379 (1963) (holding that Florida could not prohibit non-lawyers from activities authorized by federal patent law, that is, to practice before the U.S. Patent Office, even though this constituted unauthorized practice of law in that state). Circuit courts and state supreme courts have followed *Sperry*: *Surrick v. Killion*, 449 F.3d 520 (3d Cir. 2006) (lawyer suspended by state could still maintain law office in the state dedicated exclusively to his practice in federal court); *Augustine v. Dep't of Veterans Affairs*, 429 F.3d 1334 (Fed. Cir. 2005) (federal law determines whether a lawyer unlicensed in that state may represent clients in a federal administrative proceeding); *Benninghoff v. Superior Court*, 38 Cal. Rptr. 3d 759 (Ct. App. 2006) (lawyer who had surrendered his license with disciplinary charges pending could continue exclusively federal law practice there).

A few qualifications are necessary on this issue. First, if an unlicensed advocate is representing clients exclusively before federal agencies (Social Security, Veteran's Affairs, Patents, and so on), providing *any* legal advice or representation on a state law issue could still constitute the unauthorized practice of law and would not fall under the protection of federal preemption (the *Sperry* doctrine). For example, a question may arise whether a marriage or divorce were valid under state law, which could be relevant to an immigration appeal or collection of Social Security survivor's benefits—and it would be a violation for the federal-practice-only lawyer to answer this question independently. Many lawyers would find this restriction difficult to keep. Moreover, many enforcement actions for unauthorized practice of law by state disciplinary entities end before litigation and therefore do not generate case law—the disciplinary entity sends a cease-and-desist letter to an unlicensed practitioner in the state, and many recipients of such letters simply move their practice out of the state to avoid trouble with the state bar.

Second, it is hard to say whether the modern Supreme Court would uphold, or narrow, the *Sperry* decision from the early 1960s. No test case has reached the court in over fifty years. Some of the facts in the *Sperry* decision were specific to the practice of patent law, and there is some uncertainty whether the current Supreme Court would apply the same rule to other areas of law or to a different category of clients.

Nevertheless, the *Sperry* doctrine is currently the black-letter law on this issue, and an MPRE question about Rule 5.5(d) is likely to test the student's knowledge of the current precedent, rather than the uncertainty about what may happen in the future in this area. The MPRE usually contains at least one question about Constitutional Law as it relates to legal ethics.

A is incorrect. Even though the lawyer seems to be violating the state rules about unauthorized practice of law, the Supreme Court has held that federal statutes preempt state licensing requirements for lawyers.

B is also incorrect, because the place of residence for one's clients is not determinative for the question of whether a lawyer is engaged in the unauthorized practice of law. For example, a duly-licensed attorney can represent an out-of-state client who happens to have a legal matter inside the lawyer's licensing jurisdiction (whether a lawsuit or a legal transaction).

C is correct. The facts here follow those of the *Sperry* case, in which the Supreme Court held that the federal statute preempts state regulations about lawyer licensing. Rule 5.5(d) followed the *Sperry* decision and reflects its holding.

D is partly correct but incomplete. A lawyer who wishes to practice without a license in a jurisdiction under a federal statute must indeed practice federal law exclusively, which requires a high degree of specialization. At the same time, having a specialized practice is not in itself sufficient to avoid state licensing requirements for lawyers—the practice must come entirely under a federal statute that specifically authorizes non-lawyers to act as representatives or advocates before a certain federal agency.

QUESTION 21. **Living across the state line.** An attorney lives in the border town of Nashua, New Hampshire, which is a forty-five-minute drive from Boston, Massachusetts. The attorney took the Massachusetts bar exam and passed it, and now seeks admission to the bar in that state, as she has a job offer from a firm in Boston and plans to commute there every day from her home in New Hampshire. The state bar of Massachusetts has a rule that lawyers must be residents of the state in order to obtain a license to practice law there on a regular basis, so it declines her application to the bar. When the attorney challenges this decision in federal court, will she prevail?

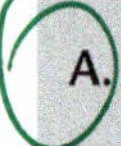

A. Yes, because the residency requirement violates the Privileges and Immunities Clause of the U.S. Constitution.

B. Yes, because the residency requirement violates the Equal Protection Clause of the U.S. Constitution.

C. No, because state courts have inherent authority to regulate the lawyers who practice in that state.

D. No, because as an out-of-state resident, she lacks standing to challenge a regulation in that state.

ANALYSIS. In *Supreme Court of New Hampshire v. Piper*, 470 U.S. 274 (1985), the United States Supreme Court held that a state's refusal to admit an out-of-state resident (New Hampshire had excluded lawyers who lived in neighboring Vermont), despite passing the state's bar exam, violated the Privileges and Immunities Clause. Similarly, the Court invalidated a residency requirement imposed by a federal court in Louisiana, in *Frazier v. Heebe*, 482 U.S. 641 (1987). Then in *Supreme Court of Virginia v. Friedman*, 487 U.S. 59 (1988), the Court struck down a state rule that let permanent Virginia residents licensed out of state waive into the Virginia bar, but required non-Virginia residents to take the state bar exam. Finally, in *Barnard v. Thorstenn*, 489 U.S. 546 (1989), the Court struck down U.S. Virgin Islands' one-year residency requirement for lawyers. Remember that residency requirements violate the Privileges and Immunities Clause rather than the Equal Protection Clause.

A is correct. The Supreme Court held such residency requirements to be unconstitutional in a series of decisions starting with *Supreme Court of New Hampshire v. Piper*, 470 U.S. 274 (1985). The basis of the decision was the Privileges and Immunities Clause.

B is incorrect. The basis for the Supreme Court's invalidation of residency requirements for lawyer licensing was the Privileges and Immunities Clause, not the Equal Protection Clause.

C is partly correct and partly incorrect. The general rule is that state courts have authority to regulate lawyers who practice in that state, but the Supreme Court has held that residency requirements violate the Constitution and are therefore impermissible.

D incorrectly invokes the doctrine of standing, which limits which individuals can properly bring a lawsuit. Even though the rule is an internal regulation within the state, an out-of-state lawyer would still have standing to challenge the residency requirement, as it would deprive that lawyer of the privileges and immunities of citizenship.

F. Rule 5.6—Restrictions on Rights to Practice

Rule 5.6 is much briefer than most of the Model Rules, and pertains only to self-imposed restraints on a lawyer's ability to practice law. Rule 5.6(a) expressly forbids non-compete agreements that are common in other industries. Lawyers cannot offer or make "a partnership, shareholders, operating, employment, or other similar type of agreement that restricts the right of a lawyer to practice after termination of the relationship, except an agreement concerning benefits upon retirement."

Rule 5.6(b) forbids a lawyer from offering or making "an agreement in which a restriction on the lawyer's right to practice is part of the settlement of a client controversy." Some corporate defendants in tort cases may try to include, as a condition of settlement, that the plaintiff's lawyer can never again practice personal injury law, in an attempt to preemptively limit the number of future lawsuits. This is improper—Comment 2 for Rule 5.6 clarifies, "prohibits a lawyer from agreeing not to represent other persons in connection with settling a claim on behalf of a client."

QUESTION 22. **Eliminating the plaintiff's lawyer.** An attorney is a notorious personal injury lawyer, widely feared by defendant corporations and insurers who must defend claims. The attorney reaches one exceptionally favorable settlement for his client, a structured settlement paying several hundred million dollars over the period of five years. The defendant has lost cases to the attorney on several occasions, and wants to avoid dealing with him in the future. The defendant demands, as a condition of settlement, that the attorney will not represent any other clients in the future in tort actions related to this defendant or even to similar businesses in that jurisdiction. The attorney's contingent fee will be large enough for him to retire comfortably to a private tropical island and never need to work again, so he is amenable to this condition of the settlement. Is the attorney subject to discipline for this agreement?

A. No, because the attorney is in a position to retire, so this is more like selling a practice to the opposing party than restricting a lawyer's ability to continue practicing law.
B. No, because the condition is part of a settlement in a case where the lawyer is receiving a contingent fee, so this is not a genuine restriction on the right to practice law.
C. Yes, because it is improper to have a settlement agreement that structures payments over such a long period.
D. Yes, the agreement violates the rules, but the attorney probably does not care about being subject to discipline if he plans to leave the practice of law.

ANALYSIS. Lawyers cannot agree, as part of a settlement on behalf of a client, to stop representing other persons, whether against that party or in general. Note that without such a rule, such a proposed condition of settlement would create a conflict of interest between the lawyer and the client in that case. The client's interest might be to take a higher settlement and let the lawyer deal with the restraint on his future practice, while the lawyer would normally refuse such a condition, even if it meant obtaining a less favorable settlement for a client. Rule 5.6 eliminates this type of situation.

A is incorrect. Even though Rule 5.6 contains an exception for lawyers retiring or selling a practice (in Section (a)), Section (b) expressly forbids such agreements as part of the settlement of a client's matter.

B is also incorrect, because the contingent fee does not change the fact that this agreement is a clear violation of the rule in Rule 5.6(b).

C uses an incorrect rationale—the agreement indeed violates the Model Rules, but not because of the structured payment plan in the settlement, which is actually commonplace in tort cases.

D is correct. The agreement violates the rules and the lawyer could be subject to discipline, regardless of whether the lawyer will care about the sanction.

QUESTION 23. **Non-compete agreements for associates.** An attorney owns his own firm in a small town, and hires an associate as a junior lawyer to help with the growing caseload. The employment agreement stipulates that the associate cannot practice law in that small town after leaving the attorney's firm. Which of the following is true regarding this arrangement?

A. Neither the attorney nor the associate are subject to discipline for such an agreement.

B. The attorney is subject to discipline for requiring this as a condition of employment, but the associate is not subject to discipline because his employer imposed the condition upon him.

C. Both the attorney and the associate are subject to discipline for such an agreement.

D. The associate is subject to discipline for accepting employment in a firm under such a condition, but the attorney is not subject to discipline, because the associate is the one who will have to execute the provision after leaving the firm.

ANALYSIS. Rule 5.6(a) forbids the non-compete agreements between employees and employers (or between partners or business co-owners) that are common today in some sectors of the economy. The rule forbids participating in the arrangement from either side—as the employer or as an employee of a firm.

A is incorrect, because both lawyers have violated Rule 5.6(a) by agreeing to a restriction on the right of the lawyer to practice law.

B is partly incorrect, because both lawyers, not merely the associate, are subject to discipline in this case for violating the rules.

C is correct. The rule says that a lawyer may not "participate in offering or making" such an agreement, so both lawyers are subject to discipline.

D is partly incorrect, because both lawyers, not just the employer, have violated Rule 5.6 by participating in this agreement.

G. Rule 8.3—Mandatory and Permissive Reporting of Misconduct

Rule 8.3 creates a mandatory reporting requirement for serious violations—in other words, lawyers or judges could be subject to discipline for failing to report other lawyers whom they know to be violating the ethical rules in a serious way. In practice, this rule is rarely the subject of enforcement actions, except occasionally against other lawyers in the same firm, who may appear to be complicit in a colleague's misconduct. For purposes of the MPRE, there are two components of Rule 8.3 that are particularly important—the duty to report (which applies only to serious misconduct or violations, not to minor infractions), and the requirement of actual knowledge. A lawyer does not have a duty to report when there is mere suspicion present.

QUESTION 24. Money laundering. An attorney knew about another lawyer's involvement in an illegal money laundering enterprise, although the money laundering was unrelated to the other lawyer's law practice or representation of clients. Eventually, when federal law enforcement officials bring criminal charges against the other lawyer, who is part of another firm, the first attorney's awareness of the situation becomes evident. Could the attorney who knew of the wrongdoing and ignored it be subject to discipline?

A. Yes, because it is a violation of the Rules of Professional Conduct to fail to report serious fraud or criminal activity by another lawyer.
B. Yes, because the lawyer who knew and did nothing was an accomplice after the fact.
C. No, because the attorney had no duty to report misconduct of lawyers in other firms.
D. No, because the attorney could have put himself in danger by reporting an organized crime effort, and lawyers do not have to report misconduct when doing so might expose the reporting lawyer to retaliation by criminal organizations.

ANALYSIS. Rule 8.3 requires lawyers to report serious misconduct by other attorneys. In this case, the attorney knows that another lawyer is committing a serious crime and violating various rules pertaining to the integrity of the profession. The lawyer has a duty to report this to the bar, and a lawyer could be subject to discipline (in theory) for failing to do so.

A is correct, because the lawyer has first-hand knowledge that the crime is taking place, and therefore has a duty to report the other lawyer to the disciplinary authorities in that state.

B is incorrect because it addresses a potential criminal charge (accomplice after the fact) that is not a feature of the Model Rules. The problem here is not that the lawyer is a co-conspirator, but that there is an affirmative duty to report misconduct.

C is also incorrect, because Rule 8.3 imposes an affirmative duty on lawyers to report violations: "A lawyer who knows that another lawyer has committed a violation of the Rules of Professional Conduct that raises a substantial question as to that lawyer's honesty, trustworthiness or fitness as a lawyer in other respects, shall inform the appropriate professional authority."

D is incorrect even though it may be true in practice. The Model Rules do not account for the possibility that a lawyer may face retaliation for reporting misconduct by other lawyers.

QUESTION 25. Just a hunch. An attorney suspects that another lawyer in his firm has violated the Rules of Professional Conduct in a rather serious matter, but has no first-hand knowledge of the situation—his suspicion rests on the fact that the other lawyer seems to be acting paranoid and evasive, and a number of strange coincidences have occurred in his cases. Does the attorney who suspects something seriously wrong is afoot have a duty to report the other lawyer to the state bar disciplinary authority?

A. Yes, but he must make an anonymous complaint to the state bar.
B. Yes, because a lawyer who knows of a violation of the rules that raises serious questions about the other attorney's honesty must report it to the state disciplinary authority.
C. No, because he does not have actual knowledge of the violation.
D. No, because lawyers do not have to report violations by other attorneys at their own firm, which would create internal divisions and mistrust between partners.

ANALYSIS. Rule 8.3 requires actual knowledge of the wrongdoing in order to trigger the mandatory reporting requirement: "A lawyer who *knows* that another lawyer has committed a violation of the Rules of Professional Conduct . . ." (emphasis added). The definition section in Rule 1.0 defines "knows" as denoting "actual knowledge of the fact in question. A person's knowledge may be inferred from circumstances." In this case, the lawyer has suspicion but not actual knowledge as defined in the Model Rules.

A is incorrect, as the reporting requirement mentions nothing about making anonymous complaints to the bar.

B is partly incorrect, even though it uses the actual verbiage of Rule 8.3(a), because it fails to mention that this is inapplicable to a situation where the attorney merely suspects another lawyer of misconduct.

C is correct, because the lawyer does not "know" about the violation in the sense that the Model Rules define that term.

D is wrong, because lawyers do have to report misconduct by colleagues in their own firms, and the failure to do so is the most likely occasion for enforcement of the reporting requirement.

H. Rule 8.1 — Bar Admission and Disciplinary Matters

Bar admission is the first subject that students encounter in most law school courses on Professional Responsibility courses, but it rarely appears as the subject of questions on the MPRE. Rule 8.1 is relatively straightforward. As part of an application for admission to the bar, or in a post-admission disciplinary action, no lawyer may knowingly make false statements of material fact to the disciplinary authority. Note that this truthfulness requirement applies to applicants to admission, lawyers subject to disciplinary proceedings or inquiries, and other individuals serving as references or recommenders. Rule 8.1 also forbids withholding information from disciplinary authorities that would be necessary to correct misapprehensions, and requires lawyers to comply with inquiries and information requests from the state bar. The comments contain predictable exceptions for honoring Fifth Amendment privileges against self-incrimination (as long as the constitutional privilege is asserted openly), and for permitting lawyers representing other attorneys before a disciplinary tribunal to follow the confidentiality requirements of Rule 1.6.

Two other points in this regard are important. First, making false statements, creating a wrong impression by withholding crucial information, or being uncooperative/unresponsive to the tribunal are separate violations from whatever actions triggered the disciplinary inquiry originally. In other words, a lawyer might successfully clear herself of the original allegations in a disciplinary proceeding and still be subject to discipline for making false statements or refusing to cooperate at some point in the proceedings. Second, false statements made during a bar admission application can be the subject of disciplinary action later, even after the lawyer has been practicing for several years — whenever the false statements come to light. Violations during a bar application can also affect subsequent bar applications in other states.

QUESTION 26. **That was then, this is now.** An attorney has been practicing for five years, but on her application to the bar five years earlier, she had stated that she had attended a particular private high school, when in fact she had attended a public high school. An unhappy client recently filed a grievance against the attorney, which was frivolous, but the state disciplinary authority had to conduct a routine, preliminary inquiry into the matter in order to make a determination that the complaint merited dismissal. The disciplinary board member assigned to the case had attended the elite private high school from which the attorney claimed to have graduated, and made a mental note of the attorney's high school when he did a cursory review of her bar admission files. He thought it was strange that he had never seen or heard her name at any alumni or reunion functions, as they had supposedly graduated the same year and the classes were small. On a hunch, the board member checked the alumni lists for the school and discovered that the attorney had lied on her application to the bar five years earlier. When asked about this issue, the attorney said she could not be subject to discipline now for the misstatement she made several years ago, and that the board lacked jurisdiction because it was unrelated to the current grievance complaint. Is she correct?

A. Yes, because she has been practicing now for five years and has demonstrated her character and fitness to practice law, making the application queries moot.
B. Yes, because it was improper for the board member to conduct a self-initiated investigation into her high school attendance merely because he had graduated from the same high school that the attorney listed on her original bar application.
C. No, because the fact that she lied about her high school makes it likely that the current client complaint has merit as well.
D. No, because if a person makes a material false statement in connection with an application for admission, it may be the basis for subsequent disciplinary action if the person is admitted.

ANALYSIS. Comment 1 for Rule 8.1 says, "Hence, if a person makes a material false statement in connection with an application for admission, it may be the basis for subsequent disciplinary action if the person is admitted, and in any event may be relevant in a subsequent admission application." There is no statute of limitations in the Model Rules, at least for false statements to the state bar. Note that previously overlooked problems with a bar application can easily come to light during the routine file review involved in handling grievances against practitioners, even if the grievance itself ends in a dismissal due to lack of merit. This question has similar facts to an actual case in which the applicant had lied about which high school he had attended, claiming he attended a private high school rather than a public high school. It was the only false statement on the application, but it became the basis for disciplinary action later.

A is incorrect. While the intervening period of good behavior might be relevant at the hearing—and might persuade a tribunal to impose a lighter sanction—the intervening time does not erase the violation during her application. A lawyer can be subject to discipline at any time for a false statement made on a bar application.

B is also incorrect. There is no rule against board members conducting their own preliminary checks into the subject of a grievance. In fact, it is perfectly natural for someone to notice a person claiming to have been a classmate and seek to refresh their memory about the person.

C is the wrong answer because the dismissed grievance is unrelated to the bar application issue, and it is unlikely that a tribunal would reopen a grievance dismissed for lack of merit or evidence merely because they uncovered an unrelated violation by the attorney in question.

D is correct. False statements on a bar application, even if discovered some time later, can be the basis for a disciplinary action against the licensed attorney.

QUESTION 27. **A clean start in another state.** An attorney obtained admission to the bar in New York and practiced there for two years. She worked for Big Firm, which has offices in five states and a few locations overseas. After her two years in the New York office, the firm transferred her to its office in San Diego, California. The attorney then applied for admission to the California bar under a reciprocity arrangement, and the state bar admitted her without making her re-take the bar exam. After practicing in California for three years, somehow the New York state bar learned that the attorney had made false statements on her original bar application about misdemeanor arrests during college. The New York bar informed the California state disciplinary authority about this problem, and the California state bar commenced disciplinary proceedings against the attorney in California. Can the attorney be subject to discipline in California for false statements made on a bar application in another state?

A. Yes, because the states depend on each other to help enforce their own attorney disciplinary rules, and California therefore has a legal duty to enforce disciplinary rules from New York.

B. Yes, because if a person makes a material false statement in connection with an application for admission, it may be relevant in a subsequent admission application or disciplinary proceeding elsewhere.

C. No, because the alleged misconduct occurred on a bar application in a non-contiguous state, so California has no jurisdiction over the matter.

D. No, because the fact that the attorney has now practiced for five years means that the estoppel doctrine prevents a state bar from revisiting her original bar application.

ANALYSIS. Comment 1 for Rule 8.1 also says, " . . . [A] material false statement in connection with an application for admission . . . may be relevant in a subsequent admission application." False statements in an application to the bar in one state can affect an application to the bar in another state, as well as subsequent disciplinary proceedings in any state.

A is incorrect. California has discretion whether to discipline lawyers for violations that occurred in other states—there is no legal duty for one state to enforce another state's rules.

B is correct. The attorney made false statements in her New York bar application, and this is relevant to disciplinary authorities in other states. California based its admission of the attorney upon her prior admission in New York, due to the reciprocity system, so the violations in the first application are imputable to the second application. A state authority can discipline a lawyer later on if it discovers violations with regard to the original application for admission.

C is wrong. It is irrelevant that the states are non-contiguous. California can claim jurisdiction because it admitted the attorney based on her existing license in New York, so fraud used in obtaining that original license directly affects California's admission decision.

D is also incorrect. There is no time limit on the relevance of prior violations for subsequent bar applications or disciplinary proceedings.

I. Rule 8.4—Lawyer Misconduct

Rule 8.4 expands the scope of potential violations that could subject a lawyer to discipline. Subsection (a) makes it a violation to violate any other section of the Model Rules (a rather redundant provision), but more importantly, adds attempt and accessory liability to the MRPC. Lawyers can be subject to discipline for even attempting to violate a rule, as well as assisting others in doing so, and offering inducements or otherwise using third parties to violate the rules at the lawyer's behest.

Moreover, Rule 8.4(b) makes it a violation for a lawyer to "commit a criminal act that reflects adversely on the lawyer's honesty, trustworthiness or fitness as a lawyer," meaning that a felony conviction is likely to result automatically in disciplinary proceedings as well, probably resulting in disbarment. Not all crimes are relevant; Comment 2 says, "Offenses involving violence, dishonesty, breach of trust, or serious interference with the administration of justice are in that category." The same comment adds that even minor crimes, if numerous enough, could give rise to a violation of this provision: "A pattern of repeated offenses, even ones of minor significance when considered separately, can indicate indifference to legal obligation."

Subsection (c) goes further still, and subjects lawyers to discipline if they "engage in conduct involving dishonesty, fraud, deceit or misrepresentation," even when the lawyer did not (or could not) face prosecution for a crime. An example would be an incident of academic misconduct, such as plagiarism or cheating on exams, in law school (prior to admission), or during a Master's of Law (that is, an "LL.M.") program after admission.

Remaining sections of Rule 8.4 prohibit actions prejudicial to the administration of justice, assisting judicial officers in violating the law, or telling clients that the lawyer has personal influence with a judge or government official that will help with the client's case.

QUESTION 28. **Simple battery.** A criminal court found that a lawyer had engaged in domestic violence against his partner, and convicted the lawyer of misdemeanor-level battery, for which he served a six-month term of probation. Could the attorney be subject to professional discipline as well?

A. Yes, because any illegal activity by a lawyer constitutes professional misconduct.
B. No, because crimes of violence have no specific connection to fitness for the practice of law.
C. Yes, because crimes of violence indicate a lack of the character traits required for law practice.
D. No, because only felonies (not misdemeanors) can constitute professional misconduct.

ANALYSIS. Comment 2 for Rule 8.4 explicitly states that any crimes "involving violence, dishonesty, breach of trust, or serious interference with the administration of justice" would "indicate lack of those characteristics relevant to law practice." Domestic violence could be the basis for suspension or disbarment.

A is incorrect because it overstates the rule. The comments for Rule 8.4 explicitly state that not all crimes constitute a violation, but only those that relate somehow to a lawyer's fitness to practice law. For example, adultery or fornication (which were still criminal offenses in some jurisdictions when they drafted the Model Rules, albeit rarely enforced), do not reflect on a lawyer's fitness to practice.

B is incorrect. Comment 2 for Rule 8.4 specifically identifies crimes of violence as indicating a lack of the character required to practice law.

C is correct. The Model Rules categorize violence along with crimes of dishonesty (fraud, perjury, and so on) in reflecting directly on the person's character and fitness to practice law.

D is incorrect. Rule 8.4 does not use the felony-misdemeanor distinction, or even the seriousness of the crime, but instead focuses on the nature of the crime itself. As Comment 2 observes, "A pattern of repeated offenses, even ones of minor significance when considered separately, can indicate indifference to legal obligation."

QUESTION 29. It's the little things. An attorney faced criminal sanctions for having over two thousand unpaid traffic and parking tickets, and several instances of failure to appear for jury duty. Could the attorney be subject to professional discipline for these minor offenses?

A. Yes, because any illegal activity by a lawyer constitutes professional misconduct.
B. Yes, because a pattern of repeated offenses, even ones of minor significance when considered separately, can indicate indifference to legal obligation.
C. No, because traffic violations or neglecting jury duty would have no specific connection to fitness for the practice of law.
D. No, because these activities do not arise from or pertain to the attorney's representation of a client.

ANALYSIS. Comment 2 for Rule 8.4 concludes, "A pattern of repeated offenses, even ones of minor significance when considered separately, can indicate indifference to legal obligation." There are recorded cases of disciplinary authorities imposing sanctions on lawyers for egregious amounts (hundreds) of traffic violations.

A incorrectly overstates the rule. Not all criminal violations constitute a violation of Rule 8.4. Only offenses that indicate a lack of the character traits needed to practice law are relevant, but an extreme pattern of small violations evinces indifference to legal obligations.

B is correct. A few tickets would not be significant, but two thousand is truly extreme. Combined with several instances of not reporting for jury duty, a disciplinary authority could conclude that there is something wrong with the attorney—or at least his attitude about obeying the law.

C incorrectly ignores the cumulative effect of numerous violations. It is true that traffic offenses or missing jury duty would normally not be serious enough to subject a lawyer to discipline, but an ongoing pattern of such offenses—especially to the extreme described here—could rise to the level of reflecting on the individual's fitness as a lawyer.

D is also incorrect. The point of Subsections (b) and (c) for Rule 8.4 is to cover actions that might occur outside a lawyer's representation of clients, but that still reflect on the lawyer's character and bring the legal profession into disrepute.

J. Rule 8.5—Disciplinary Authority; Powers of Courts and Other Bodies to Regulate Lawyers

QUESTION 30. **Punished in both states.** An attorney had a license to practice law in two jurisdictions—his home state where he lived and had his main office, and a neighboring state where he represented several clients each year. The attorney committed serious professional misconduct in his home state, and received a public reprimand from the state disciplinary authorities. All of the conduct took place in his home state, the client resided in the state, and the representation took place entirely within his home state. The lawyer's conduct would have violated the rules in either of the jurisdictions where he had a license to practice law, because it involved commingling client funds with his own money, and the states had nearly identical rules concerning this activity. After the attorney received a public reprimand in his home state, where the misconduct occurred, the state bar disciplinary authority in the neighboring state (where he also practiced) then commenced disciplinary proceedings against him as well. Ultimately, the neighboring state bar suspended his license for six months in that state, a much more severe sanction than the public reprimand he received in his home state, where the misconduct actually occurred. The attorney claims that the neighboring state bar has no jurisdiction over conduct that occurred entirely outside of the state. He also objects that the second punishment raises double jeopardy concerns. Is the attorney correct?

A. Yes, because even in cases where a second state can administer discipline over the same conduct, double jeopardy rules prevent the second tribunal from imposing a more severe sanction than the first tribunal already imposed on the lawyer.
B. Yes, because a lawyer cannot be subject to the disciplinary authority of two jurisdictions for the same conduct if it occurred entirely within one state.
C. No, because a lawyer may be subject to the disciplinary authority of two jurisdictions for the same conduct, and may receive different sanctions in each state.
D. No, because choice-of-law rules require that each state impose the same sanction.

ANALYSIS. Rule 8.5(a) says, "A lawyer may be subject to the disciplinary authority of both this jurisdiction and another jurisdiction for the same conduct." If a lawyer has a license to practice in multiple states, a violation committed anywhere could be the basis for a disciplinary action in any of those states, if it violates the professional rules in that jurisdiction. Disciplinary actions are civil-administrative in nature, not criminal, so double jeopardy does not apply.

A is incorrect. Double jeopardy applies only to criminal proceedings (and even then, it often does not apply across state lines under the "separate sovereigns" rule). Lawyer disciplinary proceedings are civil cases, occurring either in civil court or before an administrative tribunal.

B is also incorrect. Rule 8.5(a) explicitly states that the same action or conduct could subject the lawyer to multiple disciplinary actions in different states.

C is correct. The lawyer committed a violation in his home state, but other states that have licensed him to practice law may also sanction him for the same behavior—with a reprimand, suspension to practice in their jurisdiction, or even disbarment in that state. Of course, such sanctions apply only in the state that imposes them.

D incorrectly states the choice-of-law rule. The choice-of-law rule means that "the rules of the jurisdiction in which the lawyer's conduct occurred, or, if the predominant effect of the conduct is in a different jurisdiction, the rules of that jurisdiction shall be applied to the conduct." It does not require the same sanction in each state, as sanctions are a matter of discretion for each court or disciplinary tribunal.

QUESTION 31. **Regulation by the legislature.** A state legislature enacted a statute governing the licensing of attorneys and discipline for practitioners. The preamble to the statute asserts "field preemption" over the regulation of lawyers in that jurisdiction, thereby abolishing all prior rules and codes of the state bar. A lawyer comes under discipline under the new law and contests the legal validity of the enactment itself. What is the result?

A. The court will hold the law invalid because the judiciary has inherent power to regulate the attorneys who practice in its courts.

B. The court will reject the lawyer's claim about the law's invalidity and will uphold the sanction.

C. The court will refuse to hear the case because it now lacks jurisdiction over the matter.

D. The court will certify a question to the legislature to seek its decision in the matter.

ANALYSIS. The judiciary has inherent power (under common law, and probably under the separation of powers doctrine as well) to regulate the lawyers who appear in the courts representing others. Field preemption by the legislature would not survive a court challenge. Of course, legislatures have made some incursions into the regulation of lawyers. There are statutes (especially federal) permitting non-lawyers to represent certain types of parties, especially in administrative proceedings (Social Security hearings, Veterans' Benefits, Patent Office, and Immigration). In addition, some statutes impose some requirements for admission to the bar, reporting requirements by lawyers, and so on.

A is correct. Courts have resisted legislative overreaching in the regulation of lawyers, holding to the common law tradition—and the implication of the separation of powers doctrine—that courts have inherent authority to regulate the lawyers under their jurisdiction.

B is incorrect. It is unlikely that the legislation would survive a court challenge, and the sanction would be invalid if the law requiring it were invalid.

C is also incorrect. The courts will not concede that they lack jurisdiction to regulate attorneys who practice in that state.

D incorrectly invokes an imaginary procedure. Courts do not have a procedure for certifying questions to the legislature.

K. The Closer

For better or worse, the legal profession is primarily self-regulating. The judiciary (which is mostly lawyers-turned-judges) has inherent authority to regulate the attorneys who appear in its courts, which in most states it delegates in whole or in part to a state bar or similar disciplinary authority. In order to regulate the lawyers, the state bars must clearly define which individuals belong to the regulated profession as opposed to the general population. As a result, every state has rules for admission to the bar (both eligibility requirements and procedures), procedures for disciplining or delicensing lawyers, requirements for maintaining a license to practice, and so on. In addition, a number of rules about supervisory responsibility operate to prevent lawyers from using (or allowing) their subordinates, including non-lawyers, to circumvent the ethical duties that lawyers owe to their clients, to the courts, and to third parties.

QUESTION 32. **Responsibility in hiring.** A small firm employs several associates who work under the supervision of the partners, as well as three clerical staff. The most recently hired associate has a complicated situation with his license to practice law. The associate graduated from an accredited law school, successfully passed the state bar exam, and applied for admission to the bar, believing he had met all the eligibility requirements. He had no criminal record or history of academic misconduct, or any other problems meeting the traditional character and fitness requirements. The state bar approved his application and he attended his swearing-in ceremony. The state legislature, however, had recently passed a statute creating the option of a legislative veto for lawyers seeking admission to practice law in the state. The sponsors of the enactment had stated that its purpose was to prevent the grown children of illegal immigrants from becoming lawyers, even though the bar applicant might be a United States citizen "just because they happened to be born here." The associate was born in Arizona one month after his parents had moved there illegally from a country in Central America. A staff member of the relevant legislative committee flagged the associate's name from a list of recent bar licensees, along with three others in his situation. During a special session of the legislature, the state legislature exercised the equivalent of a legislative veto, narrowly passing a special act that permanently disbarred the associate and the others for the sole reason that their parents were illegal aliens. The associate received official notice of his disbarment from the Office of Legislative Counsel, not from the state bar. This occurred one week after the associate's swearing-in ceremony by the state bar, and two days after he started working at the firm. A notice of the disbarments appeared in the next issue of the state bar journal, but most of the firm was unaware of the situation, except for one managing partner in whom the associate had confided. Could the partners at the firm be subject to discipline for employing the associate as an attorney, despite challenging any such discipline in court?

A. Yes, because they have employed an associate who engaged in the unauthorized practice of law.
B. Yes, but only the managing partner, who had actual knowledge that the associate was no longer licensed to practice law, would be subject to discipline.
C. No, because the associate was duly licensed at the time that the firm hired him, and the partners cannot be responsible for an unforeseeable event that occurred afterward, such as the associate's disbarment by a special act of the legislature.
D. No, because the courts have inherent power to regulate the legal profession, and the legislature's action could not survive a court challenge.

ANALYSIS. This question ties together several different issues raised in this chapter. First, partners in a law firm are responsible for their subordinates, and it would be a violation to employ an associate who had no license to practice law. The tougher question is whether the partners (besides the managing partner) knew, or should have known. In addition, on multiple occasions in recent years, the MPRE has included one question regarding the inherent power of the judiciary to regulate the legal profession as opposed to the legislature. The general rule is that this power belongs entirely to the judiciary, but there are certainly some exceptions (such as a barratry statute or criminal penalties for the unauthorized practice of law), leaving a bit of uncertainty in this area, at least around the edges. Nevertheless, this question involves the most egregious form of intervention (or interference) that a legislature can employ, a legislative veto-special act, which students will remember from their Constitutional Law course as being invalid under many circumstances.

A is incorrect. It is true that employing non-lawyers to do legal work is a violation—assisting another in the unauthorized practice of law. Even so, the associate obtained a valid law license in the state, and the revocation of the license by a special act of the legislature (at least for a reason unrelated to the associate's own conduct) would probably be void. At the least, it is not clear enough to furnish the basis of a disciplinary action against the partners.

B is also incorrect. It is true that the Model Rules impose disciplinary liability on partners who actually supervise or manage the subordinates in question, and not partners who have no knowledge of the subordinate's wrongdoing. Even so, a disciplinary authority is likely to use a "should have known" standard (or its near equivalent, inferring knowledge from the circumstances). The publication of the disbarment notice in the state's law journal, combined with the general duty to monitor for serious violations like the unauthorized practice of law, would probably guarantee discipline for the other partners. On the other hand, as seen above, the correct answer is that none of the partners would be subject to discipline because the legislature's action is invalid.

C has the right conclusion for the wrong reason. The partners are probably not subject to discipline, but only because the disbarment is legally invalid. If the disbarment were legally valid, the partners probably would be subject to discipline.

D is correct. The judiciary has inherent power to regulate the lawyers practicing in a jurisdiction, and it is very unlikely that the legislature's action would withstand a judicial challenge, especially if the associate meets all the eligibility requirements in the state for admission to the bar (including character and fitness).

Stevenson's Picks

1. Responsibility versus liability	A
2. Not my brother's keeper	A
3. Respondeat superior	A

4. Protocols in place	A
5. Let's fix this	A
6. Dumping on the associates	A
7. Just following orders	A
8. Reasonable resolution	A
9. Nuremburg defense	A
10. Relevant factors	A
11. Duties in the cloud	A
12. Have it your way	A
13. Profit sharing for paralegals	B
14. Profit sharing and votes for paralegals	C
15. Working with Washington lawyers	C
16. The marketing guru and his contract	C
17. The disbarred lawyer-agent	B
18. One time thing	D
19. Recent graduates awaiting their bar results	D
20. Exclusively federal practice	C
21. Living across the state line	A
22. Eliminating the plaintiff's lawyer	D
23. Non-compete agreements for associates	C
24. Money laundering	A
25. Just a hunch	C
26. That was then, this is now	D
27. A clean start in another state	B
28. Simple battery	C
29. It's the little things	B
30. Punished in both states	C
31. Regulation by the legislature	A
32. Responsibility in hiring	D

7

Communications About Legal Services

CHAPTER OVERVIEW

The MPRE examiners state on their website that approximately 4 to 10 percent of the exam will be on the subjects they group under the heading "Communications about Legal Services." This percentage translates into between two and six questions out of the sixty questions on any given administration of the MPRE. This makes it one of the least-tested subjects on the MPRE, which is the reason for its placement near the end of this book. For legal practitioners, disciplinary actions for violations of advertising and solicitation are relatively rare compared to other areas, perhaps due to the fact that many states now require pre-approval of lawyer ads and websites. The low priority given to these rules by the examiners is consistent with the attention these rules receive from lawyer disciplinary authorities across the country.

On the other hand, most Professional Responsibility casebooks used in law schools feature the advertising and solicitation rules at the beginning of the course, after licensing rules, so many law students spend a disproportionate amount of class time on these rules. In addition, the U.S. Supreme Court has intervened in this area perhaps more than any other area of the professional rules for lawyers, invalidating longstanding restrictions on lawyer advertising based on Free Speech grounds. Landmark decisions by the Supreme Court always attract the attention of law professors and casebook authors, which further extends the time law students may devote to this area in their course work.

Model Rule 7.1 is a straightforward prohibition against false advertising, including half-truths designed to be misleading. Historically, most states (either by statute or bar rules) prohibited all lawyer advertising, but as mentioned above, the Supreme Court eventually held that such outright bans violated the First Amendment. At the same time, the Court has repeatedly emphasized that states could prohibit false or misleading advertising by lawyers. No questions about false advertising (i.e., Rule 7.1) have appeared on the MPRE in recent years, probably because the rule is rather simple—false or misleading advertising is impermissible. The practice questions in this chapter begin with Rule 7.2, which appears more frequently in questions on the MPRE.

A. Rule 7.2—Advertising

Rule 7.2(a) explicitly permits paid advertising (print ads, radio and television spots, billboards, and Internet). In contrast, Rule 7.2(b) prohibits most payments or incentives by lawyers for personal referrals: "A lawyer shall not give anything of value to a person for recommending the lawyer's services . . ." There are some exceptions: the normal (reasonable) payments to advertisers, purchasing another lawyer's law firm (regulated under Rule 1.17), membership fees for legal service plans and nonprofit lawyer referral services, and most importantly for test purposes, reciprocal referral agreements with other professionals. These reciprocal arrangements cannot be exclusive (either party must be free to refer people to others as well), and lawyers must inform referred clients of the existence and nature of the referral arrangement.

Rule 7.2(c) adds one more specific requirement for lawyer advertising—every advertisement in any media must include the name and office address of at least one lawyer responsible for its content. If a multiple-choice question on the test includes a quote of the text of a firm's advertisement, always check to make sure that there is a name and address for at least one of the lawyers in the firm.

QUESTION 1. **Emergency room patients.** An attorney is dating a woman whose sister works as a nurse in a hospital emergency room. The attorney gives the nurse, his girlfriend's sister, a stack of his business cards and law firm brochures, and offers to pay her $200 for any clients who hire him because of her referrals, with the understanding that she will not refer patients to any other lawyers. The nurse recommends several patients per month to the attorney for representation in personal injury claims, and one or two per month actually hire the attorney to represent them. Is such an arrangement proper?

A. Yes, because the nurse is closely related to the attorney, given that the attorney is dating her sister.
B. Yes, because the attorney is not paying the nurse on a contingent fee basis.
C. No, because a lawyer shall not give anything of value to a person for recommending the lawyer's services, with certain exceptions not applicable here.
D. No, because the fact that the attorney is dating her sister creates a conflict of interest if the nurse refers clients to the attorney.

ANALYSIS. Rule 7.2(b) prohibits paid personal referrals, although there is an exception for non-exclusive reciprocal referral arrangements between lawyers and other professionals. In this question, the lawyer is paying the nurse $200 for each referral that turns into an actual client for the lawyer, which violates Rule 7.2. Of course, it would be appropriate to have a reciprocal referral arrangement with a nurse (another professional for purposes of the rule), but only if it is non-exclusive. The facts here say that the nurse promised not to refer patients to any other lawyers, so this exception does not apply (and probably would not apply due to the payments, unless those were reciprocal as well).

A is incorrect because the relation of the nurse to the attorney is irrelevant. Except as permitted under Rule 7.2, lawyers are not permitted to pay others for recommending the lawyer's services. Even so, the attorney may agree to enter into a reciprocal referral arrangement but the facts do not indicate that the arrangement between the attorney and the nurse is a reciprocal referral arrangement. Therefore, it is not a proper arrangement.

B is also incorrect. The attorney has agreed to pay the nurse $200 for any clients that hire the attorney as a result of the nurse's referral. According to Rule 7.2, this is not a proper arrangement.

C is the correct answer. The Rules of Professional Conduct (7.2) state that a lawyer shall not give anything of value to a person for recommending the lawyer's services unless it is an exception listed in Rule 7.2(b). Here, the attorney's offer to pay the nurse for referrals is improper under the rules.

Finally, **D** is not the right answer. This answer choice is obviously wrong because there is no conflict-of-interest issue here. The issue here is the fact that the referral arrangement between the nurse and the attorney is improper.

QUESTION 2. A mutually beneficial arrangement. An attorney made an informal agreement with a physician that they would refer clients to each other when the situation seemed appropriate. They did not pay each other any money for referrals, but the relationship was explicitly reciprocal—the attorney referred patients who needed medical examinations to the physician, and when the physician had patients needing legal representation, he referred them to the attorney. The relationship was not explicitly exclusive—each was free to refer clients to others—but it happened that neither had similar reciprocal relationships with anyone else. They always informed their clients when making such referrals that they had a reciprocal relationship. Is such an arrangement proper?

A. Yes, a lawyer may agree to refer clients to another lawyer or a non-lawyer professional, in return for the undertaking of that person to refer clients or customers to the lawyer, as long as clients are aware and the relationship is not exclusive.
B. Yes, because the agreement is informal, not a written contract.
C. No, because a lawyer may not agree to refer clients to another lawyer or a non-lawyer professional, in return for the undertaking of that person to refer clients or customers to the lawyer.
D. No, because the relationship described here is de facto exclusive, even if they have not agreed specifically to keep the relationship exclusive.

ANALYSIS. Rule 7.2(b)(4) restricts reciprocal referral arrangements between lawyers and other professionals. Such arrangements are proper only if (1) the reciprocal referral agreement is not exclusive, and (2) the client is informed of the existence and nature of the agreement. In this question, it appears that the arrangement meets both of these criteria. The only point of ambiguity is that the two professionals here have not in fact referred clients to anyone else. Nevertheless, the fact that each of them has that option—neither is obligated to make referrals exclusively to the other—brings this arrangement properly under the rule.

A is the correct answer. The Rules of Professional Conduct (7.2(b)(4)) state specific instances in which a lawyer may give anything of value to a person for recommending the lawyer's services. Here, the attorney has made a reciprocal referral agreement with the physician and correctly informed clients of the arrangement. An informal agreement is permitted.

B is not the right answer because the Rules of Professional Conduct (7.2) does not require that the agreement be in writing; other forms of agreement are permitted.

C is incorrect. Under the given facts, the arrangement was proper because the attorney took the appropriate actions to make this arrangement valid. Normally a lawyer may not enter into a reciprocal referral agreement unless an exception under Rule 7.2(b)(4) applies, as it does here.

D is also incorrect because there are no facts that yield to the conclusion that the relationship is de facto exclusive. The attorney and the physician always inform their clients when making such referrals that they have a reciprocal relationship.

QUESTION 3. Honest ads. An attorney advertised in a local newspaper. His advertisement reads, "I never charge more than $200 per hour for any type of legal work, and for simple legal problems such as uncontested divorces or name changes, I charge even less." The attorney once had a particularly complicated, tedious case in another jurisdiction for which he charged $250 per hour, but he does not expect such a case to arise in the future, though his fee would be higher if it did. The attorney's advertisement fails to state that some other lawyers in the community charge substantially lower fees. The advertisement includes a pencil drawing of an unrealistically handsome, but generic-looking judge sitting behind the bench in a courtroom with a gavel in his hand. Could the attorney be subject to discipline for this advertisement?

A. Yes, because he included a drawing of an unrealistically handsome judge.
B. Yes, because it is not true that he never charges more than $200 per hour.
C. No, as long as no other attorneys in the area charge lower fees.
D. No, as long as a reasonable percentage of the attorney's cases are simple legal problems for which he charges less than $200 per hour.

ANALYSIS. This question actually involved two rules, Rules 7.1 and 7.2(a)—the latter incorporates the former by reference. While Rule 7.2 permits lawyers to use media advertising, such as the newspaper ad in this question, such ads are subject to the requirements of Rule 7.1, which forbids misleading advertising, including half-truths about the lawyer's fees. The problem here is that the claim in the ad about fees is not technically true—the lawyer did charge a higher fee on one occasion, and might do so again in exceptional circumstances.

A is incorrect. While it is possible for an advertisement to violate Rules 7.1 and 7.2 through the use of a misleading image, it is unlikely that a stock-file drawing of a generic judge would be misleading to anyone. If the drawing clearly resembled a particular local judge, on the other hand, that would be misleading, because it would imply that a local judge had endorsed or recommended this attorney.

B is the correct answer. A lawyer cannot claim that he never charges more than a certain amount per hour if the lawyer does in fact charge a higher amount in exceptional circumstances. A prospective client with an exceptionally complicated case would not infer from the ad's verbiage that his case would bill at a higher fee. If the advertisement instead had said, "Normally, I charge only $200 per hour," there would probably be no violation, but the use of absolute language in the ad means that the disciplinary authorities will hold the lawyer to an absolute standard.

C is irrelevant, so it is not the right answer. Comment 3 for Rule 7.1 says, among other things, "Similarly, an unsubstantiated comparison of the lawyer's services or fees with the services or fees of other lawyers may be misleading if presented with such specificity as would lead a reasonable person to conclude that the comparison can be substantiated." If the advertisement had claimed that the lawyer's fees were lower than every other lawyer's in the area, that would indeed be a problem (unless it was strictly and absolutely true), but the ad in this question made no such claim.

D is also incorrect, as it misstates the rule. If the lawyer's ad made an absolute claim (using words like "never" or "always"), then it must be true absolutely, with no exceptions. It is a violation even if the advertisement is true most of the time.

B. Rule 7.3—Solicitation of Clients

For purposes of the Model Rules, "solicitation" differs from advertising in that it is a direct personal contact rather than a broadcast communication such as media advertising or billboards. The prototypical example of solicitation is a direct, in-person offer by the lawyer to represent a potential client, but it also includes telephone calls to find new clients, and "live" electronic conversations such as phone texts and online chats.

The U.S. Supreme Court has taken a different approach (less friendly) to lawyer solicitation than it has to media advertising, allowing states to place more restrictions on this kind of client development. For purposes of exams, students should pay special attention to the details at the boundary of the rule, such as specific exceptions, while remembering that the default principle is that lawyers cannot make direct, person-to-person propositions to represent a prospective client who has not approached the lawyer already seeking representation. The first exception is a clause built into the rule itself—"when a significant motive for the lawyer's doing so is the lawyer's pecuniary gain." Offers to represent someone pro bono (for no fee) do not violate the rule.

In addition, lawyers can approach other lawyers offering to represent them or to take contract work from them. Other lawyers are presumably not as vulnerable to manipulation or exploitation by attorneys looking for more business. Similarly, a lawyer can contact a former client asking if the client has any new legal work for the lawyer to do, as there is already an established professional relationship in that situation. The other exception is for the lawyer's own family and close friends (i.e., personal friends, not mere social media connections). There is less potential for abuse in such situations.

Note that even in situations in which solicitations are permissible, they must be strictly truthful and not coercive. A lawyer who pressures a relative into retaining him for legal work, or who coerces a former client into hiring the lawyer for additional services, would still be in violation of the rule.

A special rule, Rule 7.3(c), applies to letters and e-mails from lawyers to potential clients. Think of these as a hybrid between solicitation and regular advertising—letters are inherently less coercive and psychologically intimidating than an actual conversation. On the other hand, senders can address letters to specific individuals, unlike most advertising. According to Rule 7.3(c), all letters offering representation to potential clients must say "advertising material" on the outside of the envelope and at the beginning or end of an e-mail. Comment 8 for Rule 7.3 says that this does not apply to "general announcements by lawyers, including changes in personnel or location."

QUESTION 4. All in the family. An attorney calls his friend, a close personal acquaintance, who was recently arrested for driving while intoxicated. The attorney advises that he saw the friend's arrest on the local police news and offers to represent his friend for the attorney's usual fee for handling such cases. The friend hires the attorney to represent him on the case. Are the attorney's actions proper?

A. Yes, because attorneys can solicit professional employment from family members, close personal friends, and persons with whom the attorney had a previous professional relationship.
B. Yes, because attorneys are not restricted from soliciting professional employment from people they know.
C. No, because attorneys are restricted from soliciting professional employment from persons who are not lawyers or the members of the attorney's family.
D. No, because attorneys are not allowed to solicit professional employment.

ANALYSIS. Normally the solicitation described in this question would be improper under Rule 7.3, but there is an important exception for family members, former clients, and close "personal friends." The question tests your knowledge of the specific exceptions to the rule.

A is the correct answer. The exception rests on the idea that a lawyer is less likely to engage in abusive practices against a former client, or a person with whom the lawyer has a close personal or family relationship. This rationale appears in Comment 5 to Rule 7.3.

B is incorrect because it is overly broad. Rule 7.3(a) gives a specific list of persons that an attorney may solicit professional employment from and it does not include the general category of everyone attorney knows.

C is completely wrong. According to Rule 7.3(a)(1)-(2), lawyers may solicit professional employment from another person who is a lawyer or persons with whom the lawyer has a close personal or family relationship.

D is also incorrect because it states the default rule without its important exceptions. Attorneys may solicit professional employment. Due to the potential abuse when a solicitation is involved, Rule 7.3 lays out the regulation for when and from whom lawyers can solicit professional employment.

QUESTION 5. **Supporting the cause.** An attorney is active within a new political movement and she has represented several members of the movement, who faced arrest or criminal charges for protesting and picketing. The attorney learns that police have arrested one of the prominent leaders of the movement for trespassing on private property during a protest, but that the movement leader is already out on bail. In response, the attorney calls the leader and offers to represent him in his case free of charge, explaining that she has experience representing other members of the movement in similar cases. The leader agrees to have the attorney represent him on a pro bono basis. The attorney wants to represent the leader because she admires him, but also because she believes it will generate terrific publicity for the firm's practice. Was it proper for the attorney to make this telephone solicitation?

A. Yes, because the attorney believes in the leader's cause and is an active member of the movement.
B. Yes, because the attorney did not charge for providing these legal services.
C. No, because the attorney made a live telephone solicitation of a prospective client.
D. No, because the attorney hopes to receive indirect benefit from the publicity that the representation will bring.

ANALYSIS. Rule 7.3 generally prohibits telephone solicitations by lawyers to prospective clients, but with an important proviso: "when a significant motive for the lawyer's doing so is the lawyer's pecuniary gain." Here, the lawyer offers to represent the leader without charge, motivated mostly by support for the cause. The fact that there will also be an indirect financial benefit in the form of publicity for the firm does not create a violation.

A is not the best answer. The attorney's belief is only partly relevant here, because the issue is whether the attorney's solicitation was proper. The more important issue is whether the lawyer's motive was pecuniary gain. The lawyer's support for the cause may help explain an alternative motive, but the most important fact is that the lawyer did not charge a fee.

B is the correct answer. The prohibition in Rule 7.3 applies only when the lawyer's main motivation is pecuniary gain, that is, a legal fee. If the lawyer offers to represent the person without charge, there is no expectation of pecuniary gain, except perhaps indirectly through publicity and referrals. Comment 5 to Rule 7.3 says that the prohibition on solicitation "is not intended to prohibit a lawyer from participating in constitutionally protected activities of public or charitable legal service organizations or bona fide political, social, civic, fraternal, employee or trade organizations whose purposes include providing or recommending legal services to their members or beneficiaries."

C is incorrect because a lawyer may make a live telephone solicitation of a prospective client as long as the lawyer has done so within the rules set forth in Rule 7.3. Based on the facts given, the attorney properly made the telephone solicitation.

D is also incorrect. The possibility of reaping an indirect benefit from pro bono work, via publicity and possibly repeat business from the client later at regular billing rates, would be too speculative to constitute a "significant motive" of "pecuniary gain."

QUESTION 6. **After the storm.** After a hurricane damaged hundreds of homes in a southeastern state, an attorney, who practices in that state, sent letters to a dozen homeowners in the affected area offering to represent them in their insurance claims arising out of the storm damage. Each letter was handwritten and personalized, and the attorney addressed each envelope by hand so that recipients would perceive it as a personal letter and would be more likely to open it and read it. At the top of the letter itself, the attorney wrote by hand the words "Advertising Material." Were the attorney's actions proper?

A. Yes, because the attorney clearly indicated at the top of the letter that it was advertising material.

B. Yes, because the attorney sent the letters only to homeowners in the affected areas who would be likely to need his help.

C. No, because the attorney did not include the phrase "Advertising Material" on the outside of the envelope.

D. No, because a lawyer should not send a solicitation letter to those who have recently experienced a tragedy and are vulnerable to manipulation or coercion.

ANALYSIS. Rule 7.3(c) requires that all letters offering to represent potential clients must say "advertising material" on the outside of the envelope and at the beginning and end of an e-mail. This allows recipients who do not want the solicitation to dispose of it without reading through it. Most non-lawyers who receive an unexpected letter from a law firm will worry that it is a complaint or demand letter (or that they are in some kind of trouble), so the rule requires that recipients can see it is merely a solicitation before reading it. Remember that Rule 7.3(c) does not apply to general announcements by lawyers, such as new hires or a new location.

A is incorrect. There is nothing wrong with the lawyer writing "Advertising Material" on the letter itself, but it must also be on the outside of the envelope, so that a recipient does not even need to open the envelope to know it is an unexpected solicitation. Note that if this were an e-mail—which has no envelope—then the lawyer must write the phrase at the beginning *and* end of the e-mail.

B is incorrect because the fact that the lawyer knows the recipients may need legal representation does not negate the requirement that the envelope indicate it is advertising material. In fact, Rule 7.3(c) specifically includes letters to "anyone known to be in need of legal services in a particular matter."

C is the correct answer. The outside of the envelope must state "Advertising Material." It is not sufficient that the lawyer included this phrase on the letter itself, inside the envelope—the purpose of the rule is to enable recipients to discard an unwanted solicitation letter without having to read it.

D is incorrect. Rule 7.3(c) contemplates that lawyers may send letters to "anyone known to be in need of legal services in a particular matter," including victims of recent storms. The Supreme Court has allowed states to impose "waiting periods" after the tragedy before lawyers can send solicitation letters to victims, and some states have adopted such rules.

QUESTION 7. **New work, old clients.** An attorney specializes in employment law, especially employer-provided benefits, as well as healthcare law. After Congress passes sweeping legislative reforms for the regulation of employer-sponsored healthcare plans, the attorney sent a letter to her former business clients offering to help them sort through the changes in employee benefit plans that the new laws would require. Nowhere did the attorney indicate that these letters were advertising materials. Could the attorney be subject to discipline for sending these letters?

A. Yes, because every written communication from a lawyer soliciting professional employment from anyone known to be in need of legal services in a particular matter shall include the words "Advertising Material" on the outside envelope.

B. Yes, because the attorney was implicitly soliciting new clients through this general professional announcement.

C. No, because the attorney sent the letters only to former clients.

D. No, because the attorney is merely offering to implement new laws enacted by the duly-elected legislature.

ANALYSIS. Rule 7.2(a)(2) creates a few categorical exceptions to the prohibition against lawyer solicitation letters, including those who have a "prior professional relationship with the lawyer"—that is, former clients. Note that Section (b) of Rule 7.3 still forbids coercive or harassing solicitations by lawyers even for former clients, and forbids lawyers from soliciting former clients who have told the lawyer not to contact them.

A is incorrect. Although the answer choice states the general rule for lawyer solicitations, it ignores the exceptions to Rule 7.3(b). According to the facts, the recipients were former clients.

B is not the right answer. Contrary to this answer choice, the facts state that the attorney was soliciting professional employment from former clients, not new clients.

C is the correct answer. Generally, lawyers are required to indicate on the outside envelope and in the letters the phrase, "Advertising Materials." Nevertheless, the recipients of the attorney's letters are former clients and thus the attorney is not required to indicate that these letters were advertising materials.

D is incorrect. The motive for a lawyer's solicitation is relevant for most prospective clients, but not for former clients.

C. Rule 7.4—Communication of Fields of Practice and Specialization

Rule 7.4 addresses a specific issue with lawyer advertising: a lawyer claiming to specialize—or to be a specialist (not the same thing)—in a certain area of law. The general rule, set forth in Rule 7.4(a), is that lawyers can always inform the public about what type of legal work they do. This includes listing areas of practice (i.e., "family law, personal injury law, and estate planning"), or, less commonly, listing areas of practice or types of cases the firm does *not* do, such as criminal law. Such information helps direct clients to a firm that does the particular kind of legal work the clients need.

On the other hand, problems arise when a lawyer claims to be "a specialist" or a special type of attorney; such claims suggest particular expertise, not merely a willingness to handle certain types of legal matters. The remaining subsections of Rule 7.4, therefore, address such claims. First, a lawyer cannot claim to be a "patent attorney" unless officially admitted to practice before the U.S. Patent and Trademark Office, which involves passing the Patent Bar examination and submitting an application for admission. This is a matter of federal law, which preempts any state regulations to the contrary. Similarly, lawyers actually engaged in Admiralty practice, another area of exclusive federal jurisdiction, may advertise that they are a "Proctor in Admiralty" or use a similar designation.

More importantly, both for legal practice and the MPRE, a lawyer cannot claim to be a "certified specialist" unless the lawyer's certification comes from an officially accredited state agency or an entity accredited by the American Bar Association. There are organizations (businesses) that claim to provide certifications to lawyers for a fee, but only those recognized by the ABA or the state bar count. The name of the certifying entity must be in the advertisement.

QUESTION 8. I won't do it. On his website, an attorney explains that he handles most areas of personal injury law, and then displays in large, bold letters: "I DO NOT REPRESENT CLIENTS IN CRIMINAL MATTERS OR DIVORCE MATTERS—PLEASE FIND ANOTHER LAWYER IF YOU ARE FACING CRIMINAL CHARGES OR NEED TO LEAVE YOUR SPOUSE." Is it improper for a lawyer to make such a statement in his website or advertising materials?

A. Yes, because a lawyer should not categorically refuse to represent needy clients in criminal matters or family law matters, as these are the most acute needs for legal representation.

B. Yes, because a lawyer should state his areas of specialization, not the areas he or she does not practice, as this information is less useful to consumers.

C. No, because a lawyer may communicate the fact that the lawyer does or does not practice in particular fields of law.

D. No, because a lawyer is required to disclose in their advertisements if they will refuse to take criminal clients or handle divorces.

ANALYSIS. Rule 7.4(a) explicitly permits an attorney to "communicate the fact that the lawyer does or does not practice in particular fields of law." Although most lawyers advertise the types of cases they *do* handle rather than the types of cases they do not, it is permissible to state publicly that a firm does not offer representation on certain types of matters.

A is incorrect. Attorney is simply informing others that he does not practice criminal nor divorce matters and has every right to do so.

B is also incorrect. Carefully re-read Rule 7.4(a). The rule permits a lawyer to indicate areas of practice in communications about the lawyer's services. If a lawyer practices only in certain fields or will not accept matters except in a specified field or fields, the lawyer may so indicate.

C is the correct answer. The question tests your knowledge of Rule 7.4(a), which states that a lawyer may communicate the fact that the lawyer does or does not practice in particular fields of law. Here, the attorney makes known to viewers of his website that he does not practice criminal nor family law. According to the rules, the attorney is not required to do so, but may choose to do so. Therefore, it is not improper for the attorney to have made this statement on his website or advertising materials.

D is not the right answer. According to the facts of this question, the attorney did indicate in his advertisements that he will likely refuse to accept criminal or divorce matters. The rules do not require lawyers to state whether they will absolutely refuse to handle certain types of matters under any circumstances. The lawyer in this case is still free to make exceptions, for example, for minor misdemeanor matters for existing clients.

QUESTION 9. **Certified by whom?** An attorney is properly certified as an immigration law specialist by a state bar organization that provides official certifications. In her advertisements, the attorney describes herself as a "Certified Specialist in Immigration Law" without identifying the certifying organization. The attorney also mentions that she speaks Spanish and Portuguese (besides English), and that her fees are very affordable. Could the attorney be subject to discipline for making such statements in her advertisements?

A. Yes, because she failed to identify the certifying organization.
B. Yes, because a lawyer should not claim in an advertisement that she has special expertise compared to other lawyers in some area.
C. No, because this lawyer is indeed a certified specialist.
D. No, because a lawyer may not obtain certification in an area of law involving federal statutes.

ANALYSIS. Rule 7.4(d) permits lawyers to claim the status of "certified specialist" only if certified by an official organization in the state (legally empowered by the state disciplinary authority or by statute), or an organization "accredited by the American Bar Association." In addition, when claiming such certification, Rule 7.4(d)(2) requires that "the name of the certifying organization is clearly identified in the communication."

A is the right answer. Here, the attorney failed to identify the organization that certified her as a specialist in immigration law.

B is incorrect because Rule 7.4 explicitly permits a lawyer to list specialty certifications in an advertisement.

C is not the correct answer because according to Rule 7.4, the attorney is still required to identify the organization that certified her as an immigration law specialist, which is missing here.

D is completely wrong. Lawyers may properly obtain certifications in different areas of law, but must meet the requirements of the Rules of Professional Conduct when disclosing such information.

D. The Closer: Advertising and Solicitation

The best rule of thumb for remembering the rules about advertising is that the First Amendment (Free Speech) protects most lawyer advertising, as long as it is entirely, strictly truthful (there is no constitutional protection for false or misleading advertising). At the same time, state disciplinary authorities can require certain common-sense disclosures in all lawyer advertisements (lawyer's contact information, jurisdictions where the lawyer has a license to practice, and so on). In contrast, there is far less constitutional protection for "solicitations"—direct communications with targeted individuals, such as phone calls, e-mails, printed letters, and face-to-face conversations. When in doubt, assume that a "live" conversation is impermissible unless the prospective client is a relative or former client of the lawyer. Mailed letters and e-mails are subject to fewer strictures than live conversations, but still must indicate to recipients that they are "advertising material" up front. States may impose reasonable "cooling periods" before contacting victims of serious tragedies.

QUESTION 10. Certified long ago. An attorney entered into an exclusive reciprocal arrangement with a local advertiser, in which the lawyer agreed to advertise her firm solely through that advertising agency, for normal market rates, and the advertising agency agreed not to take any other law firms in the region as clients. The agency ran newspaper and billboard ads based on information supplied by the lawyer, which included a claim that the lawyer was a certified specialist in immigration law, as certified by the state bar association itself. While the certification was legally valid, the lawyer had not handled a single immigration case since obtaining the certification some time ago, and has not kept abreast of major changes in immigration law in the meantime. Given the extensiveness and complexity of recent changes in the law, the attorney would no longer be able to provide competent representation in immigration matters without extensive research and study. Last week, the lawyer happened to drive by two cars on the shoulder of the road that had been in a minor collision. The attorney pulled over, got out of her car, and approached one of the drivers who were waiting for a tow truck. Handing the driver her business card, the attorney offered to represent her in any litigation over the accident, and assured her that she would charge a fair rate, and the driver gladly took it and said she might have seen one of the lawyer's advertisements. The attorney was not aware at the time that the driver was an immigrant from Europe who was in the country on a temporary work visa. The driver visited the attorney a few days later for an initial consultation, but decided not to retain the lawyer for representation because the driver's insurer had already settled the matter. Was it proper for the lawyer to offer to represent the driver in this way?

A. No, because the lawyer entered into an exclusive reciprocal arrangement with the advertiser.
B. Yes, because the driver did not end up becoming a client of the lawyer, so an agreement to provide representation never occurred.
C. Yes, because the driver appeared to be in need of representation, and gladly accepted the lawyer's card, so there was no coercion or harassment.
D. No, because the lawyer approached the driver in person at the scene of the accident and offered to represent her.

ANALYSIS. This question ties together elements from Rules 7.1, 7.2, 7.3, and 7.4. At the outset, students should have noted that the claim about being a certified specialist in immigration law is problematic. On the one hand, the claim meets the requirements of Rule 7.4(d), which covers specialty certifications, as the lawyer had indeed obtained specialist certification by an official certifying authority and apparently stated this in the ad. On the other hand, the claim was potentially misleading, because the lawyer has not kept up with major changes in a complex area of law and is not currently competent to represent clients in (at least some) immigration matters, which could violate Rule 7.1, and given that this pertains to an advertisement, Rule 7.2(a) as well. In addition, the lawyer's in-person offer to represent someone implicates Rule 7.3. Nevertheless, none of the answer options focuses on the truthfulness of the advertisement itself, so we must select the best answer from the options provided.

A is incorrect. The prohibition against reciprocal referral agreements applies only to other professions (doctors, accountants, dentists, nurses, and so on), not to advertising firms. The arrangement is for advertising, not personal referrals.

B is also incorrect. None of the restrictions on advertising and solicitation considers whether the lawyer actually represented the prospective client. Lawyers can violate the rules without ever succeeding in retaining any clients.

C wrongly focuses on the prospective client's attitude. Of course, if a prospective client has informed the lawyer of a desire not to receive any further solicitations or contact, it would be a violation for the lawyer to offer representation again. Even so, the converse does not apply—even if a prospective client enthusiastically responds to a lawyer's overtures, the lawyer's actions could still be a violation of the rules. The lawyer would still be subject to discipline.

D is the best answer. Rule 7.3 forbids lawyers from approaching prospective clients in person like this, except for relatives, close friends, and former clients, none of which apply here. It does not matter that the person did not end up retaining the lawyer after the initial consultation—solicitation is a violation whether or not it is successful.

Stevenson's Picks

1.	Emergency room patients	**C**
2.	A mutually beneficial arrangement	**A**
3.	Honest ads	**B**
4.	All in the family	**A**
5.	Supporting the cause	**B**
6.	After the storm	**C**
7.	New work, old clients	**C**
8.	I won't do it	**C**
9.	Certified by whom?	**A**
10.	Certified long ago	**D**

8

Different Roles of the Lawyer

CHAPTER OVERVIEW

The Model Rules include provisions about various roles that lawyers play when providing representation to clients—they give advice, engage in negotiations, and often prepare written reports or assessments that third parties will use in their decision making. In other words, the Model Rules recognize that legal representation includes more than simple advocacy and scrivener's tasks, and there are a few rules governing the other things that lawyers do. In addition, lawyers representing government entities (as prosecutors do), corporations, or even multiple parties in mediation have particularly complex roles as they interact with the individuals within the entities or groups they represent.

The MPRE examiners state in their published materials that questions on "Different Roles of the Lawyer" represent between two and six questions on each administration of the test, or 4 to 10 percent of the total, making it a lightly tested subject compared to others. This category of questions encompasses Model Rules 2.1, 2.3, 2.4, 3.8, 3.9, and 1.13 (listed in the order used by the examiners). Note that Rule 1.13 ("Organization as Client") often appears in Professional Responsibility courses in the chapter on conflicts of interest, but the examiners group it together with Rules 2.1, 2.3, and 2.4. This book addressed Rule 2.3 in detail already in Chapter 4, so this chapter will not revisit it.

A. Rule 2.1—Advisor

Model Rule 2.1 requires lawyers to exercise independent professional judgment and to give candid advice to their clients. It also expressly permits lawyers to give non-legal advice: "In rendering advice, a lawyer may refer not only to law but to other considerations such as moral, economic, social and political factors, that may be relevant to the client's situation." In fact, Comment 3 for Rule 2.1 suggests that when dealing with unsophisticated clients, lawyers may have a *responsibility* to communicate that "more may be involved than strictly legal considerations." Comment 5 adds more about lawyers' duties to inform their clients: on the one hand, as a general rule, "a lawyer is not expected to give advice until asked by the client." On the other hand, lawyers may have a duty to inform clients of likely adverse legal consequences of a client's proposed course of action, and to inform litigation clients of alternative forms of dispute resolution. Regarding a duty to pry into a client's affairs, Comment 5 offers a similar balancing requirement: "A lawyer ordinarily has no duty to initiate investigation of a client's affairs or to give advice that the client has indicated is unwanted, but a lawyer may initiate advice to a client when doing so appears to be in the client's interest."

QUESTION 1. **Protecting the client's feelings.** Halfway through a trial, an attorney can tell that his client is going to lose. The opposing party successfully impeached the attorney's only favorable witness, and the judge has already told the parties that he plans to follow the state's model jury instructions for this type of case, which effectively preclude the legal theory that the attorney had made the centerpiece of his case. During a lunchtime break, the client turns to the attorney and tearfully asks if they still have any chance of winning. The attorney does not want to make her cry and feels very awkward about the situation, so in order to spare her feelings, he assures the client that they still have a good chance of prevailing. The attorney is representing the client on a contingent fee basis, so he knows it will not cost the client any more in legal fees to finish the trial. At the same time, there is still an open settlement offer on the table from the other party, albeit a very small, unsatisfying settlement, which the client could accept at any time if she wants to terminate the litigation. Is it proper for the attorney to feign confidence in order to protect his client's feelings?

A. Yes, because the lawyer is working on a contingent fee basis, so finishing the case will not cost the client any more in legal fees.

B. Yes, because a lawyer should think about moral, social, and psychological factors when deciding whether to answer the client in stark, realistic terms.

C. No, because a lawyer must encourage a client to accept a settlement offer if the client would be better off doing so than by proceeding with the litigation.

D. No, because in representing a client, a lawyer shall render candid advice.

ANALYSIS. Rule 2.1 requires lawyers to "render candid advice." Such candor with clients is particularly important when there are additional costs facing a client, such as ongoing litigation expenses or forfeiting a settlement offer, as in this case. Recognizing the frequency of situations such as that described in this question, Comment 1 for Rule 2.1 says, "In presenting advice, a lawyer endeavors to sustain the client's morale and may put advice in as acceptable a form as honesty permits. However, a lawyer should not be deterred from giving candid advice by the prospect that the advice will be unpalatable to the client."

A is incorrect. Rule 2.1 applies to all lawyers even if they are working on a contingent fee basis.

B is also incorrect because a lawyer is required to give candid advice. While it is true that a lawyer can bring up non-legal factors for a client's consideration (answer **B** simply paraphrases the second part of Rule 2.1), the comments state that lawyers must communicate the information that clients need to make a decision—such as the likelihood of forfeiting an existing settlement offer and incurring more litigation costs.

C is not the right answer because it does not reflect the requirements of Rule 2.1. While a lawyer certainly has a duty to inform a client of a settlement offer, the facts in this question do not suggest that the client was unaware of the existing offer—instead, the client may have been underestimating the chances of losing at trial and forfeiting the offer. A lawyer does not have a duty to instruct a client to accept a particular offer—especially a disappointing offer, like the one described here—but rather to help the client make a realistic assessment of the options. Whether a client would be better off accepting a settlement offer is not always clear, as there may be a variety of personal reasons to continue or withdraw from the litigation.

D is the correct answer. Rule 2.1 states that a lawyer shall exercise independent professional judgment and render candid advice when representing a client. A client is entitled to straightforward advice expressing the lawyer's honest assessment. As Comment 1 observes, "A lawyer should not be deterred from giving candid advice by the prospect that the advice will be unpalatable to the client."

QUESTION 2. **Don't worry . . . .** A client repeatedly calls an attorney to discuss her pending divorce case. The client wants above-guideline child support, alimony, and a large percentage of the estate, even though the parties have only been married two years. The attorney has continuously given his honest opinion about what he believes the client is eligible to receive, and what he believes she may receive in the divorce based on his experience. The client has recently become angry with the attorney because she is unhappy with his opinion. She has even asked, "Are you working for me or my husband?" In an effort to keep the client happy, the attorney begins to tell the client what he believes she is eligible to receive when she asks, but simply states "the court will decide" when the client asks the attorney what he believes she will receive. Are the attorney's actions proper?

A. Yes, the attorney may respond to a client's requests for the attorney's opinion in any manner that will maintain the client's morale, including refusing to give advice if the attorney believes the client will not be accepting of his advice.

B. Yes, attorneys are not required to give their opinions or advice, but may, at any time, respond to clients by referring them to the appropriate legal authority or by advising them that the court will ultimately decide the issue, if applicable.

C. No, an attorney should give his honest opinion about the case when asked, even if the opinion is unsatisfactory to the client.

D. No, attorneys should always give advice to clients that encourages the client to have confidence in the client's position.

ANALYSIS. Rule 2.1 requires lawyers to provide candid advice to clients. Here, the lawyer began to appease a difficult client with a vague, almost evasive answer. It is understandable why a lawyer would feel pressured to tell a client what she wants to hear, but that is exactly why we have a rule mandating that lawyers give their clients a realistic picture of the situation.

A is an incorrect answer. A lawyer may package advice in a form that will be as acceptable as possible for a client, within the bounds of honesty, but the lawyer cannot refrain from presenting an accurate picture of the situation. Thus, this answer choice is incorrect because a lawyer cannot refuse to give advice to his client just because the lawyer believes the client will not be accepting of the lawyer's advice. The lawyer may take other measures if the lawyer does not believe he can properly represent the client any longer.

B is partly true but is not correct for the question asked. While it is true that lawyers may tell clients that the outcome of the case depends on the court's decision, and that the court has a range of discretion, a lawyer must inform a client about the likely outcome of the client's litigation.

C is the correct answer because it properly reflects the requirement stated in Rule 2.1: "A lawyer shall exercise independent professional judgment and render candid advice when representing a client."

D is not correct. It is appropriate for lawyers to try to boost the morale of a client during litigation, but not to give the client false hope or a false sense of security about the expected outcome.

QUESTION 3. Don't lecture me. An attorney represents a client, who lost his criminal appeals and is now serving a life sentence in a federal penitentiary. The client confesses to the attorney that he (the client) committed a murder for which a jury incorrectly convicted another (innocent) man. The client says he is happy that someone else took the fall for that crime and that he will never tell anyone. The attorney lectures the client about the morality of this situation, allowing an innocent man to face life imprisonment or even capital punishment for a crime that the client committed, and pleads with the client to reveal the truth. Was it proper for the attorney to bring morality into his consultation with the client, and to sermonize on this point for a few moments?

A. Yes, because in rendering advice, a lawyer may refer not only to law but to other considerations such as moral factors.
B. Yes, because the attorney will have an obligation under the Model Rules to disclose the information if the client does not reveal the truth.
C. No, because in rendering advice, a lawyer may refer only to legal and financial considerations, and not to personal views about morals or politics.
D. No, because urging the client to reveal information that could overturn a final jury verdict undermines the finality of court decisions and the public's confidence in the legal system.

ANALYSIS. The facts are similar to two actual cases—in both instances, a client refused to come forward and let an innocent person face a murder conviction and life sentence in prison. Rule 2.1 says that it is proper for a lawyer to bring in moral, social, and other factors when giving legal advice. While a client may not agree, it is not a violation for the lawyer in this question to urge the client to do the right thing, especially when the consequences for an innocent third party are so serious.

A is the correct answer. Comment 2 for Rule 2.1 observes, "Purely technical legal advice can sometimes be inadequate. It is proper for a lawyer to refer to relevant moral and ethical considerations in giving advice." Ethical considerations "impinge upon most legal questions and may decisively influence how the law will be applied," so it is appropriate for the lawyer to include such factors in a discussion of the client's options.

B is not the correct answer. The traditional rule is that a lawyer shall not reveal information relating to the representation of a client unless the client gives informed consent, although several states now permit lawyers to betray a client's confidence in certain circumstances, and a few states explicitly allow lawyers to disclose confidential client information to prevent the incarceration of an innocent third party.

C is incorrect. Rule 2.1 explicitly permits lawyers to include non-legal factors in their legal advice to clients.

D is also incorrect. Rule 2.1 requires a lawyer to exercise independent professional judgment and render candid advice, and this trumps abstract concerns about preserving an incorrect verdict for the sake of stability in the system.

QUESTION 4. **My client is a suspicious character.** A client hired an attorney to represent him in a simple real estate matter. When the attorney asked some standard questions about the financial arrangements for the sale and purchase of the property, the client was somewhat evasive on a few points, but provided the information necessary to complete the legal work for the transaction. The attorney also heard from a friend that the client frequently cavorted with prostitutes. The attorney finds the client rather suspicious and has many unanswered questions, but none surrounding the transaction that occasioned the representation. Does the attorney have an ethical duty to inquire into the affairs of a suspicious client?

A. Yes, because it is possible that the client is engaging in some kinds of illegal activity, and it is important to uncover whatever that might be.
B. Yes, because the attorney has a right to know what kind of person he is representing in this simple real estate transaction.
C. No, because a lawyer must never invade the privacy of a client in any way.
D. No, because a lawyer ordinarily has no duty to initiate investigation of a client's affairs or to give advice that the client has indicated is unwanted.

ANALYSIS. Comment 5 for Rule 2.1 says, "A lawyer ordinarily has no duty to initiate investigation of a client's affairs or to give advice that the client has indicated is unwanted, but a lawyer may initiate advice to a client when doing so appears to be in the client's interest." Lawyers often have clients whose personal decisions might seem imprudent or socially unacceptable, but the lawyer does not have an automatic duty to function as the client's life coach or to pry into a client's other matters that are unrelated to the representation.

A is not the correct answer. The alleged prostitution transactions that the client is involved in are unrelated to the representation. Thus, the lawyer has no duty to initiate investigation of the client's affairs.

B is incorrect. Although engaging in prostitution activities may be illegal (depending on the facts and the jurisdiction), the question does not state that the client's course of action is likely to result in substantial adverse legal consequences to the client. Thus, the lawyer does not have a duty to initiate investigation of the client's affairs.

C is also incorrect because it overstates the rule in absolute terms. A lawyer may initiate advice to the client when doing so appears to be in the client's interest. It is not true that a lawyer may "never" invade the privacy of a client (whatever that means), but certainly there is usually no duty to do so.

D is the correct answer. Here, the facts state that the attorney has unanswered questions that are not related to the transaction that occasioned the representation. Thus, the lawyer has no duty to offer advice because the client's course of action is not related to the representation.

QUESTION 5. Risky business. A client hires an attorney to help with the legal documents necessary to liquidate most of his investments so that he can use the cash to fund a new business venture. The client explains that he plans to quit his regular job and start a new career working from home as a "day trader," buying and selling stocks online every day in hopes of making large profits. The client has no experience or training in finance or investments, but he attended a seminar that featured testimonials from others who claimed to have made millions as day traders. The attorney thinks this is a foolish idea, but the client does not ask the attorney for his advice. Does the attorney have an ethical duty to caution the client against his seemingly reckless decision?

A. Yes, because a lawyer has a duty to offer sound advice and not wait for a client to ask questions to solicit the specific information.
B. Yes, if the attorney suspects that the client will eventually have trouble paying his legal fees.
C. No, because many day traders are indeed successful, and this client could be one of the fortunate ones.
D. No, because a lawyer is not expected to give advice until asked by the client.

ANALYSIS. Comment 5 for Rule 2.1 opens with a general rule of thumb followed by a caveat: "In general, a lawyer is not expected to give advice until asked by the client. However, when a lawyer knows that a client proposes a course of action that is likely to result in substantial adverse legal consequences to the client, the lawyer's duty to the client under Rule 1.4 may require that the lawyer offer advice if the client's course of action is related to the representation." In this question, the client's proposal is to undertake a notoriously risky line of work at the expense of his regular (presumably more secure) job. It would be going too far, though, to say that this is "likely to result in substantial adverse consequences to the client," which would obligate the lawyer to interject a word of caution. A few people succeed at day trading, and others who fail are able to minimize their losses or return to a secure job easily—it depends on the person.

A is incorrect. This answer contradicts the statement in Comment 5 for Rule 2.1—lawyers normally do not have a duty to offer advice unless the client asks for it, with some exceptions.

B is incorrect. The lawyer's duty to give honest legal advice does not depend on whether he expects the client to pay. If the client is not paying the bills as agreed, the lawyer may have the option of withdrawing from the representation. As long as the representation continues, though, the lawyer's duties to the client remain in force.

C is not the right answer. Although this statement may be true, it is not the proper reasoning as to why the lawyer does not have a duty to caution the client against his seemingly reckless decision. There is a general rule that lawyers do not have a duty to advise clients. Of course, the fact that the client has some chance of success at his risky venture probably means that there is no "likelihood of substantial adverse legal consequences" that would create a duty for the lawyer to speak up, but even so, this is but one factor that could have other offsetting facts in a given case. Answer **D** is a better answer because it reflects the general rule.

D is the correct answer. Here, a client has asked an attorney for help with legal documents to liquidate investments and the client has not asked the attorney for advice with his new business venture. The lawyer has discretion about whether to warn the client about the risks of failure in the proposed venture—there is no duty to warn in this case.

QUESTION 6. **Disinheriting the daughter.** An attorney agreed to prepare a will for a client, a wealthy widow with three grown children. An earlier will divided her estate equally between her children, but the client now wants to modify the will to disinherit her only daughter, who disobeyed the client's wishes by marrying outside their nationality. The daughter is also a lawyer and is married to a lawyer, and the estate is substantial. The client's two sons are both working as manual laborers and they struggle financially. In the past, there had been some tension between the brothers and their sister, although the relationships seem to be cordial now. The attorney believes that disinheriting the daughter will ensure that the daughter and her husband will contest the will after the client's death, and will rupture the tenuous relationship between the siblings. The client did not ask for the attorney's advice about disinheriting the daughter, she just insisted on it. The attorney initiated a debate about it, explaining that he believed it could be against the client's best interests and would cause unnecessary acrimony between her children. Was it proper for the attorney to initiate such advice when the client did not ask for it?

A. Yes, because a lawyer may offer unsolicited advice to a client when doing so appears to be in the client's interest.
B. Yes, because a lawyer has a duty to refer not only to law but also to other considerations such as moral factors that may be relevant to the client's situation.
C. No, because a lawyer is not expected to give advice until asked by the client, and should normally wait until asked for such advice, especially when the advice is not strictly a statement of the law on a subject.
D. No, because a testator has a sacred right to devise her estate as she wishes.

ANALYSIS. Comment 5 for Rule 2.1 concludes, "A lawyer ordinarily has no duty . . . to give advice that the client has indicated is unwanted, but a lawyer may initiate advice to a client when doing so appears to be in the client's interest." (*See also* the recent ABA clarification in ABA Formal Op. 05-434, note 15.) There is no prohibition against an attorney offering unsolicited advice for the benefit of the client.

A is the correct answer. Here, the attorney is aware of the consequences that are likely to result if the client proceeds to disinherit her daughter and believes the unnecessary hassle can be avoided and be dealt with strategically. Thus, it was proper for the attorney to initiate the advice to the client because the advice was in the client's interest.

B is not the correct answer. This answer choice does not address the real issue of the question. The issue is not whether a lawyer may refer to moral factors but whether it was proper for the attorney to initiate advice to the client when the client did not ask for advice.

C is also not the correct answer. This answer choice is only half-correct. Even though there is no duty for a lawyer to give advice until asked by the client, there is also no prohibition against unsolicited advice.

D is incorrect. Although it is true that a testator holds this right, the testator in these facts happens to be the attorney's client. It was proper for the attorney to initiate advice to the client because it was in the client's interest to hear the attorney's advice.

QUESTION 7. **Whether to appeal.** An attorney represented a client in tort litigation against a pharmaceutical company over injuries allegedly resulting from one of the company's drugs. During a pretrial hearing about the admissibility of certain evidence, the court ruled against the attorney and ordered that the evidence was inadmissible at trial. The attorney then contacted a reporter from a prominent newspaper and gave him a lengthy interview explaining the case, discussing the upcoming trial, and giving the reporter the very evidence that the court had held should be inadmissible at the trial. The newspaper ran the story on the same day that jury selection began for the trial. Opposing counsel moved to disqualify the attorney due to misconduct in the matter, that is, the public disclosure of the inadmissible material in an attempt to taint the jury pool. The court agreed to disqualify the attorney on the eve of the trial. Another firm was already representing the client as co-counsel, so that firm agreed to continue with the trial work alone. The attorney filed an interlocutory appeal, which he lost at the appellate court and appealed to the Supreme Court. Delaying the trial with this interlocutory appeal was clearly against the client's interest, but was necessary for the attorney to continue to handle this big case. Is it proper for the attorney to recommend to the client that they appeal his disqualification, if it is not clearly in the client's interest to do so?

A. Yes, because the lawyer's interests and the client's interests presumptively align in litigation.

B. Yes, because the other lawyer might not obtain as favorable a result for the client as the attorney would.

C. No, because the decision to appeal should turn entirely on the client's interest.

D. No, because the disqualification was for lawyer misconduct rather than a conflict of interest.

ANALYSIS. Rule 2.1 requires lawyers to exercise *independent professional judgment,* which includes separating the lawyer's own interests from what would be best for the client. The Supreme Court addressed a situation like this in *Richardson-Merrell, Inc. v. Koller,* 472 U.S. 424, 435 (1985).

A is incorrect because there are no facts presented to support this reasoning. Instead, the facts suggest that the attorney's actions are clearly not in the interest of the client. The lawyer's duty is to the client, not to himself.

B is also incorrect. It is speculative to assert that another lawyer might not do as well as the current attorney, because it is just as possible (given these scanty facts) that another lawyer would do even better. The facts suggest that the delay runs counter to the client's priorities, so the lawyer should follow the client's priorities and withdraw from the case.

C is the correct answer. Here, the facts state that the attorney's actions are clearly not in the best interest of the client. Thus, it was not proper for the attorney to delay the trial.

D is incorrect. The reasoning for the disqualification is irrelevant here because the facts state that delaying the trial with an interlocutory was clearly against the client's interest. The attorney's actions do not align with the general rule that a lawyer shall exercise independent professional judgment and act in the client's interest.

B. Rule 2.4—Lawyer Serving as Third-Party Neutral

Sometimes, lawyers serve as neutral negotiators between two parties—usually with potential litigants in the mediation setting, but it could also be as a negotiator or "fixer" in a business transaction. Whether mediating between litigants or negotiating a business deal between potential collaborators to a transaction, the lawyer's goal is to help forge an agreement. This creates potential misunderstandings with the parties, as one or more might think the lawyer is on "their side" or looking out for their interests. Rule 2.4, therefore, imposes a simple duty on the attorney: "A lawyer serving as a third-party neutral shall inform unrepresented parties that the lawyer is not representing them." In recent years, the MPRE has tested on this rule less frequently than on Rules 2.1, 2.3, or 1.13.

QUESTION 8. The former mediator. An attorney, who often serves as a court-appointed mediator, received an appointment to mediate the divorce case between a husband and wife. The case settled in mediation and the divorce became final soon after. A year later, the husband sought to retain the attorney to represent him in a modification suit against his ex-wife. The attorney accepted the case and sent a letter to the ex-wife advising her that her ex-husband had retained him to represent him in a modification suit. Are the attorney's actions proper?

A. Yes, an attorney who previously served as a third-party neutral may represent any party in a suit connected to the previous matter if the attorney provides proper notice to the other party in writing.

B. Yes, an attorney who previously served as a third-party neutral may represent any party in a suit connected to the previous matter if the previous case occurred more than one year before the third-party neutral began representation of one of the parties.

C. No, an attorney who previously served as a third-party neutral is required to obtain informed consent, confirmed in writing, from all parties to the proceeding prior to representing a party in a suit connected to the previous matter.

D. No, an attorney who previously served as a third-party neutral shall not represent any party in a suit connected to the previous matter.

ANALYSIS. Comment 4 for Rule 2.4 addresses this type of scenario: "A lawyer who serves as a third-party neutral subsequently may be asked to serve as a lawyer representing a client in the same matter. The conflicts of interest that arise for both the individual lawyer and the lawyer's law firm are addressed in Rule 1.12." The operative provision in Rule 1.12, in turn, says, " . . . [A] lawyer shall not represent anyone in connection with a matter in which the lawyer participated personally and substantially as a judge or other adjudicative officer or law clerk to such a person or as an arbitrator, mediator or other third-party neutral, unless all parties to the proceeding give informed consent, confirmed in writing." In other words, a lawyer who served as a mediator cannot later represent one of the parties against the other in the same or related matter.

A is incorrect. Although the attorney sent the ex-wife a letter notifying her that he would be representing her ex-husband, the facts do not state that the attorney has obtained consent, confirmed in writing from the ex-wife. Therefore, the attorney's actions are presumptively improper.

B is also incorrect because the rules do not have a time limit (such as one year) on the prohibition against representing one side in a matter after previously serving as a third-party neutral.

C is the correct answer. The lawyer in this question served as a third-party neutral between the husband and wife, so he cannot later represent one against the other in a suit to modify the agreement.

D is incorrectly overbroad. Rule 2.4 actually allows a lawyer who has previously served as a third-party neutral to subsequently represent a client in the same matter, on the condition that he first obtains written consent, confirmed in writing, from the other party.

QUESTION 9. **The good deal.** A husband and wife are attending court-ordered mediation with an attorney, who is serving as the neutral mediator. The husband has retained counsel, but the wife has not. During mediation, the wife asks the mediator for his advice, and asks whether he believes that the husband's offer is a "good deal" for her. The attorney explains that his position as mediator only allows him to facilitate the negotiating process. The wife continues to seek the attorney's advice about the settlement proposals the husband makes. The attorney finally tells the wife what she is getting is a decent percentage of the estate and that he believes it to be a "good deal" for her. The attorney also informs the wife again that he does not represent her and that anything he says is merely general information, not legal advice. Are the attorney's actions proper?

A. Yes, attorneys serving as mediators may permissibly give their opinions about settlement offers to clients, as their experience as mediators offers insight that would not be obtainable by clients elsewhere.

B. Yes, attorneys serving as mediators are required to inform parties that their role is to facilitate the negotiation process, and may then give general advice as long as they inform the party that any advice given should be taken as general information, not as legal advice.

C. No, the lawyer should decline to advise her, and instead explain more carefully the difference between the lawyer's role as a third-party neutral and a lawyer's role as one who represents a client.

D. No, attorneys may not give legal advice or their opinions to unrepresented persons who do not have an attorney also in attendance to further advise the unrepresented person.

ANALYSIS. Rule 2.4(b) requires a lawyer acting as a third-party neutral to be careful about leaving either party with the wrong impression that the lawyer is there to represent them. This question describes a particularly awkward situation for mediators—one party has his own counsel present for the mediation, while the other party is unrepresented, and the mediator is the second lawyer in the room, but without an individual client. It is natural for the unrepresented party to start treating the mediator as her lawyer in the situation, and it is particularly important for the mediator to clarify his neutral role. Neutrality includes refusing to advise one side to accept the other party's offer.

A is not the right answer. The Model Rules do not clarify exactly what legal opinions a third-party neutral may offer to individuals during a mediation, but deciding for one party whether the other party's settlement offer is a "good deal" is clearly the type of advice Rule 2.4 intended to avoid, because it goes to the conclusion of the matter.

B is not correct. Rule 2.4 does not give clear guidance about what type of advice a third-party neutral may offer, but advising someone whether the other party's offer is a "good deal" is not general advice, but specific advice.

C is the correct answer. The attorney should have known that the wife did not fully understand the attorney's role in the matter when she continued to ask for his advice after he told her the first time that he was not representing her.

D is overbroad and therefore incorrect. It is not clear that lawyers can never offer opinions or advice at all when acting as mediators, so this answer is too absolute. The reason the lawyer's conduct was improper here is because of the specific advice he gave, which a neutral third party should not give.

QUESTION 10. **A deeply divided law school faculty.** A law school suffers from deep divisions among its faculty. One group of the faculty dislikes the Dean and wants to force his resignation with a vote of no confidence and pressure on the Board of Trustees. The other group is loyal to the Dean and resents their disloyal colleagues, whom they consider unprofessional. The controversy surrounding the law school's Dean overlaps with faculty divisions over hiring practices, tenure, and whether the school should try to emulate top-tier law schools in order to boost their national rankings, or if they should focus instead exclusively on pedagogy and preparing the students for the practice of law after graduation. The divisions are so great that each faction has threatened to quit, or take other drastic action that would imperil the school's existence, if their side does not prevail. The Board of Trustees obtains an agreement from both factions on the faculty that they will hire an attorney to function as a third-party neutral to attempt to broker a compromise between the factions on the faculty. The attorney is an alumnus of the law school and offers to serve in this capacity without charging legal fees. He claims that he is not representing the Board, the Dean, or either side of the balkanized faculty. He begins to schedule private conferences with each faculty group, the Dean, and the Board, as well as meetings attended by representatives from each faction of the faculty to have deliberations and consider possible compromises. The attorney also insists that he is not an arbitrator or mediator because no litigation over the dispute is pending or even contemplated at this point. Is it proper for the attorney to serve in this capacity?

A. Yes, because a lawyer can serve as a third-party neutral when the lawyer assists two or more persons who are not clients of the lawyer to reach a resolution of a dispute or other matter that has arisen between them.
B. Yes, because in this situation, the lawyer represents all of the parties jointly for purposes of the Model Rules, and all the parties have consented to any potential conflicts of interest.
C. No, because it is unclear whom, if anyone, the lawyer represents in this situation, so it is impossible to ascertain the lawyer's duty of loyalty.
D. No, because the lawyer is an alumnus of the law school and therefore is not truly neutral in the dispute.

ANALYSIS. This question highlights the fact that the "third-party neutral" concept in Rule 2.4 covers more than official arbitrators and mediators. Third-party neutrals also assist with business transactions (such as the negotiations involved in corporate mergers and acquisitions) between parties with divergent interests, and to resolve disputes like the one described in this question. Here, neither side has necessarily threatened litigation—and litigation is not likely to result even if the third-party neutral is unsuccessful. Instead, resolving the conflict would preserve the institution from disruption or dissolution, much like saving a business partnership after a conflict has arisen between partners. Even if the direst consequences were never to materialize for this law school—maybe nobody will actually quit—resolving the conflict or smoothing over some of the points of tension could foster institutional cohesiveness and teamwork that would enable the school to function better in the future.

A is the correct answer. Rule 2.4(a) applies and these warnings are appropriate. Aside from representing clients in dispute-resolution processes, lawyers often serve as third-party neutrals. Whether a third-party neutral serves primarily as a facilitator, evaluator, or decision maker depends on the particular process that the parties select or the court mandates.

B is incorrect. The facts provided do not state that the attorney represents all the parties jointly. The attorney was hired to serve as a third-party neutral and has made it clear that he represents neither side.

C is also incorrect. The facts state that the attorney has claimed that he does not represent the Board, the Dean, nor either side of the balkanized faculty. Presumably, the attorney represents the institution overall, which could include its alumni, the students, the brand name, and so on.

D is not the right answer, because the lawyer's connection to the institution does not necessarily give him a conflict of interest or even a bias toward either faction of the faculty. If anything, being an alumnus gives the lawyer an interest in preserving the institution as an entity, which fits well with the job of resolving the dispute to keep the school from coming apart.

C. Rule 1.13—Organization as Client

Lawyers sometimes represent organizations and not just individuals, and this presents its own set of ethical challenges. The first question a lawyer must ask when dealing with members of an organization she represents is: "Who is the client?" When representing a company or other organization as an in-house lawyer, the client is the organization, and not the constituent members. Of course, an organization must act through its constituent members like its officers or directors. This means that the lawyer communicates with members of the organization to give advice and render legal services. Even so, those members are not the lawyer's clients in any individual capacity. Thus, to the extent that a constituent is not duly authorized, or not acting on behalf of the organization, or has interests adverse to the organization, that person is not the client, and the attendant duties of confidentiality and privilege may not apply under those circumstances.

The lawyer has a duty to explain the identity of the client to constituent members who seek the lawyer's advice. A lawyer should be clear and unequivocal that he represents the company and not the individual. When a constituent is acting in a manner that would be detrimental to the organization or is unlawful, and the lawyer becomes aware of the wrongful conduct, the lawyer has a duty to the organization to confront the individual. The lawyer must explain how the individual's conduct is harmful to the company, and urge the individual to change his conduct to conform to the law. If that member refuses to listen or alter his behavior, the lawyer may need to go up the chain of command, starting with the member's immediate supervisor, to correct the conduct that could harm the company. If the infraction remains uncorrected and there is a substantial risk of significant harm to the organization, a lawyer may go to the authorities in order to protect the company from illegal conduct by its members. A lawyer must weigh the seriousness of the crime and potential for harm involved when deciding whether to go to the authorities. See Rule 1.3, comment 4. If a lawyer is discharged or withdraws for trying to correct malfeasance, he must inform the higher-level members of his discharge or withdrawal, taking reasonable steps to make sure that the organization's highest authority is aware of his discharge or withdrawal. See comment 8.

Sometimes, an organization brings a lawyer into a situation to defend members of an organization or to conduct an investigation about possible wrongdoing. Under these circumstances, the lawyer's duty of confidentiality remains intact for the information gathered as part of his investigation.

QUESTION 11. **Clash of the titans.** An attorney worked for a corporation as its in-house counsel. Hostility breaks out between the Chief Executive Officer (CEO) and the Chief Financial Officer (CFO), with each threatening to sue the other over allegations of slander, libel, trespass to chattel, and so on. Does this personal clash between top managers present the attorney with a conflict of interest?

A. Yes, because as representative of the corporation, he also necessarily represents each of the top managers or directors, so both of these individuals are the lawyer's clients.
B. Yes, because both the corporation as an entity and the Chief Executive Officer are necessarily clients of the lawyer, and the clash with the Chief Financial Officer is essentially a clash with the corporation.
C. No, because a lawyer representing an organization as a client cannot have a conflict of interest, as conflicts are strictly between natural persons.
D. No, because a lawyer employed by an organization represents the organization acting through its duly authorized constituents, so the lawyer represents neither of these officers individually.

ANALYSIS. Rule 1.13(a) says, "A lawyer employed or retained by an organization represents the organization acting through its duly authorized constituents." In this question, the attorney works as in-house counsel representing the corporation, not the individual managers who are at odds. The attorney has no duty of loyalty to either one, but instead must look out for the best interest of the corporation. Of course, in practice one or the other manager might be the attorney's direct supervisor or have the ability to fire him, which can affect how the lawyer may interact with different individuals on a day-to-day basis.

A is wrong because it is an incorrect statement of law. An attorney representing a corporation does not represent the constituents of that corporation in their individual capacities. (Rule 1.13(a).) In the scenario set forth above, the CFO and CEO have a dispute—a "personal clash"—that is not related to the business of the corporation, nor is there any indication in the question that either of the individuals was acting as an authorized representative of the company regarding the conduct at issue.

B is incorrect because the CEO is not necessarily the client of the lawyer. A CEO or a CFO may be clients of the corporate lawyer to the extent that the conduct under review was duly authorized and could be said to be the conduct of the corporation. Nevertheless, neither the CEO nor the CFO is a client of the lawyer when acting in their individual capacities.

C is wrong because it is an incorrect statement of the law. It is possible to have a conflict between two clients that are not natural persons, whether those clients are both corporations, or if one is a corporation and the other is a natural person. A corporation is a legal entity, which must act through its duly authorized members. Even though a lawyer represents the organization acting through its duly authorized constituents, when an action or an agent is not duly authorized, the person acting outside her authority is not the client of the lawyer; only the corporation and those acts that are the corporation's acts are part of the lawyer's representation.

D is correct. A lawyer representing a corporation represents the corporation, not its constituents, unless those constituents are (1) duly authorized and (2) acting for the corporation. In the facts above, neither the CFO nor the CEO is purportedly acting for the corporation, and therefore the lawyer does not represent either of them for their individual conduct.

QUESTION 12. **Trouble with the FEDs on the horizon.** An attorney worked for a corporation as in-house counsel. The attorney discovered that the Chief Financial Officer falsified the corporation's quarterly earnings report in order to prop up the firm's share price, as the CFO's compensation is partly in stock options. The attorney knows that these misrepresented earnings appeared in the filings to the Securities and Exchange Commission, and will eventually result in severe regulatory fines or civil liability for the corporation. The attorney thus reasonably believes that the violation is reasonably certain to result in substantial injury to the organization. The attorney confronted the CFO, but this proved unfruitful, and then he proceeded up the corporate chain of command, eventually going to the Chief Executive Officer and the Board of Directors. The officers and directors refused to address the problem because they thought it would send their stock prices into a freefall and make the corporation vulnerable to a hostile takeover from corporate raiders. Would it now be proper for the attorney to become a whistleblower and reveal the problem to the relevant government authorities?

A. Yes, as long as the attorney protects the identities of all those involved and does not reveal the names of the wrongdoers, as they are his clients.

B. Yes, because the attorney has exhausted all other reasonable avenues to address the problem internally, so the lawyer may reveal information relating to the representation whether or not Rule 1.6 permits such disclosure.

C. No, because the lawyer has a duty of confidentiality to the corporation, and this information relates directly to the attorney's representation.

D. No, because the attorney has a duty of confidentiality to the corporate officers and directors personally, and may not disclose information relating to his representation of them without their consent.

learns of a wrongdoing

ANALYSIS. Rule 1.13(c) has an exception for extreme circumstances when a company's activities clearly risk hefty sanctions from government regulators, and the lawyer has exhausted the internal options for addressing it—not even the Board will take action. In such a case, the lawyer must protect the corporation itself—that is, the owners or shareholders—by reporting the problem to the proper authorities.

A is incorrect because it contains an incorrect statement of law. An attorney representing a corporation does not represent the constituents of that corporation in their individual capacities, but rather represents the organization. Thus, the wrongdoers are not his clients, because they are not authorized to commit crimes in the name of the company.

B is correct. The in-house lawyer was not retained to investigate an alleged violation of law or to defend the organization or its officers for specific conduct described above. Further, the conduct described above is sufficiently serious, and the consequences significantly dire, such that the lawyer confronted the alleged wrongdoers to encourage them to rectify the situation, and has gone up the chain of command with his concerns. Because those actions have failed, the lawyer may reveal information to the extent necessary to prevent reasonably certain substantial harm to the company, which may include revealing the identity of the wrongdoers to the authorities.

C is wrong because the fact pattern above states that the attorney is an in-house attorney and does not mention that he was retained to conduct an investigation into specific wrongdoing or to defend the company or its officers from charges related to that alleged wrongdoing. Thus, the exception in Comment 7 does not apply.

D is incorrect because a lawyer representing a corporation represents the corporation, not its constituents, unless those constituents are (1) duly authorized and (2) acting for the corporation. In the facts above, the corporate officers engaging in criminal activity, were not duly authorized and were not acting for the corporation. Further, as explained above, the in-house lawyer was not retained for their defense or to conduct an investigation concerning this matter.

QUESTION 13. Now that we're already in trouble. A large corporation was under investigation by a government regulatory agency over possible violations of securities law. The corporation hired an attorney to represent it in the matter, and authorized the attorney to make a full internal investigation to discover the merits of the accusations. The attorney discovered that a high-level manager had falsified quarterly earnings reports, a clear violation of the law that could expose the corporation to devastating sanctions and civil liability. The attorney confronted the officer involved, but this proved unfruitful, and then he proceeded up the corporate chain of command, eventually going to the Chief Executive Officer and the Board of Directors. The officers and directors refused to address the problem because they thought it would send their stock prices into a freefall and make the corporation vulnerable to a hostile takeover from corporate raiders. Would it now be proper for the attorney to become a whistleblower and reveal the problem to the relevant government authorities?

A. Yes, because the attorney has exhausted all other reasonable avenues to address the problem internally, so the lawyer may reveal information relating to the representation whether or not Rule 1.6 permits such disclosure.

B. Yes, as long as the attorney protects the identities of all those involved and does not reveal the names of the wrongdoers, as they are his clients.

C. No, because the attorney has a duty of confidentiality to the corporate officers and directors personally, and may not disclose information relating to his representation of them without their consent.

D. No, because the attorney has a duty of confidentiality to the corporation, and the corporation hired the attorney to defend the organization against a claim arising out of an alleged violation of law.

ANALYSIS. Rule 1.13(d) says that the whistleblower duties outlined in an earlier section of the rule "shall not apply with respect to information relating to a lawyer's representation of an organization to investigate an alleged violation of law, or to defend the organization or an officer, employee or other constituent associated with the organization against a claim arising out of an alleged violation of law." Here, the corporation is already under investigation and hired the lawyer to represent it during the enforcement proceedings. This situation changes the lawyer's role, and makes the duty of confidentiality paramount.

A is incorrect because the lawyer has been retained to represent the company against possible enforcement of securities violations, so the lawyer may not become a whistleblower under these circumstances. This falls under the exception in Subsection (d) and is discussed in Comment 7. Where, as here, the lawyer has been retained to represent the organization and/or its officers against a claim arising out of an alleged violation of the law, the lawyer must not reveal information relating to the representation.

B is incorrect for the same reasons that answer **A** is incorrect, and the rule does not contain an exception for the fact that the lawyer protects the identities of all those involved. Answer **B** is also wrong because it states that the individuals are his clients. The officers are his clients only to the extent that their interests are aligned with the organization's interests. Protecting individuals' identities is in the individual interests of the officers, not necessarily the interest of the organization.

C is wrong because it states that the individual officers and directors, personally, are his clients. The officers and directors are his clients only to the extent that their interests are aligned with the organization's interests.

D is correct because the lawyer was hired specifically to represent the corporation regarding a violation of the law. Under Rule 1.13(c), the obligations to apprise the chain of command about wrongdoing is not applicable because the lawyer has been retained as part of the process to deal with the defense of the actions in question taken by the officers or directors in their capacities as the representatives of the company.

QUESTION 14. **Corporate counsel and the tortfeasor employee.** An attorney represents a corporation. One of the corporation's delivery trucks, driven by a corporation employee, had a tragic accident with a school bus full of children, and many children died. The delivery truck driver suffered severe injuries, but survived, and spent three weeks recovering in the hospital. In preparation for the wrongful death lawsuits by the deceased children's families, the corporation's attorney visited the truck driver in the hospital and interviewed him about the accident. The attorney did not explain that he was not representing the driver, or that the driver should retain his own lawyer. The unsophisticated driver may have assumed that his employer's lawyer was also looking out for his (the driver's) interests. The driver made some incriminating admissions to the lawyer about being slightly intoxicated at the time of the accident and having been careless while driving. He also admitted that at the time of the accident, he had taken the corporate delivery truck off its assigned route to attend to some personal business for about twenty minutes. Could the attorney be subject to discipline in this case?

A. Yes, because he shares in the corporation's collective responsibility for the deaths of those innocent children.
B. Yes, because in dealing with an organization's employees, the lawyer should explain the identity of the client when the lawyer should reasonably know that the organization's interests are adverse to those of the employee with whom the lawyer is dealing.
C. No, because it is not yet clear whether the driver's interests are adverse to the corporation's interests, or whether the corporation will be responsible through respondeat superior.
D. No, because a lawyer does not have an obligation to remind every employee in a corporation that the lawyer represents the organization rather than the individuals within the organization.

ANALYSIS. This question draws its facts from an actual case on this point. Rule 1.13(f) says, "In dealing with an organization's directors, officers, employees, members, shareholders or other constituents, a lawyer shall explain the identity of the client when the lawyer knows or reasonably should know that the organization's interests are adverse to those of the constituents with whom the lawyer is dealing." Here, the lawyer for the corporation is interviewing an employee who caused an accident. It will eventually be in the corporation's interest to deny responsibility and claim that the employee acted outside the scope of his employment, so the employee's self-incriminatory statements could constitute admissions against interest for purposes of shifting all the liability to him.

A is incorrect because the lawyer in not subject to discipline under the ethical rules for tortious actions of his clients or their employees where he had no part in the action that resulted in the harm.

B is correct. According to Rule 1.13(f), a lawyer has the obligation to explain the identity of the client to the organization's directors, officers, employees, or other constituents when the lawyer has reason to believe that the interests of the constituent is adverse to the interests of the company. Here, the facts provide that the lawyer is representing the corporation. He is interviewing the driver of a truck who was severely injured while driving a company vehicle and caused an accident with multiple fatalities. At a minimum, the lawyer should expect that it is highly likely that the driver's interests are or may be adverse to the company's interests. Therefore, he had a duty to explain that he represented the company and not the individual truck driver when he interviewed him at the hospital.

C is wrong because the lawyer must identify who his client is when he knows or reasonably should know that the organization's interests are adverse to the interests of the employee. Here, as stated above, the truck driver was injured and could sue the company under workers' compensation or some other theory. Thus, on its face, the situation has high likelihood of the truck driver having adverse interests to the company. Additionally, the truck driver exposed the company to significant liability, raising the possibility that the driver would have interests adverse to those of the company.

D is incorrect because it directly contradicts Rule 1.13(f).

QUESTION 15. **The people want to know.** An attorney represented a large corporation as a defendant in a toxic tort action. The matter had received little media attention and the corporate officers who retained the attorney emphasized the need to be discreet as long as possible, so that the pending litigation would have a minimal effect on stock prices. The representation necessitated that the attorney interview some of the employees involved in the incident that gave rise to the litigation, including some of the lowest-level unskilled laborers. A few of these individuals, as well as their co-workers whom the lawyer did not interview, asked the lawyer for details about what was happening with the case. The lawyer felt that they had a right to know about the case as it could affect the company, and their jobs, so he explained who the plaintiffs were, how strong the evidence appeared to be on each side, and the potential liability the company was facing. Could the attorney be subject to discipline for sharing this information with the company employees?

A. Yes, but only for sharing it with the employees whom he did not need to interview.

B. Yes, because a lawyer may not disclose to company employees any information relating to the representation except for disclosures explicitly or impliedly authorized by the organizational client in order to carry out the representation.

C. No, because a lawyer should disclose to the company employees any information relating to the representation unless the officers explicitly forbid the disclosures as necessary to carry out the representation.

D. No, because when a lawyer represents a corporation, every employee of the corporation is the client of the lawyer, and has a right to the information.

ANALYSIS. Comment 2 for Rule 1.13 says that constituents of an organizational client are not necessarily the clients of the lawyer: "The lawyer may not disclose to such constituents information relating to the representation except for disclosures explicitly or impliedly authorized by the organizational client in order to carry out the representation or as otherwise permitted by Rule 1.6." Here, the lawyer should not discuss the case with lower-level employees, even though the outcome of the case could affect their jobs. Most of the decisions of upper management in large corporations could affect future salaries or layoffs, but such decisions are within the management's purview, and do not have to be discussed with everyone who might have an indirect stake in the issue.

A is incorrect because the lawyer has a duty to keep information about the lawsuit confidential, and there is no indication that the company expressly or impliedly authorized the lawyer to disclose information about the plaintiffs or the strengths or weaknesses of the company's case to the employees. This duty of confidentiality extends to those he interviewed as well as to their co-workers whom he did not interview.

B is correct because the lawyer has a duty to keep information about the lawsuit confidential, and there is no indication that the company expressly or impliedly authorized the lawyer to disclose information about the plaintiffs or the strengths or weaknesses of the company's case to the employees.

C is wrong because it is an incorrect statement of the rule. The rule states that a lawyer may not reveal confidential information to constituents unless he has express or implied authorization to do so. Answer **C** would allow disclosures unless such were explicitly forbidden. The attorney, on his own initiative, decided that the employees deserved to know about the details and strategy of the lawsuit, but there is no indication of any permission for him to inform them, as required by the rules.

D is incorrect because the lawyer represents the corporation, not the corporation's employees. An attorney representing a corporation does not represent the constituents of that corporation in their individual capacities. An employee's "need to know because it affects their job" is an individual interest, not an organizational interest, and every employee does not have an unqualified right to information concerning a company's legal disputes.

D. The Closer

There are several contexts during the course of representation in which lawyers must communicate with persons other than their own clients—opposing parties who have their own counsel, unrepresented individuals, constituents (such as employees) of a corporate client, and parties for whom the lawyer serves as a neutral mediator. In each of these contexts, the lawyer must strike a delicate balance of preserving the client's interests and avoiding exploitation of the other person.

QUESTION 16. **The dreaded conversation.** An attorney served as in-house counsel for a corporation, and uncovered illegal actions taken by a particular senior manager (not the Chief Executive Officer or any comparable officer or director, but an individual with decision-making authority and several direct subordinates in the organization). The senior manager had a reputation for being arrogant and unreasonable, and he and the attorney had clashed on several occasions and were barely on speaking terms. At the same time, the senior manager was exceptional in his area of expertise and was an asset to the company despite his unpleasant demeanor. The attorney summoned the nerve to confront the senior manager about the problem as graciously as possible, and the senior manager's initial response was to be dismissive, saying that he was unaware of any laws or regulations that he might have violated. The attorney walked away from the conversation discouraged and planned to take the matter up with the corporate officers, and perhaps the Board of Directors. Before doing so, he reconsidered and returned to the manager, and patiently explained to him the relevant laws and regulations that the manager had violated. The senior manager begrudgingly accepted the attorney's advice and took all necessary measures to rectify the wrongdoing and prevent any long-term repercussions. The senior manager also insulted the attorney, called him incompetent for not bringing up the matter earlier, and suggested that the attorney's incompetence was due to the attorney's ethnic background. Could the attorney be subject to discipline for not referring the matter of the illegal actions to a higher authority in the corporation?

A. Yes, because the senior manager continued to insult him and behave like a bigot even after the attorney proved that the manager's actions violated the law.

B. Yes, because referral to a higher authority in the corporation is part of the lawyer's professional duty under the Model Rules.

C. No, because the manager took the lawyer's advice.

D. No, because a lawyer for a corporation represents not only the corporation itself, but all the managers within the corporation, so the lawyer had a direct client-attorney relationship with the manager.

ANALYSIS. Comment 4 for Rule 1.13 says, "... [I]f the circumstances involve a constituent's innocent misunderstanding of law and subsequent acceptance of the lawyer's advice, the lawyer may reasonably conclude that the best interest of the organization does not require that the matter be referred to higher authority." Remember that the manager is not the lawyer's client—and in a sense, the lawyer is dealing with an unrepresented person in the corporation.

The corporation itself is the client. Thus, if the manager had remained recalcitrant, the lawyer would have had a duty to report it up the chain of command, a step at a time, until someone with authority addressed the matter. Nevertheless, the manager accepted the lawyer's reproof, albeit grudgingly, and not without insulting the lawyer out of spite. The parting insults, though serious (and highly inappropriate), do not change the answer—what matters is that the lawyer obtained a change in behavior that rectified the problem, so there was no need to escalate it further.

A is wrong because the constituent reconsidered the matter and took all necessary steps to rectify the wrongdoing and prevent long-term repercussions, so no referral is needed. According to the rule, an attorney is supposed to consider the seriousness of the wrongdoing and the likelihood of substantial repercussions to the company when deciding whether to refer a matter up the chain of command. Insults and rude behavior do not rise to the level of unlawful conduct that should be referred up the chain of command, and as stated, the employee rectified the situation that posed a legal problem to the company.

B is incorrect because referral up the chain of command is not automatic. First, the attorney should try to speak with the errant employee to correct the behavior. Here, the employee eventually agreed to rectify the situation, so there was no need to go up the chain of command. An attorney is supposed to consider the seriousness of the wrongdoing and the likelihood of substantial repercussions to the company when deciding whether to refer a matter up the chain of command, and here, the problem was resolved so the likelihood of substantial harm to the company is absent under these facts.

C is correct. The facts here indicate that the employee agreed with the attorney to rectify the wrongdoing and to prevent long-term repercussions. An attorney is supposed to consider the seriousness of the wrongdoing and the likelihood of substantial repercussions to the company when deciding whether to refer a matter up the chain of command, and here, the problem was resolved so the likelihood of substantial harm to the company is absent under these facts.

D is wrong because a lawyer representing a corporation does not represent the corporation's constituents, but only the company and those acts that are duly authorized and on behalf of the company. The lawyer does not have a direct attorney-client relationship with the employee, but instead has a duty to the company to ensure that all employees are acting pursuant to the law. The rules therefore require that the lawyer refer wrongdoing up the chain of command if the employee is recalcitrant. In this scenario, however, the employee changed his behavior and prevented any further harm. Thus, even though the lawyer need not refer the matter up the chain of command, it is not because the lawyer must keep communications between the lawyer and the employee confidential; to the contrary, the lawyer's duty is to the organization, not the employee.

Stevenson's Picks

1.	Protecting the client's feelings	D
2.	Don't worry . . .	C
3.	Don't lecture me	A
4.	My client is a suspicious character	D
5.	Risky business	D
6.	Disinheriting the daughter	A
7.	Whether to appeal	C
8.	The former mediator	C
9.	The good deal	C
10.	A deeply divided law school faculty	A
11.	Clash of the titans	D
12.	Trouble with the FEDs on the horizon	B
13.	Now that we're already in trouble	D
14.	Corporate counsel and the tortfeasor employee	B
15.	The people want to know	B
16.	The dreaded conversation	C

9

Transactions and Communications with Persons Other Than Clients

CHAPTER OVERVIEW

A. The Closer

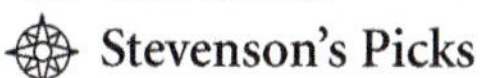

Model Rules 4.1 through 4.4 govern the interactions lawyers have with people other than their clients—opposing parties/counsel, unrepresented individuals, and even third parties whose lives the lawyer could affect indirectly by serving a client. There is a general requirement of truthfulness (Rule 4.1), which is consistent with other integrity rules such as candor to the tribunal. Rule 4.2 primarily forbids lawyers to speak directly to opposing parties without their lawyer present (if they are represented), while Rule 4.3 forbids lawyers from manipulating or exploiting opposing parties who are unrepresented by counsel.

For purposes of examination questions, probably the trickiest provisions are those buried in Comments 6 and 7 for Rule 4.2. Comment 6 permits lawyers to seek a court order to communicate with a represented person directly under extreme circumstances, and Comment 7 deals with interactions with constituents of a corporation (directors, employees, former employees, etc.) when the corporation itself is the other party. The MPRE examiners publicly report that questions on Rules 4.1 through 4.4 constitute 2 to 8 percent of the MPRE, which means students should expect to see between one and three questions on the test from all of the rules combined. Rules 4.2 and 4.3 seem to be the most heavily tested of this group.

QUESTION 1. **The former employee.** In anticipation of trial, a plaintiff's lawyer contacts several former employees of the defendant corporation and interviews them about the day-to-day operations of the company and the chain of command for addressing complaints. The lawyer does this without permission from the defendant's attorney. Was this proper?

A. Yes, consent of the organization's lawyer is not required for communication with a former constituent of the organization that is a represented opposing party.

B. Yes, because being a party to litigation means that the company waived its right to prevent opposing counsel from privately interviewing their present or former employees.

C. No, consent of the organization's lawyer is always required for communication with a present or former constituent of the organization that is a represented opposing party.

D. No, because it is improper for the lawyer to inquire into the private, behind-the-scenes workings of a company, merely looking for dirt or gossip to use against the company during litigation.

ANALYSIS. Comment 7 for Rule 4.2 says, "In the case of a represented organization . . . Consent of the organization's lawyer is not required for communication with a former constituent." Normally, a lawyer cannot communicate directly with anyone in a represented organization, but this does not apply to former employees, as in this question.

A is correct. Former employees are not constituents of the corporation for purposes of the Model Rules, and the lawyer may contact them directly without permission from the corporation's attorney.

B is incorrect because it contradicts Rule 4.2, which forbids lawyers from communicating directly with litigants who have representation by counsel.

C is too absolute, therefore incorrect. While it is generally true that lawyers must obtain consent from an organization's counsel before communicating directly with the entity's constituents, there is a caveat found in Comment 7, which says that former employees are not constituents and permission from the entity's lawyer is not necessary.

D is the wrong answer. Lawyers often investigate the inner workings of a company that is the opposing party in a lawsuit, to develop evidence in the case and to identify the true wrongdoers.

QUESTION 2. **My old friend, the opposing party.** A lawyer represents the defendant in litigation over a car accident. The plaintiff, who was driving the other car, was a childhood friend and neighbor of the lawyer—they still keep in touch. As the defendant's lawyer has known the plaintiff since childhood, he calls the plaintiff, who has retained counsel as well, to see if they can resolve the case without going to trial. Is the lawyer subject to discipline for calling his lifelong friend?

A. Yes, the Model Rules prohibit in-person solicitation of settlements, and this includes real-time electronic communication such as telephone calls, texts, or chat.

B. Yes, as a lawyer shall not communicate about the subject of the representation with a person the lawyer knows to be represented by another lawyer in the matter, unless the lawyer has the consent of the other lawyer or is authorized to do so by law or a court order.

C. No, the Model Rules do not prohibit communication with a represented person, or an employee or agent of such a person, concerning matters outside the representation.

D. No, the courts and disciplinary boards strongly favor settlement before trial as a matter of public policy.

ANALYSIS. Rule 4.2 is one of the shortest rules in the MRPC, but it imposes a strict standard—lawyers simply cannot communicate about the case with the other party directly if the lawyer knows the other person has representation by counsel—unless the other person's lawyer consents or a court order authorizes the communication. The great fear is that lawyers will call the opposing party directly behind their lawyer's back and manipulate the person into settling the case or mistrusting their lawyer if the matter continues. Students should assume the rule applies regardless of any extenuating circumstances, but should also note the conditions that frame the rule, as these specific clauses lend themselves to multiple-choice test questions. The lawyer must have "knowledge" that the other person has a lawyer, which means actual knowledge, though a disciplinary board may infer actual knowledge from the circumstances. The rule forbids communication "about the subject of the representation," meaning a lawyer who knows the other party in social contexts could still talk to the person about unrelated matters. If a question presents extenuating circumstances (such as the opposing counsel disappearing for weeks at a time), look to see if the lawyer obtained a court order authorizing the direct communication, which is the appropriate remedy in extenuating circumstances.

A is incorrect. The Model Rules do not prohibit in-person solicitation of settlements, but Rule 4.2 does require that the other lawyer be present or consent to the communication. This answer is tricky because it conflates verbiage of Rule 7.3, addressing solicitation of prospective clients, with the rule about communications with another party.

B is correct. Even though the opposing party is the lawyer's longtime friend, once the friend has retained counsel, it is improper for the lawyer to call him directly offering to settle the case.

C quotes a valid rule, but it is inapplicable to these facts. Comment 4 for Rule 4.2 uses similar verbiage to clarify the point that lawyers may indeed communicate with other parties about matters outside the representation, but here, the lawyer is offering to settle the case.

D is also incorrect. Even though it is true in the abstract that courts (and state bar associations) favor settlement before trial, this does not negate the prohibition in Rule 4.2. If the lawyer wants to settle the case, he should contact opposing counsel.

QUESTION 3. **Straight to the top.** While preparing for a trial over workplace discrimination, the plaintiff's lawyer contacts the owner and chief executive officer (CEO) of the defendant corporation and interviews her about the day-to-day operations of the company and the chain of command for addressing personnel complaints. The owner/CEO is not personally involved in the matter of the pending litigation—she actually never met the plaintiff warehouse worker who claims to be the victim of workplace discrimination, she is not on the witness list to testify at trial, and nobody has suggested that she was responsible for the wrongdoing. Even so, she has the power to settle the case or stipulate to a judgment amount, so the plaintiff's lawyer talks to her directly. The lawyer does this without permission from the corporation's attorney, whom the company's general counsel hired; general counsel is an employee three steps below the CEO in the organizational chart. Was this communication by the plaintiff's lawyer proper?

A. Yes, because the rules allow a lawyer to communicate with the constituent of a represented organization (opposing party) who has authority to obligate the organization with respect to the matter.

B. Yes, because the CEO is three steps above the employee who hired the outside counsel, and therefore clearly has authority to overrule outside counsel's permission or lack thereof.

C. No, the rules prohibit a lawyer from communicating with the constituent of a represented organization (opposing party) who has authority to obligate the organization with respect to the matter.

D. No, because the CEO clearly would not have first-hand knowledge of lower-level personnel problems in the company's warehouse, although asking the owner/CEO for a settlement was proper.

ANALYSIS. Comment 7 for Rule 4.2 says, "In the case of a represented organization, this Rule prohibits communications with a constituent of the organization who supervises, directs or regularly consults with the organization's lawyer concerning the matter or has authority to obligate the organization with respect to the matter or whose act or omission in connection with the matter may be imputed to the organization for purposes of civil or criminal liability." In other words, when the other party (in litigation *or* a transaction) is a corporation, a lawyer cannot communicate directly with the management, thereby circumventing the corporation's legal counsel.

A is incorrect. This states the exact opposite of the mandate set forth in Comment 7 to Rule 4.2.

B may be true as a fact, but is wrong as a rule. The fact that the CEO ranks higher than the organization's lawyer and has legal power to bind the organization is exactly why the Model Rules prohibit attorneys from circumventing the corporation's legal counsel to communicate directly with directors, officers, or managers.

C is correct. Even though the executive is not involved in the litigation, she has the power to bind the corporation. If she agrees to a settlement, the other lawyer could legally hold the corporation to that agreement (depending on the facts, of course) or make a damaging admission against interest. The lawyer must communicate through the corporation's counsel unless the other lawyer consents to the communication, which is unlikely.

D is incorrect. The individual's lack of knowledge about the case actually matters less than the person's legal authority to bind the entity with a settlement agreement or an admission. In fact, the CEO's lack of familiarity with the matter makes the individual more susceptible to manipulation or exploitation by the opposing attorney, highlighting the need to include corporate counsel in such communications.

QUESTION 4. A chance encounter between adversaries. The plaintiff and the defendant in a lawsuit run into each other in the supermarket and start discussing their case without their lawyers present. Both have been shocked at the mounting litigation costs, and at how long the case has gone on. The plaintiff volunteers to withdraw his case if the defendant will withdraw his counterclaims and pay whatever filing fees are involved in such a voluntary dismissal. Later, when each party reports this to their respective lawyers, the plaintiff's lawyer is very upset. The plaintiff mentioned that the defendant said his own lawyer (defense counsel) had helped give him the idea by asking at their first consultation, "Why haven't you and the plaintiff simply resolved this on your own, without resorting to litigation?" The plaintiff's lawyer reports the defendant's lawyer for misconduct, claiming that opposing counsel merely used his client as an agent to communicate with the plaintiff without the latter's lawyer present. Is the defendant's lawyer subject to discipline, based on these facts?

A. Yes, because parties to a matter must not communicate directly with each other, and a lawyer is prohibited from advising a client concerning a communication that the client might make.

B. Yes, because the lawyer clearly manipulated his client into communicating directly with the opposing party without opposing counsel present.
C. No, because the plaintiff is the party who actually agreed first to withdraw his claim, so the defendant's lawyer cannot be responsible for any communication thereafter.
D. No, because the parties to a matter may communicate directly with each other without their lawyers being present or consenting to the conversation.

ANALYSIS. Comment 4 for Rule 4.2 says, "Parties to a matter may communicate directly with each other, and a lawyer is not prohibited from advising a client concerning a communication that the client is legally entitled to make." Even though a lawyer may not contact the other party directly without their counsel's permission, the parties can talk to each other and may even decide to settle a matter without consulting their attorneys. At the same time, a lawyer *cannot* instruct his client to approach the other side directly to transmit a message from the lawyer, merely as a way of circumventing the rule.

A is incorrect. This contradicts the provisions in Comment 4 for Rule 4.2, which explicitly permit parties to communicate directly with each other and permit lawyers to advise their clients on what to say (or not say) during such conversations.

B is incorrect because it exaggerates what the lawyer did. The facts in the question do not indicate that the defendant's lawyer was manipulative at all—instead, this is a perfectly normal question to ask a client, in order to understand the nature of the relationship between the parties and their personal history.

C is also incorrect. The lawyer in this question did nothing wrong, but which party actually initiates the discussion is not relevant for purposes of Rule 4.2 For example, Comment 3 for Rule 4.2 says, "The Rule applies even though the represented person initiates or consents to the communication. A lawyer must immediately terminate communication with a person if, after commencing communication, the lawyer learns that the person is one with whom communication is not permitted by this Rule." Thus, if the plaintiff (represented by counsel) calls the defense attorney directly, even to ask a question about the case or to inquire about how to reach the other party, the attorney cannot speak to the person, and must politely terminate the conversation immediately.

D is correct. Even though the parties have each retained lawyers to represent them, they can talk directly to each other without their lawyer present and without their lawyer's consent. Of course, many lawyers would discourage their clients from doing so, to avoid the risk of making a damaging admission against interest.

A. The Closer

Of all the provisions in Rules 4.1 through 4.3, perhaps the most important are to remember that lawyers cannot communicate directly with other parties represented by counsel (subject to a few qualifications). The other crucial point is that when dealing with unrepresented parties, the lawyer must make clear whom he represents (that he is not disinterested or trying to help the other party), as required under Rule 4.3.

There is also a crossover provision connecting the two rules. Comment 9 to Rule 4.2 says, "In the event the person with whom the lawyer communicates is not known to be represented by counsel in the matter, the lawyer's communications are subject to Rule 4.3." The Model Rules mean *actual knowledge* when they refer to the lawyer "knowingly" taking some action. As the definition section in Rule 1.0 says, "'Knowingly,' 'known,' or 'knows' denotes actual knowledge of the fact in question. A person's knowledge may be inferred from circumstances."

QUESTION 5. **It starts with a phone call.** A business owner hires a lawyer hoping to enforce a non-compete agreement against a former employee at their technology firm. According to the client, a rumor started going around just this past week that the former employee either had started his own consulting practice nearby or was working for a nearby competitor. Each scenario, if true, could violate the non-compete agreement. The employee left the client's company on bad terms about three weeks ago. The client provides a copy of the non-compete agreement, and speculates that the former employee may have forgotten about the agreement (which he signed fifteen years ago), and may even be oblivious to the fact that he is violating it. The lawyer decides that the first step is to call the former employee and ask him whether he has found another job yet or has started his own business. The lawyer assumed that the former employee would not have retained counsel yet to challenge the non-compete agreement, given the client's comments about him, and the brief time since the events had unfolded. The former employee answers the phone, and after the lawyer identifies himself as counsel for the business client, the former employee explains that he has started his own rival company, and that he believes the non-compete agreement is invalid under state law. When the lawyer asks why it would be invalid, the former employee says that his own lawyer says that recent changes in state law make the previous agreement void, and that they plan to challenge the agreement in court. The lawyer asks him to have his own lawyer contact him so that they can discuss possible settlement for the dispute. Has the lawyer acted properly?

A. No, the prohibition on communications with a represented person applies regardless of the lawyer's knowledge, because the burden is on every lawyer to determine whether an opposing party has representation before making contact.
B. No, because one can easily infer from these facts and circumstances that the lawyer actually knew the former employee had representation.
C. Yes, as the prohibition on communications with a represented person only applies in circumstances where the lawyer knows that the person is in fact represented in the matter to be discussed, and this means that the lawyer has actual knowledge of the fact of the representation.
D. Yes, if the non-compete agreement has a binding arbitration clause, as matters covered under alternative dispute resolution (arbitration, mediation, or a non-judicial referee) do not implicate the prohibition on communication with opposing parties.

ANALYSIS. Even though there is a strict prohibition against lawyers talking to opposing parties whom the lawyer knows to have retained legal counsel, the operative word for purposes of this question is "knows." In such a case, the lawyer must then comport with the requirements of Rule 4.3, which forbid the lawyer from giving the impression of being neutral or disinterested in the matter. Here, it appears that the lawyer reasonably surmised that the other party had not yet retained his own legal counsel, given the client's comments, and the fact that the person had left his job only three weeks before and had been busy starting a new career. If the former employee had gone to work for another firm, it would be unusual for him to have representation, and if he were acting as a consultant, he may not have bothered hiring a lawyer yet for the formalities of incorporating his own consulting business. The facts here suggest the lawyer complied with Rule 4.3 as well—the conversation was too short and one-sided for the lawyer to give an impression of being disinterested; in addition, he identified himself immediately as representing the person's former employer.

A is incorrect. Rule 4.2 explicitly includes a knowledge requirement (actual knowledge) for the rule to apply. It does not impose a duty to confirm the person is unrepresented beforehand, though it may be prudent to do so.

B is factually incorrect. The facts and circumstances described in the question do not lead to an inference that the lawyer had actual knowledge before the phone call that the other person had already obtained legal representation.

C is correct. The lawyer did not have actual knowledge that the other party had representation. Even if a more cautious lawyer might have tried to confirm that beforehand, nothing from the circumstances creates an inference that the lawyer actually knew the individual had obtained his own legal counsel.

D is the wrong answer. The binding arbitration clause is irrelevant to the lawyer's duties regarding other parties known to have retained legal counsel. The rule would still apply, but in this case the lawyer's lack of knowledge makes Rule 4.2 inapplicable.

Stevenson's Picks

1. The former employee	**A**
2. My old friend, the opposing party	**B**
3. Straight to the top	**C**
4. A chance encounter between adversaries	**D**
5. It starts with a phone call	**C**

10

Rule 1.15—Safekeeping Property

CHAPTER OVERVIEW

A. The Closer

 Stevenson's Picks

Rule 1.15 governs the handling of client money and property. The most important substantive rule to remember is that lawyers must not commingle client funds with the lawyer's own funds (or the firm's operating funds) in the same account. Instead, lawyers must deposit client money (whether it comes from the client or comes from another party for the client) in a separate client trust account. Meticulous recordkeeping is also a requirement, as one would expect. Lawyers may deposit just enough additional money to cover any bank fees on the account, but cannot add additional funds as a "buffer." Lawyers can put funds from multiple clients together in the same client trust account, though. The account must be in the same state unless the client consents to using an account elsewhere.

The trickiest part of the rules in this area involves disputes over portions of the funds, as when a lawyer receives a settlement check for the client from the opposing party, and the client suddenly disputes the lawyer's contingent fee percentage or some of the other expenses in the case. In such cases, the lawyer should keep the disputed portion—and *only* the disputed portion—in the client trust account until the matter is resolved. Whatever amount is indisputably owed to the client or the lawyer (that is, both agree at least on that sum), the lawyer should disburse immediately. The same applies to third-party judgment creditors who inform the lawyer that the client's money should go directly to them—the lawyer must hold the disputed portion of the funds until there is a judicial resolution of the dispute.

Questions about safekeeping client funds (that is, the provisions of Rule 1.15) appear on every administration of the MPRE—usually two per exam.

The examiners state (on their website) that this area constitutes 2 to 8 percent of each MPRE, which means students should expect between one and three questions about this subject on each MPRE.

QUESTION 1. **Across state lines.** An attorney represented a seller in a business transaction involving industrial equipment. When the deal was complete, the purchaser sent the attorney a check for $7,000, the agreed-upon purchase price, with a letter directing the attorney to forward the money to his client (the seller). The attorney notified his client immediately that the check had come in. The client was traveling at the time, and asked the attorney to hold the funds until he returned from his trip. The attorney had only recently moved to this jurisdiction and opened a new firm, did not yet have a client trust account at any banks in the area, so he deposited the check in the client trust account in the neighboring state, where he had practiced until recently. He told the client that the funds would be in a separate client trust account, and explained that it would be out of state, and the client consented. As soon as the check cleared, the attorney wrote a check to the client for the full amount from the client trust account, which the client picked up in person. Did the attorney act properly in this case?

A. Yes, because a lawyer may deposit client funds in an out-of-state client trust account if the client gives informed consent to this arrangement.
B. Yes, because the client asked the attorney to hold the funds temporarily, and the attorney faithfully delivered the entire sum to the client with his own check.
C. No, because a lawyer should not have accepted the check at all, but should have instructed the purchaser to write the check out to the client himself, and deliver it directly to the client.
D. No, because client funds must be kept in a separate account maintained in the state where the lawyer's office is situated, unless the client explicitly consents to another arrangement.

ANALYSIS. Rule 1.15(a) says, "Funds shall be kept in a separate account maintained in the state where the lawyer's office is situated, or elsewhere with the consent of the client or third person." It would be improper for an attorney to keep client funds in an account in another state without the client's consent—but here, the client consented. The consent does not have to be in writing.

A is correct. The crucial fact here is that the client consented to the arrangement, which according to the Model Rules, makes it permissible to hold client funds in an out-of-state account.

B incorrectly ignores the required protocols for handling client funds. It is not sufficient that the client ends up with the money or that the lawyer fulfilled the client's overall goals. The Model Rules impose strict rules about holding client funds. A client could consent to a lawyer holding funds in an out-of-state account, for example, but could not consent to a lawyer commingling the client's funds with the lawyer's own money.

C is incorrect. Lawyers regularly act as intermediaries when funds pass between parties to litigation or parties in a transaction.

D has the right rule, but the wrong conclusion. This is a correct expression of the rule, but the answer should be "yes"—the lawyer followed the rule in this case.

QUESTION 2. The buffer. An attorney has a busy transactional practice and frequently must handle client funds, either for making commercial purchases, sales, leases, dispute settlements, or other transfers. The attorney faithfully deposits client money in a separate trust account and does not commingle the funds with his own, except that he deposits enough of his own money in the account to cover the monthly bank service charges. He also put $1,000 in the account when he opened it and left it there, as a buffer in case there were any accounting errors, so the clients would never experience inconvenience due to the account being inadvertently overdrawn. The attorney keeps complete, accurate records of all deposits and withdrawals for seven full years, after which he destroys the records to preserve client confidentiality. Is the attorney acting improperly?

A. Yes, because the attorney did not keep records for a long enough period.

B. Yes, because the attorney should not have deposited the $1,000 buffer from his own funds in the account.

C. No, because the lawyer may deposit the lawyer's own funds in a client trust account for the purpose of paying bank service charges on that account.

D. No, because the attorney keeps property of clients or third persons that is in a lawyer's possession in connection with a representation separate from the lawyer's own property, in a separate account maintained in the state where the lawyer's office is situated.

ANALYSIS. Rule 1.15(b) says, "A lawyer may deposit the lawyer's own funds in a client trust account for the sole purpose of paying bank service charges on that account, but only in an amount necessary for that purpose."

A is irrelevant to the fact pattern. While Rule 1.15 does include record-keeping requirements, the problem here was commingling funds, not the length of time the attorney kept records.

B is correct. The lawyer should not have put extra money in the account as a "buffer," regardless of his good intentions. Instead, lawyers should keep sufficiently meticulous records to avoid overdrafts. If lawyers could add their own funds merely to buffer the client accounts, too many would use it as a way to commingle their own funds with the clients' money. There are even some reported cases of lawyers parking money in client accounts in order to evade taxes or to avoid judgment creditors when the lawyer was nearing bankruptcy.

C incorrectly omits the last clause of the rule, which is the part that makes this transaction improper. It is true that lawyers may deposit enough of their own funds in client trust accounts to cover bank fees, but no more than is necessary for that purpose.

D ignores the fact that some commingling of funds occurred here. Even though the lawyer properly created a client trust account to keep the client's funds separate from his own, he then deposited an unnecessary sum of his own funds into the account to serve as a "buffer," which is impermissible.

QUESTION 3. **When the client disputes the fee.** An attorney represented a client in a contention litigation matter, at the end of which the attorney received a settlement check for an agreed-upon amount from the opposing party ($100,000). The client had agreed to the amount but was unsatisfied and blamed the lawyer for the disappointing settlement amount. The attorney called the client to inform her that the check had arrived, and explained that he would forward the amount minus his fees and the expenses, which constituted half of the amount (the jury consultants and experts in the case had turned out to be very expensive). The client was furious and said that the expenses should have been included in the attorney's contingent fee, and that the attorney was not entitled to the original contingent fee in any case because the case had never gone to a verdict and had settled for a mediocre amount. Pursuant to their retainer agreement, the client and attorney agreed to schedule arbitration over the disputed fees and expenses as soon as possible, which realistically would be three or four months later. In the meantime, the attorney kept the money in the client trust account until they could resolve the dispute. Was this proper?

A. Yes, because the client has disputed the expenses and a portion of the contingent fee, so it is prudent to hold the entire sum until they reach a resolution.

B. Yes, because the lawyer put the money in a separate client trust account and did not commingle it with his own funds.

C. No, because the attorney should have paid the client $50,000 immediately and held only the remainder until the dispute was resolved.

D. No, because the attorney should have paid the client all the money immediately and collected the fees and expenses from the client later, depending on the amount determined in arbitration.

ANALYSIS. Rule 1.15(e) says, "When in the course of representation a lawyer is in possession of property in which two or more persons (one of whom may be the lawyer) claim interests, the property shall be kept separate by the lawyer until the dispute is resolved. The lawyer shall promptly distribute all portions of the property as to which the interests are not in dispute." This is a frequently tested scenario on the MPRE—a client disputes the bill, and the lawyer must decide how much of the funds to disburse to the client even before the resolution of the disagreement.

A is incorrect. Even though a dispute has arisen between the lawyer and the client over the funds, the Model Rules require the lawyer to disburse immediately whatever portion they both agree should belong to the client.

B ignores additional duties beyond keeping separate accounts. It is true that a lawyer must not commingle the funds, but the lawyer's duties do not end there. The lawyer should hold the disputed portion in the client trust account and disburse the rest.

C is correct. Rule 1.15(e) requires lawyers to disburse the undisputed portion of the funds to a client immediately, and to withhold only the portion that is still in dispute.

D is incorrect. Rule 1.15 actually instructs the lawyer to hold on to the disputed portion until the resolution of the disagreement. As a policy matter, many clients will turn out to be judgment-proof later when the lawyer tries to recover the fees from the client (if he disbursed all the funds at once despite the dispute).

QUESTION 4. **Client dispute with a third-party judgment creditor.** An attorney received from the opposing party $150,000 as a settlement for the attorney's client. Before the attorney could disburse the funds to the client, a third-party judgment creditor with a court-ordered lien against the client contacts the lawyer demanding disgorgement of the client's funds to satisfy the amount of the judgment, from a matter in which the lawyer did not represent the client. The client instructs the attorney to give the money to the client immediately and not to give anything to the third-party judgment creditor. Preliminary inquiries suggest that the third-party judgment creditor has a valid court order to execute on the client's assets. The attorney did as the client instructed him to do, disbursing the funds promptly to the client, and informed the judgment creditor to take up the matter with the client directly. Did the attorney act properly?

A. Yes, because the attorney should not unilaterally assume to arbitrate a dispute between the client and the third party.
B. Yes, because the attorney has a duty of loyalty to the client, and no duty to the third-party judgment creditor.
C. No, because the attorney should immediately have disbursed the funds to the judgment creditor.
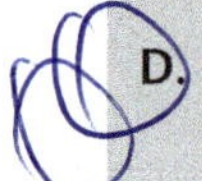
D. No, because in this type of situation, the lawyer must refuse to surrender the property to the client until the claims are resolved.

ANALYSIS. Rule 1.15(e) says, "When in the course of representation a lawyer is in possession of property in which two or more persons (one of whom may be the lawyer) claim interests, the property shall be kept separate by the lawyer until the dispute is resolved." The previous question addressed the situation in which the dispute is between the client and the lawyer over the lawyer's share of the award, while this question focuses on the fact that many clients have disputes with third parties who could assert a legal claim to some, or all, of the award.

A is incorrect. Even though this quotes verbiage from Comment 4 for Rule 1.15, the comment overall says that the lawyer must simply hold the funds until there is a resolution—which is not the same as presuming to arbitrate the dispute.

B is too absolute. Lawyers do have a duty of loyalty to the client, but there are also rules imposing duties to third parties and to courts. Comment 4 says, "A lawyer may have a duty under applicable law to protect such third party claims against wrongful interference by the client."

C is also too absolute. The lawyer has duties to protect the rights of third parties, but it is also possible that the third party does not have a valid legal claim on the funds.

D is correct. As Comment 4 for Rule 1.15 says, the rule "recognizes that third parties may have lawful claims against specific funds or other property in a lawyer's custody, such as a client's creditor who has a lien on funds recovered in a personal injury action." It goes on to instruct as follows: "A lawyer may have a duty under applicable law to protect such third party claims against wrongful interference by the client. In such cases, when the third-party claim is not frivolous under applicable law, the lawyer must refuse to surrender the property to the client until the claims are resolved."

A. The Closer

Rule 1.15 covers the handling of client funds and other property, and the provisions are primarily procedural rather than substantive—the requirement of separate client trust accounts (no commingling of funds), recordkeeping and reporting, timely disbursement, and so on. Unlike other sections of the Model Rules, Rule 1.15 does not have a variety of rules for different situations, so for examination purposes, students will not have to choose between alternate rules for specific fact situations. The main variable provision is that clients can consent to their funds being in an out-of-state account; otherwise, client funds must remain in the state (a point tested on a recent MPRE). The overarching rule running throughout all the provision is straightforward—lawyers holding money or property for clients must conscientiously protect the client's interests.

QUESTION 5. **Tie us over for the weekend.** A client retains an attorney to handle a criminal matter. The client delivers a retainer check to the attorney on Friday afternoon. The retainer check will only cover the work the attorney anticipates he will begin and complete the following Monday. Because the following Monday is a banking holiday, if the attorney deposits the retainer check into his client trust account on Friday afternoon, he will not have access to the funds until Tuesday. The attorney deposits the retainer check into his business checking account and pays himself on Friday before the firm closes with those funds. Is the attorney subject to discipline?

A. Yes, attorneys shall not accept amounts paid in advance for criminal matters.

B. Yes, attorneys shall deposit amounts paid in advance into a client trust account and the attorney shall not withdraw the funds until fees are earned or expenses are incurred.

C. No, if an attorney believes the funds will be earned within a short period, the attorney may deposit the amount he anticipates will be earned directly into his business account.

D. No, when an event out of an attorney's control, such as a bank holiday, causes the funds to be unavailable when the attorney anticipates he will need to withdraw the funds, the attorney may deposit the amount he reasonably believes will be earned or needed for expenses into his business account instead of the client trust account.

ANALYSIS. Rule 1.15(c) says, "A lawyer shall deposit into a client trust account legal fees and expenses that have been paid in advance, to be withdrawn by the lawyer only as fees are earned or expenses incurred." Commingling funds is simply impermissible under any circumstances except the one narrow exception (covering the bank fees on a trust account).

A is incorrect. A lawyer may indeed accept funds in advance for criminal and other matters—in fact, this is the norm for criminal defense attorneys.

B is correct. The lawyer is obligated to deposit the funds as soon as possible in a separate client trust account. The fact that the funds will be inaccessible for a few business days does not matter.

C is incorrect. There is no provision in the Model Rules for attorneys temporarily commingling funds in the way described here.

D posits a false exception to the rule against commingling funds. As reasonable as an exception for bank closures may sound, there is no such provision or exception in the Model Rules.

Stevenson's Picks

1. Across state lines	**A**
2. The buffer	**B**
3. When the client disputes the fee	**C**
4. Client dispute with a third-party judgment creditor	**D**
5. Tie us over for the weekend	**B**

Index

CPSIA information can be obtained
at www.ICGtesting.com
Printed in the USA
BVOW08s2240120817
491847BV00004B/14/P

9 781454 862154